JOURNAL FOR THE STUDY OF THE OLD TESTAMENT SUPPLEMENT SERIES
208

Sheffield Academic Press

Out of Eden

Reading, Rhetoric, and Ideology in Genesis 2–3

Beverly J. Stratton

Journal for the Study of the Old Testament
Supplement Series 208

To Terry, Jesse, and Sara

Published by Sheffield Academic Press Ltd
Mansion House
19 Kingfield Road
Sheffield, S11 9AS
England

Printed on acid-free paper in Great Britain
by Bookcraft Ltd
Midsomer Norton, Bath

British Library Cataloguing in Publication Data

A catalogue record for this book is available
from the British Library

ISBN 1-85075-575-2

CONTENTS

ACKNOWLEDGMENTS

I would like to thank several people who read and commented on earlier drafts of some chapters: Mark Gravrock, Jean Larson Hurd, Diane Jacobson, Carol Schersten Lahurd, Linda Lehner, Barb Lund, Daniel Lyman, Kristine Carlson Wee, and members of the Luther Seminary scripture seminar.

My work would not have been possible without the support of the mathematics and religion departments at Augsburg College. Thanks also to Augsburg's graphics center and interlibrary loan department for prompt and courteous service. Kathy Swanson and Lynne Lorenzen provided advice and counsel in times of stress. I thank them for their friendship. Thanks to Doug Green for reading and critiquing earlier drafts of several chapters, and for allowing me to audit and converse with him about his critical theory class. A special thanks to Earl Alton— friend, mentor, colleague, designated 'nag', willing and capable 'naive reader', and encourager for his constant affirmation and support of my work.

Thanks to my dissertation readers, Lisa Albrecht, Mary Knutsen, and Richard Nysse for their advice, encouragement, criticisms, questions, and honesty. A special thanks to my adviser, Terry Fretheim, for his support of my work through all of its stages.

Finally, thanks to my children Terry, Jesse, and Sara for getting along with me and without me these many years and to my husband, Tom, for his love, his support, and the hundreds of hours he has spent as parent in charge.

ABBREVIATIONS

ABD	D.N. Freedman (ed.), *Anchor Bible Dictionary*
ANQ	*Andover Newton Quarterly*
AUSS	*Andrews University Seminary Studies*
BA	*Biblical Archaeologist*
BASOR	*Bulletin of the American Schools of Oriental Research*
BETL	Bibliotheca ephemeridum theologicarum lovaniensium
Bib	*Biblica*
BibRev	*Bible Review*
BJRL	*Bulletin of the John Rylands University Library of Manchester*
BTB	*Biblical Theology Bulletin*
BZ	*Biblische Zeitschrift*
CBQ	*Catholic Biblical Quarterly*
CTM	*Concordia Theological Monthly*
ExpTim	*Expository Times*
GTJ	*Grace Theological Journal*
HTR	*Harvard Theological Review*
HUCA	*Hebrew Union College Annual*
IBC	Interpretation: A Bible Commentary for Teaching and Preaching
Int	*Interpretation*
JAAR	*Journal of the American Academy of Religion*
JANES	*Journal of the Ancient Near Eastern Society*
JBL	*Journal of Biblical Literature*
JETS	*Journal of the Evangelical Theological Society*
JFSR	*Journal of Feminist Studies in Religion*
JR	*Journal of Religion*
JSNT	*Journal for the Study of the New Testament*
JSOT	*Journal for the Study of the Old Testament*
JSOTSup	*Journal for the Study of the Old Testament*, Supplement Series
JSS	*Journal of Semitic Studies*
JTS	*Journal of Theological Studies*
KB	L. Koehler and W. Baumgartner (eds.), *Lexicon in Veteris Testamenti libros*
NIB	L.E. Keck (ed.), *New Interpreter's Bible*
NRT	*La nouvelle revue théologique*
NTS	*New Testament Studies*

OBT	Overtures to Biblical Theology
RB	*Revue biblique*
RevScRel	*Revue des sciences religieuses*
SBL	Society of Biblical Literature
SBLBSNA	SBL Biblical Scholarship in North America
SBLDS	SBL Dissertation Series
SBLMS	SBL Monograph Series
SBLSS	SBL Semeia Studies
SJT	*Scottish Journal of Theology*
TS	*Theological Studies*
TToday	*Theology Today*
USQR	*Union Seminary Quarterly Review*
VT	*Vetus Testamentum*
VTSup	*Vetus Testamentum*, Supplements
WBC	Word Biblical Commentary
WTJ	*Westminster Theological Journal*
WW	*Word and World*
ZAW	*Zeitschrift für die alttestamentliche Wissenschaft*
ZTK	*Zeitschrift für Theologie und Kirche*

INTRODUCTION

Interpretations matter. They mattered in the garden of Eden. The couple's interpretation of their world and of God's words led to their life-changing actions. Interpretations matter out of Eden. Interpretations matter because they affect people's lives, especially when we view the Bible as authoritative.

Interpretations of the Adam and Eve story, in particular, have affected women's lives for centuries. Interpreters have read signals of women's inferiority in the text: woman's secondary creation, her creation from the man's body and for him (to be his helper), her naming by the man, God's speaking first and primarily to him, and certainly God's words to the woman in Gen. 3.16 that she will have pain in childbearing and that the man will rule over her. Over the centuries, such readings of Genesis 2–3 have prompted, or at least served as an excuse for, women's exclusion from full participation in religious communities.[1] They have reinforced women's secondary status in economic and political life and served as a resource for those who would limit women's effective domain to concerns of home and family. Interpreters have argued from this text against women's use of drugs during labor to lessen their pain in childbearing. Perhaps worst of all, interpretations of this text have legitimated men's domination of women, even to the point of sanctioning physical abuse. Surely, feminists would be wise to consider how interpretation functions in relation to Genesis 2–3.

Interpretation of any text functions in relation to the aims and methods of interpretive communities. I am a member of several communities whose interests and purposes vary and sometimes seem to conflict. This work is, in part, an attempt to be whole—to integrate who I am and how I think as a Christian feminist scholar. I do this by interpreting this particular Genesis 2–3 text.

As a scholar, I have chosen, for this project, to address Genesis 2–3

---

1. Genesis 2–3 serves as a shorthand for Gen. 2.4–3.24 and Genesis 1 for Gen. 1.1–2.3 throughout.

using literary methods.[1] I use reader-response criticism in Chapters 1 and 2, narratology (with insights from rhetorical criticism and speech act theory) in Chapter 3, and intertextuality and ideological criticism in Chapter 4. (See the chart at the end of the introduction.) While I offer critical summaries to introduce these various literary approaches, my goal is not to further understandings of the methodologies or to advance new techniques in relation to them. Rather, I learn from these critical theories and apply them to this biblical text. I expect scholars to find that I have read Genesis 2–3 in new ways, but not in the sense of proposing a new reading of the whole text that I think should displace all others.[2] I have, however, stepped outside of the two traditional strands of interpretation of the narrative in terms of either creation and fall or growth. Asking alternate questions of the text has allowed me to read it with different nuances.

As a feminist, I address this text because traditional interpretations of Genesis 2–3 have contributed significantly to the ways Christianity has (mis)understood women. The major feminist components of the book are the themes for three of the chapters: in Chapters 2, 3, and 4, respectively, these are knowledge, language, and difference. In the introductory section of each of these chapters, I offer analyses of feminist scholarship in relation to these themes.

As a Christian, I struggle with what often seems to me like the organized church's inattention to the voices of those on the margins, to the cries of feminists and others who think that we should be living differently. As a Lutheran, being justified by grace through faith, I think we are free to serve our neighbors' needs and should be doing a better job of it—not for our salvation, but for our neighbors' well-being.

Communities of feminists and communities of Christians should be able to talk with one another about how each group sees the world and the ways that we live in it today. Yet I experience each community

---

1.   I seek to learn about these methods, to experiment with them and learn their limitations and strengths, to see how they may or may not be useful in reading a text. I do not intend by this choice to suggest either that literary methods are superior or that historical scholarship is optional.

2.   Against interpretive battles as the goal of criticism and favoring conversation, compassion, collaboration, concurrence, and community, see J.J. Sosnoski, 'A Mindless Man-driven Theory Machine: Intellectuality, Sexuality and the Institution of Criticism', in L. Kauffman (ed.), *Feminism and Institutions: Dialogues in Feminist Theory* (Oxford and Cambridge, MA: Basil Blackwell, 1989), pp. 55-78.

primarily as rejecting the other, which puts me on the margins of both. My work, then, is an attempt to combine these ways of seeing the world. It is an endeavor to contribute voices toward a conversation[1] about what we do when we interpret scripture and about reading Genesis 2–3 in relation to questions and concerns of contemporary communities.

By focusing on Genesis 2–3, a foundational text for Christians and a problematic one for many feminists, this book encourages discussion between these groups. It invites feminists who do not think of the Bible as scripture, and who perhaps view it as dangerous, to read a biblical text and find it helpful. It invites Christians who take the Bible seriously also to take seriously the contemporary context of our world as it is analyzed by feminists. It attempts to think about women's and men's lives and God's relation to the world in ways that make sense to me as a Lutheran feminist scholar. I do not intend or expect my work to convert a non-believing feminist or to make a Christian skeptical of feminism start to advocate it. My goal, rather, is to facilitate the opening of conversations where these two groups can begin to understand what each thinks is at stake in our ways of living in the world.

Interpretation got humanity into trouble in the garden. It was also part of seeking wisdom. Interpretation continues both to delight and to frustrate us, and we are stuck with it. Interpretation is exciting and dangerous, but in any case, it is an inevitable part of what it means to be human. The question, which I think the garden story places before us, is how we will live with our knowledge of good and evil, with our recognition that we are embedded in language that both shapes and reflects what we think, with our various understandings of the differences among us, and with the facts that we *do* interpret and that we *will* sometimes violate God's command. By placing this story at the beginning of the Bible, the shapers of the canon may be urging us to think about how we interpret God's word. My thesis, then, is about interpretation: Genesis 2–3 claims that interpretation matters, that there are consequences for the actions we take on the basis of our interpretations, and that we should engage this process carefully.

---

1. The book focuses on what feminist scholarship and literary critical theories bring to conversations about this Genesis text and about the interpretive process generally. I will need to work later on what Christian perspectives contribute to the conversation and on how the 'text' as scripture interacts with these communities, both being shaped by them and critiquing their positions.

As mentioned above, the book is organized so that each chapter has a particular theme, and each uses different feminist and literary-critical theories to explore issues of interpretation in relation to this Genesis text. The book offers not so much an argument for a particular claim as an integrative study.[1] It combines feminist theories and literary-critical scholarship to interact with questions of contemporary communities about interpretation in relation to Genesis 2–3. The chapters are arranged to build upon one another toward Chapter 4, where the questions of what is at stake in how we interpret the world and this text become critical.

Chapter 1 offers a close reading of the entire Genesis 2–3 narrative, focusing particularly on God. The chapter also surveys important scholarship on Genesis 2–3. It begins to distinguish narrative levels, and it demonstrates the temporal nature of reading. The chapter's main purpose is to raise a variety of questions, some of which are explored in subsequent chapters. These questions suggest a multiplicity of interpretive interests—the kinds of features we might consider as we interpret this (or any) text. The chapter suggests also that among the most important interpretive interests for biblical texts is God.

Chapter 2 reviews recent feminist work on Genesis 2–3; it presents as plausible two opposing feminist views of the woman in the garden. The first approach views her as a model moral thinker who interprets her world and learns from her mistakes. The second reading views the entire narrative and the woman's role in it as governed by patriarchy. The chapter demonstrates that interpretations can oppose one another, even when they emerge from the same interpretive community, for example, feminist biblical scholars.

Chapter 3 continues an intentionally ambivalent reading of the text, this time focusing on language. The chapter argues that Genesis 2–3 is conscious that language shapes our understanding of reality. Rhetorical

---

1. Ernest L. Boyer argues for doing research 'at the boundaries where fields converge', for 'making connections across the disciplines, placing the specialities in larger context, illuminating data in a revealing way, often educating nonspecialists, too'. He contends that 'graduate study must be broadened, encompassing not only research, but integration, application, and teaching too. It is this vision that will assure, we believe, a new generation of scholars, one that is more intellectually vibrant and more responsive to society's shifting needs.' See *Scholarship Reconsidered: Priorities of the Professoriate* (Princeton: The Carnegie Foundation for the Advancement of Teaching, 1990), pp. 19, 18, 74.

and narratological study of Genesis 2–3 in this chapter demonstrates that texts affect interpreters by drawing them into a story through narrative techniques. Texts shape readers as narrators shape characters. Story-tellers know that their audiences appreciate the flexibility and fun of language, hence the puns and word plays. Interpreters can be drawn in by a text, and they can step back from it to understand its rhetorical moves. By its rhetorical sophistication, the Genesis text presents language in an ambiguous and flexible way: as power and possibilities, danger and delight.

Given the ambiguity of language, Chapter 4 insists that texts are read and understood within interpretive communities, which are shaped by various ideological commitments, lived experiences, and intertexts. This chapter reads Genesis 2–3 through the lens of feminist scholarship on 'difference', particularly the notion of 'compulsory heterosexuality'. It sees Genesis 2–3 as attempting to naturalize a male view of reality as the way the world is—an attempt that is largely, though not entirely, successful. Through intertextual readings of Genesis 2–3 with the Cain and Abel story and with wisdom literature, the chapter also begins to address how we might carefully engage the interpretive process and the rhetorical power of texts as we live our lives 'out of Eden'.

The overall shape of my work, by not claiming a particular single 'meaning' for the Genesis 2–3 text, suggests that perhaps 'settling' a text by understanding it is *not* what interpretation should be about, that at least in some cases it may be better to converse with a text. Perhaps more important than sending a message of doom or even of sin and grace, Genesis 2–3 challenges us, as readers, to think—to consider the choices we face, the ways we interpret our world (our trees of knowledge), and the ways we experience our relationships with God. It reminds us through persuasive speech and playful word plays that our interpretations have effects.

Chapter	ONE	TWO	THREE	FOUR
Theme	God in the story	Knowledge	Language	Difference
Feminist theories		Feminist epistemologies	Feminist theories about language	'Compulsory heterosexuality'; interlocking differences
Literary and critical method(s)	Reader-response criticism	Feminist criticism and reader-response	Narratology; (rhetorical criticism; speech act theory)	Ideological criticism; intertextuality
Discussion of Gen. 2–3 text	Partial review of Gen. 2–3 literature	Review and analysis of feminist work on Gen. 2–3	Language as power, possibilities, danger and delight	Attempts to naturalize a male view of reality as the way the world IS
Movement toward thesis	Raises questions; promotes reading as an event in time, based on one's prior experiences	Presents two opposing views of woman in garden as plausible	Language shapes understanding of reality: it is ambiguous and flexible	Language occurs within communities of discourse; chapter begins to address living 'out of Eden' by reading Gen. 2–3 with Gen. 4 and wisdom literature

THESIS: Genesis 2–3 claims that interpretation matters, that there are consequences for the actions we take on the basis of our interpretations, and that we should engage this process carefully.

Chapter 1

READING AND THE GARDEN STORY

The primary goal of this chapter is to read the garden story, Gen. 2.4–
3.24, in a way that raises questions and makes observations that will
prompt discussion in the later chapters. The reading offered here
attempts to capture one reader's responses and questions (mine) *as* the
reading happens. The goal in the chapter is not to explain, understand,
or interpret the text as a whole, but to point toward moments of
difficulty and areas where interpretation of the text will need to address
reader questions.[1]

My reading builds on the work of feminist scholars before me. Like
the question and claims of the serpent in the garden story itself, feminist
biblical scholarship has opened a way for new visions and alternative
interpretations. By challenging several aspects of standard interpretations
(even feminist ones), my reading of Genesis 2–3 in this chapter also
opens paths for fresh walks through the garden story. One particular
path, only lightly trodden in recent years, is the theological one. In this
chapter's reading of the garden story I focus on God: what readers can
know about God in the narrative, what they might like to know about
God that the narrator does not reveal, and, in general, how readers may
experience the God of the garden.

A brief survey of the issues, terminology, and range of approaches in
reader-response criticism provides a helpful introduction to this chapter's
discussion of Genesis 2–3. The next chapter continues the reader-
response approach. There I consider how knowledge and experience are
factors both in the Genesis text and in the interaction between readers

---

1. I invite my readers to read Genesis 1–3, jotting notes about questions and
responses, before reading further. Readers will then more easily be able to compare
their practice with the theories I discuss.

and texts. I also introduce specifically feminist reading aims, though they are evident in my reading here as well.[1]

Reader-Response Criticism

Brief History of Reader-Response Criticism

Readers and hearers have been responding to texts and stories ever since there have been texts and stories, so in some ways the history of reader-response criticism is the entire literary history or history of interpretation of a text.[2] A history of readers' and hearers' responses to literature in general reveals some surprising results. For example, the interpretive interest in 'meaning' is a relatively recent phenomenon: classical and renaissance critics were interested in literature's rhetorical power to affect people and to influence their moral and political action in the world.[3]

Critical attention to a reader's responses and to how to incorporate those responses into an interpretation of a text has become significant in the twentieth century. Reader-response criticism in America grows out of the work of I.A. Richards and Louise Rosenblatt in the 1920s and 1930s.[4] In Europe it developed primarily in terms of reception criticism.[5]

---

1.   I have elected to separate the feminist understandings, aims, and strategies of reader-response criticism from the discussion here simply to avoid swamping this chapter with methodology. Clearly my feminist perspective cannot be separated from my understanding of reader-response criticism. It is explicit in Chapter 2.

2.   B.J. Malina makes this point in reference to the Bible: 'Reader-Response Theory: Discovery or Redundancy?', *Creighton University Faculty Journal* (Omaha) 5 (1986) p. 63.

3.   J.P. Tompkins offers a historical perspective, making this point; see 'The Reader in History: The Changing Shape of Literary Response', in J.P. Tompkins (ed.), *Reader-Response Criticism: From Formalism to Post-Structuralism* (Baltimore: The Johns Hopkins University Press, 1980), pp. 301-20.

4.   I.A. Richards, *Practical Criticism* (New York: Harcourt, 1929) and L. Rosenblatt, *Literature as Exploration* (New York and London: D. Appleton-Century Company, 1938).

5.   H.R. Jauss termed his theory *Rezeptionsästhetik*. W. Iser contrasts his own theory of aesthetic response (*Wirkungstheorie*), which has its roots in the text, with *Rezeptionsästhetik* that Iser says arises from readers' judgments. See the preface to Iser's *The Act of Reading: A Theory of Aesthetic Response* (Baltimore: The Johns Hopkins University Press, 1978), p. x. R.C. Holub introduces both Jauss's and Iser's theories with attention to their predecessors and related models and issues in *Reception Theory: A Critical Introduction* (New York and London: Methuen, 1984).

The discipline has grown in the past two decades. There are now journals entirely devoted to reader-response theories, and a wide range of professional societies give attention to them.[1]

Varieties of Reader-Response Criticism

The variety of reader-response methodologies seems almost as vast as the number of readers of literature.[2] In a recent survey, Richard Beach organizes them into categories: experiential, psychological, social, cultural, and textual.[3] Experiential theories emphasize what readers actually think and do while they are reading. Louise Rosenblatt's interest in aesthetic response and David Bleich's 'subjective criticism' attend to the role of a reader's experiences.[4] Experiential theories are more likely than others to consider readers' feelings.[5] Psychological theories focus on readers'

1.   See the journal *Reader: Essays in Reader-Oriented Theory, Criticism, and Pedagogy*. In biblical studies, numerous articles and books and two issues of Semeia have been devoted to reader-response criticism: R. Detweiler (ed.), *Reader Response Approaches to Biblical and Secular Texts* (Semeia, 31; Decatur, GA: Scholars Press, 1985) and E.V. McKnight (ed.), *Reader Perspectives on the New Testament* (Semeia, 48; Atlanta: Scholars Press, 1989).

2.   In addition to the Tompkins collection, cited above, see S. Suleiman and I. Crosman (eds.), *The Reader in the Text: Essays on Audience and Interpretation* (Princeton: Princeton University Press, 1980), which organizes reader-response criticism by disciplinary approach. Research and theories on gender differences in readers' responses and feminist reader-response interpretations of literary texts are included in E.A. Flynn and P.P. Schweickart (eds.), *Gender and Reading: Essays on Readers, Texts, and Contexts* (Baltimore: The Johns Hopkins University Press, 1986).

3.   R. Beach offers an up-to-date introduction and bibliography for the field, including pedagogical approaches for attending to readers, and research on the responses of actual readers in *A Teacher's Introduction to Reader-Response Theories* (Urbana, IL: National Council of Teachers of English, 1993).

4.   See L. Rosenblatt, 'The Poem as Event', *College English*, 26, 2 (November 1964), pp. 123-28; 'Towards a Transactional Theory of Reading', *Journal of Reading Behavior* 1 (Winter 1969), pp. 31-47; and *The Reader, the Text, the Poem: The Transactional Theory of the Literary Work* (Carbondale and Edwardsville: Southern Illinois University Press, 1978). See also D. Bleich, *Readings and Feelings: An Introduction to Subjective Criticism* (Urbana, IL: National Council of Teachers of English, 1975) and *Subjective Criticism* (Baltimore: The Johns Hopkins University Press, 1978).

5.   J.P. Tompkins makes a case for including attention to feelings and gives an example of how to incorporate them into an interpretation in her essay 'Criticism and Feeling', *College English* 39 (1977), pp. 169-78.

psychological and cognitive development. Some critics, like Norman Holland (and many of his colleagues at SUNY Buffalo) are interested in a reader's identity formation, based on Freud's psychoanalytic theories.[1] Holland uses the acronym DEFT to summarize his method's understanding of reader-response as involving *d*efense, *e*xpectation, *f*antasies, and *t*ransformation. Matters of cognitive or moral development play a role in psychological theories.[2] Social theories include Stanley Fish's notion of 'interpretive communities' that both shape and constrain reader responses and interpretations.[3] Shared conventions of communication such as those presupposed by speech-act theory are another aspect of social reader-response theories.[4] Cultural theories of reader response consider such matters as the role of literary canons and the effects of gender, race, and class. The claims of post-structuralists, like those of the French theorists Roland Barthes and Michel Foucault about how a reader is already shaped by cultural codes and assumptions, parallel Fish's notions of interpretive communities.[5] Finally, all reader-response theories include ideas about the text and its role. Textual theories of reader-response criticism developed in part in reaction to the New Criticism's abhorrence of what it termed the 'affective fallacy'.[6]

1.   See Holland's essay 'Unity Identity Text Self' in *Reader-Response Criticism*, pp. 118-33 or his book *5 Readers Reading* (New Haven: Yale University Press, 1975). Holland's early work has been rightly criticized by J.K. Gardiner for ignoring the role of gender in his theory and as part of the reader's identity; see 'Psychoanalytic Criticism and the Female Reader', *Literature and Psychology* 26 (1976), pp. 100-107. Holland and L.F. Sherman address gender in 'Gothic Possibilities', in *Gender and Reading*, pp. 215-33.

2.   These include W. Perry's scheme for the intellectual development of college students, L. Kohlberg's theory of moral development, and their various critiques. Beach gives brief summaries and essential bibliographies for these theories in *A Teacher's Introduction*, pp. 77-82.

3.   S. Fish first introduced this term in his essay 'Interpreting the *Variorum*', *Critical Inquiry* 2 (Spring 1976), pp. 465-85. See the discussion of Fish and textuality in Chapter 4.

4.   I discuss speech-act theory in Chapter 3.

5.   For issues and bibliography relevant to post-structuralism in relation to reader-response criticism, see Beach's chapter on cultural theories in *A Teacher's Introduction*. I converse with post-structuralist theories but do not focus on them.

6.   Proponents of the 'affective fallacy' lament a confusion between a literary work and its results or effects, fearing that attention to affect would lead to the disappearance of the work in favor of the pure subjectivism of readers. See W.K. Wimsatt, Jr, and M.C. Beardsley, 'The Affective Fallacy', in *The Verbal Icon: Studies in the*

These textual theories address a whole range of matters as they relate the reader to the text: phenomenology, narrative and genre conventions, rhetoric, semiotics, intertextuality, and postmodernism.[1]

A second way to categorize reader-response theories is in terms of how they understand the roles of text and reader in the reading process. The theories range on a continuum from 'objective' to 'subjective'. 'Objective' theories would include that of E.D. Hirsch, who assumes that meaning (as contrasted with significance) is universal and that interpretations can be validated, though not verified.[2] Wolfgang Iser's understanding of the reader filling in gaps and resolving indeterminacies assumes that the text governs the reader. Stanley Fish, when he is actually interpreting a text, also exemplifies this attitude. His reader regularly miscalculates meanings and stumbles over line endings at the whim of the text.[3] The reader is still active in these 'objective' theories, but always subject to the text's control. Meaning resides in or beneath the text or in the author's conscious or unconscious intention. 'Objective' versions of reader-response theory have some affinities with structuralism (and hence post-structuralism and deconstruction).

A purely 'subjective' reader-response criticism would insist that interpretations are entirely idiosyncratic, that reading depends solely on an individual's experiences, and basically that the reader controls the text. The subjective and psychoanalytic criticisms of Bleich and Holland fall in this realm. Subjective criticism has affinities with intertextuality and ideological criticism since the texts that a reader has read and the ideas she holds will affect her interpretation.[4]

Several theorists adopt a middle position, allowing roles for both text

Meaning of Poetry, W.K. Wimsatt, Jr (ed.) (n.p.: University of Kentucky Press, 1954), pp. 21-39.

1.   Among these matters, I address rhetoric in Chapter 3 and intertextuality in Chapter 4. Feminist theories and applications of reader-response criticism, like feminism itself, overlap all of these approaches. I discuss them initially in the next chapter.

2.   E.D. Hirsch, Jr, *Validity in Interpretation* (New Haven: Yale University, 1967).

3.   See, for example, S. Fish, 'Literature in the Reader: Affective Stylistics', chap. in *Is There a Text in this Class?* (Cambridge and London: Harvard University Press, 1980).

4.   Though I do not consider myself primarily a subjective reader-response critic, I address Genesis 2–3 in terms of intertextuality and ideological criticism in Chapter 4.

and reader in the reading and interpreting process. Neither controls the other, but both participate in an interaction or transaction that constitutes the formation of the 'work'.[1] Mary Louise Pratt describes the transaction this way.

> The text produces (operates on, transforms, interprets) ideology; the reader produces (operates on, transforms, interprets) the text. Such a formulation avoids reifying either text or reader, and captures our sense of reading as a creative, making activity rather than a simple process of re-ception, re-production, re-presentation.[2]

Genre itself is a feature of the reader–text interaction. Jonathan Culler gives the example of a joke to explain the balance of reader and text.[3] A joke requires a listener's laughter at the punch line to earn its genre designation as a joke. But whether the joke *is* a joke or not is *not* a decision the listener makes, except in retrospect, since his laughter is either spontaneous or absent. Fish's notion of interpretive communities belongs in this middle region of the spectrum.[4] A particular interpretive community will select strategies and rules for evidence in discussing meaning and interpretation that depend on its own aims and interests. Thus, what 'meaning' is and the choice of whether the reader or the text governs the interpretive process are ultimately decisions the interpretive community makes.[5]

1.   Here, I am using Rosenblatt's distinctions of 'text' as the ink marks on the page and 'work' as the literary entity created by the reader–text transaction. Rosenblatt prefers John Dewey's term 'transaction' over interaction, which she likens to the collision of two (fixed) billiard balls. I find her work/text distinction more helpful than Fish's insistence that there is no text until it is created by the reader. Fish's 'text' is like Rosenblatt's 'work', but Fish has no term for talking about the words on the page.

2.   M.L. Pratt, 'Interpretive Strategies/Strategic Interpretations: On Anglo-American Reader Response Criticism', *Boundary 2* 2 (1982), p. 207.

3.   J. Culler, 'Readers and Reading', chap. in *On Deconstruction: Theory and Criticism after Structuralism* (Ithaca: Cornell University Press, 1982), p. 73.

4.   Fish's theoretical position thus differs from his practice, which I noted above tends to locate control in the text.

5.   For a helpful discussion of meaning in relation to interpretive interests see S. Fowl, 'The Ethics of Interpretation or What's Left Over After the Elimination of Meaning', in D.J.A. Clines, S. Fowl, and S. Porter (eds.), *The Bible in Three Dimensions: Essays in Celebration of Forty Years of Biblical Studies in the University of Sheffield* (JSOTSup, 87; Sheffield: Sheffield Academic Press, 1990), pp. 379-98.

I situate my own use of reader-response theory toward the 'subjective' side of the middle area of the 'objective'/'subjective' continuum. In terms of Beach's categorization, I am interested primarily in experiential and textual theories of reader-response. My feminist perspective requires that I attend to the psychological, social, and cultural contexts that inform reading. I see myself as exercising some influence over the reading process, since I have chosen many of the interpretive communities which regulate the questions and strategies that I employ. I am not a sociologist, nor is my work in educational research, so I do not attempt to verify my position through experimental studies.[1] As a feminist, I have interests beyond the act of interpretation itself: I want to change the world. My feminist perspective means that I am interested in actual contemporary readers and in the particular role that gender plays in the reading process. It also makes me aware of ways that psychological, social, and cultural factors are influenced by and shape notions of gender.

Preparation for Reading

Nature and Purpose of this Reading

In the remainder of this chapter I offer a slow reading of the garden story in Gen. 2.4–3.24. I use the word 'slow' deliberately, to emphasize, along with reader-response critics, the importance of reading as an activity that occurs *through time*. By stopping regularly while reading the text to consider my own questions and responses and to imagine the observations, ideas, and reactions of other potential readers, I reflect on how various readers might experience the garden story. This first reading raises issues, many of which I address later in the thesis.

In this reading I consider several reader perspectives, those of a first-time contemporary reader, an experienced contemporary reader familiar with other biblical narratives, an early Hebrew hearer of the story, and a Hebrew reader or hearer familiar with biblical (and perhaps other)

---

1.   Nevertheless, I do hope to apply my work to classroom teaching. I suspect there are strong correlations between a particular reader-response theory's attitudes about whether reader or text more strongly affects the reading process and the kind of pedagogy and understanding of teacher authority evident in the classroom. For related discussion, see my 'Dirtying Our Hands: Ideologies, Pedagogies, and Scriptures', presented to the Society of Biblical Literature's Ideological Criticism Group, Chicago, 21 November 1994.

narratives.[1] I consider potential historical perspectives and comment on scholarly debates to suggest how the information and perspectives of trained readers offer interpretive possibilities. As my comments in this chapter sketch only briefly, any exegete's debt to previous scholarship on Genesis 2–3 is enormous. I engage the work of these scholars with respect and thanks. My eagerness to challenge their positions and to flavor the discussion in different ways grows out of this respect.

Who is the Reader?

As a feminist, I recognize the importance of my own social location, so it seems appropriate to describe my context as the reader of Genesis 2–3. I read as a college religion professor, married mother of three young children, and recent graduate student, struggling with this text to write this work. I read as a feminist, recently aware of my partiality, my privilege, and my responsibility as a white, heterosexual, upper-class, educated American. I read as a Christian lover of the Bible, thirsting to hear God speak in and through biblical texts to today's readers and believing communities. I read as a biblical feminist eager to reclaim even the most seemingly irredeemable texts and anxiously aware that the Bible's implied audience is often male and that its original social contexts were undeniably patriarchal.[2]

A reader's own faith stance affects her or his reading posture. Responses of readers who are nominally Jewish or Christian differ from those of readers who believe the God of the Bible still acts in the world. Avowed atheists and Christians who are uncomfortable with what they perceive as the 'angry, warlike God of the Old Testament' may make

---

1.   My comments about the perspectives of first time contemporary readers include questions and observations that scholars have long ceased noting. I ask readers to be patient, and to try again to imagine with me what it might be like to read this Genesis text through the eyes of a new reader.

2.   Even P. Trible, who argues in 'Depatriarchalizing in Biblical Interpretation', *JAAR* 41 (1973), pp. 30-48, that the Bible bears within itself its own 'depatriarchalizing' tendencies, admits its original patriarchal social context. Essays by C. Meyers and A.L. Wordelman give a nuanced discussion of the Bible's social contexts; see 'Everyday Life: Women in the Period of the Hebrew Bible', and 'Everyday Life: Women in the Period of the New Testament', respectively, in C.A. Newsom and S.H. Ringe (eds.), *The Women's Bible Commentary* (Louisville and London: Westminster/John Knox and SPCK, 1992), pp. 244-51, 390-96. S. Durber discusses some potential implications of the Bible's implied reader being male in her essay 'The Female Reader of the Parables of the Lost', *JSNT* 45 (1992), pp. 59-78.

different assumptions about God and react differently to the portrayals of God in these narratives than theologians of the church and feminist biblical scholars. I am presupposing, at a minimum, that readers are willing to give the story a chance, that they are open to engaging the text to see whether a new understanding of God emerges. I am also assuming in this section that most people begin a book at the beginning. So while I discuss primarily Gen. 2.4–3.24, I can expect readers to have read Gen. 1.1–2.3 as well.

Text and Translation of Genesis 2.4–3.24

Because my readings of Genesis 2–3 work closely with particular words, it is important to establish carefully the text on which they are based. Unlike New Testament scholarship that works from a critically recon-structed text, the practice for most Old Testament studies has been to adopt the Masoretic text, except where textual corruptions are evident or where variants in the versions suggest that a reconstructed 'original' would be superior. Since there are no significant textual problems, I follow this practice by basing my translation of Gen. 2.4–3.24 on the Masoretic text. Matters of text criticism are noted in the appendix.

I have translated Gen. 2.4–3.24 into a fairly smooth English, while preserving, as much as possible, the Hebrew word order, except that I usually translate the standard Hebrew syntax of verb, subject, object, modifier into the standard English order: subject, verb, modifier, object. When the Hebrew deviates from its usual word order, I indicate the emphasis by italics. I also italicize unnecessary pronouns that show emphasis. For the benefit of English readers, I designate the plural pronoun 'you' and the possessive 'your' with a parenthetical (pl). I translate the same root word consistently so that repetitions and inclusios are more obvious in English. Readers interested in further details should consult the heavily annotated translation in the appendix.

> (2.4) These are the generations of the heavens and the earth when they were created, on the day YHWH God made earth and heavens. (5) When no bush of the field was yet on the earth and no grass of the field had yet sprouted, for YHWH God had not caused it to rain upon the earth, and there was not a man to work the ground, (6) but *a stream* would go up from the earth, and it watered the whole face of the ground, (7) then YHWH God formed the man out of dust from the ground, and breathed into his nostrils living breath, so that the man became a living being.
>
> (8) Then YHWH God planted a garden in Eden, to the East, and he put there the man whom he had formed. (9) And YHWH God made to sprout from

the ground every tree [that is] desirable to see and good to eat, and the tree of life in the middle of the garden, and the tree of the knowledge of good and evil. (10) And *a river* would go up from Eden to water the garden, and from there it divided and became four branches. (11) The name of the first is Pishon; it is the one that goes around the whole land of Havilah, where there is gold; (12) and the gold of that land is good. There is bdellium there and shosham stone. (13) And the name of the second river is Gihon. It is the one that goes around the whole land of Cush. (14) And the name of the third river is Hidqel (Tigris). It is the one that goes east of Asshur. And the fourth river is the Euphrates.

(15) Then YHWH God took the man and settled him in the garden of Eden to work it and to guard it. (16) And YHWH God commanded the man saying, 'Of every tree of the garden you may surely eat, (17) but of the tree of the knowledge of good and evil you shall not eat of it, because on the day that you eat of it you will surely die'.

(18) Then YHWH God said '[It is] not good [that] the man be alone; I will make for him a helper as his counterpart'. (19) So YHWH God formed out of the ground every animal of the field and every bird of the heavens, and he brought [them] to the man to see what he would call them, so that whatever the man called the living being, that is its name. (20) So the man gave names to all cattle and birds of the heavens and to every animal of the field, but [as] for the man he did not find a helper as his counterpart. (21) So YHWH God caused a deep sleep to fall upon the man, and he slept. Then he took one of his ribs, and he closed [with] flesh its place. (22) Then YHWH God built the rib that he had taken from the man into a woman, and he brought her to the man. (23) And the man said,

'This one, this time,
    bone of my bones and flesh of my flesh;
this one shall be called woman,
    for from a man was taken this one'.

(24) Therefore a man leaves his father and his mother and clings to his woman, and they become one flesh. (25) And the two of them were naked, the man and his woman, and they were not ashamed.

(3.1) Now the serpent was more shrewd than all the animals of the field that YHWH God had made. So it said to the woman, 'Really, did God say "you (pl) may not eat from any tree of the garden"?' (2) And the woman said to the serpent, 'of the fruit of the trees of the garden we may eat, (3) but, of the fruit of the tree that is in the middle of the garden, God said, "You (pl) shall not eat from it and you (pl) shall not touch it lest you (pl) die"' (4) Then the serpent said to the woman, 'You (pl) will not surely die. (5) For God knows that on the day you (pl) eat of it your (pl) eyes will be opened and you (pl) will be like God, knowing good and evil'.

(6) Then the woman saw that good [was] the tree for eating and that a delight it [was] to the eyes and [that] the tree was desirable for insight; so she took of its fruit, and she ate. Then she gave [some] also to her man [who was] with her, and he ate. (7) And the eyes of them both were opened, and they knew that naked [were] they. So they sewed fig leaves, and they made for themselves coverings.

(8) Then they heard the voice of YHWH God, walking around in the garden at the breezy time of the day, and they hid themselves, the man and his woman, from (the face of) YHWH God among the trees of the garden. (9) And YHWH God called to the man and said to him, 'Where are you?' (10) And he said, '*Your voice* I heard in the garden, and I was afraid because naked [am] *I*, so I hid'. (11) And he said, 'Who told you that naked [are] *you*? Of the tree which I commanded you not to eat of it did you eat?' (12) And the man said, 'The woman whom you gave [to be] with me, *she* gave to me of the tree, and I ate'. (13) Then YHWH God said to the woman, 'What [is] this [that] you have done?' And the woman said, '*The serpent* tricked me, so I ate'.

(14) So YHWH God said to the serpent,
'Because you have done this,
cursed are *you* among all the cattle
and among all animals of the field.
Upon your belly you will go,
and dust you will eat all the days of your life.
(15) *Enmity* I will make between you and the woman
and between your seed and her seed.
They will strike your head,
and *you* will strike their heel.

(16) To the woman he said,
'I will greatly multiply your toil and your pregnancies;
with toil you will bear children.
To your man will be your longing,
and he will rule over you'.

(17) And to [the] man he said,
'Because you have listened to the voice of your woman
and you have eaten of the tree
[about] which I commanded you saying,
"you shall not eat of it",
cursed [is] the ground on your account,
with toil you will eat of it
all the days of your life;
(18) thorns and thistles it will sprout for you,
and you will eat the grass of the field.

(19) By the sweat of your face, you will eat bread
until you return to the ground,
for from it you were taken.
For *dust* [are] *you,*
and to dust you will return.

(20) And the man called the name of his woman Eve, for *she* was the
mother of all living. (21) Then YHWH God made for [the] man and for his
woman tunics of skins, and he clothed them. (22) And YHWH God said,
'Behold, the man has become like one of us, knowing good and evil; and
now lest he send out his hand and take also from the tree of life and eat
and live forever...' (23) So YHWH God sent him out of the garden of
Eden to work the ground from which he was taken. (24) And he drove out
the man, and he stationed to the east of the garden of Eden the cherubim,
and the flame of the turning sword to guard the way to the tree of life.

Reading the Garden Story

A Transitional Verse: Genesis 2.4

The narrator leads readers into the paradise narrative with what scholars
call the *tôlēdôt* formula: 'these are the generations'.[1] To a first time
reader the line may sound strange. What does it mean to talk about 'the
generations of the heavens and the earth'? Generations typically have to
do with people and the cycle of being children, bearing children, having
grandchildren, growing old, and dying.

Genesis 1 was at least moderately concerned with generation.[2] God
called forth from the earth and deemed good the 'plants yielding seed',
and the fruit trees 'bearing fruit with the seed in it'. God blessed them
and told the sea creatures and birds to reproduce. God also blessed the
humans and told them to be fruitful and multiply. But though the
commands for procreation were given and humankind was specifically
made male and female in order that it might have this reproductive
capacity, creation in that story seems to end with God resting and
specifically *without* any generations. There has been no procreation, no
children, grandchildren, growing old, or dying. The *tôlēdôt* formula may

---

1.   T. Stordalen correctly analyzes the whole of 2.4 as transitional: 'Genesis 2.4:
Restudying a *locus classicus*', *ZAW* 104 (1992), pp. 163-77.
2.   Some scholars even see in its orderly repetitive pattern a similarity to the
genealogies that come later in Genesis. C. Westermann, *Genesis 1–11: A
Commentary* (trans. J.J. Scullion S.J.; Minneapolis: Augsburg Publishing House,
1984), p. 16.

suggest to a first-time reader that perhaps the generations and regeneration are to come in this next story.

To hearers of the garden story as it was first told, the *tôlēdôt* formula may have functioned in other ways as well. Perhaps it served simply to introduce a story, much like 'once upon a time' does for contemporary English-speaking story hearers. Or it may have been an indication of a different form or genre, perhaps signaling that a history of a particular character was going to be recounted.[1] Experienced readers of biblical narrative (i.e. not first-time readers) may expect a long, repetitive list of names and life spans to follow,[2] or they may recognize that the formula indicates a shift to a new focus for the story.[3] Trained readers (biblical scholars) know that the *tôlēdôt* formula refers to what is to come as the progeny of the subject,[4] which in this case is the heavens and the earth.[5]

As the verse continues in 2.4b, the narrator seems to focus our attention on one particular day: 'on the day...' Readers of Genesis 1 may reasonably wonder whether they are going to get a more detailed analysis of one of the six days of creation already described in that chapter. Readers more familiar with Hebrew may recognize this phrase as an idiom for 'when'.

In Genesis 1 the deity was known as 'God', so a contemporary reader unfamiliar with the Bible may be somewhat puzzled at the name 'LORD God' in this introductory verse.[6] Without having read the Bible translation's preface or having had other instruction, an English reader would not know that the word LORD, with its unusual capitalization, stands for the Hebrew personal name for God, YHWH. A casual English reader from a Jewish or Christian background might not even notice the change in what God is called, seeing the addition of 'LORD', if it is noticed at all, as just another proper religious way to talk about God.[7]

1. See Stordalen, *'locus classicus'*, p. 176.
2. In the primeval narrative, Genesis 1–11, see Gen. 5.1; 10.1; 11.10.
3. For example, the shift to Noah in 6.9 and to Abraham in 11.27.
4. See Stordalen, *'locus classicus'*, pp. 170-71. Westermann, *Genesis 1–11*, p. 26 also understands the phrase in terms of birth, but he treats Gen. 2.4a as summarizing Gen. 1.1–2.3.
5. Experienced readers, like first-time readers, may remain puzzled as to just how the heavens and the earth can be the progenitors of the creatures and events in the story that follows.
6. While I refer primarily to my own translation, I do on occasion refer to standard translations by their usual abbreviations.
7. A more careful or informed first-time reader would recognize the shift in

God and the Garden: Genesis 2.5–14[1]
As the story itself begins in 2.5, the narrator gives readers a first insight
into this LORD God. Early Hebrew listeners may be the best prepared
to guess what kind of a story this will be. They might have recognized,
in the desolate picture as the story begins, echoes of other popular
ancient Near Eastern creation myths. Knowing these similar stories
might also influence their expectations of God in the story.[2]

The parallel structure of the four parts of 2.5 answers in the second
part of the verse questions that the first part may raise for readers:

> 2.5a   When no bush of the field was yet on the earth
> 2.5b   and no grass of the field had yet sprouted,
> 2.5c   for YHWH God had not caused it to rain upon the earth,
> 2.5d   and there was not a man to work the ground...

God's not causing it to rain upon the earth in 2.5c explains to readers
why 'no bush of the field was yet on the earth' in 2.5a, just as there not
yet being a man to work the ground in 2.5d may clarify why 'no grass
of the field had yet sprouted' in 2.5b. The narrator leads readers to

divine appellation, but might not know what significance it has. Readers of other
biblical narratives may already know that LORD stands for YHWH and that YHWH is
the God who revealed God's self and name, YHWH, personally to Moses and to the
people of Israel. These experienced readers may wonder about how Israel's story is
connected with the one to come. Hebrew hearers of the story may feel particularly at
home since the coming story is about *their* God. Still, the combination YHWH God
may sound strange to experienced Hebrew readers, occurring as it does so rarely in
the biblical texts. (See J. L'Hour, 'Yahweh Elohim', *RB* 81 (1974), pp. 524-56 for
discussion.) YHWH God is *not* one of the standard ways to talk about God, so one
suspects the narrator may be trying to make a special point or to create a particular
effect by talking of God in this way.

1.   I hesitate to use titles for the reading in this chapter because titles always
shape reading and sometimes give away the punch line. While titles are dangerous,
especially for a reading 'through time' like this one, they are also helpful for keeping
track of where we are in the story, so I will use them.

2.   Scholars know a host of ancient Near Eastern creation stories with ties to the
Genesis texts. For the stories themselves, see J.B. Pritchard, *Ancient Near Eastern
Texts Relating to the Old Testament* (Princeton: Princeton University Press, 3rd edn,
1969). For an analysis of their similarity to Genesis texts see Westermann, *Genesis
1–11*, or S.R. Lieberman, 'The Eve Motif in Ancient Near Eastern and Classical
Greek Sources' (PhD Thesis, Boston University, 1975). The Akkadian myth *Enuma
Elish* begins similarly to 2.5 'When on high the heaven had not been named...' and
continues with other realities that were 'not yet'. Its portrayal of the deities and their
motives and role in creation, however, is strikingly different from Genesis 1–3.

believe that God is the causer of rain. Readers may also wonder if God is responsible for the absence of someone to work the ground, especially if they remember the creation of humans by God and their mandate to subdue the earth in Gen. 1.26-28.

The stream in Gen. 2.6 may be only indirectly related to the narrator's portrayal of God. Is it an alternative to God's sending rain? Does it insure that the ground is adequately wet for the forming of man[1] from the dust? The narrator's picture of God forming man in 2.7 is striking. Experienced readers note that the verb *yāṣar* used to depict God's action is also used in other biblical texts for the shaping done by potters. The anthropomorphic picture of God intensifies as the narrator describes God breathing the breath of life into the human body.

The narrator's human-like picture of God continues as God shifts from being potter to horticulturalist. God plants 'a garden in Eden' in 2.8. Readers know from Genesis 1 that God called the earth to bring forth plants and trees. In Genesis 2–3, God is actively involved in planting, but there are no details about the garden—at least not yet. So, readers may wonder what kind of a garden it is and why God plants it. In Genesis 1 God planted 'plants yielding seed' and trees bearing 'fruit with the seed in it' (Gen. 1.12, NRSV) and gave them to the humans for food (Gen. 1.29). Did God plant a similar garden here as food for them? Are the conditions good for a garden? Remembering readers might wonder whether the dry desert-like wasteland of 2.5 has been amply and adequately watered by the stream of 2.6?

And where is Eden? 'In the east' is not a terribly descriptive clue from the narrator. Why did God choose that place? What does Eden mean, modern readers may wonder? Hebrew readers may understand the word Eden as suggesting delight. Experienced Bible readers may know other things about Eden or God's garden.[2] Readers familiar with ancient Near Eastern texts might associate a garden with the king, who tended the garden for the deity.[3]

---

1.   See the translation note on 2.5 in the appendix and the discussion on pp. 102-104 for why I use 'the man' throughout most of this reading rather than human, 'earth creature' or other alternatives.

2.   Gen. 4.16, 2 Kgs 19.12 and Isa. 37.12 know Eden as a place. Isa. 51.3, Ezek. 28.13, 31.8-9, 36.35 and Joel 2.3 know it as a garden or garden of God. Genesis 13.10 refers to the garden of the Lord, and garden language is prominent in the Song of Songs.

3.   G. Widengren, *The King and the Tree of Life in Ancient Near Eastern*

Certainly readers will wonder how this garden is related to the newly formed man, especially since 2.5 noted his absence as a worker of the ground. The narrator answers some of these readerly questions and tells more about God's relationship to the man as 2.8 continues. God puts the man in the garden. God seems, here, like a child playing, first shaping the mud to make a person, then planting a garden and putting the mud creature in it.[1] The narrator's picture of God forming, planting, and placing no longer has the transcendent, orderly quality of the story of Genesis 1. To think of God playing in the muck may seem too extreme, but the narrator certainly pictures this God as more embodied (breathing in 2.7) and 'down to earth' (2.8) than the bodiless, commanding voice of Genesis 1.[2]

The narrator gives readers some details in 2.9 about the garden: God plants trees. The narrative also begins to take a human perspective as readers hear that the trees are 'desirable to see and good to eat'. Since readers know from Genesis 1 that fruit trees were for human consumption, and nothing has been said so far in Genesis about God eating food, readers deduce that these trees were planted for the man's benefit. Presumably, it is the man's sight and food that the verse has in mind. God takes care of human needs in this story, as God did in the earlier account of creation. God provides not only for the man's nourishment, the narrator suggests, but also for his aesthetic pleasure. This version of the story has so far not repeated God's giving of the trees to the man for food, however. Readers may reasonably suppose, from the prior account in Genesis 1, that this provision remains in force. They may also observe and wonder why God has not yet spoken in the Genesis 2–3 story to this man whom God created.

Rather than God giving all the trees to the new man for food, which Genesis 1 might lead readers to expect, the story adds details. Two trees are named,[3] and at least one of them is located: 'the tree of life in the

Religion (Uppsala: A.B. Lundequistska Bokhandeln, 1951).

    1.   H. Bloom also recognizes the scene as mud play. See H. Bloom and D. Rosenberg, *The Book of J* (New York: Grove Weidenfeld, 1990), p. 28.

    2.   Perhaps the distinction between the creation accounts in Genesis 1 and 2 is not as sharp as scholars often make it. There is a transition in the portrayal of God. The God at the end of the first account, who has an 'image' and 'likeness' and who rests from work, is closer to the bodied God of the rest of Genesis 2–3.

    3.   Scholars attempting to reconcile what happens with the trees later in the story have speculated about whether earlier versions of the tale had one tree or two. It seems clear, as the story now stands, that it refers to two trees. For a discussion of the two

middle of the garden, and the tree of the knowledge of good and evil'. Are these trees among those described as 'desirable to see and good to eat' that God had planted? Readers will certainly wonder about what these names mean.

What is the tree of life? A first-time English reader of Genesis has no clues from the text about this special tree. A reader's own cultural experience may stretch to bring up potentially related images of a fountain of youth. Experienced Bible readers know that wisdom is described as the tree of life in Prov. 3.18 and that the New Testament book of Revelation expects the tree of life to be made available again to the righteous in the end times.[1] Early readers of Genesis in ancient Palestine may recall that kings were often responsible for watering a ritual tree with the water of life.[2]

The tree of the knowledge of good and evil will be even more of a puzzle to modern Western readers. Except perhaps for this Genesis story, our cultural myths do not include trees of knowledge or wisdom. An effect of this narrative detail on modern readers may be to make us ask why the narrator is bringing up good and evil at this point. These readers might also wonder what the man knows about good and evil. What is the significance of these trees? Does God make all of these trees available to the man for food as God did in Genesis 1? Their names are the only hints the narrator gives about these trees. God's purposes for the two specially named trees, in relation to the man, are unknown.

The narrator keeps the emphasis on detail going in 2.10-14, and the suspense mounts. Readers learn nothing new in these verses about God since God is not mentioned directly. Readers may start to wonder about the direction of the story. Verses 7-9 seemed to focus on the new man and his immediate environment. Now the story seems to zoom out, considering the garden in relation to the whole earth. Is the story shifting focus? Where will it go from here? Were readers mistaken to think that the man might be a special focus of attention? And how is God, the

---

trees and how they function in the composite narrative, see Westermann, *Genesis 1–11*, pp. 211-14.

1.   Proverbs also equates the tree of life with the 'fruit of the righteous' in 11.30, with 'desire fulfilled' in 13.12, and with 'a gentle tongue' in 15.4. See also Rev. 2.7; 22.2, 14, 19.

2.   Widengren, *The King and the Tree of Life*, p. 19. For J. Barr, the tree of life shapes the direction of the story; see *The Garden of Eden and the Hope of Immortality* (Minneapolis: Fortress Press, 1992), p. 59.

chief maker in the creation accounts so far, connected to these rivers?

In trying to make sense of a story that may seem to have gone off course, readers may wonder whether God made the rivers. Nothing was said specifically in Genesis 1 about rivers. The story so far in Genesis 2 has mentioned God's not yet causing rain, and in 2.6 it notes a 'stream', whose origin is unknown, as a water source. Alternatively, the narrator may gain credibility in these meandering verses about winding rivers. The scope and level of detail suggest the narrator has expansive knowledge, and the dazzling description of jewels in unknown lands may capture the reader's attention. The rivers mentioned move from unknown to more familiar.[1] They are described less as they become better known, and the reader's estimation of the narrator's ability may rise accordingly. A narrator who knows so much may be particularly reliable, or he may be recognized as an adept weaver of tales. The significance of 2.10-14 for the story may be puzzling for readers, who might ponder these verses as they continue reading.

God and Humans in the Garden: Genesis 2.15-25

Having made readers wonder, at least momentarily, about what is going on, the story of the man resumes. The narrator reminds readers that God put the man in the garden, and links this placement to the lack mentioned in 2.5. Readers are pleased, finally, to have a question answered. The man that God made *will* supply the ground's lack since he is made to work and guard the garden.

Another question about divine intent and God's relationship to the man is answered in 2.16. God finally speaks, for the first time in this story, and the speech is familiar. Just as God gave food in Genesis 1, here too God provides every tree of the garden to the man for food. But the narrator describes the permission here in a modified fashion. The verb is different: 'commanded'. In the earlier version (Gen. 1.29) God called the gift to human attention ('See... '), but here God commands. The tone of the narrator's word 'commands' in 2.16 differs from God's earlier mandate in 1.28 to be fruitful, subdue and exercise dominion, introduced by the simple word 'said'. God, in this story, commands. How does God's command here differ from God's blessing in Genesis 1, readers might wonder? The word might remind experienced Bible readers of God's commands to Israel at Sinai.

---

1.   Both ancient and modern readers are likely to be unfamiliar with the name Pishon, while some may recognize the Tigris and Euphrates.

The full force of God's command, and the shock to the reader comes in 2.17 with the 'but': 'but of the tree of the knowledge of good and evil you shall not eat of it...' The puzzling tree of the knowledge of good and evil also reappears. Eating of it is prohibited under pain of death. The narrator provides no explanation for this unexpected prohibition, no comment on why this tree or its knowledge should be dangerous, no hints of God's aims or motives in proscribing it, not even a clue about whether the man understood God's command or the warning of death.

Nor does the story give us as readers any narrative experience with death. Nothing has died yet that was created in Genesis 1, as far as we know anyway. The man in this story has not seen death; at least the narrator has not told us about it. But neither does the man express any surprise, dismay, or consternation at God's command or at God's comment about death.

As readers, we may be puzzled, fearful, or enraged at what may seem to be an arbitrary command of God, with what might seem to us to be an unduly severe punishment or consequence. Why should the man not eat from this particular tree? What does the knowledge of good and evil have to do with the prohibition? Why should such a severe warning or threat (and which of these is it?) accompany the prohibition? We readers live in a world where people *do* die, and, however well we may understand or explain death, we often fight and hate its arrival. Thus, while readers may react strongly to God's pronouncement, we might also wonder what, if anything, the man knows of death and whether death was part of life in the garden.[1] Alternatively, we may note that God has allowed (even commanded) eating from almost all of the trees. A single limitation may seem unproblematic in view of God's largess.

Though up to this point the narrator has given no clues about the role that the tree of the knowledge of good and evil will play in the story, readers may begin now to be suspicious. That tree was mentioned and dropped from attention once before in 2.9 as the narrator wandered off to discuss the rivers. Given the potentially startling prohibition of the mysterious tree in 2.17, readers will expect to hear more about it as the story continues.

But not right away. In 2.18, the narrator leaves readers dangling in suspense about what God is doing with the tree in order to step back

---

1.   See Barr, *Garden*, for a discussion of mortality as a presupposition in the garden.

again and give us a God's-eye view of the situation. Having become accustomed in Genesis 1 to regular divine evaluations of the creation in the repeated phrase 'and God saw that it was good', readers will recognize the divine evaluation of the garden scene 'it is not good... ' They will also certainly notice the negative difference in God's assessment. Why, a reader may wonder, is something *not* good? God made it. Everything God made before was 'good' or 'very good'. How can God make something that is not good?

As the verse continues, readers learn that what is not good is the man's being alone. Readers of Genesis 1 may wonder what happened to all the fish, birds, and animals that God had already created. They may begin to wonder now, if they had not already, whether they are reading an alternate account or a supplement to the Genesis 1 story. Readers might then pause to remember that if a new story has begun in Gen. 2.5 then the animals have not been specifically created. The garden, it seems is populated only with the man, presumably ordinary trees, and the two specially named trees. There are no other creatures, at least not mentioned, so perhaps not yet made. And God has deemed this situation 'not good'. Readers may also wonder at this point what the man thinks about his aloneness since the narrator has so far given no indications of the man's perspective.

God not only evaluates the situation, God vows to do something about it. God decides to make the man 'a helper as his counterpart'.[1] Reader speculations about what the man needs help doing or why he needs a counterpart are based on what the narrator has said so far and on readers' own experiences. Perhaps the man needs a counterpart to fulfill the command given earlier to be fruitful and multiply.[2] As sexually aware readers, we know that the man cannot procreate alone. If we read the paradise story independently of Genesis 1, however, this option seems less likely. In the garden version, God has given no command to the man to procreate, and the narrator has given no clues that the man is sexually aware. Of course, God may have just at this point realized that the man could not procreate alone, deemed this infertility 'not good' in terms of God's purposes, and decided to remedy the situation before issuing such a command. Is God so absent-minded? The narrative

---

1.   'Counterpart' captures the oppositeness and likeness of *kᵉnegdô*.

2.   This is the position of D.J.A. Clines in *What Does Eve Do to Help? and Other Readerly Questions to the Old Testament* (JSOTSup, 94; Sheffield: JSOT Press, 1990). I discuss woman's role as helper on pp. 96-98.

suggests that perhaps God is figuring things out, to some extent, as the creation proceeds.

A more reasonable option for what help the man needs might be to consider what could be the narrator's view: the man needs additional farm labor.[1] The narrator has suggested three times now to readers that the man is to work or serve the ground: first by noting the lack of a man to do so in 2.5; second, indirectly, by describing in 2.8 how God formed the man and put him in the garden (readers infer that the man will fill the ground's lack of a worker); and finally, directly, by stating in 2.15 that 'God took the man and settled him in the garden of Eden to work it and guard it'. That God's judgment 'it is not good that the man be alone' refers to the man's task of serving the garden seems to be a more obvious reader choice, within this story at least. Farmers, certainly, would recognize the importance of a family as part of the labor force in maintaining the crops. But if the helper is created to help the man with the job of working and guarding, why does God's reported evaluation of the situation in 2.18 not follow directly on the narrator's reminder in 2.15 of God's agricultural intentions for the man?

The reader turns to the narrator, hoping for help in sorting out these questions about the man's helper. The narrative, however, continues with a description of God's activity, again universal in scope. So 'out of the ground', just like the man, readers will remember, God forms 'every animal of the field and every bird of the heavens'. In the earlier story (in Genesis 1) the animals were to share the humans' vegetarian food supply. What will they eat here? Will God permit and prohibit trees to them too, readers may wonder? Will the animals be the needed helpers? The narrator does not say, nor does God speak directly at this point. In the earlier account the humans were to exercise dominion over the birds and animals. Will the man have dominion over them here? So far, the narrator has said nothing about what this mud boy may have said or done, dominating or otherwise. Readers may presume that he heard God's command in 2.16-17, though the narrator has given no clue yet that he listened. We recall that he did not respond.

The narrative suggests that God may be curious about the man's response to these newly-formed earth creatures. God brings them 'to

---

1. C. Meyers suggests that the whole narrative is concerned with the difficulties of beginning agriculture as pioneers in an uncultivated land. At least part of the helper's role would then be agricultural in nature. See *Discovering Eve: Ancient Israelite Women in Context* (New York: Oxford University Press, 1988).

the man to see what he would call them'. Apparently the man can speak, though the narrator is careful to hide his direct speech from readers at this point. We see the scene instead from a God's eye view. As readers we wait with God to hear what the man will call the animals. God apparently hears the names since, the narrator tells us, God agrees that 'whatever the man called the living being, that is its name'. As readers, however, we get no details. We do not hear whether the man chose the names hippopotamus and elephant (in Hebrew of course). We hear nothing of the man's response to the tiger or giraffe. We do not know whether the man was looking for a mate or a fellow gardener, or whether he was looking for anyone at all. As readers we rely, reluctantly perhaps, on the narrator for clues to this first human's ideas and feelings, but we get little information: 'whatever the man called the living being, that is its name.'

This episode does suggest some things about God, at least. If we can trust the narrator, God is willing, perhaps even anxious, to involve the man in the creation process. Readers remember that in the earlier account (following the NRSV) God gave the names day, night, sky, and earth to the light, darkness, dome, and dry land.[1] The animals were not named in that story. Rather than keeping all the authority, God may have decided to involve humans,[2] and in the paradise account we hear that God allows the man to name God's artwork. What this naming entails or implies is not specified in this story.[3] So, the narrator continues, the man gives 'names to all cattle and birds of the heavens and to every animal of the field'. The man seems to go along with God's plan, naming in 2.20 even the cattle that the narrator neglected to tell us earlier in garden story that God had made. A careful reader may wonder somewhat about the narrator's reliability. Why did the narrator skip the cattle in the earlier list? Maybe such details are not important, or maybe it is a clue that not every type of creature that God made and the

---

1.   Very careful readers will have noted that God did not name anything else in the first story. In particular God did not name the animals, though the story has probably established that naming is important and is God's prerogative.

2.   For a persuasive reading of Genesis 1–11 as having as its theme the self-limitation of God, see H. Shank, 'The Sin Theology of the Cain and Abel Story: An Analysis of Narrative Themes within the Context of Genesis 1–11' (PhD diss., Marquette University, 1988).

3.   Scholars have recently debated the importance of naming and where it occurs in Genesis 2–3. I discuss naming on pp. 100-102.

man named is specifically listed here. The man is certainly no longer alone, in any case, or so it would seem.

There is a narrative 'but' again, however, at the end of 2.20: 'but [as] for the man he did not find a helper as his counterpart.' Other translations may aid or confuse the English reader at this point.[1] Just who is assessing this situation? Is God deciding that none of the animals are suitable for the man? Does the man evaluate the situation himself? Is it the narrator's verdict being reported in the passive voice as the NRSV might suggest?

In any case, the narrator continues the story from God's perspective, giving no direct indications of the man's responses to the animals. The visions we may have of the man shouting 'no! no!' or shaking his head in rejection or dismay as the animals are brought forward for naming (and as potential partner candidates?) are not available in the text. We just don't know what he thinks.

God, apparently, is dissatisfied with the affair so far and embarks on a new plan. The narrator fills us in on the details. This narratorial attention suggests that this particular creation may be a far more sophisticated and complicated operation than God's fashioning of the animals from the ground. God the hypnotist or anesthesiologist begins, causing 'a deep sleep to fall upon the man'. God the surgeon continues, extracting a rib and sewing up the man's side. God the architect finishes the job, building the rib into a woman, for God as zookeeper to bring to the man.[2]

Readers wonder about the woman. What does she look like? Is she pretty? Is she strong? Why was she made from the man's body rather than from the ground, and why was she made from a rib in particular?[3]

---

1.   Cf. NRSV: 'there was not found a helper as his partner.' See the translation note on 2.20 in the appendix.

2.   Once we readers hear the man's response and the narrator's aside in the next two verses we may, with the rabbis and G. von Rad, prefer to read God's bringing of the woman to the man as portraying God as the father of the bride. Rabbinic midrashim contribute details about how God decked out the woman with a fancy hairstyle and jewels. See *Gen. R.* 18.1 and G. von Rad, *Genesis: A Commentary* (Philadelphia: The Westminster Press, rev. edn, 1972), p. 84. For other aspects of Jewish exegesis of Genesis 2–3 see the essays by S.N. Lambden and P. Morris in P. Morris and D. Sawyer (eds.), *A Walk in the Garden: Biblical, Iconographical and Literary Images of Eden* (JSOTSup, 136; Sheffield: Sheffield Academic Press, 1992).

3.   A. Bledstein recognizes the use of 'rib' as a pun on 'the lady of the rib', the Sumerian goddess Ninti: 'The Genesis of Humans: The Garden of Eden Revisited', *Judaism* 26 (1977), p. 192.

Why, for that matter, has no human been born in the more usual
fashion? Will the woman help the man tend the garden? Will she help
him procreate? How is she different from all of the mud creatures that
someone deemed unsuitable as partners? What will the man think of
her? Will he name her as he did the animals? Will he recognize her, or
will God decide her adequacy as the man's partner?

'At last', the reader might say (with some translations of 2.23), the
man finally speaks. At last the man has a voice, and not only a voice but
thoughts, feelings, and a sense of humor as well. His joy bursts out in an
exclamation of delight as he recognizes 'this one' (which appears three
times in the Hebrew) as bone of his bones and flesh of his flesh. The
recognition is dramatized since the narrator uses the man's direct
discourse to report it. The man names the new creature woman (ʾiššâ) in
a pun on man (ʾîš).[1]

Though neither the man in his speech, nor God, who seems recently
to have disappeared from view,[2] says so directly, the narrator's next
aside suggests that perhaps the woman is the desired, awaited, intended
helper. In 2.24, the narrator explains, in a reader aside, what sounds like
a common ancient custom about marriage. Is this verse the climax of the
whole story? Does 2.24 suggest the sexual union of the garden couple in
addition to the habitual mating of men and women in the narrator's
time, and, if so, does the couple's joining as one flesh undo God's
recently wrought separation of the man and woman? Is this union the
remedy for the not-goodness of man's aloneness that God had
previously noted? Is it God's intention for human sexuality? Is the
woman's role as helper simply to meet the man's sexual needs, or does
this verse suggest a mutuality in male-female relations?[3]

The narrator continues the story in 2.25, again seemingly in God's
absence, with a comment on the couple's nudity and lack of shame.
Readers may wonder why the couple would be ashamed. In 2.23, the
man was obviously delighted and seemingly unembarrassed with what
he saw. The woman's thoughts and feelings are hidden by the narrator,
however, so readers do not know her reactions to him, to her own
nakedness, to life, or to God (if she is aware of God). Perhaps the couple

---

1.   See translation notes on 2.5 and 2.23 and Chapter 3 for discussion of puns.

2.   God may have disappeared because ancient conventions had only two
characters on stage at any one time. See B. Vawter, *On Genesis: A New Reading*
(Garden City, NY: Doubleday, 1977), p. 79.

3.   I discuss many of these questions in Chapter 4.

should be ashamed of being naked in each other's presence since they are strangers. Hebrew readers, like their contemporary counterparts, would recognize that except for bedroom scenes, nudity is prohibited (to varying degrees) in 'civilized' culture.[1] The narrator's comment about nakedness and unashamedness, then, is a hint about societal aspects of human relations.

Other Views of God in the Garden: Genesis 3.1-7
The comment about nakedness is also a segue to the next part of the story, where the narrator introduces a new character, the serpent,[2] described by means of a pun on the couple's nakedness. The couple was naked *ʿᵃrûmmîm*, and the serpent is crafty *ʿārûm*. Both words share the same three consonants *ʿrm*. The serpent is not only related to the couple's nakedness, however. The narrator also describes it[3] as one of the animals of the field, in fact as being more shrewd than all of the animals of the field 'that YHWH God had made'. The reader may well draw some inferences from this last remark. As one of the animals of the field, the serpent would have been made from the ground, brought to the man, named by him, and presumably deemed inappropriate as a helper or partner for the man.

What, we may wonder as readers, is this creature doing in the story? The man has a helper now, or at least the not-goodness of his aloneness seems to have been remedied (though whether the woman is the planned counterpart and the precise nature of her helping may still be unclear). Other unresolved issues may also come to mind. God issued a command about trees that the story has not taken up. Perhaps the serpent has something to do with that. Maybe the serpent is related specifically to whatever is meant by 'the knowledge of good and evil'.

1. But see M. Oduyoye's analysis of the significance of nakedness and clothing in African cultures in *The Sons of the Gods and the Daughters of Men: An Afro-Asiatic Interpretation of Genesis 1–11* (Maryknoll, NY: Orbis, 1984).

2. For more background and various assessments of the serpent, see R.S. Hanson, 'The Snake and I', chap. in *The Serpent Was Wiser: A New Look at Genesis 1–11* (Minneapolis: Augsburg, 1972) and K.R. Joines, 'The Serpent in Gen. 3', *ZAW* 87 (1975), pp. 1-11.

3. I use the neuter pronoun for the serpent, as we normally do in English for animals. The sex of the serpent is not specified in the story, so presumably it is not relevant, but for other possibilities see Bledstein, 'The Genesis of Humans', p. 196. Vawter also notes the serpent's connection with the Canaanite god Baal as a fertility symbol in *On Genesis*, p. 71.

The serpent's arrival as a new and unknown character forces readers again to try to make some connections with other parts of the story and eventually, perhaps, to rely on the narrator.

And we may rely on the narrator. In fact, since the narrator provides no aside about the strangeness of serpents talking, readers may willingly accept the narrator's nonchalant attitude about talking snakes and think little of it. Such a creature may affect our thoughts about the historicity of the story, but probably no more than the strange birth of the woman. Certainly a talking snake is no more unusual than a woman being born from a man. If we were not convinced earlier of the narrative's fictive qualities, we are subtly reminded of them again by the crafty, speaking snake.

Unlike the man who waited sixteen verses for a chance (or motive?) to speak and unlike the woman, whose perspective and voice are still unknown to the reader, the narrator lets this serpent speak right away. In fact, readers seem to come upon the scene in 3.1 as the serpent and the woman are in the middle of a conversation. We have the impression that they may have been talking for some time, though the narrator does not say so explicitly. Instead, the narrator captures the serpent's speech beginning with a pausal word: 'Well...' or 'Indeed...' or '*Really*, did God say...' The serpent's question catches our attention and makes us look back in the story.[1] If, as careful readers, we reconsider God's command in 2.16-17, we notice how the serpent's question differs from God's statement, reported earlier by the narrator. While God began with permission freely to eat 'of every tree of the garden', the serpent questions the availability of *any* tree. Whereas earlier God suggested that death would follow from eating from the one forbidden tree, which God names as the tree of the knowledge of good and evil, the serpent in 3.1 mentions neither the name of the tree nor the potential consequences of eating from it.

Many scholars feel quite free to part from the narrator's portrayal of the serpent.[2] Perhaps because of their knowledge of ancient Near Eastern parallels and later developments in the history of interpretation

---

1.   J.F.A. Sawyer notes that the serpent's question is the first in the Bible. See 'The Image of God, The Wisdom of Serpents and the Knowledge of Good and Evil', in Morris and Sawyer (eds.), *A Walk in the Garden*, p. 69. I discuss the significance of the serpent's question in Chapter 3.

2.   For neutral portrayal of the serpent, see T.E. Fretheim, 'Is Genesis 3 a Fall Story?', *WW* 14 (1994), pp. 149-51.

of this story, or perhaps simply from their own puzzlement, they attribute knowledge and motives to the serpent that the narrator shrouds in silence. For example, one commentator says that the serpent is duplicitous,[1] another that it twists God's words.[2] This assumes that the serpent knew God's words,[3] even though the animals had not yet been created in the story when God spoke in 2.16-17, and there is no direct indication that God or anyone else told the serpent or any animals of the permission and prohibition. Again, critics often presume that the serpent is trying to seduce or trick the woman,[4] and they may wax eloquent about why the serpent chose her as its victim.[5] The narrator gives no direct indications of the serpent's motives, suggesting neither that it wants to trick the woman, nor speculating on why it converses with her rather than her man.[6] The serpent could just as easily be trying to get information it does not have.

In any case, the serpent asks the woman what God said. While the woman may not know, the serpent's question prompts readers to

1.   Vawter, *On Genesis*, p. 81. Several scholars in addition to Vawter (p. 71) assume the serpent is tempting the woman. See, for example, Bledstein, 'The Genesis of Humans', p. 143; D. Damrosch, *The Narrative Covenant: Transformations of Genre in the Growth of Biblical Literature* (San Francisco: Harper & Row, 1987), p. 140; Shank, 'The Sin Theology', p. 107. For an alternative perspective, see D.R.G. Beattie, '*Peshat* and *Derash* in the Garden of Eden', *Irish Biblical Studies* 7 (1985), pp. 62-75, who contends that the serpent told the truth and that scholars squirm about admitting that God lied.

2.   W. Brueggemann, *Genesis* (IBC; Atlanta: John Knox Press, 1982), p. 48.

3.   P.L. Wismer contends that the serpent's statement claims 'exact knowledge of the divine command' in 'The Myth of Original Sin: A Hermeneutic Theology Based on Genesis 2-3' (PhD dissertation, University of Chicago, 1983), p. 173.

4.   M. Fishbane, 'Genesis 2.4b-11.32/The Primeval Cycle', chap. in *Text and Texture: Close Readings of Selected Biblical Texts* (New York: Schocken Books, 1979), p. 20.

5.   See W. Park, 'Why Eve?', *St. Vladimir's Theological Quarterly* 35 (1991), pp. 127-35 and A. Gardner, 'Genesis 2.4b-3: A Mythological Paradigm of Sexuality or of the Religious History of Pre-exilic Israel?', *SJT* 43 (1990) 14, who explain the woman as the logical choice because of Israelite women's involvement with Canaanite fertility religions.

6.   The narrator does not say the woman falls because she is weaker, as D. Bonhoeffer contends in *Creation and Fall: A Theological Interpretation of Genesis 1-3* (trans. J.C. Fletcher; London: SCM Press, 1959), p. 76; nor is the woman tempted first because she is 'the perfection', as G. Tavard claims in *Woman in Christian Tradition* (Notre Dame: University of Notre Dame Press, 1973), p. 13.

remember (or to look back and see) what *we* know God said in 2.17. The woman's response, whose 'we' actually answers the serpent's plural 'you', suggests that she knows of the permission, which she understands as referring to the *fruit* of the trees.

Attentive readers may well wonder at this point how the woman knows anything at all of God's permission and prohibition to eat from the trees. After all, as we readers heard the story, she was just a rib in the man's side when God made this speech. That she knows *something* is not in question, only *how and what* she knows are at issue. Did the man tell her? Did God tell her? How, if at all, did what she heard differ from what the narrator describes God speaking originally? Did the woman's interlocutor make the alterations in the command as she reports it to the serpent, or did she interpret what she heard, making her own modifications?

In 3.2 the woman continues describing the prohibition, adding details. First, she locates the forbidden tree 'in the midst of the garden', a fact the narrator implies and readers infer from 2.9, but which the man could not have heard because God did not say in 2.17. Of course, the man or the couple presumably knew which tree God intended, so this detail is not entirely out of place. The woman's next addition also suggests interpretation on her part: she adds the phrase 'nor shall you touch it'. Commentators again differ on whether the woman heard the prohibition this way from the man or whether she alters God's words (presumably faithfully and accurately reported to her by her man). It is the rare commentator, remarking on the woman's addition at this point, who assigns any positive qualities to this act or to her.[1]

The serpent then 'contradicts' God's comment about the resulting death.[2] The narrator does not report the serpent's remark as a contradiction, however. Instead, readers are told merely what the serpent 'said' in 3.4. Whether to deem it a contradiction, or simply the serpent's perspective on how eating and living generally work, is left to us to conclude. As readers we may be relieved, and actually hope, that the serpent is right. If a death sentence seemed capricious to readers in 2.17, its denial here is welcome.

---

1.   Trible describes the responding woman as 'intelligent, informed, and perceptive': *God and the Rhetoric of Sexuality* (Philadelphia: Fortress Press, 1978), p. 110.
2.   N.M. Sarna, *The JPS Torah Commentary: Genesis* (Philadelphia: The Jewish Publication Society, 5749/1989), p. 25.

The serpent also makes its own speculation about what would happen as a result of the forbidden eating, and it gives its thoughts the credibility of what 'God knows'. By choosing direct discourse with little comment at this point, the narrator leaves in the shadows any intentions or motives the serpent may have had in making this claim.[1] The alternative to death that the serpent proposes is ambivalent. The serpent neither touts being 'like gods, knowing good and evil' as a status to which the woman should aspire, nor does it caution her against divine-likeness as something to be avoided. Perhaps the serpent does not know the implications of such knowledge or god-likeness.

In any case, the narrator paints the woman as showing no 'uptake'[2] of the serpent's alternative. The explanation given in 3.6 for her decision to eat the fruit, while it mentions eyes, is not based on a yearning for open eyes *or* on a desire to be like deities.[3] It certainly is not described

1. Commentators regularly remark on the serpent's special knowledge in 3.1-6. For example, Sarna claims that the serpent 'deliberately misquotes God': *Genesis*, 24. Similarly, von Rad describes the serpent's question in 3.1 as 'a complete distortion', *Genesis*, p. 88; and Vawter calls it a 'deliberate caricature', *On Genesis*, p. 78. The story, however, gives no evidence that the serpent has any inside information. Rather, by describing the serpent as 'shrewd', 'crafty', or 'subtle', the narrative suggests that the serpent is able to make judicious (and perhaps tricky) use of the knowledge it does have. As the narrative will bear out in 3.7 and 3.22, it is inappropriate to refer to the serpent's remarks at this point as lying.

2. J.L. Austin's discussion of speech-act theory refers to 'uptake' as amounting to 'bringing about the understanding of the meaning and of the force of the locution'. See *How to do Things with Words* (ed. J.O. Urmson and M. Sbisà; Cambridge, MA: Harvard University Press, 2nd edn, 1975), p. 117. R.M. Fowler illustrates this idea regularly in *Let the Reader Understand: Reader-Response Criticism and the Gospel of Mark* (Minneapolis: Fortress Press, 1991). I discuss speech-act theory in Chapter 3.

3. See Westermann, *Genesis 1–11*, p. 249 and J. Barr, 'The Authority of Scripture: The Book of Genesis and the Origin of Evil in Jewish and Christian Tradition', in G.R. Evans (ed.), *Christian Authority: Essays in Honour of Henry Chadwick* (Oxford: Clarendon Press, 1988), p. 65; contra A.J. Hauser, 'Genesis 2–3: The Theme of Intimacy and Alienation', in D.J.A. Clines, P.R. Davies, and D.M. Gunn (eds.), *Art and Meaning: Rhetoric in Biblical Literature* (JSOTSup, 19; Sheffield: JSOT Press, 1982), p. 27; and B. Och, 'The Garden of Eden: From Re-Creation to Reconciliation', *Judaism* 37 (1988), p. 350. H.C. White explains that the inside view of the woman's thoughts conceals her inadmissible desire to be like God: 'Direct and Third Person Discourse in the Narrative of the "Fall"', in D. Patte (ed.), *Genesis 2 and 3: Kaleidoscopic Structural Readings* (Semeia, 18; Chico, CA: Scholars Press, 1980), p. 101. For implications of being like deities, see

as an act of ambition, pride, or hubris.[1] The woman is not trying to overstep her bounds of creatureliness.

If as readers we trust the narrator's portrayal of the woman's decision[2] (and, as Chapter 3 will show, all the narrative rhetoric works to encourage our trust), then we must take seriously the reasons the narrator provides in 3.6 for her action: she saw that the tree was good for food, that it was a delight to the eyes, and that the tree was 'desirable for insight'. The narrator here portrays the woman as possessing skills in evaluation that parallel those of God in deeming creation 'good' in the first creation story and the man's aloneness 'not good' in this one. The narrator in Genesis 1 had God describe creation as 'good', and in both Genesis 1 and Genesis 2 the trees are intended for food. The woman confirms the earlier narrator's picture (though as a character she is, of course, unaware of doing so) as she merges God's evaluative 'good' in Genesis 1 with the trees' divinely intended purpose as food in 2.9. While the woman is thus unaware of the rightness of her judgment (at least as it parallels God's), we readers know she is correct.

Similarly, the woman recognizes the tree as a delight to the eyes. Readers recall the man's delighted response at the appearance of the woman, though we do not know whether the woman was aware of (or if she was how she responded to) the man's assessment of her and, presumably, her beauty.[3]

A.J. Bledstein, 'Are Women Cursed in Genesis 3.16?' in A. Brenner (ed.), *A Feminist Companion to Genesis* (The Feminist Companion to the Bible, 2; Sheffield: Sheffield Academic Press, 1993), p. 145.

1.   Barr, *Garden*, p. 13; J.G. Williams, 'Genesis 3', *Int* 35 (1981), p. 275; and Wismer, 'The Myth of Original Sin', p. 262 concur; contra D.J.A. Clines, 'Prefatory Theme', chap. in *The Theme of the Pentateuch* (JSOTSup, 10; Sheffield: JSOT Press, 1978), p. 69 and G.W. Coats 'The God of Death: Power and Obedience in the Primeval History', *Int* 29 (1975), p. 231.

2.   C.A. Newsom has suggested the possibility of being an 'assenting reader': 'Cultural Politics and the Reading of Job', *Biblical Interpretation* 1 (1993), p. 121. D.J.A. Clines urges readers extract themselves from the ideology of the text: 'Metacommentating Amos', in H.A. McKay and D.J.A. Clines (eds.), *Of Prophets' Visions and the Wisdom of Sages: Essays in Honor of Norman Whybray on his Seventieth Birthday* (JSOTSup, 162; Sheffield: JSOT Press, 1993), p. 158. See S. Fowl on why texts don't have ideologies to be resisted: 'Texts Don't Have Ideologies', *Biblical Interpretation* 3 (1995), pp. 15-34. I discuss resisting reading in Chapter 2, narrative rhetoric in Chapter 3, and the role of ideology in interpretation in Chapter 4.

3.   Following the rabbis. See *Gen. R.* 18.1.

Finally, the woman's judgment about the tree's qualities adds a third feature, whose precedent in the story can only be inferred from the serpent's remarks. The tree is 'desirable for insight'. Does this insight mean having open eyes? Does it mean being like God? Does it mean knowing good and evil? The serpent named all these things. Is one or all of them what the woman means by insight? And why should such insight, (or knowledge, god-likeness, or vision if that is what it means) be desired? As readers, we may wonder whether the serpent's assertions are true, whether the woman is making a good decision. If we have succumbed to the narrator's portrayal of the situation, however, we are convinced that the woman is capable of making a decision and that she not only *can* but *has* considered the consequences. Her action is certainly not rash, though it may be bold.

She takes the fruit and she eats it. Well, what happens? Does she die? Not instantly. Will God respond to her deed? As we read, our suspense (and perhaps our annoyance at the narrator) mounts. We readers want to know the consequences, so recently debated, of her act, but the narrator describes subsequent actions instead, leaving us to wait.

After eating, the narrator tells us, the woman gives '[some] to her man [who was] with her'. How long did she wait? Did she stop to see what would happen to her, or did she quickly try to involve him? What *did* happen to her, we still want to know, or did nothing happen yet? Does she have any particular motives or intentions in giving fruit to her man? Does he ask for it? Does he want it? Does she explain to him the advantages that the narrator suggests made her decide to eat it? Does the man argue against eating it? After all, he heard the prohibition directly from God, or so the narrator has led us to believe. Does the couple even talk with one another at all? We readers have overheard no conversations between them so far.[1] Does the man have mixed feelings about eating the fruit? Does he feel anxious or guilty about doing it? Will he even do it? We don't know yet. We have to keep reading.

Furthermore, we may wonder how the man got there if his presence came as a surprise. The man's being with the woman is probably less surprising to the Hebrew reader, who has clearly heard the serpent's plural verbs (to a plural 'you') throughout the discussion. Upon reflection, English readers might also have recognized his presence in the woman's 'we' statements. The 'with her' in 3.6 leaves no doubt that he

---

1. The man's exclamation in 2.23, since it elicits no response from the woman, is not a conversation.

is at her side, at least at this point in the narrative, and it suggests that he was there and aware of the whole conversation.[1]

The narrative compels us to continue: 'and he ate'. The contrast between the woman's long and careful deliberations about whether to eat the fruit and the man's unreflective (at least from the narrator's perspective) act are even more striking in the Hebrew where his action is a single word![2]

While the story reports that each of them ate of the forbidden tree, readers might notice that the narrator does not explicitly characterize either the woman's or the man's eating as 'sin' or 'rebellion'. The narrative uses none of the Hebrew words for sin.[3] Is the story interested in sin? Does it intend to portray rebellion?[4] Or is the couple's action better described as stemming from curiosity? Might the narrator's lingering in 3.6 over the woman's deliberations suggest thoughtfulness and reason, rather than rebellion, as leading to her decision? God and God's prohibition *are* noticeably absent from her considerations. Does this absence suggest that the woman acted out of pride or rebellion? Being like gods or disobeying God are not explicitly part of her

1.   Contra presumptions of RSV, JPS, NEB, REB, TEV, and Speiser's translations that omit the phrase 'with her'. Vawter conveniently leaves the phrase 'with her' from 3.6 in an ellipsis as he explains why the serpent's conversation has taken place primarily with the woman: *On Genesis*, p. 79. Other commentators (e.g. Brueggemann, *Genesis*; Fishbane, 'Genesis 2.4b-11.32'; von Rad, *Genesis*) ignore the phrase and its implications for the man's complicity. Westermann also leaves the phrase 'with her' out of his discussion, though he speaks of the communal nature of the sin: *Genesis 1–11*, pp. 249-50. G.J. Wenham notes the phrase as indicating that the man's action was decisive: *Genesis 1–15* (WBC; Waco, TX: Word Books, 1987), p. 76. Women commentators regularly remark on this phrase: L.D. Blake in E.C. Stanton (ed.), *The Woman's Bible* (New York: European Publishing Company, 1898; repr., Seattle: Coalition on Women and Religion, 1974), p. 26; Trible, *God and the Rhetoric*, p. 113. See J.M. Higgins, 'The Myth of Eve: The Temptress', *JAAR* 44 (1976), p. 646 for a detailed set of arguments for the man's presence throughout the whole serpent-woman dialogue.

2.   Trible deems his unreflective act 'belly oriented': *God and the Rhetoric*, p. 113.

3.   The word 'sin' first appears in the biblical text in relation to Cain's deliberations and potential action in 4.7.

4.   B. Och suggests that 'writers who have interpreted the act of disobedience as one of rebellion against God have been influenced more by the fruitfulness of their imagination than by the substance of the narrative'. See 'The Garden of Eden', p. 143.

reasoning, but should readers infer them? The narrator is considerably more reticent in describing the man's motivations. What might this silence mean?[1]

Regardless of how we interpret the couple's motives, we still wonder at the consequences of their actions, though perhaps with less fear since the woman seems not to have died instantly. Will anything happen to the couple? Will they gain insight, knowledge, god-likeness, or vision? We do not wait long for a first answer to these questions.

The story continues apace in 3.7, 'the eyes of them both were opened...' They now have the vision, the first of the serpent's claims, 'and they knew...' Perhaps this is the knowledge the serpent suggested; 'that naked [were] they'. Nakedness is probably not the knowledge readers were expecting, however. How is knowing nakedness related to the insight or god-likeness the serpent promised? Has the couple been duped?

Readers have seen nakedness in the story before. The couple was naked but not ashamed. Are they ashamed now? What about the knowledge of good and evil? Did the couple get that? And did they become like God? Perhaps the next phrase will answer these remaining or revived questions. We may have others as well. How does the couple respond to their new vision and their new knowledge? Do they like what they now see and know?

The narrator does not tell us their feelings. Instead, the story quickly reports their next act: 'they sewed fig leaves, and they made for themselves coverings'. Readers must get involved in the story to try to understand this action. Did the couple gain new knowledge that suggested they should cover themselves? Did new knowledge reveal that nakedness was 'bad' and that clothing was 'good'? Do the man and woman cover themselves because they are somehow newly aware of sexual differences? Or are they differently aware of the significance of sexual differences? Is the couple aware of their disobedience, and is this awareness related to their clothing of themselves? Perhaps the couple is embarrassed or ashamed to be in one another's presence. The narrator is again silent (perhaps annoyingly so to the reader) about the couple's thoughts and feelings after their action and whatever unspecified immediate consequences it may have had for them. But perhaps, given

---

1.   On the implications of the couple's silence during their crucial act, see White, 'Direct and Third Person Discourse', in Patte (ed.), *Genesis 2 and 3*, p. 102.

the couple's unashamed nakedness of 2.25, their actions here speak louder than words.

God's Voice in the Garden: Genesis 3.8-19

The woman and man have taken action together: in eating the fruit, experiencing its effects, and next in hearing 'the voice of YHWH God, walking around in the garden at the breezy time of the day'. The anthropomorphic God is back on the scene, again down to earth, this time walking in the garden. The narrator's portrayal of divine evening strolls suggests that these may have been a common occurrence. Readers may speculate about whether God and the couple regularly took walks together. Remembering God's earlier prohibition and warning, readers might again be anxious about the aftermath of the couple's wrongdoing. The couple did not die instantly. Will God now kill them? Does God even know what they have done? Will the man and woman tell God? How will God respond?

Since no game of hide-and-seek has been announced, the couple's scurrying into the trees suggests some anxiety on their part, especially given their prior covering with foliage. Perhaps they think that if they are out of sight God will not know anything about what they have done. The narrator tells us only that the couple hid themselves 'from (the face of) YHWH God'. As usual, readers get no inside information about the couple's thoughts or motives in concealing themselves. Do they feel guilty or ashamed? Though the narrator does not spell it out, this seems likely.

Since the couple has disappeared from view, God takes the initiative, asking, 'Where are you?' This is God's first question in the Bible. Is it a rhetorical question, like that spoken by a parent of a toddler who is easily visible as she crouches behind a couch to avoid going to bed? Does God know where the couple is?[1]

Careful readers (especially those able to see or hear the singular 'you' of the Hebrew) will notice that God speaks only to the man, and they may wonder why. Is God only interested in the man and not in the woman? Maybe God is shy around women. (God did seem to vanish in 2.22 after delivering the woman to the man.) The only one readers know to have had a conversation with the woman is the serpent. In 2.23

---

1. Wenham, *Genesis 1–15*, p. 77 makes a similar comparison of God to a parent and observes that the rhetorical nature of the questions has been noted since the targums, contra Gunkel's position that the questions were real.

the man exclaimed in her presence, but he did not talk *to* or *with* her, at least not as the narrative records the story. God spoke to the man in 2.16-17 (again, not in conversation), but we have no indication that God has *ever* spoken with the woman.[1] Perhaps God speaks to the man alone because it was the man alone who heard the initial prohibition. The narrative, as usual, does not provide any explanation. Perhaps none would have been needed in ancient Israelite culture if men were assumed to speak on behalf of their families.

The man does not hesitate to respond, though he does fail to say 'Here am I' as experienced readers of Hebrew biblical narratives might expect in response to God's call.[2] The man heard the voice of God (a voice that presumably was familiar), and he was afraid because of his nakedness, so he hid. Following God's example(?), the man ignores the woman too and speaks only for himself. And there is considerable 'self' in his statement. English readers note the fourfold repetition of 'I', and readers of the Hebrew text notice use of the optional personal pronoun *ʾanōkî*, emphasizing the man's nakedness.

Readers also notice an absence, as God does. The man says nothing about his forbidden action. He does seem to have a new experience of God however. Now he is afraid of God, or at least afraid of being naked in God's presence, while presumably earlier he was not. Neither the man in his statement nor God in response explains whether nakedness in God's presence is unacceptable or why it should be frightening.

God's response allows the man's fears to persist. God does not comfort him or tell him not to be afraid, as experienced Bible readers would expect a divine messenger to do. God does acknowledge the man's changed awareness of his nakedness, however. God's next question, 'Who told you that you are naked?' suggests that the man's nakedness was not something the man knew about when God last spoke to him. It also implies that he would not have found out about it if

1. Of course, God does eventually question and pronounce judgment on the woman in 3.13,16, but even then they do not have a conversation that goes beyond a single question and reply. For a convenient chart of direct discourse in Genesis 2–3, see J.D. Crossan, 'Response to White: Felix Culpa and Foenix Culprit', in Patte (ed.), *Genesis 2 and 3*, pp. 107-11.

2. H.C. White observes this in 'Direct and Third Person Discourse', p. 103. The patriarchs Abraham (in Gen. 22.1, 11) and Jacob (in Gen. 31.11 and 46.2) respond appropriately to divine or heavenly voices.

someone had not told him. And it may suggest that the man should
have thought about to whom he was listening.

Often commentators assume that the man and woman knew about
their nakedness at the end of Genesis 2 since the narrator comments on
it in 2.25. Here is where a careful distinction between 'story' and
'discourse' levels of the narrative may be helpful.[1] At the 'discourse'
level, we as readers were informed by the narrator in 2.25 that the
couple was naked and not ashamed, but at the 'story' level, neither the
characters themselves, in their direct speech, nor the narrator, in
describing their actions or perspectives, suggests before 3.7 that they
know their nakedness. The narrator could have said in 2.25 that the man
and his wife both *knew* that they were naked (as the narrator does in
3.7), but it is precisely their knowledge that is at issue. We cannot
assume that the characters in the story know what we as readers of the
story embedded in the narrator's discourse know. So it seems that one
change resulting from the eating of the forbidden tree is that the couple
now *knows* their nakedness.[2]

We may pause a little longer with God's first question: 'Who told you
that you are naked?' Who might be logical candidates? Readers have
only met a few characters: God, the man, a whole host of animals (if
these can reasonably be considered characters), the woman, and the
serpent. Does God think that one of these, presumably an animal or the
woman, would have told the man about his nakedness? Could the
woman have done it? Again, 3.7 suggests that the couple only knew
about their nakedness *after* their eating, but perhaps that means that
each of them knew their own individual nakedness then. Might the
woman have known the man's nakedness (and he hers) earlier? If she
knew his nakedness, then she could have told him that he was naked.
Who else could have? Perhaps the serpent or another talking animal.

Why is God interested in the agent of the man's knowledge? God
seems to be more concerned with carrying out an investigation than

1.   Reader-response critics, following S. Chatman and other literary theorists,
distinguish between the 'story' level, where the tale transpires between the characters,
and the 'discourse' level that includes the whole shape of the narrator's presentation
of that story to readers. See Chatman's *Story and Discourse: Narrative Structure in
Fiction and Film* (Ithaca, NY: Cornell University Press, 1978) or any of R. Fowler's
discussions of reader-response criticism listed in the bibliography.
2.   This new knowledge may suggest that the couple's seeing after their eyes
were opened in Gen. 3.7 differed somehow from what it was before.

with the man's fears or concerns. The narrator gives us no clues, however, about the tone of God's queries. God's tone might have conveyed something like 'don't worry about being naked, that's not important'. Alternatively, God might be extremely angry, anxious to quash the troublesome party. The narrator gives no indications at this point about whether God is pleased, disturbed, unhappy, or accepting of the couple's actions and the resulting new knowledge of their nakedness.

And does God really want an answer to this question about who told the man? Since God waits for no response (or the narrator allows none), we suspect that God is more interested in the next question: did the man eat from the forbidden tree? Again, God's question may seem unnecessary. Doesn't God know what the couple did? Is God really trying to find out what happened? Modern readers' notions of divine omniscience may get in the way here. The man's response to God's questions suggests that he thought God may really have needed the information. At least the man does not seem to presume God's foreknowledge.

The man's response answers God's two questions in order. The 'who' is 'the woman whom you gave to be with me', and the confession 'and I ate' (echoing the narrator's final 'and he ate' of 3.6) answers God's question about eating. Is the man's phrase 'whom you gave to be with me' a subtle accusation of God, as some commentators suggest?[1] Or is it merely an identification (as if there were other women roaming the garden?) of the woman who, as yet, has no proper name? Could the man simply be reporting straightforwardly (from his perspective, of course) what took place? Need the question and the response to it imply any direct or indirect accusation on God's part or the man's?

God's question to the woman might be heard as carrying a far more obvious accusatory tone: 'What is this that you have done?' Readers might well wonder what God is getting at. Just what is the 'this' to which God refers? Is God upset? Is God angry that the woman ate from the forbidden tree? Is eating the problem? Is God angry because the woman gave fruit to the man?

Or maybe a readerly assumption of God's anger at this point is inappropriate. After all, God does not exactly fly off the handle. (Experienced readers know that the curses come later in the story.) Perhaps the tone of God's question is just one of seeking information. The man and woman were creatures whom God had formed, breathed

1.   Bonhoeffer, *Creation and Fall*, p. 84; Wismer, 'The Myth of Original Sin', p. 189.

into, taken, put, and commanded, whose situation God had found 'not good' and then remedied, for whom God had formed animals, whom God had anesthetized, operated on, and built, whom God had brought together now that they had been separated from the original one being. When God was last on the scene, it was *God* who had been doing just about everything. Maybe God is just trying to get used to the idea that these beings are now acting on their own. As the narrator has reported to readers in God's absence, the man and woman are now emerging as subjects of their own verbs.

As readers, *we* know about the woman's intelligent conversation with the serpent. We know that the woman and man have begun to act in the ways God has acted. We know that the woman 'saw that the tree was good' in 3.6 (as God had seen good aspects of creation in the Genesis 1 story). We know she 'took' and she 'gave' the fruit, as God had 'taken' the man (2.15) and later the rib (2.21) and had, according to the man, given (3.12) the woman to him. We know the couple had also sewed fig leaves and 'made' coverings (3.7), whereas earlier in the story it was God who had formed the man (2.7) and the animals (2.19), and who had 'made' a helper (2.18) and all the animals of the field (3.1). We know that the man and the woman *hid themselves* (3.8), rather than having *been put* by God in the garden (2.8,15) or being brought by God to the man (2.22). In short, we readers know that these mud and flesh creatures are now the subjects of active rather than passive verbs. But we do not know whether God knows any of this. God has been off stage. So God's question may imply anger, accusation, or annoyance, but it may also simply be inquiring or investigating the events. Like the returning mother in *The Cat in the Hat*, God may only want to find out what went on in the garden that day.[1]

Or maybe God's question is asking the woman to interpret what it is that she has done. The woman's response in 3.13 shows that she has thought about the matter. She does not simply report the actors and actions as the man seems to have done; she interprets. She says that the serpent 'tricked' her. This word suggests that she recognizes her action as something she ought not to have done (it is, thus, a confession as well), since she would not otherwise have done something she was

---

1.   The mother asks 'Tell me. What did you do?' and Sally and her brother '…did not know / What to say / Should we tell her / The things that went on there that day?' See Dr Seuss, *The Cat in the Hat* (New York: Random House, 1957) p. 60.

'tricked' into doing. It also suggests that she had been persuaded,[1] indicating that she had made up her own mind about her action. Her remark need not be construed solely as passing the buck to the serpent, since the word 'tricked' suggests her own complicity in addition to the serpent's external agency.

What does the woman think now about her previous actions? What effect has listening to God's interrogation of the man had on her? Does she feel guilt or remorse at having disobeyed God or simply a tinge of regret at having been tricked? The narrator again does not reveal the woman's thoughts, emotions, or reactions to her situation.

The narrative pattern of talking first to the man and then to the woman might suggest that we should expect God to turn to the serpent next for an explanation, in which case, God's failure to question the serpent may come as a surprise. On the other hand, God's interest in the animals in this story has been limited to their relation to the man. God did not earlier speak to any of the animals, at least as far as we know, in the way God spoke to the man. Though in 3.1 the serpent seems to have known something of God's prohibition, the narrative does not say that *God* knew that the serpent knew this. God does not seem particularly interested in the serpent or the other animals.

The narrator has shown some interest in the garden, noting at the outset in 2.5 that God had not yet sent rain and implying that God had not yet made a man to work the ground. But while the narrator's interests may include the garden or land as a whole, God's focus throughout is on the man. Thus the narrative, from God's perspective, is anthropocentric,[2] perhaps even androcentric.[3] God forms the man, breathes into the man, plants a garden in which to put the man, makes trees to grow which God permits and prohibits for the man, provides an occupation for the man, commands the man, determines that aloneness is not good for the man, forms birds and animals and brings them to the man, gives the divine prerogative of naming to the man, causes a deep

---

1.   I discuss her persuasion further in Chapter 3.

2.   J.L. McKenzie makes this observation: 'The Literary Characteristics of Genesis 2–3', *TS* 15 (1954), p. 557. So does von Rad, *Genesis*, p. 77. While the point seems obvious, especially in contrast to Genesis 1, P.H. Santmire argues against an anthropocentric reading of the creation narratives: 'The Genesis Creation Narratives Revisited: Themes for a Global Age', *Int* 45 (1991), pp. 366-79.

3.   P. Bird views the J account as androcentric: 'Genesis I–III as a Source for a Contemporary Theology of Sexuality', *Ex Auditu* 3 (1987), p. 38.

sleep to fall on the man, performs surgery on the man, and creates a woman, bringing her to the man. When God comes back on the scene after the couple's fruit eating, God calls to the *man*, asks where *he* is, who told *him* about *his* nakedness, and asks whether *he* has eaten from the tree from which God had commanded *him* not to eat. God's focus is almost entirely on the man, both before and after the eating.

Readers may wonder about the roles of the woman and the serpent in the story.[1] Are they merely devices of the plot?[2] Is God interested in them at all? We may have to read further to find out. After the woman's statement, God neither questions the serpent nor allows it to speak.[3] Instead, God launches into what turns out to be a lengthy monologue.

God's speech to the serpent begins with a reason: 'because you have done this'. But again, readers may wonder just what the 'this' refers to. Does God accept the woman's claim that the serpent tricked her. Is God responding to the serpent because of the serpent's reported deception? Readers know that the serpent and the woman had a conversation; we also heard the content of that conversation and may have inferred some subtle accusations about God in it. But does God know anything about the serpent's dialogue with the woman or about anything untoward the serpent might have suggested? Is the fact of conversation itself the reason God refers to here? Maybe God's 'this' to the serpent refers to the effects or results of the conversation or deception. Maybe the 'this' means causing the forbidden eating. If so, then God would be blaming the serpent and thus not crediting the woman with responsibility even for her own misdemeanor.[4]

---

1.   In fact, historical critics have suggested that an original disobedience story involved only the man. See Vawter's discussion of a garden story and a creation-fall story, to which the creation of woman was a later addition, in *On Genesis*, pp. 64-65. Westermann treats Genesis 2–3 as an artful composite of two types of narrative, creation and crime and punishment: *Genesis 1–11*, pp. 18-19, 190-91.

2.   Trible sees the serpent as a mere 'literary tool... a device in plot', *God and the Rhetoric*, p. 111. Likewise, Brueggemann calls the serpent simply 'a device to introduce the new agenda': *Genesis*, p. 47. For an opposing position see Gardner, 'Genesis 2.4b-3: A Mythological Paradigm', p. 11.

3.   Von Rad, *Genesis*, p. 92 notes the absence of the serpent's trial but does not explain its significance. T.E. Fretheim attributes absence of the interrogation to its function as leading the humans to an admission of guilt: 'The Book of Genesis', *NIB* 1.362.

4.   This view is perhaps supported later in 3.16 by God's failure even to say

Whatever readers might speculate about the 'this' which provokes the serpent's sentence, God's curse may come as a surprise. After all, we know (though God may not, since the woman and man did not tell God) that the serpent only talked with the woman, asking her questions and suggesting alternative possibilities. We know that the woman and the man made their own decisions to eat, however much they may feel in retrospect that they were pressured or tricked. *We* were there. We saw and heard what it may seem that God did not. God's response to the serpent, thus, may even seem out of line, too extreme. Why should the serpent be cursed?

The curse itself takes us back to the introduction of the serpent. The narrator described it in 3.1 as 'more shrewd than all the animals of the field'. Like the narrator's description, the curse now relates the serpent to the animals. The serpent was introduced as more shrewd than all the animals, and now it is more cursed. It will go upon its belly, God says. How did the serpent get around before, we may wonder? And it will eat dust, not a very nourishing diet, but probably intended metaphorically anyway. Are the references to belly and eating related to the humans' crime of eating? 'All the days of your life' may be a puzzling phrase since nothing has actually died yet in the story, though readers may still be sitting on pins and needles waiting for the first fatal shot to be fired. Presumably snakes are mortal (and always have been). We may wonder again whether humans are mortal as well, remembering that God mentioned (threatened? warned about?) death in connection with the prohibited eating in 2.17, but still having no direct evidence that they are.

God's punishment of the serpent includes enmity between the serpent and the woman. Everyone has seemed fairly friendly so far. At least they have been getting along in the story. Perhaps God thinks that the serpent and the woman have been a little *too* friendly. Like a protective parent, perhaps God wants to shield this daughter from the unseemly influence of a disreputable character, the serpent. Does God know more about this serpent than the woman does? Does God know more than the narrator reveals to readers? The enmity God envisions may be designed to prevent further illicit or dangerous conversations between the woman and the serpent.

The enmity is not limited to this particular serpent and woman, however. God has the offspring in mind as well. This comment about

'because you have done [some unspecified and ambiguous] this' to the woman in her sentence.

'seed' is the first direct indication in the paradise story (beyond the mention of generations in the introductory verse, and the narratorial aside about father and mother in 2.24) that any of the creatures were reproducing.[1] The man and the woman were naked together in 2.25, and, if we determine that the narrator's aside about marriage customs in 2.24 applies to the newly created couple as well, they may have clung to one another and become one flesh, but any resulting pregnancy has yet to be announced. We certainly have not heard about any babies in the garden, but apparently there may be some.

According to 3.15, the relationship of the woman's and serpent's offspring will include mutual striking, crushing, or bruising.[2]

> *Enmity* I will make between you and the woman
> and between your seed and her seed.
> *They* will strike your head,
> and *you* will strike their heel.

Precisely who the parties are is ambiguous.[3] Though I have translated it as 'they', the Hebrew masculine singular pronoun 'he', or perhaps better 'it' for the collective 'seed', is unnecessarily present in 3.15b for the first head-striking party. What God is getting at in this particular specification is not clear. Whom is God talking about?

Is some cosmic battle intended? The story gives no indication (except perhaps to those originally astute hearers who could not avoid the ancient Near Eastern echoes) that the serpent is anything other than an animal 'of the field that YHWH God had made'. So it would be strange at this point to hint at an otherworldly dimension. Perhaps more mundanely, all of this may simply reflect an ancient and modern observation that people generally view and treat snakes as enemies, crushing them and being bitten. However, the violent language and use of divine voice rather than narratorial comment suggest that more than simple etiology may be at stake.

Having now mentioned her offspring, God turns to the woman. God gives no explanation for her sentence, no 'because', not even a vague or ambiguous 'this'. She is simply told how God will change her toil and

---

1.   M. Buber and J. Barr concur that the couple was probably sexually active in the garden. See Buber, *Good and Evil: Two Interpretations* (New York: Charles Scribner's Sons, 1952), p. 83 and Barr, *Garden*, p. 67.

2.   The verbal root *šûp* is the same for both parties.

3.   See the translation note on 3.15 in the appendix.

childbearing. Readers of Genesis 1 will recognize that while the human race in that account was told to 'multiply', in 3.16 it is the woman's toil and pregnancies that will multiply.[1] Moreover, the woman is not simply told that this will happen; rather, God speaks to her directly and says 'I will' do this. Why will God do this? What is the nature of God's involvement in this change? The woman's punishment, if that is how we should interpret God's words to her, may seem out of proportion with her misdeed. Alternatively, God's response may indicate appropriate frustration or sorrow that we humans could not be obedient in even so small a matter.

It may seem strange for God to multiply pains that have not yet occurred. At least we have not heard that the woman has had any children. Any reader or hearer of the story, however, surely knows that human pregnancy and birth involve discomfort, great labor, and pain. Is God the source of this unease, or of its increase into agony? Why does God assign toil to the woman?

The last half of the verse does not improve the situation, at least for many modern readers. The woman's longing will be for her husband, and (or 'but' since the Hebrew conjunction can be translated either way) he will rule over her. We heard earlier from the narrator (in 2.24) that a man is willing to leave his parents (an indication that the story's original hearers were, of course, familiar with generations, parents and children) in order to cling to his woman. The man of 2.24 clearly desires the woman in the narrator's depiction. Now the narrator has God suggest to readers through direct discourse that women will desire their men. Is God orchestrating women's desire? predicting it? prescribing it? describing it? redirecting it? Does the woman get to decide for herself what or whom she will desire? Moreover, men can or will rule over women. What does this mean, and why should it occur? These are certainly questions of modern readers, even if they would not have arisen in the same way in ancient societies.[2]

Actually, God's speech is directed to the particular woman of the story, but the generic language used to describe the woman and the man in the story and their status as the first human beings conspire to make readers view the couple as representatives for all humanity.[3] Women

1. See the translation notes on 3.16 in the appendix.
2. Further attention will be given to aspects of gender relations related to this verse and to Genesis 2–3 as a whole in Chapters 2 and 4.
3. Vawter, *On Genesis*, pp. 72, 89 and von Rad, *Genesis*, p. 100 support a

readers, then, may be particularly troubled by this verse. What kind of a god *is* YHWH God in this story? Just what does this God think of women?

The man does not fare much better. The reason for his punishment is at least explicit, though it may be unsettling for contemporary readers. The man is sentenced because he has listened to the voice of his woman. 'Listening to the voice of' translates the Hebrew literally, but not help-fully since the phrase also means 'obeying'. The problem is not that the man was in the same corner of the woods as his woman; it is not that he was within earshot of her words. The man is being judged because he 'obeyed' his woman. It sounds like God is miffed that the man did not obey God. But *did* the man 'obey' his woman?

We readers must stop to ask just where God gets God's information. After all, the narrator has not allowed us to eavesdrop on any conver-sation between the man and the woman. Much to the consternation of many commentators, who assume its presence, there was *no* scene where the woman lured, tricked, tempted, seduced, or for that matter even said a word to the man, either to command or to persuade his eating.[1] Nor does the man blame her for doing any of these things. What the narrator has told us, and what the man's response to divine questioning confirms, is only that the woman gave fruit to her husband and that he ate. She did not command him to eat it so that he could 'obey' her. The narrator does not even say that she tells him to eat it, or that she suggests he take a nibble. So, just what is God talking about in this explanation? Does God have the facts straight?

The obedience to his wife is only part of the man's sentenced crime, however. God correctly reminds the man that he has eaten from the tree about which God had commanded him (and, if we can trust the narrator's thoroughness, readers know that *only* the man directly heard the command from God) not to eat of it. God is right on this score. But does the punishment fit? Why is the ground cursed because of the man's disobedience? Is cursing the ground simply a way to make life

universal interpretation of the story as does D. Louys, *Le jardin d'Eden: Mythe fondateur de l'Occident* (Paris: Cerf, 1992), p. 50 (my translation): 'The important thing is that each one is able to say: This (hi)story is mine, I was in the Garden of Eden—insofar as I am man, as I am woman'. I discuss potential ideological effects of this generic language in Chapter 4.

1.   See Higgins, 'The Myth of Eve: The Temptress', for a summary of how interpreters habitually accuse the woman of such actions.

difficult for the man, as painful labor and childbearing make life difficult for the woman? Is God angry with the man and woman (not to mention the serpent)?

The elaboration of the ground's curse and its effects on the man's toil suggest that making life difficult for him may be just what God has in mind. Phyllis Trible, has distinguished between reading these verses as *de*scriptive and *pre*scriptive.[1] While the distinction may be helpful and I might like to agree with her, Trible does not argue for it on the basis of the text. She merely claims its validity. Had God wanted simply to explain to the people about the way life is, God could have conducted a special informational seminar before turning the new couple loose in a snake-filled garden. We cannot escape the divine intent suggested by these verses simply by saying that life would have been better for the woman and man if they had obeyed the rules. While that may be true, they did not obey, and an easy life is no longer, apparently, the situation. Given the magnitude of suffering inscribed in these verses, the theological and anthropological questions concern the divine and human roles in bringing this suffering about. In particular, what is the force of God's 'I will...' in 3.15-16? These divine words are not tangential to the matter. I suspect that the *de*scription/*pre*scription dichotomy cannot be as neatly posed or settled as Trible would have it.

Returning to the details of the punishment, the man's 'toil' in 3.17 echoes the woman's in 3.16.[2] As with the serpent's curse, reference to the man's eating subtly reminds readers and the man of the nature of his disobedience (if a fivefold repetition of the word 'eat' or 'eating' in the three verses can be called subtle). The man's mortality also surfaces again as he is reminded that he will return to his dusty origins.[3] Being

1. I wonder whether Trible's distinction (*God and the Rhetoric*, p. 128) arises not so much from a view that reality has a built-in moral order as from a theological concern to avoid implicating God in patriarchy. I discuss her claim in the next chapter.

2. The NRSV unfortunately obscures this relationship by translating 'pangs' in 3.16 and 'toil' in 3.17. NIV does a better job since it uses 'pains' in 3.16, reflecting the plural, and 'painful toil' in 3.17.

3. J. Galambush finds numerous helpful parallels among the three judgments, especially as each creature's punishment connects it with its origin: the serpent and man from the dust are returned to dust, and the woman, likewise, returns to her source, the man. See ' *ʾādām* from *ʾᵃdāmâ*, *ʾiššâ* from *ʾîš*: Derivation and Subordination in Gen. 2.4b-3.24', in W.P. Brown, and J.K. Kuan and M.P. Graham, (eds.), *History and Interpretation: Essays in Honour of John H. Hayes* (JSOTSup, 173;

worn out by the toil of the previous verses, both readers and the man may look forward to this settled end.

So what do the creatures think of their assigned fates? The narrator again gives us no direct access to their reactions (thus not giving voice to what may be our own). Whether the woman and man are penitent, mourning, enraged, acquiescent or merely puzzled at God's pronouncements, we do not know. As readers, we may have experienced several of these reactions, or others, upon hearing God's monologue in 3.14-19.

Living and Leaving the Garden: Genesis 3.20-24

Our only clue to the human response comes in the form of the man's next reported action in 3.20: 'the man called the name of his woman Eve, for *she* was the mother of all living'.[1] Now just what does this naming suggest? Is it a neutral getting on with life? Is it a rebellion against the harshness of God's sentences? Is the man in effect saying to God, 'you predict a hard life, but *live* we will!' or is the 'mother of all living' comment the narrator's assessment of the woman's role?[2] Is the man submitting, on behalf of his woman and in disregard of the pain and dangers such childbearing entailed for her, to God's proclamation that she *would* bear children.[3] Is the man's naming an act of domination,[4] also affirming God's punishment of the woman in 3.16. And what about the woman? Again we do not hear what she thinks about any of the recent events, the interrogation, the sentences, or the man's naming of her.

The narrative continues in 3.21 with what may seem to be a disconnected and unnecessary report of an unmotivated divine action. God makes (resuming God's command of the prerogative of making that had

---

Sheffield: Sheffield Academic Press, 1993), pp. 40-41.

1.   Barr notes that 'it has long been suggested, though never clearly proved or evaluated, that the name Eve was related to an Aramaic *ḥwyh* and similar Arabic cognates, which mean 'snake', and that the mythological ancestor of Eve was some sort of 'serpent goddess' who was, perhaps, the goddess of life.' See *Garden*, p. 65.

2.   Von Rad sees the man's statement as an act of faith, an 'embracing of life': *Genesis*, p. 96.

3.   R. Hinschberger views the man's statement as an acceptance of the new order: 'Une lecture synchronique de Gn 2–3', *RevScRel* 63 (1989), p. 9.

4.   Trible acknowledges that the man exerts dominance over the animals by naming: 'Depatriarchalizing', p. 38. She insists, however, that the man does not name the woman until 3.20. I discuss naming on pp. 100-102.

been illicitly, and some commentators say pitifully,[1] usurped by the humans in 3.7) clothing for the man and his wife, and God clothes them. Theologians are quick to see this making as a caring action on God's part and to see in it a mitigation of the recently pronounced divine punishments.[2] Is new clothing really meant to lessen the dire sentences God has imposed in 3.14-19? And what does the snake think of God clothing its new enemies with animal skins?

Perhaps a more reasonable alternative is to see in God's action an attempt to make real for the humans the idea of death. They have just declared their intent to go on living (forever?) through this 'mother of all living', Eve. Perhaps God wants them to understand something of what death is about. The skin clothing God provides will serve as a constant reminder to the people of the death they too will suffer at the end of their difficult lives.[3]

Another possibility is that God wants to remind the couple of their humanity. It is humans, after all, who wear clothing.[4] They are not animals; they should be dressed. They are also not gods, as they might have thought they would become, given the serpent's persuasion. Either of these last two interpretations would also explain why God is suddenly concerned about God-likeness and about the tree of life in 3.22. But I'm getting ahead of the story.

God's first remark after clothing the couple is that 'the man has become like one of us'. Who is the 'us'? Neither the narrator's introduction nor the first few words of God's reported speech makes this clear. The man has become like God. One wonders whether the woman did too. Is *hā-ʾādām* being used generically now to refer to both the man and the woman?[5] Feminists might interpret God's use of 'the man' as a (false) generic, a linguistic signal of the man's rule over his

---

1. Galambush, ' *ʾādām* from *ᵃdāmâ* ', p. 39.
2. See D.J.A. Clines, 'Prefatory Theme', whose 'sin-speech-mitigation-punishment' pattern builds on the work of von Rad and Westermann.
3. R.A. Oden, Jr notes that until the sixteenth century (including Luther) the garments were to serve the couple as a reminder of their fall; see 'Grace or Status? Yahweh's Clothing of the First Humans', chap. in *The Bible Without Theology: The Theological Tradition and Alternatives to It* (San Francisco: Harper & Row, 1987), p. 96. R.J. Ratner argues similarly that the skins served to make the idea of death real for the couple; see '"Garments of Skin" (Genesis 3.21)', *Jewish Bible Quarterly* 18 (1989), pp. 74-80.
4. See Oden, 'Grace or Status?', p. 104.
5. I discuss the use of *ʾādām* in the next chapter.

woman. If it is not intended as a generic, then God's use of 'man' suggests that God has forgotten or is ignoring the woman entirely. This alternative is consistent with God's initial woman-ignoring response to the couple's disobedience.

Readers of the earlier account might think that this becoming 'like one of us', like God (and the heavenly beings?), is a good thing since that was God's creative intention in Genesis 1. (The echoes of the earlier passage are strong, so we may quite legitimately consider its effects on the reading of this story.[1]) If we view Genesis 2–3 as a complement to the earlier story in Genesis 1 or an elaboration of certain of its aspects, then we have in 3.22 an indication that the creation of humans in God's image (or better 'likeness' since God took care of the 'image' part in Gen. 1.27) is now complete. Becoming like God in this story has some meat to it, however; it involves the ambiguous and ambivalent phrase 'knowing good and evil'. It is this knowledge that God's very speech now confirms as (part of?) what it means to be like God.

But God does not seem pleased about the man's God-likeness in this story. In fact, God sounds concerned, perhaps even fearful or jealous. God is worried for some reason that the man might eat from the tree of life. We readers may have wondered what happened to that tree. Or perhaps, like the human couple, we were distracted into thinking only about the tree of the knowledge of good and evil that occupied the center of our story. We never really heard much about this enigmatic tree of life, and now it is back, only to be quickly put out of sight and off limits again.

God is concerned that the man will eat from this tree. Granted, the man does not have a good track record as far as eating from prohibited trees is concerned, but God has never prohibited eating from this particular tree. In fact, maybe the couple has already eaten from it,[2] though the sense of the verse suggests that God is concerned to prevent a *first* eating. God wants to prevent the humans from stretching out a hand, taking, and eating from this tree lest they 'live forever'. Why is

---

1. See L.A. Turner ,'The Primeval History', in *Announcements of Plot in Genesis* (JSOTSup, 96; Sheffield: Sheffield Academic Press, 1990), pp. 21-49 and Sawyer, 'The Image of God', who also insist on reading the stories together.

2. Some scholars make sense out of this possibility by suggesting that continuous eating from the tree was necessary for its life-preserving effects. See R. Gordis, 'The Knowledge of Good and Evil in the Old Testament and the Qumran Scrolls', *JBL* 76 (1957), pp. 123-38.

this tree and the potential immortal life of humans suddenly of concern? We never find out. Just as God in the 'story' sends the couple out from the garden in 3.23, in the 'discourse' of the next sentence in 3.24 the narrator excludes God's reasoning from our readerly curiosity. But unlike the human couple in the story, we readers of the 'discourse' now have an idea about what they are missing, and we do not know why. The man and woman were not privy to the narrator's discourse about the garden in Genesis 2, nor, we may reasonably assume, do they hear God's self-musings in 3.22 about their own God-likeness. They are sent out of the garden, not knowing that they will therefore miss the chance to eat from the tree of life.[1] The human pair in the story does not know what they are missing, only what awaits them. We know both.

The man is sent forth 'to work the ground from which he was taken'. Again we wonder whether to interpret the word as generic. The rest of the phrase suggests that a generic interpretation is unlikely. The woman, after all, was taken from the man, not directly from the ground, nor is her assigned task to work the ground.[2] We may still wonder whether Eve accompanied the man as he left the garden, but the next verse does not clarify the situation. The action merely intensifies. God does not just send the man out, but drives him out, and stations the heavenly bouncer,[3] complete with turning sword, at the door to prevent his unauthorized return and access to the mysterious tree of life. The paradise story comes to a flaming finish. To find out about Eve's fate and about life out of the garden, we have to keep reading. But that reading will be part of a later chapter.

Conclusions: God in the Garden

Our slow reading of the garden story enables us to make several observations about God. God creates—even shrewd, crafty creatures. God speaks, commands, evaluates, adjusts, experiments, judges, punishes, curses, and banishes. God is in charge of the rain. God seems to have strange, miraculous powers: to make animals and man from the dust, to do surgery on the man, and to build a woman from a rib. God also

1. Barr, *Garden*, claims that the lost chance for immortality is the point of the entire story.
2. Unless we incorporate into the literary reading Meyers's anthropological focus that requires agricultural labor from the whole pioneer family.
3. The cherubim are no cherubs, as unsuspecting English readers might think.

intervenes in human affairs, causing enmity and multiplying toil in childbearing.

At the same time as God is clearly powerful, this God also has a name, YHWH God. This is a 'down to earth' God, a God who plays in the mud, forms animals and humans, and strolls in the garden. God is intimate with the earth, planting trees and a garden. God is also intimate with humans (or at least with the man). God breathes into the man's nostrils, provides food, gives commands, values the man's opinions about names, involves the man in creation through naming, clothes the couple and banishes them. God seems less interested in the woman. God's intimacy with the man extends to God's remarking that the man (the couple?) has become like God. This story portrays primarily an anthropocentric (perhaps androcentric?) God.

While Genesis 2–3 reveals several things about God, it hides many others, particularly God's motives and goals. We do not know why God plants a garden, forms a man, gives a command of permission and prohibition, determines man's aloneness is not good, or builds a woman. Neither do we know why God stays off stage rather than intervening to prevent the disobedience. We are not sure whether God's plans for dealing with the humans changed after their disobedience or during the course of the inquest. We do not know why God cursed the serpent, whether God ordains or allows man's domination of woman, or why God clothes the couple or prevents eating from the tree of life. Perhaps we are not supposed to know, but as readers we will wonder.

Chapter 2

KNOWING AND EXPERIENCING (IN) THE GARDEN

Chapter 1 introduced the garden story, commenting slowly, raising a variety of questions, and elbowing room among the standard interpretations for other experiences of reading the garden narrative. This chapter focuses on one aspect of being human that is of concern both in the Genesis 2–3 text itself and for feminist theory and criticism: knowledge and experience.

In contrast to Chapter 1, where feminist concerns and methods were implicit in the reading, here they are explicit. I begin with a brief discussion of several kinds of feminism and a typology of how feminist scholarship challenges and interacts with a discipline. Next, I give examples of this typology at work in both feminist literary scholarship and feminist epistemologies. Then I use methods and insights from these discussions to engage Genesis 2–3 in terms of knowledge and experience and in relation to feminist literary and epistemological theories. First, I consider how feminists have rehabilitated the woman in the story as someone who uses her knowledge, interpreting her experience in making decisions. I also consider how feminist interpreters have experienced Gen. 3.16 as troublesome and how they have explained God's announcement to the woman. Next, I read the story, not to rehabilitate it or the woman, but to expose the patriarchy many feminists see in it.

Feminisms and Feminist Scholarship

Feminists and Womanists

There is no single definition of feminism, but a variety of feminisms. Feminisms agree in their commitment to work to free women from oppression. They differ in what they think women's oppression is, what they think its causes are, and the solutions or kinds of liberation they seek.[1]

Liberal feminists are typically satisfied with the societal systems in which they live, but they observe structural impediments to women's progress within those systems. For them, women's oppression consists in the customary and legal constraints that limit women's entry or success in the public world.[2] Liberal feminists suggest that false beliefs about women being less capable than men lead to policies of exclusion and to social rules that privilege men over women. Liberal feminists assume that men and women are essentially the same, but know there are impediments to their equality. Their goal is gender justice, making the rules of the game fair so that no one is systematically disadvantaged. They seek civil rights and equal opportunity, and they want to free women and men from oppressive gender roles.

Radical feminists[3] identify women's oppression as the way that the sex/gender system of male dominance and female subordination has made women's biology enslaving, when it should be a source of power. Symptoms or examples of women's oppression include witch burning, foot binding, suttee, purdah, clitoridectomy, pornography, sexual harassment, battering of women, prostitution, and rape.[4] Radical feminists acknowledge basic differences between men and women and see the cause of women's oppression as men's control over women's bodies. They seek solutions in reproductive freedom, celebrating women's sexuality, activism (such as 'Take Back the Night' marches), and creation of 'womanspaces', sometimes promoting women's separation from men.

Postmodern feminists challenge the notion of difference (or sameness)

---

1.   My discussion of feminisms is abstracted from R. Tong, *Feminist Thought: A Comprehensive Introduction* (Boulder and San Francisco: Westview Press, 1989).

2.   Liberal feminists also acknowledge men as fellow victims of sex-role conditioning.

3.   On the relationship between 'cultural feminism' and 'radical feminism', see L. Alcoff, 'Cultural Feminism Versus Post-structuralism: The Identity Crisis in Feminist Theory', *Signs: Journal of Women in Culture and Society* 13 (1988), p. 411. Tong does not discuss cultural feminism.

4.   M. Daly's *Gyn/Ecology: The Metaethics of Radical Feminism* (Boston: Beacon Press, 1978) analyzes various ways the sex/gender system has victimized women's bodies. A. Lorde contends, however, that Daly ignores the differences between the oppression of white and Black women: 'An Open Letter to M. Daly', in *Sister Outsider* (Trumansburg, NY: The Crossing Press, 1984), pp. 66-71. I discuss radical feminist perspectives further in Chapter 4.

between men and women that the radical and liberal feminists claim.[1] This movement grows in part out of the work of French post-structuralist thinkers Jacques Lacan, Jacques Derrida, and Michel Foucault, and includes French feminists Julia Kristeva, Hélène Cixous, Luce Irigaray, and Monique Wittig. Postmodernism doubts many of the standard assumptions of modernism: the existence of self, foundations through reason or objectivity, unchanging truth, universal reason, non-contingent autonomy, apolitical knowledge, neutrality of science, and realism (including correspondence theories of truth and the transparency of language).[2]

Feminism in general has an uneasy relation with postmodernism for several reasons. While postmodernism offers capable deconstructive critique, it seems to offer no positive constructive possibilities.[3] Its notion of the world as a text and its emphasis on the 'endless play of difference' treats some realities, like racial oppression and the experiences of victims of abuse or sexual assault, too lightly. Mary Hawkesworth points out that '[r]ape, domestic violence, and sexual harassment (to mention just a few of the realities that circumscribe women's lives) are not fictions or figurations that admit of the free play of signification.'[4] To address its shortcomings, some feminists propose alternatives within postmodernism (e.g. 'ludic postmodernism' versus 'resistance post-modernism'),[5] while others advocate positionality.[6]

1. Tong discusses several other categories of feminism that I omit here: Marxist, psychoanalytic, existentialist, and socialist feminism.

2. J. Flax, 'Postmodernism and Gender Relations in Feminist Theory', *Signs: Journal of Women in Culture and Society* 12 (1987), pp. 624-25.

3. L. Alcoff, 'Cultural Feminism Versus Post-structuralism', p. 420.

4. M.E. Hawkesworth, 'Knowers, Knowing, Known: Feminist Theory and Claims of Truth', *Signs: Journal of Women in Culture and Society* 14 (1989), p. 553.

5. T.L. Ebert distinguishes ludic postmodernism, which addresses 'reality as a theatre for the free-floating play (hence the term 'ludic') of images', from resistance postmodernism, which 'views the relation between word and world... as the effect of social struggles.' See 'The "Difference" of Postmodern Feminism', *College English* 53 (1991), p. 887.

6. Alcoff describes positionality as feminists' 'claiming of their identity as women as a political point of departure': 'Cultural Feminism Versus Post-structuralism', p. 432. She notes on p. 434 that '[w]hen women become feminists the crucial thing that has occurred is not that they have learned any new facts about the world but that they come to view those facts from a different position, from their own position as subjects.' I discuss positionality more fully below in terms of standpoint epistemologies.

All of these types of feminism have a history of being exclusive themselves. Although feminism in the 1970s grew out of the civil rights work
of the 1960s, feminist agendas have often been limited to the visions of
white, heterosexual, middle-class feminists. Women of other races, poor
women, and lesbian women have felt and have been marginalized. These
women continually call various (un-prefixed) feminist movements to
account for the way they ignore differences among women.[1]

Dissatisfied with the un-prefixed term 'feminist', Alice Walker coined
the term 'womanist' as being more appropriate to her visions from and
for women of African American heritage. One of Walker's definitions of
'womanist' is

> From *womanish*. (Opp. of 'girlish', i.e., frivolous, irresponsible, not
> serious.) A black feminist or feminist of color. From the black folk
> expression of mothers to female children, 'You acting womanish', i.e., like
> a woman. Usually referring to outrageous, audacious, courageous or
> *willful* behavior. Wanting to know more and in greater depth than is
> considered 'good' for one. Interested in grown-up doings. Acting grown
> up. Being grown up. Interchangeable with another black folk expression:
> 'You trying to be grown.' Responsible. In charge. *Serious.*[2]

Walker provides other definitions as well, and notes that 'Womanist is to
feminist as purple to lavender'.[3]

Walker's emphasis on the breadth and depth of womanist concern,
courage, and responsibility fits well with Barbara Smith's definition of
feminism.

> Feminism is the political theory and practice that struggles to free *all*
> women: women of color, working-class women, poor women, disabled
> women, lesbians, old women, as well as white, economically privileged
> heterosexual women. Anything less than this vision of total freedom is not
> feminism, but merely female self-aggrandizement.[4]

1.   See E.K. Minnich's *Transforming Knowledge* (Philadelphia: Temple
University Press, 1990) on the conceptual philosophical errors we make when we
identify some groups with prefixes while allowing others to stand unmarked as the
presumed norm or ideal. See also my discussion of 'difference' in Chapter 4.

2.   Walker introduced the term 'womanist' in the preface to her book *In Search
of Our Mother's Gardens: Womanist Prose* (New York: Harcourt Brace Jovanovich,
1983), p. xi, emphasis hers. 'Mujerista' is a similar term used by women from Latin
American countries or heritage.

3.   Walker, *In Search of Our Mother's Gardens*, p. xii.

4.   B. Smith, 'Racism and Women's Studies', *Frontiers* 5 (Spring 1980), p. 48,
emphasis hers.

When I use the word 'feminist' in this book, I intend Smith's and Walker's visions of feminism and womanism as courageous, responsible and actively working to promote the freedom and living of *all* women.[1]

The approaches that feminist biblical scholars take toward reading the Bible, and Genesis 2–3 in particular, depend on the type of feminism to which they subscribe and on how they understand feminism intersecting with their discipline, as the next section describes.

McIntosh's Interactive Phases for Curricular Re-Vision

Feminist and womanist struggles for a better world occur in the classroom and on campuses as well as in the streets and in legislative offices. The so-called 'new scholarship on women' has not only become a staple of Women's and Gender Studies programs, it has also flavored and nourished every discipline. It is developing new tastes among students and is beginning to transform primary, secondary, and college curricula.[2]

Peggy McIntosh outlines a typology of five interactive phases that describes how such scholarly and curricular change commonly occurs within a discipline.[3] I first sketch these phases briefly and then illustrate them further in terms of feminist literary criticism and feminist epistemologies, both of which are relevant for the ensuing interpretations of knowing and experiencing (in) the garden story.

1. Ultimately a new vision for all humanity is involved, men and women. Promoting the life and well-being of all people will necessitate eliminating as 'conferred dominance' some of these 'privileges' that are undesirable for anyone to have. It will also mean working to share with others those privileges that are 'unearned entitlements' that everyone should enjoy. For a readable, eye-opening discussion, from a white woman's perspective, of how re-vision also requires acknowledging and understanding our own racism, see P. McIntosh, 'White Privilege and Male Privilege: A Personal Account of Coming to See Correspondences Through Work in Women's Studies', Working Paper, 189, available from the Wellesley College Center for Research on Women, Wellesley, MA 02181.

2. For an introduction to the wealth of scholarship on what is usually called 'curriculum transformation', see J.F. O'Barr (ed.), *Reconstructing the Academy*, a special issue of *Signs: Journal of Women in Culture and Society* 12, 2 (1987) and the American Council on Education book edited by C.S. Pearson, D.L. Shavlik, and J.G. Touchton, *Educating the Majority: Women Challenge Tradition in Higher Education* (New York: Collier Macmillan, 1989).

3. My discussion summarizes P. McIntosh, 'Interactive Phases of Curriculum Re-Vision: A Feminist Perspective', Working Paper 124, available from the Wellesley College Center for Research on Women.

McIntosh begins with a discipline as it is usually understood. History is her sample discipline; she calls this first phase 'woman*less* history'. Here, women are absent from the curriculum, but no one notices their absence.

In the second phase, women's absence is noted, and scholars find and add 'women worthies' to fill the void. This compensatory scholarship shows that women as well as men meet the standards of greatness in the discipline. The structures of the discipline itself, however, remain unchallenged. McIntosh calls this phase 'women *in* history'. Supplementing an unaltered discipline is also derogatorily called the 'add women and stir' method by feminists impatient with its usual long-term ineffectiveness.

While there is a great deal of work to be done in recovering women as the objects of scholarship, phase two scholarship generally leads to a third phase that McIntosh refers to as 'women *as a problem, absence, or anomaly* in history'. This third phase begins when scholars recognize that a discipline's structures only awkwardly fit the many women's lives they are trying to add.[1] The discipline itself must be changed. For example, feminist historians found that historical periodization did not accurately describe women's experiences: periods of 'Renaissance' or 'Enlightenment' for privileged men were periods of greater restriction for women and nonprivileged men.[2] Similarly, theories of 'moral reasoning' based on white, upper-class, male college students led to low estimates of most women's moral development.[3]

Often the problematization of women within a discipline's traditional structuring leads to scholarly attempts to re-vision it from women's perspectives. McIntosh terms this fourth phase 'women *as* history'. Here, scholars engage disciplinary discussions from the perspectives of women's lives. For example, what women do is considered to *be* history. Women's Studies programs often emphasize this fourth phase (women's

---

1.   See Minnich, *Transforming Knowledge*, for a discussion of how the standard understandings in most disciplines are based on false universalization of the few as the norm or ideal.

2.   J. Kelly, 'Did Women Have a Renaissance?', chap. in *Women, History and Theory: The Essays of Joan Kelly* (Chicago and London: University of Chicago Press, 1984).

3.   See S. Harding, 'Is Gender a Variable in Conceptions of Rationality? A Survey of Issues', *Dialectica* 36.2-3 (1982), pp. 225-42, and C. Gilligan, *In a Different Voice: Psychological Theory and Women's Development* (Cambridge, MA and London: Harvard University Press, 1982).

writing, women's art, women's history, etc.) because women have been so systematically excluded from standard curricula.[1]

McIntosh's fifth phase involves redefinition of the discipline. She calls it 'history *redefined or reconstructed to include us all*'. I do not think any disciplines have been so redefined yet, but feminist and womanist scholars are working at this phase in addition to continuing their essential work in the previous three phases.[2]

Part of including 'us all', and perhaps problematic in McIntosh's description of the phases, is recognizing that the term 'women' can make overgeneralizing errors similar to those that traditional scholarship has made. Women come in all ages, classes, sexual orientations, and races. They have different cultures, customs, and religions and live in different countries. Some have been colonized, others colonizers. Feminist scholarship, like the women's movement in general, continually has to come to terms with its own racism, heterosexism, classism, and other exclusionary practices.[3]

While it must regularly pause to critique itself, feminist scholarship concerning gender and cultural diversity is affecting pedagogies[4] and is

1.   Following Minnich, *Transforming Knowledge*, p. 32, I use the word 'excluded' deliberately. Women were not simply omitted. Rather, Minnich observes, 'the reasons why it was considered right and proper to exclude the majority of humankind were and are built into the very foundations of what was established as knowledge.'

2.   McIntosh expects that curriculum transformation will easily take 150 years, but she hopefully notes that any project worth doing will take more than a lifetime to complete.

3.   For a critique of feminist phase theories as too reformist, see P. Hill Collins 'On Our Own Terms: Self-Defined Standpoints and Curriculum Transformation', *NWSA Journal* 3 (1991), pp. 367-81. Collins advocates beginning with the lives of Black or other marginalized women and moving from there to reframe the concepts and epistemologies of the disciplines.

4.   See the bibliography by C. Shrewsbury in a special issue of *Women's Studies Quarterly* on feminist pedagogy: 21.3-4 (1993), pp. 148-60; L.A. Goetsch, 'Feminist Pedagogy: A Selective Annotated Bibliography', *NWSA Journal* 3 (1991), pp. 422-29; C. Bunch and S. Pollack, *Learning Our Way: Essays in Feminist Education* (Trumansburg, NY: The Crossing Press, 1983); M. Culley and C. Portuges (eds.), *Gendered Subjects: The Dynamics of Feminist Teaching* (Boston: Routledge & Kegan Paul, 1985); J. Gore, *The Struggle for Pedagogies: Critical and Feminist Discourses as Regimes of Truth* (New York: Routledge, 1993); and the journals *Feminist Teacher* (published by Indiana University) and *Radical Teacher* (published by the Boston Women's Teachers' Group), especially nos. 41, 42.

being incorporated into curricula,[1] including religion and theology. Though feminists are now urging replacement of the term in the title, Arlene Swidler and Walter Conn's *Mainstreaming* is an early example of curriculum transformation efforts in theology and religious studies.[2]

Feminist Literary Criticism

Phases of Feminist Literary Theory

Feminist literary criticism is in many ways very old,[3] but it has flourished since the early 1970s. Its interaction with 'mainstream' (now sometimes called 'malestream') literary criticism exhibits the interactive phases of McIntosh's theory for curricular re-vision. Although much of feminist criticism attends primarily to the work of women authors, because of its greater relevance for biblical study my discussion here emphasizes the critical perspectives and methods feminists have used in studying male-authored classics.

1.   Men unfamiliar with feminist scholarship will appreciate the introduction by A. McDavid, 'Feminism for Men: 101 Educating Men in "Women's Studies"', *Feminist Teacher* 3.3 (1988), pp. 25-33. Scholars interested in classroom and curricular re-vision might contact the Association of American Colleges' Project on the Status and Education of Women, 1818 R St., NW, Washington, DC 20009, whose many helpful short papers include R.M. Hall with B.R. Sandler, 'The Classroom Climate: A Chilly One for Women?', 1982, and 'Evaluating Courses for Inclusion of New Scholarship on Women', 1988. See also L. Fiol-Matta and M.K. Chamberlain (eds.), *Women of Color and the Multicultural Curriculum: Transforming the College Classroom* (New York: Feminist Press, 1994).

2.   A. Swidler and W.E. Conn, *Mainstreaming: Feminist Research for Teaching Religious Studies* (Lanham, MD: University Press of America, 1985) has essays on world religions, Bible, history, systematic theology, and ethics. See also Joanna Dewey, 'Teaching the New Testament from a Feminist Perspective', *Theological Education* 26, 1 (1989), pp. 86-105. On recent feminist biblical scholarship, see J.C. Anderson, 'Mapping Feminist Biblical Criticism: The American Scene, 1983-1990', *Critical Review of Books in Religion* (1991), pp. 21-44; E. Schüssler Fiorenza (ed.), *Searching the Scriptures* (2 vols.; New York: Crossroad, 1993–1994); and the ten volumes of the Feminist Companion to the Bible Series, edited by A. Brenner (Sheffield: Sheffield Academic Press, 1993–1995).

3.   As forerunners of feminist literary criticism, S. Schibanoff describes both the interpretations of Chaucer's character Alysoun of Bath and the critical writing of Christine de Pisan in the late 1300s. See 'Taking the Gold Out of Egypt: The Art of Reading as a Woman', in E.A. Flynn and P.P. Schweickart (eds.), *Gender and Reading: Essays on Readers, Texts, and Contexts* (Baltimore and London: The Johns Hopkins University Press, 1986), pp. 83-106.

Kate Millett's 1969 publication of *Sexual Politics* was 'an event' in the women's liberation movement and something of a watershed for feminist literary criticism.[1] Millett's manifesto liberated women literary critics to read standard literary works differently. Feminist critics now choose alternative subjects for analysis, bringing forgotten women characters into view. They recognize that the implied reader of many texts is male and deliberately resist being 'immasculated' by a text.[2] By contrasting the portrayal of women characters with women's own values and experiences, feminist critics see texts in new ways and discern different significances in them. What is new about literary scholarship in the hands of feminists in McIntosh's phase two, 'women *in* literature', is not the critical methods themselves; these are still to a large degree the same as those other critics employ. Rather, the angle of vision is changed.

The second phase also includes recovering women authors and analyzing their concerns and how they write. Thus, feminist scholars begin, in McIntosh's third phase, to be uncomfortable with the traditional literary canons, whose criteria (established through circular reasoning on the basis of works by male authors) regularly exclude women's literature. Feminist scholars recognize women as a 'problem, absence, or anomaly' in both literary works and literary interpretive practices. They begin to challenge the methods and canons of traditional literary study. Does structuralism rely too heavily on binary dualisms, which often result in what Minnich calls 'hierarchically invidious monism'[3] that leaves women always on the bottom? Does deconstruction too readily undo and dismiss difference? Is post-structuralism too playful, neglecting harsh realities of life and ignoring needs for political change? Have reader-response and rhetorical theories considered the role of experience and how it shapes women's responses and mediates the effects of literature on women?

Out of the movements of feminist aesthetics and feminist critique[4] in

1. K. Millett, *Sexual Politics* (New York: Doubleday and Company, 1969).
2. J. Fetterley, *The Resisting Reader: A Feminist Approach to American Fiction* (Bloomington: Indiana University Press, 1978), p. xx.
3. Minnich, *Transforming Knowledge*, p. 53.
4. E. Showalter provides a typology of feminist criticism's growth as paralleling that of Afro-American literary criticism; see 'A Criticism of Our Own: Autonomy and Assimilation in Afro-American and Feminist Literary Theory', in R. Cohen (ed.), *The Future of Literary Theory* (New York and London: Routledge, 1989), pp. 347-69. Her categories for feminist literary theory roughly parallel McIntosh's phases: androgynous (phase 1), female aesthetic (phase 2) and feminist critique (phase 3), and gynocritics and gynesis (phase 4). She thinks gender theory (phase 5?) will be next.

phase three grew a new emphasis on analyzing the specificity of women's writing, which Elaine Showalter terms 'gynocritics' and an attention to theorizing from women's perspectives, which Alice Jardine calls 'gynesis'.[1] Developing out of French feminist theory, gynesis focuses on 'the textual consequences and representations of sexual difference', primarily in the realms of body and language.[2]

Gynocritical analyses of women writers and feminist criticism of gynocriticism suggest that interpretation itself may be gendered, since it is based at least in part on the different life experiences of women. For example, Susan Glaspell's story 'A Jury of Her Peers' relates how a group of men surveying the scene of a homicide do not notice the clues that their wives recognize from women's everyday experience.[3] Baffled at the domestic disorder, the men retreat to a more familiar barnyard territory. To their wives, however, the house's disarray tells a desperate, lonely tale of the woman who had lived there and explains what led her to kill her husband.

I suspect that feminist literary criticism is nowhere near McIntosh's fifth phase, where the discipline is redefined and reconstructed to include us all.[4] In part this is due to the generally slow response of male critics to consider feminism. Feminists recognize grudgingly that powerful literary critics are predominantly male. They alternately lament the failure of these critics to acknowledge the legitimacy of feminist literary theory

---

1.   E. Showalter, 'Women's Time, Women's Space: Writing the History of Feminist Criticism', in S. Benstock (ed.), *Feminist Issues in Literary Scholarship*, (Bloomington: Indiana University Press, 1987), p. 37. See also A. Jardine, *Gynesis: Configurations of Woman and Modernity* (Ithaca and London: Cornell University Press, 1985).

2.   Showalter, 'Women's Time, Women's Space', p. 37.

3.   The story is available in M.A. Ferguson's *Images of Women in Literature* (Boston: Houghton Mifflin, 1973), pp. 370-85. See A. Kolodny's discussion of this story and gendered interpretation in 'A Map for Rereading: Or, Gender and the Interpretation of Literary Texts', *New Literary History* 11 (1980), pp. 451-67 and J. Fetterley's 'Reading about Reading', 'A Jury of Her Peers', 'The Murders in the Rue Morgue', and 'The Yellow Wallpaper', in Flynn and Schweikart (eds.), *Gender and Reading*, pp. 147-64.

4.   For more recent discussion of feminist literary theory, see R.R. Warhol and D. Price Herndl (eds.), *Feminisms: An Anthology of Literary Theory and Criticism* (New Brunswick, NJ: Rutgers University Press, 1993).

and warn against feminists expending too much energy trying to capture male critics' attention.[1]

Feminist criticism has been successful, however, in developing practices that combine critical theories with fresh perspectives and essential attention to values. Showalter observes that male critics seem to have recognized that feminist criticism 'offers the mixture of theoretical sophistication with the sort of effective political engagement they have been calling for in their own critical spheres'.[2] In this sense, feminist literary scholarship is not a particular method; rather it employs many methods. As Annette Kolodny states, it is

> an acute and impassioned *attentiveness* to the ways in which primarily male structures of power are inscribed (or encoded) within our literary inheritance; the consequences of that encoding for women—as characters, as readers, and as writers; and, with that, a shared analytic *concern* for the implications of that encoding not only for a better understanding of the past, but also for an improved reordering of the present and future as well.[3]

Some Techniques of Feminist Literary Criticism
I conclude this discussion of feminist literary criticism by listing several of the attitudes and techniques that feminist criticism employs when reading and interpreting not only women's writing, but even what many would deem offensive, anti-feminist texts.

Feminists acknowledge our aims and presuppositions.[4] We lift up women characters, attend to women's likely responses, and consider how women are problematic or absent in texts. We realize that our

---

1. Many feminists are interested in male scholarship and in male critics' responses to feminist scholarship, but we are also realists about the typically low male interest in feminist criticism and pragmatists with respect to how we, as feminists, will spend our time.

2. E. Showalter, 'Critical Cross-Dressing: Male Feminists and the Woman of the Year', *Raritan* 3 (1983), p. 131.

3. A. Kolodny, 'Dancing Through the Minefield: Some Observations on the Theory, Practice, and Politics of a Feminist Literary Criticism', *Feminist Studies* 6 (Spring 1980), p. 20, emphasis hers.

4. Of, course, none of the techniques or strategies listed here are limited to feminists. I include particular items here because they are almost always explicitly important to feminist critics, while they may be only occasionally or only implicitly present in non-feminist criticism. I also use 'we' and 'our' in this section, including myself among the feminist critics.

social locations, biases, and individual experiences shape our readings, so we are conscious of the danger of false universals. While feminists insist on using gender as a category of analysis in interpretation, we recognize that it can never be isolated from other categories like class, sexual orientation, and race. Women may more easily hold together, and in tension, these various aspects of our lives and our literary responses.[1]

Feminist strategies for dealing with antifeminist texts range from ignoring them to counter-reading. At one extreme, feminists may simply refuse to read offensive texts, denying their importance or authority.[2] Or we might despoil them, raiding a text for its hidden treasures or at least salvageable material. For example, with regard to antifeminist biblical texts, we might claim masculine language as generic if that seems advantageous and plausible,[3] or we might use a text as a tool to reconstruct the sociocultural context of women's lives behind the text.

Modern readers have a different situation than readers of the oral cultures that preceded us. Previous hearers could remember texts selectively and update them for relevance to contemporary cultural contexts as they passed texts on orally.[4] Readers today are constrained by the relative fixity of written texts. Feminist readers may work to discredit and disestablish inappropriately biased standard (and dominant) interpretations. We may read a text from new directions, rereading it imaginatively and artistically, or 'leaning into' it through a technique Jean Kennard calls 'polar reading', to learn more about ourselves and

1.   E. Flynn's research on gender differences in reader-response suggests that women more readily discern relationships and resolve tensions in literature: 'Gender and Reading', in Flynn and Schweikart (eds.), *Gender and Reading*, pp. 267-88. K.H. Swanson's research confirms Flynn's observation about women readers noting relationships, but Swanson also finds that women's interpretations are more 'cognitively complex' than men's. See 'The Relationship of Interpersonal Cognitive Complexity and Message Design Logics Employed in Response to a Regulative Writing Task' (PhD dissertation, University of Minnesota, 1990).

2.   Actually destroying the text is not an option in our print and electronic culture. See Schibanoff, 'Taking the Gold Out of Egypt' for an interesting account of how one translator's conscious decision to exclude antifeminist material from his translation was 'corrected' before publication by a contemporary who noticed the omission.

3.   E. Schüssler Fiorenza advocates this in 'Missionaries, Apostles, Coworkers: Romans 16 and the Reconstruction of Women's Early Christian History', *WW* 6 (1986), p. 422.

4.   This was Alysoun of Bath's strategy in Chaucer's tale. See Schibanoff, 'Taking the Gold Out of Egypt'.

the text.[1] Certainly we are conscious of traditional reading practices that encourage our 'immasculation' or 'colonization' by the text. For our survival, we may need to become what Judith Fetterley calls 'resisting' readers.[2]

Reading 'As a Woman' and Resisting Reading
'Resisting reading' by feminists[3] grows out of the recognition that women have been trained to read *as* men.[4] Not only do literary critical practices encourage women's reading as men, but the male implied readers of the texts themselves also do so. In order to read a text by adopting the role of its male implied reader, women are 'immasculated'.[5] We are 'seduced and betrayed by devious male texts'.[6] Too often, the experiences of women's lives shape neither the literary expectations of canonical texts nor the critical theories we use to address them.

The phrase 'reading as a woman' is old. Christine de Pisan in the middle ages was accused of reading 'like' a woman, that is, misunderstanding through 'envy, pride, or foolishness'; she responded by

1. J.E. Kennard, 'Ourself behind Ourself: A Theory for Lesbian Readers', in *Gender and Reading*, pp. 69-71. Kennard explains polar reading as, for example, occurring when a woman reader attempts to identify as fully as possible with a male character instead of resisting the text. Rather than denying herself, the reader 'redefines herself in opposition to the text' (p. 77).

2. Fetterley, *The Resisting Reader*, p. xxii.

3. Feminists are not the only ones to engage in resisting reading. Old Testament scholar D.J.A. Clines offers several versions of resisting reading. Clines describes 'reading from left to right', that is, reading a text in our contemporary context, not only in the author's or character's context. See 'Reading Esther From Left to Right: Contemporary Strategies for Reading a Biblical Text', in D.J.A. Clines, S. Fowl and S. Porter (eds.), *The Bible in Three Dimensions: Essays in Celebration of Forty Years of Biblical Studies in the University of Sheffield* (JSOTSup, 87; Sheffield: Sheffield Academic Press, 1990), pp. 31-52. Clines also explains a process he calls 'reading against the grain' that lifts up features often not noticed in a text. See his essay 'The Story of Michal, Wife of David, in Its Sequential Unfolding', in D.J.A. Clines and T.C. Eskenazi (eds.), *Telling Queen Michal's Story: An Experiment in Comparative Interpretation* (JSOTSup, 119; Sheffield: JSOT, 1991), pp. 129-40.

4. C. Heilbrun, 'Millett's *Sexual Politics*: A Year Later', *Aphra* 2 (1971), p. 39.

5. Fetterley, *The Resisting Reader*, p. xx.

6. J. Culler, 'Reading as a Woman', portion of the chapter 'Readers and Reading' in *On Deconstruction: Theory and Criticism after Structuralism* (Ithaca: Cornell University Press, 1982), p. 52. Culler analyses Fetterley's assessment of what happens to women readers.

developing techniques for reading 'as' a woman, recognizing that 'readers inevitably recreate the texts they read in their own images'.[1] Male critics continue to describe feminist criticism by using the phrase 'reading as a woman'.[2] Jonathan Culler discusses reading as a woman as part of his argument for deconstruction.[3] He notes three 'moments' in feminist reader-response criticism: first, criticism building on the real experiences of women,[4] second, reading as a woman as a hypothesis to displace 'the dominant male critical vision',[5] and third, reading as a woman 'to investigate whether the procedures, assumptions, and goals of current criticism are in complicity with the preservation of male authority, and to explore alternatives'.[6] Robert Scholes critiques Culler's discussion of reading as a woman in his own essay, strangely titled 'Reading Like a Man'.[7] Scholes notes that feminist literary criticism is based on ethical-political concerns.[8] Feminist literary critics, he contends, read as 'class-conscious member[s] of the class *woman*'[9] and write not only for other literary critics, but also 'on behalf of other women',[10] conscious of their responsibility.

Reading *as* a woman can be described using McIntosh's phases. In phase two, reading as a woman uses traditional (male) standards to point out omissions, by paying attention to what male critics ignore. In phase three, it observes problems with the male standards and practices that often lead to exclusion of women and women's concerns. Reading as a woman in phase four involves considering women's lives and defining

1. Schibanoff, 'Taking the Gold Out of Egypt', pp. 95, 96.

2. In addition to Culler and Scholes (cited below), see also D. Boyarin's review of Sternberg and Bal: 'The Politics of Biblical Narratology—Reading the Bible Like/As a Woman', *Diacritics* 20, 4 (1990), pp. 31-42. D. Fuss insists on feminism as a chosen subject-position in her essay: 'Reading Like a Feminist', *differences* 1 (Summer 1989), pp. 77-92.

3. Culler, 'Reading as a Woman'.

4. Culler, 'Reading as a Woman', p. 51.

5. Culler, 'Reading as a Woman', p. 57.

6. Culler, 'Reading as a Woman', p. 61.

7. See R. Scholes, 'Reading Like a Man', in A. Jardine and P. Smith (eds.), *Men in Feminism* (New York: Methuen, 1987), pp. 204-18. From Scholes's title I expected him to discuss what it meant for him to read as a male critic; he does not do so. This essay is the essence of chapter 2 in R. Scholes, *Protocols of Reading* (New Haven: Yale University Press, 1989), which I cite here.

8. Scholes, *Protocols of Reading*, p. 94.

9. Scholes, *Protocols of Reading*, p. 94, emphasis his.

10. Scholes, *Protocols of Reading*, p. 93.

methods of reading and critical practices that are specifically suited to them. Eventually this work may lead to phase five in which women and men redefine criticism to include everyone. Reading as a woman means always including gender as an analytic category (assuming that the gender of characters, narrator, author, and readers all matter in the analysis and interpretation of a work);[1] recognizing women as a class, even as we rebel against this categorization; and working for better lives for women as a class, and hence against the oppressions of racism, classism, heterosexism, agism, ablism, and other 'isms' that many women and men face.

The notion of 'reading as a woman' highlights the fact that reading is actually done by people rather than by the various types of hypothetical readers posited by some reader response critics. Walter Slatoff notes that experience is inevitably a factor in real reading.

> One will, if one is a good reader, bring to bear all the knowledge and experience one has which will aid the work in fulfilling its intentions, and one will exclude as best one can knowledges, experiences, and associations which are clearly inappropriate, but if one is reading as a human being one will also inevitably bring to bear attitudes, feelings, vantage points, and perceptions which the work has not called for. One will wonder and speculate about their relevance and appropriateness and in so doing may come to feel some degree of tension between oneself and the work. But that seems to me a fine price to pay in order to be a real rather than ideal reader.[2]

Feminist criticism explicitly brings experience to the surface as a factor in reading. Culler notes that 'the question of the woman reader poses concretely and politically the problem of the relation of the experience of the reader when reading to other sorts of experiences',[3] and Scholes considers women's attempts 'to use their own experience as authority for reading or writing'.[4]

One type of reading as a woman is resisting reading. Resisting reading by feminists may include a variety of perspectives and practices. As resisting readers we uncover what is hidden, expose biases and

1.   For an example of such gender analysis in biblical studies, see A. Brenner and F. van Dijk-Hemmes, *On Gendering Texts: Female and Male Voices in the Hebrew Bible* (Leiden: Brill, 1993).

2.   W.J. Slatoff, *With Respect to Readers: Dimensions of Literary Response* (Ithaca: Cornell University Press, 1970), p. 78.

3.   Culler, 'Reading as a Woman', p. 42.

4.   Scholes, *Protocols of Reading*, p. 98.

stereotypes, and explore power relations. We note how women are characterized differently than men and whether a text is addressed primarily to men. We aim to understand the rhetoric of a text, sometimes in order to subvert it. We resist a text or its standard interpretations in order to disrupt the immasculation they may intend. We acknowledge the political role and power of literature and expose the partiality of supposedly universal truths. We consider the gender assumptions of a text and of our own cultures and question those values and assumptions. We are willing to break taboos and to rename, reimage, and reimagine reality. We value and pay attention to our own experience and develop interpretations in conversation with others.

Resisting reading is an important resource for feminists. It helps us see and think clearly and honestly, if we can exorcise the power of 'the male mind that has been implanted in us'.[1] As Alice Walker's Shug tells Celie, '[y]ou have to git man off your eyeball, before you can see anything a'tall'.[2] Resisting reading also challenges us not to be satisfied with the persistent 'play' of deconstruction by making room for the real experiences of women and acknowledging the importance of values for feminist hopes for transforming the world.

Feminist Epistemologies

Like literary studies, feminist theories about knowledge can be sorted according to McIntosh's phase theory. Three basic types of epistemologies, roughly corresponding to McIntosh's phases two, three and four, are commonly referred to as feminist empiricism, feminist postmodernism, and feminist standpoint theories. Due to the influence of positivism, especially in science, many of these theories developed recently as part of discussions in the philosophy of science.

Feminist empiricism suggests that problems with knowing result not from bad models or methodologies but from their poor application or practice. Feminists operating within this epistemology notice biases in conclusions which, for example, result from insufficient attention to women or from faulty generalization based on samples whose subjects were primarily men.[3] In the sciences and social sciences, as with other

---

1. Fetterley, *The Resisting Reader*, p. xxii.
2. A. Walker, *The Color Purple* (New York: Washington Square Press, 1982), p. 179.
3. For example, C. Gilligan's early work on moral development (see p. 72 n. 3)

disciplines, this sort of feminist work (McIntosh's second phase) generally leads to calls for changes in models and methodologies.

Feminists both affirm and are wary of postmodernism. Like post-modernists, feminists have been quick to point out several problems in standard epistemologies. Building on her work in curriculum transformation, feminist philosopher Elizabeth Minnich exposes the errors of false universalization: faulty generalization, circular reasoning, mystified concepts, and partial (in both senses of the word) knowledge. In recognizing that some particular groups have served as the norm and ideal for all of humanity and that concepts and ideas developed on the basis of such false universalization are faulty and pervasive, Minnich shares with postmodernists generally a critical suspicion of claims about truth and reality. (Women are a problem for standard epistemologies, as in McIntosh's phase three.)

Still, feminists are also skeptical of postmodernism. They note that postmodernism can easily play into the existing power structures.[1] Jane Flax observes that if

> there is no objective basis for distinguishing between true and false beliefs, then it seems that power alone will determine the outcome of competing truth claims. This is a frightening prospect to those who lack (or are oppressed by) the power of others.[2]

The reluctance of postmodernists to engage openly in political discussions has made it less appealing as a basis for feminist theory.

Feminist standpoint theorists recognize the inevitable biases that postmodern critics are quick to point out. They also recommend that

challenged the theories of Lawrence Kohlberg, which were generalized from a sample of men. In working with women, Gilligan noted different moral voices emerging: an ethic of responsibility and care rather than one of rights and impartiality. Similarly, the work of Mary Belenky and her colleagues corrects or supplements William Perry's work on intellectual development by noting that women's thinking often involves connection rather than separation. Their work with women in a variety of life situations observes perspectives or styles emerging in women's intellectual development that differ from the positions or stages Perry developed from a sample of primarily upper-class male students at Harvard. See M.F. Belenky, B. McVicker Clinchy, N.R. Goldberger, and J.M. Tarule, *Women's Ways of Knowing: The Development of Self, Voice, and Mind* (New York: Basic Books, 1986), p. 9.

1. Hawkesworth, 'Knowers', p. 557. Not only have feminists been leery of postmodernism, but prominent postmodernist thinkers have been notorious in their neglect of gender relations as a cultural constraint.

2. J. Flax, 'Postmodernism', p. 625.

women be research subjects, as the feminist empiricists propose. Standpoint theorists, whose stance grows out of Marxism, maintain that truth exists, but insist that it is more accessible to those on the margins.[1] Their position is like McIntosh's fourth phase: what women know *as* women forms the basis for standpoint epistemology.

Sandra Harding argues for a feminist standpoint epistemology that would acknowledge (with the postmodernists) that knowledge is socially situated and that it is grounded, not in women's experiences, biology, or in what women say, but in women's *lives*. Harding has developed the notion of 'strong objectivity.'[2] Strong objectivity argues that

> it is reasonable to think that the socially situated grounds and subjects of standpoint epistemologies [for example, the everyday lives of those on the margins] require and generate stronger standards for objectivity than do those [standard epistemologies] that turn away from providing systematic methods for locating knowledge in history.[3]

Patricia Hill Collins argues for an afrocentric feminist epistemology that lifts up Black women's knowledge prior to oppression, their common experience of oppression, and their concrete experience that includes

1.   To get a quick and humorous sense of the importance of knowledge from women's lives, see G. Steinem, 'If Men Could Menstruate', in her *Outrageous Acts and Everyday Rebellions* (New York: Signet, 1986), pp. 382-86. A lengthier, role-reversing satire is G. Brantenberg's *Egalia's Daughters: A Satire of the Sexes* (Seattle: The Seal Press, 1977, 1985). In a more serious vein, see the discussion of truth from the margins in b. hooks, *Feminist Theory: From Margin to Center* (Boston: South End, 1984).

2.   Harding contrasts strong objectivity with 'weak objectivity', which she describes as the unexamined value-neutrality claims of positivism: *Whose Science? Whose Knowledge? Thinking from Women's Lives* (Ithaca, NY: Cornell University Press, 1991), p. 147. Donna Haraway describes positivist claims as 'the God trick', by which she means knowledge from no place at all. See her 'Situated Knowledges: The Science Question in Feminism and the Privilege of Partial Perspective', *Feminist Studies* 14 (1988), pp. 575-99.

3.   S. Harding, 'Rethinking Standpoint Epistemology: What Is "Strong Objectivity"?', in L. Alcoff and E. Potter (eds.), *Feminist Epistemologies* (New York and London: Routledge, 1993), p. 50. Harding also observes that strong objectivity acknowledges the historical character of beliefs; it accepts cultural, sociological, and historical relativism, but rejects epistemological relativism (denying the possibility of criteria for judging competing claims); it aims to investigate, but not to control, the subject-object relationship; and it looks at the self from another's more distant, critical perspective, thereby thinking and acting as 'outsiders within'. See *Whose Science?*, pp. 151, 156, 160.

practical wisdom and knowledge for survival.[1] This epistemology is based on an ethic of care; it requires personal accountability; and it insists on dialogue for assessing knowledge claims.[2] Collins's proposal is Aristotelian in attending to the character of the knower (ethos) and recommending a place for persuasion and emotions (pathos), in addition to using reason (logos).[3]

Feminists discussing epistemologies display a wide range of interests. They consider the effects of subjectivity and of standpoints. They explore the notion of 'strong objectivity' and problematize any epistemic priority for gender, and even gender itself, as an abstract category. Some argue for social and communal, rather than individual knowledge, perhaps even allowing competing, multiple, local standards rather than seeking global ones. They ask about embodied knowledge, consider how women's 'know-how' has been devalued (termed 'old-wives tales') in favor of propositional 'know-that' knowledge. They propose feminist engagement *outside* the academy in order to test theories. They defy the philosophical myth that politically or socially motivated philosophy is necessarily 'bad' philosophy, and they insist on including politics and analyzing attendant values of all theories. They are not simply intellectually curious, but have emancipatory goals.[4]

Reading the Garden Story 'As a Woman'

How do feminist literary critical practices and feminist epistemologies apply to the garden story? In the remainder of this chapter I read the garden story in the company of many women readers, noting first how feminist critics have used standard methods of literary criticism within the dominant theological interpretation of the story to lift up positive aspects of the woman as a character in the story. Secondly, I consider how women readers both rebel at and attempt to understand the notion of male domination of women that Gen. 3.16 seems to imply. Thirdly, I demonstrate how it is possible for feminist readers to read the garden story as a patriarchal text.

1. P. Hill Collins, *Black Feminist Thought: Knowledge, Consciousness, and the Politics of Empowerment* (London: HarperCollins Academic, 1990), pp. 206, 208.

2. Collins, *Black Feminist Thought*, pp. 212, 215, 217.

3. Collins, *Black Feminist Thought*, pp. 218, 215.

4. This summary of the range of interests of feminist epistemologies reflects the essays in Alcoff and Potter, *Feminist Epistemologies*.

Rehabilitating the Woman

The garden woman has been much maligned throughout the centuries.
Jean Higgins summarizes well the ways commentators regularly describe
the woman:

> We have seen that Eve tempted, beguiled, lured, corrupted, persuaded,
> taught, counseled, suggested, urged, used wicked persuasion, led into
> wrongdoing, proved herself an enemy, used guile and cozening, tears and
> lamentations, to prevail upon Adam, had no rest until she got her husband
> banished, and thus became 'the first temptress'.[1]

Feminists' ability to rehabilitate the woman, thus, relies primarily on
reading the text with different presuppositions about the woman. Lillie
Devereux Blake laid a foundation for recent feminist rereading of the
text when she noted in *The Woman's Bible* that Eve's conduct is
'superior to that of Adam' and that Adam remains silent during the
woman's conversation with the serpent.[2] Elizabeth Cady Stanton likewise observes that 'the unprejudiced reader must be impressed with the
courage, the dignity, and the lofty ambition of the woman'.[3] Rehabilitating the woman will involve a reassessment of both her and her
conversation partner, the serpent.

The woman's active role in the garden narrative is fairly brief. God
comments on a need for her immediately after the prohibition in 2.17,
creates her and delivers her to the man's appraising eyes in 2.21-22. The
narrator notes the naked and clothed states of the man and his woman
in 2.25 and 3.21 and mentions their knowledge of nakedness, covering,
and hiding in 3.7-8. The woman is questioned by God, replies, and is
sentenced in 3.13, 16. Of the 46 verses in the narrative, the woman is
included or implied in 25 verses (2.22–3.21), mentioned in 16 verses
(2.22, 23, 25; 3.1-8, 13, 15, 16, 20, 21), and active in only 6 verses (3.2-
3, 6-8, 13).[4] Her big scene, however, is the conversation with the serpent
in 3.1-6.

The serpent has been much maligned over the centuries. A careful

---

1. J.M. Higgins, 'The Myth of Eve: The Temptress', *JAAR* 44 (1976), p. 641.
2. L.D. Blake, *The Woman's Bible* (ed. E.C. Stanton, *et al.*; New York:
European Publishing Company, 1898; reprinted, Seattle: Coalition on Women and
Religion, 1974), p. 26.
3. E.C. Stanton, *The Woman's Bible*, p. 24.
4. The man, by comparison, is included or implied in 37 verses (2.7-8; 2.15–
3.24), mentioned in 23 verses (2.7-8, 15, 16, 18-23, 25; 3.6-10, 12, 17, 20-24), and
active in only 7 verses (2.23; 3.6-8, 10, 12, 20).

reading of the text, however, shows that at worst the serpent is morally ambiguous. It dares to talk about God, even to ask questions about God. It speaks words (in 3.4-5) that seem to contradict God's earlier pronouncements (2.17), but that turn out to be true. The couple does not die; their eyes are opened (3.7); they do become (at least somewhat) like God (3.22); and they know good and evil (3.22).

If we understand the narrative symbolically, we can think of the serpent as 'representing anything in God's good creation that is able to facilitate options for human will and action'.[1] The serpent does *not* directly tempt the woman (or the man with her). It never suggests that she should eat from the forbidden tree. It *does* ask questions that provoke the woman's response, that cause her to think and reflect, to consider her options. Then, apparently, it stands back silently to watch. Phyllis Trible's portrayal of the woman and man in this scene is apt.[2] The woman actively engages in conversation and reflection, while the man participates silently and passively. Like an able teacher, the serpent simply lays out some possibilities before its students, the vocal woman and the silent man. It urges critical thinking on their part by offering perspectives and implying choices they may not have considered. Then it leaves them to draw their own conclusions.

While we may be willing to redeem the serpent, to exempt it from the disdain it has suffered for centuries at the pens of interpreters, it might be more difficult to rehabilitate the woman's image. Given the focus on knowing and thinking in this chapter, I consider the woman as a thinker. I contend, in the paragraphs that follow, that the woman is a connected knower, that she acts independently, that she interprets, and that she is a model moral thinker.

The Woman as Knower and Actor. First, the woman is a 'connected knower'.[3] Human relationship is part of her being from the moment she enters the story. The woman is not created from the ground as the man is. She knows no human life alone in the garden with God or with the animals. She is constantly among various companions: God, the man,

1.   T.E. Fretheim, 'Is Genesis 3 a Fall Story?', *WW* 14 (1994), p. 149.
2.   P. Trible notes that the woman is 'intelligent, informed, and perceptive'; she 'speaks with clarity and authority'. See *God and the Rhetoric of Sexuality* (Philadelphia: Fortress Press, 1978), p. 110. In contrast, Trible observes (on p. 113) that the man's presence is 'passive and bland'. See my discussion on pp. 47-48 on why it is likely that the man is present throughout 3.1-6.
3.   The term comes from Belenky, *et al.*, *Women's Ways of Knowing*.

and the serpent. Her scene with the serpent includes the man all the way through, even though the narrator's explicit mention of his presence is reserved until the end of the episode in 3.6. The serpent speaks to her using plural pronouns and verbs, and she replies in the same fashion. The woman also operates with an ethic of care. Having judged the tree to be good, delightful, and desirable, the woman shares its food, beauty, and wisdom with her man. Together the couple's eyes are opened; together they know their nakedness; together they sew coverings for themselves; and together they hear and hide from God. Even after the sentences, the woman's desire will be for her man (3.16). The woman knows and experiences her life in relationship with her man. She is what Belenky and colleagues would call a 'connected knower'.

Secondly, the woman acts independently. While experiencing her life as a relational being, the woman acts without consulting either her man or God. She has apparently been conversing for some time with the serpent when in 3.1 the narrator lets readers in on the conversation. If the man had been involved in the discussion before we readers begin hearing it, he drops out now. Though part of a human pair, the woman continues the dialogue alone, and it involves theological discussion. She does not consult the man for his (perhaps more directly obtained) understanding of what God has said, nor does she turn to God for help sorting out the possibilities the serpent's further questions have raised in her mind. She ponders and acts alone, before turning to include her man in her decision.

The Woman as Interpreter. Thirdly, the woman interprets. The inside view of her thoughts in 3.6 is the most striking instance of the woman's interpretive capabilities, but if we read carefully, we see that she interprets throughout the story.[1] The woman has interpreted the prohibition before we hear her recital of it in 3.2-3. Presumably she has heard earlier from God or from the man about the forbidden tree and the reason (or warning or threat) associated with its prohibition. Her interpretation of this prohibition is evident in her understanding that even touching the tree is not allowed.

---

1. There may be some question about how to assess 3.6a. Here the narrator provides an inside view into the woman's thought process before she takes and eats the fruit. While the narrator's report of her thoughts mediates them differently to readers than her direct speech does elsewhere in the chapter, we can probably trust the narrator's portrayal equally well in either format.

In Gen. 3.6, the woman interprets both her environment and the serpent's remarks. The woman evaluates the tree itself. She sees that the tree is good for food and pleasing to the eye. Her assessment is correct since it agrees with the narrator's description of the tree in 2.9. The woman also interprets the serpent's idioms and metaphors in 3.5 about having their eyes opened, being like gods, and knowing good and evil, when she notes, as part of her reasoning in 3.6, that the tree is to be desired for insight. That is, the woman seems to understand the phrase 'knowing good and evil' positively, as insight. To know good and evil is to be like God. It is divine insight. Having their eyes opened will make this desirable insight available to the couple. Thus, the woman evaluates the serpent's perspective and reasoning as trustworthy. The serpent had also announced that the couple would not die, and the woman believes the creature enough to risk tasting the forbidden fruit. Having done so, she may also interpret what (if anything) has happened to her as being sufficiently safe to risk sharing the fruit with her man as well.[1]

The woman continues interpreting in 3.13. There, the divine question itself suggests that God expects interpretation from her. In spite of the man's lengthy responses, God's questions to him can be read as requiring only very short answers. 'Where are you?' expects a place, 'who told you...?' a name, and 'did you eat...?' a simple yes or no. His responses report actions. In contrast, God's question to the woman seems to require an explanation. God asks not simply whether she ate, but prompts her to explain what it is that she has done. Her response includes reflection on actions.

The woman's reply to God's question suggests that she has paid attention to God's questioning of the man, reflected on her actions, reconsidered her evaluation of the serpent and perhaps of God, and learned from her mistaken decision to eat from the tree. All of these possibilities emerge from the woman's observation that the serpent 'tricked' her.[2] The woman does not say that the serpent 'made me do

---

1.   The man may also be interpreting the conversation and the woman's action and its effects before he eats, but in contrast to the woman, the narrator provides no sustained inside view to suggest this reading.

2.   Translations of *hiššîʔanî* as 'deceived me' (NIV, REB), 'beguiled me' (RSV, KJV), or 'duped me' (JPS) carry similar nuances. All suggest that an action now recognized as inappropriate was thought to be reasonable (due to false assumptions) when it was undertaken. All indicate that the woman now evaluates her prior interpretation as a mistake.

it'. She does not blame the serpent. She was not coerced, and she knows it. Neither does she blame the man for standing by mutely, not intervening to prevent her wrongful action. Nor, in contrast to the man, does the woman subtly attempt to implicate God by saying that the serpent who tricked her is one whom God had created and left with her to talk unsuspectingly in the garden.

The woman does not claim that the serpent 'tempted' her. Being tempted would suggest that the woman was attracted to the forbidden eating. It would also imply that she entertained the possibility of disobedience *against* her better judgment. One is only 'tempted' to do something that one knows at the time that one should not do. The reasoning in 3.6 suggests, in contrast, that immediately before her action the woman considers the implications of eating the fruit. She seems at the time to make a reasonable choice. She knows of the prohibition, certainly, but she has also heard persuasive arguments from other perspectives, and she has made her own observations that lead to her considered decision.[1]

The woman's use of the word 'tricked' indicates that she felt her decision was made with good intentions, not out of rebellion or wrongful desire. It also shows that she *now* understands the situation differently. Looking back on her interactions with the serpent, the woman now recognizes the negative effect its words had on her. Whatever the serpent's intentions, its words helped to persuade the woman to make a choice that she has by 3.13 come to regret. Saying that the serpent 'tricked' her shows that the woman now understands her choice and her action to have been a mistake, one from which she has already learned. It is not clear when the woman realizes her choice was a bad one.[2] Perhaps she recognized it as soon as the couple's nakedness led them to cover themselves. Maybe she understood the nature of the problem when they hid from God. Perhaps hearing and reflecting on the man's replies to God's questions helped the woman recognize her

---

1.   The woman's considered decision could involve conscious rebellion against authority, in this case God's command. The narrator's inside view into the woman's thoughts in 3.6 does not include rebellion, however. The narrator's reticence to mention rebellion stands in contrast to the practice in the remainder of the OT. There, prophets, leaders, God, and the narrator regularly evaluate Israel's rebellion negatively. So, the narrator's silence about rebellion may suggest that it is not a primary concern in Genesis 3.

2.   Nor is it clear *what* the 'trick' was for the woman, only *that* it was.

misdeed. The woman's use of the word 'tricked' acknowledges that the ultimate responsibility for her actions is her own; it also attempts some explanation that indicates her new understanding.

The Woman as Moral Decision-Maker. Finally, the woman is a moral decision-maker. Evelyn and James Whitehead have developed a fourfold model for moral discourse. It involves attending, asserting, deciding, and acting.[1] The model recognizes that, even when a person or group follows these steps, the decisions made will be wrong about half the time. The process of deliberation and decision, however, will have been useful, and an individual or group can learn easily from a mistake and go on to make new decisions by building on the attending and asserting that has already been done. The woman demonstrates many features of the Whitehead's model for good moral decision-making.

First, the woman 'attends'. She has listened to the man's appraisal of her in 2.23. Presumably she has heard from the man or from God about the prohibition, which she clearly knows in some fashion by 3.2. She gives her full attention to the serpent's questions, and 'asserts' her response carefully, including her own interpretation. She attends again to the serpent's further remarks in 3.4-5, showing thoughtful consideration in her interpretation of them in 3.6. Next, having attended and asserted, the woman considers the options and makes a reasoned decision, which she then 'acts' to carry out, including her man as well. The woman continues 'attending' to the situation and to the interchange between God and her partner. In her own response to divine questioning she 'asserts' once more, indicating that she has recognized that her earlier decision was a mistake, one from which she has already learned.

Confronting a Troublesome Verse: Genesis 3.16. While feminist scholars are generally pleased with what they view as the positive portrayal of the woman's intellectual and moral decision-making abilities in the garden story, they are generally less comfortable with God's pronouncement to the woman in 3.16. In fact, Susan Lanser argues that this

---

1. J.D. Whitehead and E.E. Whitehead, *Method in Ministry: Theological Reflection and Christian Ministry* (Minneapolis: Seabury, 1980). The Whiteheads' model of theological reflection has been applied to the context of moral decision-making; they draw from B. Lonergan, *Method in Theology* (New York: Herder & Herder, 1972).

is the point where Bal's and Trible's readings reach their *aporia*—the impasse, the silence, that unravels the argument. For finally neither can explain why male dominance should be the particular consequence of a transgression for which both man and woman are equally, as they argue, responsible.[1]

Feminist attempts to rehabilitate the woman must confront Gen. 3.16.

Some scholars like Carol Meyers, Adrien Bledstein, and Anne Gardner address this verse and the story as a whole in the context of its ancient setting.[2] Meyers treats the entire narrative in terms of three genres: as a myth about existential conditions to be applied universally, as an etiology explaining the status quo, and as a wisdom tale, describing to Israelites involved in pioneering agriculture the paradoxical and harsh aspects of life.[3] Because the emphasis throughout the story is on the means of sustenance, as the repetition of words related to eating indicates, Meyers reads 3.16 in a setting of pioneering agriculture. She offers a careful and detailed translation of the verse:

> I will greatly increase your toil and your pregnancies;
> (Along) with travail shall you beget children.
> For to your man is your desire,
> And he shall predominate over you.[4]

1. S.S. Lanser, '(Feminist) Criticism in the Garden: Inferring Genesis 2–3', in H.C. White, (ed.), *Speech Act Theory and Biblical Criticism* (Semeia, 41; Decatur, GA: Scholars Press, 1988), p. 75, emphasis hers.

2. See C. Meyers, *Discovering Eve: Ancient Israelite Women in Context* (New York: Oxford University Press, 1988); A.J. Bledstein, 'Are Women Cursed in Genesis 3.16?' in A. Brenner (ed.), *A Feminist Companion to Genesis* (The Feminist Companion to the Bible, 2; Sheffield: Sheffield Academic Press, 1993), pp. 142-45; and A. Gardner, 'Genesis 2.4b–3: A Mythological Paradigm of Sexuality or of the Religious History of Pre-exilic Israel?', *SJT* 43 (1990), pp. 1-18.

3. Meyers, *Discovering Eve*, pp. 79, 80, 91.

4. Meyers, *Discovering Eve*, p. 118. This translation differs slightly (as noted below) from the one Meyers proposes in an earlier essay 'Gender Roles and Genesis 3.16 Revisited', in C.L. Meyers and M. O'Connor (eds.), *The Word of the Lord Shall Go Forth: Essays in Honor of David Noel Freedman in Celebration of His Sixtieth Birthday* (Philadelphia: American Schools of Oriental Research, 1983), p. 344, emphasis mine:

> I will greatly increase your *work* and your pregnancies;
> (Along) with *toil* shall you *give birth to* children.
> *To* your man is your desire,
> And he shall predominate over you.

Meyers notes that women contribute to sustenance for the pioneering community both through their agricultural work and by bearing children to add to the labor pool.[1]

From detailed lexical and syntactic considerations, Meyers tries to minimize the connections between Gen. 3.16 and childbearing.[2] She observes that none of the normal childbearing terms are used, though they were available. Meyers is quick to point out the connection between the disobedient eating and the repetition of eating terms built into the punishments. She views this emphasis on eating as an indication that sustenance is what was at issue for the community. Though she observes the discussion of eating throughout the chapter, Meyers does not comment on Cassuto's suggestion that Gen. 3.16-17 uses alternative words for pain, toil, or suffering (ʿiṣṣābôn and ʿeṣeb) in childbearing and in farm labor precisely as a word play on the tree (ʿēṣ) that caused the couple's trouble.[3] In line with her theory that the context is one of pioneering agriculture, Meyers limits the scope of man's dominion over woman in 3.16b to the reproductive arena.[4] Because of the dangers childbirth entails, the woman may prefer not to bear so many children. Yet her desire moderates her reluctance, and her man dominates over her in sexual matters in any case. A high birthrate serves the interests of the emerging nation.

Gardner and Bledstein discuss Genesis 3 in the context of ancient Near Eastern parallels and the attraction of Canaanite fertility religions, especially for Israelite women. Bledstein argues for an alternate translation of part of 3.16 on the basis of cognates in other ancient Near Eastern languages and the parallel construction in Gen. 4.7. She translates 3.16b as 'You are powerfully attractive to your husband, But he can rule over you (3.16)'.[5] Bledstein says that the Hebrew word tᵉšûqātēk usually translated 'your desire', has an Akkadian cognate kuzbu that means 'attractiveness, charm, sexual vigor'.[6] It indicates not the woman's active desire for her husband, but that the man finds her

1. Meyers, *Discovering Eve*, p. 105.
2. Meyers, *Discovering Eve*, pp. 102, 106, 108.
3. U. Cassuto, *A Commentary on the Book of Genesis: Part I From Adam to Noah Genesis I–VI 8* (trans. I. Abrahams; Jerusalem: The Magnes Press, 1961), p. 65.
4. Meyers, *Discovering Eve*, p. 116.
5. Bledstein, 'Are Women Cursed?', p. 144.
6. Bledstein, 'Are Women Cursed?', p. 143.

desirable. Bledstein contends that the Hebrew verb *mšl*, usually translated 'rule', should be translated in 3.16 in a way parallel to its use in 4.7. Thus, Bledstein argues that the imperfect verb indicates *not* that the man *will* rule over the woman, but that he *can*, just as God's warning to Cain in 4.7 suggests that Cain is able to rule over sin whose desire is for him. Thus, for Bledstein, the verse reminds the woman that she is human and that she will give birth as humans do, through pain; she has not become 'like the gods', who give birth without suffering.

In contrast to Meyers's wisdom tale supporting the nation's need for pioneering agriculture or Bledstein's contrast between divine and human means of giving birth, Gardner views the entire story in terms of Canaanite fertility religions.[1] Seen against its ancient Near Eastern background and Israelite setting, Gardner understands the text as supporting patriarchy in various ways. She admits that Genesis 2–3 is sexist in implicating primarily the woman, but she explains the reason for this bias. The story cautions husbands to control wives and warns about potential loss of land for disobedience. It reflects the moral and cultic impurity of women during the monarchy (a period when, Gardner claims, no heroines are mentioned in the Bible).[2] The story accomplishes its polemic against fertility religions by its mundaneness. In the garden narrative, the trees are ordinary trees, not symbols of the goddess Asherah, and it is Yahweh, not the goddess, who controls women's fertility.[3] Gardner contends that, by modifying the Mesopotamian tales to make a woman the protagonist, the Yahwist points to his motive: discrediting the women who 'were especially attracted to the worship of the goddess and introduced their menfolk to her cult'.[4]

While the proposals of Meyers, Bledstein, and Gardner may explain how the text came into being in its present shape and how it may have affected early hearers, they are less helpful in offering suggestions for how we should read Gen. 3.16 today. Should we simply treat the text as a historical artifact whose only role today is to explain ancient agriculture, mythology, or cultic practices? The text's own history of interpretation and scriptural status prohibit a purely historical reading.

Phyllis Trible focuses her attention on the inner dynamics of the text itself rather than looking behind the narrative for an explanation of the

---

1.   Gardner, 'Genesis 2.4b-3', p. 2.
2.   Gardner, 'Genesis 2.4b-3', p. 16.
3.   Gardner, 'Genesis 2.4b-3', p. 14.
4.   Gardner, 'Genesis 2.4b-3', p. 14.

verse. She also wants to read the text theologically and hopes that it can continue to be our story today. She goes to great lengths to insist that it is the text's interpretations, not the text itself, that are sexist. Trible follows Claus Westermann in seeing God's words in 3.14-19 not as *pre*scriptions of divine intentions for human social relations and human relationship to the world, but as *de*scriptions of consequences of the couple's deed for life after the 'fall'.[1] An advantage of this kind of interpretation, some argue, is that by clearly separating creation and 'fall' it preserves mutuality in gender relations as God's intention for the created order.[2] A potential disadvantage is that it reads the story as an event in the early history of the world,[3] one which, because of its primeval nature, we can expect neither to undo nor to repeat. A further problem with this reading, as noted in Lanser's comment cited above, is its failure to take seriously God's active role in making the statements.

Reading With Opened Eyes (and Seeing Patriarchy)
If the patriarchy of the story were limited to Gen. 3.16, feminist interpreters could probably decide to accept one or another of the explanations that attempt to make the verse palatable, thus redeeming the whole story. But while some feminists reading the garden story attempt, with varying degrees of success, to rehabilitate the woman, others see in the story a level of patriarchy that can only be exposed, not redeemed.[4] When Pamela Milne, for example, questions whether a

1. Trible, *God and the Rhetoric*, p. 128; C. Westermann, *Creation* (trans. J.J. Scullion, S.J.; Philadelphia and London: Fortress Press and SPCK, 1974), p. 100.

2. But see R.M. Richardson, 'The Theology of Sexuality in the Beginning: Genesis 3', *AUSS* 26 (1988), pp. 121-31 for arguments about God's order of creation involving hierarchy as well. J.T. Walsh does not address Trible's work, but arrives at a conclusion opposite hers concerning the role of hierarchy in the text: 'Genesis 2.4b–3.24: A Synchronic Approach', *JBL* 96 (1977), pp. 161-77. See also my discussion in Chapter 4.

3. Westermann's basic understanding of the story as primeval narrative places it 'on the other side of our historical experience'; see *Genesis 1–11: A Commentary* (trans. J.J. Scullion, S.J.; Minneapolis: Augsburg, 1984), p. 276. While Westermann thus claims that the Genesis 2–3 narrative is not the beginning of history (p. 42), he also acknowledges the role the story plays in Genesis 1–11 as a prologue to Israel's history (pp. 65-66). Trible does not discuss the text's genre in terms of history.

4. There are many definitions of patriarchy. E. Schüssler Fiorenza's definition is both classical and broadly applicable: patriarchy is 'a complex pyramidal political structure of dominance and subordination, stratified by gender, race, class, religious

feminist reading of Genesis 2–3 is possible, she is really asking whether a feminist can read the story positively.[1] In denying this possibility, Milne and other feminists engage in the feminist scholarship that McIntosh describes as finding women to be a 'problem, absence or anomaly' in the discipline. In this section, I discuss this feminist view. The woman's portrayal is problematic, and patriarchy is inscribed in the story in three areas: the man/woman relationship, the priority of the man in the story, and the woman's relationship with God.

a. *The Man/Woman Relationship*
Scholars generally recognize that the man's and woman's relationship is troubled *after* the couple's eating, but gender relations are also disturbed *before* their offense. In fact, the relationship of the man and woman demonstrates aspects of what feminists describe as patriarchy throughout the garden story, in terms of the narrator's descriptions of each of the individuals separately and of the couple in relationship. In this section, I justify the following specific claims. First, the woman is created *for* the man, to be his helper. Second, she is derivative from the man. Third, he rules over her. Fourth, the man names the woman.

Woman as Helper. God decides in Gen. 2.18 that it is not good for the man to be alone, so God eventually creates the woman *for* the man. In this story, she is not created for her own sake, but in order to meet some divinely discerned needs of the man. Feminists have sensed that the woman's creation is something of an 'afterthought'.[2] Moreover, the woman is created as a *helper* for the man. Trible attempts to redeem this label. She argues, in her classic 'Depatriarchalizing' essay, against its use as a status marker at all. Later, in *God and the Rhetoric of Sexuality*, Trible suggests that the term *'ēzer* is a sign of superiority because God is regularly described with this word.[3] Clines notes the contradiction in

---

and cultural taxonomies and other historical formations of domination'. It is appropriate in recognizing that patriarchy is embodied differently in different times and cultures. See her book *But She Said: Feminist Practices of Biblical Interpretation* (Boston: Beacon, 1992), p. 115.

1. P.J. Milne, 'Eve & Adam: Is a Feminist Reading Possible?', *BibRev* 4 (June 1988), pp. 12-21, 39.

2. E.C. Stanton, *The Woman's Bible*, p. 20.

3. Trible, 'Depatriarchalizing in Biblical Interpretation', *JAAR* 41 (1973), p. 36 and *God and the Rhetoric*, p. 90, as noted by Clines, 'What Does Eve Do to Help?' chap. in *What Does Eve Do to Help? and Other Readerly Questions to the Old*

Trible's two approaches, arguing that the word either presumes a notion of ranking or it does not.[1] He contends that regardless of the status of the person who takes it on, the role of helper has an inferior connotation.[2]

Clines wants to shift the question, however, from the status of the helper to what the woman actually *does* as a helper. Trible contends that the woman 'alleviates [the man's] isolation through identity'.[3] Bonhoeffer sees her as embodying and helping to bear the creaturely limit God has imposed.[4] Francis Watson suggests that the woman's 'first role is to meet the man's sexual needs'.[5] Phyllis Bird specifies that the woman helps the man in terms of procreation.[6]

Clines agrees with Bird's assessment; the woman helps the man with what he could not do alone: procreate. Clines insists that the woman's help could not be ordinary or it would not be mentioned at all.[7] She does not imaginatively help the man name the animals, since she is not yet on the scene when their naming occurs, nor does she help him with his farm labor.[8] Clines observes that the woman's help is not of an intellectual nature either: 'after the sin of the couple he [God] does not punish the woman by threatening her with demotion to intellectual inferiority or by rendering her incapable of keeping up interesting conversation with her partner'.[9]

Clines contends that the woman helps her mate with procreation, with carrying out God's command from Gen. 1.28 to 'be fruitful and multiply' as evidenced also in the offspring she bears in Gen. 4.1-2. Clines argues that it is precisely for this reason that the man recognizes

---

Testament (JSOTSup, 94; Sheffield: JSOT Press, 1990), p. 28.

1. Clines, 'What Does Eve Do to Help?', p. 28.
2. Clines, 'What Does Eve Do to Help?', p. 30.
3. Trible, *God and the Rhetoric*, p. 90.
4. D. Bonhoeffer, *Creation and Fall: A Theological Interpretation of Genesis 1–3* (trans. J.C. Fletcher; London: SCM Press, 1959), pp. 60-61.
5. F. Watson, 'Strategies of Recovery and Resistance: Hermeneutical Reflections on Genesis 1–3 and its Pauline Reception', *JSNT* 45 (1992), p. 99.
6. P. Bird, 'Genesis I–III as a Source for a Contemporary Theology of Sexuality', *Ex Auditu* 3 (1987), p. 38.
7. Clines, 'What Does Eve Do to Help?', p. 33.
8. Clines, 'What Does Eve Do to Help?', pp. 34, 33. Clines makes no mention of Meyers' work on Gen. 3.16, which argues precisely that part of what the woman is sentenced to do is agricultural toil.
9. Clines, 'What Does Eve Do to Help?', p. 35.

the woman in Gen. 2.23 *as his mate*. This is why the garden story is concerned with nakedness. That the woman's help is procreation explains God's sentencing the woman in terms of pregnancy. Clines observes that 'God regards Eve as primarily a child-bearing creature'[1] and notes that Adam gets the point also when he names Eve in 3.20 in terms of her reproductive abilities. Finally, Clines shores up his argument for woman's procreative help by noting that Augustine and Aquinas, in this case at least, seem to have got it right.[2]

Woman as Derivative. The woman is created *from* the man.[3] She is thus derivative, not primary. Moreover, some feminists charge that the man is portrayed as having usurped the normal birth process where all individuals are born from women.[4] Once born of man, the woman immediately becomes the object of male gaze. Readers gaze on her as well. Seduced by the man's poetry in Gen. 2.23, we appraise our own imaginative visions of the perfect garden woman (or familiar artistic depictions of her naked body that the story calls to mind).[5] On hearing herself described three times in 2.23 as a 'this', the woman does not protest being referred to as an object. The man's poem not only shows his delight in the woman, but also reminds readers that she is a member of the 'marked' class: her 'woman' derives from his 'man'. The man's

1. Clines, 'What Does Eve Do to Help?', p. 35.
2. All of the arguments in this paragraph come from Clines, 'What Does Eve Do to Help?', pp. 35-37. I think procreation alone is an insufficient explanation of the woman's help in Genesis 2–3. I include Clines's argument as a plausible reading of the narrative, indicating what feminists regard as the patriarchal nature of the text in its defining woman only in terms of her reproductive capabilities.
3. I give arguments on pp. 102-104 for why we should understand the first human as a man rather than as a human or 'earth creature'.
4. M. French, *Beyond Power: On Women, Men, and Morals* (New York: Ballantine Books, 1985), p. 267. C. Froula also finds Adam's role as a male mother strange; see 'Rewriting Genesis: Gender and Culture in 20th Century Texts', *Tulsa Studies in Women's Literature* 7.2 (1988), p. 199. The Bible's separate account of the creation of woman seems to be unique among ancient Near Eastern texts: S.R. Lieberman, 'The Eve Motif in Ancient Near Eastern and Classical Greek Sources' (PhD thesis, Boston University, 1975), p. 100.
5. Appraisal of woman's nakedness in this garden scene is not as obviously pornographic as when readers join David's observation of Bathsheba touching herself while bathing. See J.C. Exum, 'Raped by the Pen', chap. in *Fragmented Women: Feminist (Sub)versions of Biblical Narratives* (Valley Forge, PA: Trinity Press International, 1993), p. 174.

naming of the woman[1] in this verse continues his depiction as the definer, the labeler, the categorizer. He determines the norms to which she is subject. Contemporary feminists recognize, in the woman's derivative status and her depiction as an object, aspects of patriarchy in the man/woman relationship even *before* the couple's misdeed.

Man's Rule over Woman. There seems to be a measure of mutuality in the story in 2.25–3.8, but this mutuality falls apart under stress. As soon as God questions the man about the events that have transpired, the man thinks only of himself. When the going gets tough, the man blames the woman for his action. The woman either does not confirm or deny the man's depiction of the problem or she is not allowed (by the narrator or by God) to do so. The woman does not support the man's story, nor does he confirm hers. Mutuality has vanished.

The woman's sentence in 3.16 indicates that the unequal treatment already begun before the forbidden eating is now being institutionalized. The woman is either restricted completely to hearth and home, if we read a hendiadys, 'pain in childbearing', in 3.16, or, if we read with Meyers, the woman works a double shift. She contributes her toil to the hard work of pioneering agriculture, and she is still responsible to be mother and wife on the home front. Yet she does not rule even in this limited domain. The man will rule over her.

The man's rule is extensive. It includes control of the woman's sexuality since his rule is related to her desire. Presumably the man's control extends to her reproductive capacities as well, given his insistence in 3.20 that Eve will be the mother of all living. The man is in charge of the woman's sustenance also, since he clearly has the breadwinner role in this account (3.19). Even if we read the imperfect in 3.16 with Bledstein as simply indicating the man's capability (he 'can' rule over you),[2] the woman is no better off. In fact, this translation may be even more threatening—sounding, as it does, like a warning reminder of the man's physical prowess. In this case, in addition to the man's rule over the woman's sexuality, reproduction, and sustenance, his dominion includes physical domination over her. The verse has been read over the centuries as permitting the abuse of women's bodies.[3] If the woman is

1. See, pp. 100-102 on the man's naming of the woman.
2. Bledstein, 'Are Women Cursed?', p. 144.
3. M.F. Stitzinger, 'Gen. 1–3 and the Male/Female Role Relationship', *GTJ* 2 (1981), p. 44. See also J.M.K. Bussert, *Battered Women: From a Theology of*

threatened with battering by a domineering man, her desire for him is itself her enemy, trapping the woman into a relationship upon which she is dependent, but perhaps leading to her death.[1] There are no restraining orders on the man's means of ruling the woman. Nor is she given a divine mark, like Cain in Gen. 4.15, to insure her protection.

Man's Naming of Woman. The man's renaming of the woman in 3.20 shows that he accepts his dominant role and that he will control the woman's sexuality, in this case by committing her to motherhood. The narrator confirms the man's authority to name the woman by using the name Eve in his report in 4.1. That verse also shows that the man plays the dominant sexual role. He is the subject of the sentence and the act, the one who 'knew', while she is the object and possession, 'his woman'.[2] Gen. 4.1 also foreshadows what will be the primary roles of women in Genesis. They are described almost exclusively as objects of sexual desire, future mates, mothers, or women anxious to bear children.[3] The woman in the garden story sets the stage for these portrayals.

Trible claims that the man does not name the woman until 3.20, but when he does so there he 'reduces the woman to the status of an animal (2.19)'.[4] Trible's arguments in this matter are strained. She observes that the word 'name' is missing in 2.23 from the standard Hebrew naming formula 'called the name', which is present in 2.19, 20. Thus, she contends that the man does not name the woman in 2.23, but only recognizes sexuality.[5] The text itself argues against Trible's claim;

Suffering to an Ethic of Empowerment (New York: Lutheran Church in America: Division for Mission in North America, 1986), pp. 10-11.

1. Women stay in abusive relationships not only out of desire or love for their partners, but because they are economically dependent and/or they fear for themselves (and/or their children).

2. Certainly the man 'knowing' the woman is one of the standard biblical ways for describing sexual intercourse, but like the others, e. g. he went in to (into) her, it views lovemaking as a male activity and from the man's perspective.

3. The shrewdness, wit, and other characteristics that Genesis women are able to portray occur within these roles.

4. Trible, *God and the Rhetoric*, p. 133. M. Bal agrees with Trible and denies any sexist ideology in the text until 3.20: 'Sexuality, Sin, and Sorrow: The Emergence of Female Character (A Reading of Genesis 1–3)', in S.R. Suleiman (ed.), *The Female Body in Western Culture: Contemporary Perspectives* (Cambridge, MA: Harvard University Press, 1986), p. 324.

5. Trible, *God and the Rhetoric*, p. 99.

Gen. 2.19 says that whatever the man called any living creature would be its name, so the man's calling the woman 'woman' in 2.23 indicates that 'woman' is her name.

Others have argued against Trible's position. Lanser notes that ordinary discourse is often abbreviated when clear inferences can be presumed. This is the case, she contends, with the man's naming of the woman in 2.23 after the scene of his naming of the animals.[1] Clines observes, based on God's naming of creation in Genesis 1, that a name is no less a name when it is indicated in the text simply by the verb 'call'.[2] He also contends that since what the man calls her is a noun, rather than simply a descriptive adjective, it can credibly be thought of as a name.[3] George Ramsey reviews other instances of the naming formula and notes that it indicates naming whether or not the word 'name' is included.[4] He goes on to suggest that name-giving is *not* about domination, however. Adrienne Munich, in contrast, thinks that domination is precisely the point.[5] Noting that mothers are typically the first namers for their children, Munich suggests that '[a]s an extreme effort to obliterate any female role in shaping language, the fable's reversal [in having the man both birth and name the woman] detaches woman from her function'.[6]

Summary. We have seen that feminist efforts to the contrary have not been able to eliminate the patriarchy evident in the man/woman relationship throughout the story. The woman is created as the man's helper. She is created precisely for him and is derivative from him. The man exercises his authority over her not only after the fruit-eating incident, but also before by naming her in 2.23.

1. Lanser, '(Feminist) Criticism in the Garden', p. 73.
2. Clines, 'What Does Eve Do to Help?', p. 38.
3. Clines, 'What Does Eve Do to Help?', p. 39.
4. G.W. Ramsey, 'Is Name-Giving an Act of Domination in Genesis 2.23 and Elsewhere?', *CBQ* 50 (1988), p. 29.
5. A. Munich, 'Notorious Signs, Feminist Criticism and Literary Tradition', in G. Greene and C. Kahn (eds.), *Making a Difference: Feminist Literary Criticism* (London and New York: Methuen, 1985), p. 241. Clines agrees, seeing the naming of the woman in both 2.23 and 3.20 as signifying 'his authority over her'. See 'What Does Eve Do to Help?', p. 39.
6. Munich, 'Notorious Signs', p. 241.

b. *The Priority of the Man.*

The man occupies a central position throughout the narrative. His prominence is evident in the use of masculine pronouns and the potentially generic term *ʾādām*. The man was also created first. God cares about his needs, and God expects obedience from him to the command. The sections below clarify and argue each of these claims.

The Term ʾādām. First, the text's use of language presumes a male priority and norm. In attempts to be inclusive, some translations stumble over the Hebrew's use of *ʾādām* and its corresponding masculine verbs and pronouns. For example, in 2.7 the Revised English Bible says that God 'formed a human being', but then it continues by saying that God breathed into 'his' nostrils. Readers today notice this equation of human and male.[1]

Phyllis Trible's position on the use of *ʾādām* in Genesis 2–3 suits her insistence on the simultaneous creation of man and woman. Trible argues that when *hā-ʾādām* first appears in 2.7 it should be translated generically because it refers to a sexually undifferentiated creature.[2] While Trible's translation of *hā-ʾādām* as 'earth creature' in 2.7 helpfully highlights this creature's formation out of the ground (*hā-ʾadāmâ*) her theory requires some gymnastics to account for the use of *hā-ʾādām* later in the story. Trible contends that *hā-ʾādām* refers to the 'earth creature' as it existed before the surgery in 2.22. After this point Trible recognizes that *hā-ʾādām* refers to the human being who is now clearly a male.[3] Finally in 3.22-24, Trible notes that the word refers generically to both the man and the woman.[4]

Critics observe problems with Trible's reading of *ʾādām*. Brevard Childs notes that *ʾādām* is used similarly before and after the supposed 'split', suggesting that, in fact, there was no simultaneous creation of sexuality.[5] Susan Lanser agrees that the text provides no clues to an

---

1.   Underlying the REB's attempts at inclusivity, Hebrew and Greek both have words (*ʾādām* and *anthrōpos*) that can be used to refer to humanity or to a person in general, while maintaining separate nouns for male human beings (*ʾîš* and *anēr/andros*). Like the word 'man' in English, however, Hebrew 'generic' words can be used to refer to (male) men but never exclusively to women.

2.   Trible, *God and the Rhetoric*, pp. 80, 98.

3.   Trible, *God and the Rhetoric*, p. 98.

4.   Trible, *God and the Rhetoric*, pp. 134-35.

5.   B. Childs, *Old Testament Theology in a Canonical Context* (Philadelphia: Fortress Press, 1985), p. 190.

altered meaning of ʾādām.[1] Richard Hess argues that ʾādām is used in several different ways: generically in Genesis 1, as a title for the garden-tiller in Genesis 2–3, and as a proper name by Gen. 4.25.[2] David Clines suggests that the 'simple and mindless androcentricity' of the Hebrew Bible would have presumed the male as 'the obvious representative of humanity'.[3] The explicitly sexually differentiated terms ʾîš and ʾiššâ do not persist throughout the story. Instead, Clines notes, ʾādām reappears, even as the namer of his ʾiššâ in 3.20.[4]

There are other reasons to maintain that the creature from whose side God built the woman was already a (male) man. First, it is the ʾādām in 2.18 whose aloneness God deems not good and for whom God decides to make a counterpart. If we accept Trible's notion of the undifferentiated earth creature, it would be this strange not-quite-human being that needs a counterpart. God does not propose to divide an earth creature into two beings who are counterparts for each other. Rather, God decides to make a counterpart for the ʾādām, for the already existing (hu)man being. Second, in 2.21-22, God takes a rib from the man (ʾādām), that is, from the existing (earth?) creature, which God builds into the woman and brings to the man (ʾādām). The ʾādām remains ʾādām both before and after the surgery. Contra Trible, he is not an earth creature before the separation and a male human being afterwards. Third, the man's poetic recognition in 2.23 of himself (ʾîš) as male, in contrast to the woman (ʾiššâ) as female, is made by the same (ʾādām) who has been the subject all along.[5] The creature has not changed physically; sexuality has not been newly created, as Trible maintains.[6] Rather the man now seems happy to understand his

1. Lanser, '(Feminist) Criticism in the Garden', p. 72.

2. R.S. Hess, 'Splitting the Adam: The Usage of ʾādām in Genesis I–V', in J.A. Emerton (ed.), *Studies in the Pentateuch* (VTSup, 41; Leiden and New York: Brill, 1990), pp. 1-4.

3. Clines, 'What Does Eve Do to Help?', pp. 41, 40.

4. Clines, 'What Does Eve Do to Help?', p. 40.

5. In fact, Gen. 2.23 suggests that the ʾādām understood himself to have been a male ʾîš even *before* the creation of the woman since he says that she was taken from ʾîš).

6. Gardner, 'Genesis 2.4b–3', p. 7, notes that Trible argues against her own assertion of the sexually undifferentiated nature of the ʾādām before the appearance of the female when she contends that 'both the man and the woman were made from raw materials and processed by God and were therefore equal', probably referring to Trible, 'Depatriarchalizing', p. 37.

sexuality, his embodied humanness, in a different way. Finally, through-out Genesis 3, the narrative (and even God in 3.22) persists in referring to the man, now clearly male, as *ʾādām*.

Man as Focus of God's Attention. Since the first creature in the story is a (male) man from the beginning, we see that man was created first and that God cares about the man's needs. God provides the breath of life, beautiful trees for pleasure, food for sustenance, work, life-preserving commands that set appropriate boundaries, and helpers to alleviate loneliness, all for the man. God shares creating capacity with the man by allowing him to name the animals. At the end of the story, God does clothe both the man and his woman, but she is mentioned almost as a possession. God's ongoing concern and the resulting expulsion is expressed in terms of the man. (Readers only infer the woman's inclusion from 4.1.)

Commandment for the Man. Furthermore, God's commandment is initially given only to the man. The command is given before the woman is created.[1] The prohibition is never explicitly repeated to the woman in our hearing. We do not know how the woman hears the command. The man or God may have repeated the command to her, or she may have overhead them conversing about it. If she was not explicitly told, should the woman have presumed that the command included her?[2]

The aftermath of the eating suggests that the man's violation of the command is paramount (at least for the narrator). There are no reported

---

1. D. Jobling points this out, noting that a more logical order for a creation and fall story would have been to finish the creation (by creating the woman) before giving the command. Such a placement would still enable some commentators to see the command as part of God's creation, while providing an even better segue to the ensuing 'fall' story. Especially given the probable growth and development of this story in oral and written forms, the placement of the prohibition before the creation of the woman deserves notice and explanation. See 'Myth and Its Limits in Genesis 2.4b–3.24', chap. in D. Jobling, *The Sense of Biblical Narrative: Structural Analyses in the Hebrew Bible II* (JSOTSup, 39; Sheffield: JSOT Press, 1986), p. 21.

2. Women always, whether consciously or unconsciously, have to interpret whether language spoken to or about 'men' includes them as women. Sometimes who is included in 'men' is interpreted in precise opposition to the original intentions of a text's writers. For example, courts now interpret the United States constitution's words about 'all men are created equal' as including Blacks, women, and non-landed white men.

immediate effects of the woman's eating. Only when the man has *also* eaten does anything happen to the couple.[1] God questions the man first and perhaps only questions the woman because of the man's response. God directly asks only the man about violating the command. God does not interrogate the woman specifically about either her eating or her violation of the command. It almost seems as if God is not concerned in the interrogation about the woman's relation to the command, though God is certainly interested in how the man has responded to it. Similarly, while delivering the sentences, God prefaces the consequences for the man (and even for the serpent) with a 'because', while the woman's fate is presented with no explanation. The man's sentence refers to eating and specifically mentions his violation of the command. The woman's sentence mentions neither command nor offense.

c. *The Woman and God*
An Indirect Relationship. Just as the woman's relationship to the command is secondary and indirect in the story, so is her relationship with God. God's involvement with the woman derives from God's relationship to the man. God creates the woman second, not without considered reflection to be sure. It was not good for the man to be alone. But God's creation of the woman, almost as an afterthought, suggests that God's initial thoughts may have been that the man alone could perhaps have been adequate for God's purposes. God does not create the woman in order that *God* might be in relationship with her. She is created as the *man*'s helper. God's bestowal of the woman on the man and God's subsequent abandonment of the couple in the narrator's account suggest no particular interest in the woman on God's part.

God does not provide for the woman's needs separately from the man's. It seems that God has breathed life into the woman too, though the narrator gives us no scene of the divine breathing into her nostrils as we had about the man. If God thinks about the woman's needs at all, presumably God's provisions of beauty, food, work, boundaries, and companionship for the man will somehow satisfy his woman as well. Nor does God evaluate the resulting situation from the woman's (or even the couple's) perspective and deem it good. Perhaps the man's poetry in 2.23 is to serve that function.

---

1. G.J. Wenham observes that 'his eating is the last and decisive act of disobedience, for immediately the consequences of their sin are described'. See *Genesis 1–15* (WBC; Waco, TX: Word Books, 1987), p. 76.

God's Inattention to the Woman. God barely speaks to the woman, at least in the presence of readers. God may have repeated the command to the woman, but if so, we readers have not heard it. The woman claims in 3.3 that 'God said' some different things about the commandment from what readers learned in 2.16-17. She describes the tree differently and indicates that even touching it is forbidden. God may have spoken with both the man and the woman during what 3.8 suggests were perhaps regular evening strolls, but again the narrator does not allow readers to know how much time has passed between the creation and the couple's eating of the fruit. We do not know how close God and the couple may have become during these potential daily walks. When God questions and sentences the couple, God's speech to the man uses nearly four times as many words as his remarks to the woman.[1]

God leaves the woman on her own to be misguided by the serpent. In contrast to God's provision for the man, God does not make a helper for the woman. (The story does not say that the couple is mutually to help each other. Even if we try to think of the man as a helper, he fails the post by standing silently while the woman alone considers the serpent's claims.) God does not intervene to prevent trouble for the woman as God intervenes for the man in 3.22-24 to keep him from eating from the tree of life or as God later warns Cain directly about the dangers of sin.[2]

God's Treatment of the Woman. God disrupts or announces the disruption of woman's relationships. God creates enmity between the woman's children and the serpent's offspring. God proclaims the man's rule over the woman. The man is in trouble with God in 3.17 precisely for listening to his woman.

God treats the woman in what continues to be stereotypical fashion, emphasizing solely her motherhood, sexuality, and body. God sentences her as a mother by referring to her children in 3.15-16. She is a sexual being whose desire is for her man. Her punishments affect her body, where she will feel the increased toil, pregnancies, and pain of childbirth.

1.   Even the serpent hears twice as much from God as the woman. God speaks sixty-three words to the man in 3.9, 11, 17-19, sixteen words to the woman in 3.13, 16, and thirty-three words to the serpent in 3.14-15.
2.   The contrast between how God responds to the woman's temptation and to Cain's hints that perhaps the potential value of direct intervention is something that God learns from the events in the garden.

Conclusion

This chapter reviewed varieties of feminist thinking. Feminists view women's problems differently and thus propose multiple solutions. Similarly, feminist epistemologies and literary criticism take varied forms. Feminist empiricists adopt the standard practices of a discipline. This type of feminist literary scholarship applies usual methodologies but focuses their attention on women. Feminist postmodernists recognize that women do not fit standard models. As literary critics, these feminists expose faulty generalizations and challenge traditional canons and methodologies. Feminist standpoint theorists understand knowledge as socially situated; they privilege voices on the margins. These scholars recognize that they have been trained to read as men. They employ techniques of 'resisting reading', which build on their lives and experiences as women to counteract and to disrupt what would otherwise be their 'immasculation' by male-focused texts or reading practices.

Interpretations of Genesis 2–3 exhibit various phases of feminist scholarly re-vision. Many interpretations pay little particular attention to the woman's role in the story. Those that address the woman attempt either to portray her positively or to expose the patriarchy of the text. Gen. 3.16 proves to be particularly problematic, and scholars confront it in several ways. Meyers explains the verse in terms of the demands that ancient pioneering agriculture placed on women. Bledstein hears it saying that women will give birth as humans, not painlessly like gods, and that men are physically stronger, but need not dominate women. Gardner sees an anti-woman bias in the text resulting from a polemic against Canaanite fertility religions. Trible follows standard interpretations at this point by accepting 3.16 as an unfortunate result of the 'fall'.

By reading with different presuppositions about women, this chapter viewed the woman in the story positively, as a 'connected knower', a thoughtful interpreter, and a model moral decision-maker. The chapter also presented the opposite position: reading patriarchy as evident throughout the text, not just as the result of the couple's disobedience. Man was created first (*ʾādām* is not simply an 'earth creature') and is the focus of God's attention. Woman's relationship with God is minimal at best. The man/woman relationship is uneven: she is a helper and derivative; he rules over her and names her.

The theoretical discussions and interpretive examples surveyed and critiqued in this chapter suggest that how readers hear, understand, and interpret texts depends in part on the presuppositions they hold, the methodologies in which they have been trained, and the ways they choose to focus their attention. Interpretations depend on what and how we know.

Chapter 3

SUBTLE RHETORIC—WORD PLAYS IN THE GARDEN

'Sticks and stones can break my bones, but words…'
'And God said, 'Let there be…
'In the beginning was the word…'

Words matter. God's language is powerful, creative language. Human language expresses many of our deepest desires and feelings. It enables us to communicate, and even to think, our thoughts and ideas. It marks us as social beings, and it may mark us differentially, as contrasting hospital nursery signs 'I'm a boy' or 'It's a girl' suggest.[1]

Feminists raise several questions about language. They wonder about the determinacy of meaning and about the relationship between language and reality. Does language shape reality? Is it determined by reality? Is language a resource? Do men control language; are women disadvantaged of language? Are women related to language differently than men? Does language 'fit' men better than women? Are variations in language usage a matter of difference or of dominance? How is language related to sexual difference, to our embodied selves, to gender identities?[2]

Language: An Issue in the Garden

The garden narrative in Genesis 2–3 is also interested in the nature and role of language. Speech distinguishes the human creature who names from the animals who are named (2.19-20). God's word of command in 2.16-17 sets the story in motion. Precisely what God said and what God's speech means is the topic of discussion for the woman and the

1. D. Cameron, *Feminism and Linguistic Theory* (New York: St. Martin's, 2nd edn, 1992), p. 161.
2. Feminists are primarily concerned with how a particular language is used (that is with discourse) rather than with language as an abstract system.

serpent in 3.1-5. The serpent's rhetoric, in conversation with the woman, occasions the couple's eating. Interpretation of God's speech in 3.1-6 forms the hinge in the story. Rhetorical ethos, who told the man of his nakedness (3.11) and to whom he listened (3.17), is a matter of divine concern. Interest in language appears not only in the fabula and story, but at the text level: the text delights in the sound of language and in word plays.[1]

Scholars have recognized the importance of language as an aspect of the garden story. John Dominic Crossan sees the narrative as describing the beginnings of differentiation and hence of language and writing.[2] Michael Fishbane concurs, pointing out that through differentiation the man in the garden story orders the world symbolically with words. 'In so doing, man-the-steward, like God-the-creator, creates a world with words.'[3] Such creative linguistic play is at the heart of our humanness. Claus Westermann highlights the important role of language: 'Man discovers, defines, and orders his world with the naming of the animals. It is speech that makes the world human.'[4] Gerhard von Rad recognizes in Gen. 2.19-20 the importance of language as part of our intellectual life.

> This naming is thus both an act of appropriative ordering, by which man intellectually objectifies the creatures for himself. Thus one may say that something is said here about the origin and nature of language. The emphasis is placed not on the invention of words but on that inner appropriation by recognition and interpretation that takes place in language. Here, interestingly, language is seen not as a means of communication but as an intellectual capacity by means of which man brings conceptual order to his sphere of life.[5]

---

1.   I introduce 'fabula', 'story', and 'text' as technical terms in the discussion of narratology.

2.   J.D. Crossan, 'Response to White: Felix Culpa and Foenix Culprit,' in D. Patte (ed.), *Genesis 2 and 3: Kaleidoscopic Structural Readings* (Semeia, 18; Chico, CA: Scholars Press, 1980), p. 110.

3.   M. Fishbane, 'Genesis 2:4b-11:32/The Primeval Cycle', chap. in *Text and Texture: Close Readings of Selected Biblical Texts* (New York: Schocken Books, 1979), p.18.

4.   C. Westermann, *Creation* (trans. J.J. Scullion; Philadelphia and London: Fortress Press and SPCK, 1974), p. 85.

5.   G. von Rad, *Genesis: A Commentary* (Philadelphia: The Westminster Press, rev. edn, 1972), p. 83.

Some feminist critics, claiming that mothers are usually the first namers as part of their usual child-rearing activities, see this story as 'an extreme effort to obliterate any female role in shaping language'.[1]

In addition, aspects of the history of interpretation of Genesis 2–3 (for example, as providing arguments for women's silence and against women's teaching) suggest that inquiry into women's and men's differential relation to language in the garden narrative is appropriate. Given the text's standard interpretation as concerning human willful disobedience to an obvious and reasonable divine command, study of divine-human rhetoric in the story is warranted as well. Genesis 2–3 shows that God's discourse with human beings requires responsible interpretation.[2] My study of the narrative rhetoric of Genesis 2–3 in this chapter shows that it presents language as ambivalent, as offering both power and possibilities, both danger and delight.

This chapter adopts the format of the first two chapters, briefly presenting feminist and methodological concerns before addressing these to the Genesis text. Feminist attention to language issues varies from American feminists' pragmatic concerns with language use to French feminists' interest in the role of the subject and body in psychoanalytic theories.[3] In addition to feminist issues about language, rhetorical criticism, speech act theory, and narratology provide methodological tools for examining the Genesis text's use of language. The first portion of this chapter deals briefly with these issues and tools, not attempting to advance the conceptual or methodological discussions in these areas, but

1. A. Munich, 'Notorious Signs, Feminist Criticism and Literary Tradition', in G. Greene and C. Kahn (eds.), *Making a Difference: Feminist Literary Criticism* (London and New York: Methuen, 1985), p. 241.

2. I am indebted to B. Zelechow's discussion of language in the garden narrative for helping focus my own interpretive concerns. See his essay: 'God's Presence and the Paradox of Freedom', in A. Loades and M. McLain (eds.), *Hermeneutics, the Bible, and Literary Criticism* (New York: St. Martin's Press, 1992), pp. 162-76.

3. I use the terms 'American' and 'French' feminists broadly to distinguish two different types of concerns about language, as discussed below. The 'American' group, while generally referring to feminists in the United States, would also include for example, the British scholar D. Spender. See her *Man Made Language* (London and Boston: Routledge & Kegan Paul, 2nd edn, 1980). Similarly, while 'French feminists' is often a shorthand reference to three particular French feminists, H. Cixous, L. Irigaray, and J. Kristeva, the spectrum of their concerns about language would also include other French speaking scholars and others influenced by French deconstruction.

making their key concerns and terminology available for use in the study of the garden narrative.

Language about Language: Background Issues and Methodologies

American Feminists and Language Use

As befits their generally pragmatic and political stance, feminists in the United States are interested primarily in how language is used and the effects it has.[1] They generally accept a version of the Sapir-Whorf hypothesis, that language not only reflects but *shapes* reality.[2] American feminist research identifies the gender asymmetry of language use in vocabulary and conversational styles and roles, and it promotes and facilitates the use of nonsexist language.

Feminists point out the gender asymmetry of language use. American language use is unbalanced in terms of the visibility of women and the amount and nature of gender specific vocabulary.[3] Often, women's

1.   The following books contain general overviews of American feminists' research and discussions of language and include lengthy (often annotated) bibliographies: B. Thorne and N. Henley (eds.), *Language and Sex: Difference and Dominance* (Cambridge, MA: Newbury, 1975); B. Thorne, C. Kramarae, and N. Henley (eds.), *Language, Gender and Society* (Cambridge, MA: Newbury House, 1983); S. McConnell-Ginet, R. Borker, and N. Furman (eds.), *Women and Language in Literature and Society* (New York: Praeger, 1980); and F.W. Frank and P.A. Treichler, (eds.), *Language, Gender, and Professional Writing: Theoretical Approaches and Guidelines for Nonsexist Usage* (New York: The Modern Language Association of America, 1989). See also the journal *Women and Language News* published at 244 Lincoln Hall, 702 S. Wright, University of Illinois, Urbana, IL 61801.

2.   Linguists E. Sapir and B. Whorf formulated this hypothesis in the 1940s: 'that language shapes the perception of reality as much as reality shapes language'; see Frank and Treichler, 'Introduction: Scholarship, Feminism, and Language Change', in *Language, Gender, and Professional Writing*, p. 3. For the original discussion, see B.L. Whorf, *Language, Thought, and Reality: Selected Writings of Benjamin Lee Whorf* (ed. J.B. Carroll; Cambridge: M.I.T. Press, 1956).

3.   For example, men and masculine pronouns are far more prominent in children's schoolbooks than women and feminine pronouns. One study showed that masculine pronouns outnumbered feminine pronouns by a four to one ratio and that men were specifically referred to seven times as often as women. See Thorne, Kramarae, and Henley, 'Language, Gender and Society: Opening a Second Decade of Research', in *Language, Gender and Society*, pp. 9-10. This imbalance is significant because women's differential visibility in texts and media influences their perception of career opportunities and their preferences for employment. See Frank and Treichler,

invisibility is due to the use of so-called 'generic' masculine language and pronouns. Some people claim that the term 'man' and the masculine pronoun 'he' include women, but feminists point out how such language functions at best ambiguously.[1]

Vocabulary is another arena of gender asymmetry in language. Feminists point out that women are often deprecated by language and that they are defined by, and in terms of, men. Sally McConnell-Ginet describes these differences as 'significant lexical gaps (*henpecked* but no *cockpecked*), lexical asymmetries (*mothering* is a long-term affair but *fathering* the act of an instant), and nonparallel distribution of items… (*cleaning lady/garbage gentleman*)'.[2] Other examples of sexual asymmetry in vocabulary include, for example, a predominance of terms for promiscuous women over those for promiscuous men[3] and terms for

'Introduction', in *Language, Gender, and Professional Writing*, pp. 8-9.

1.   W. Martyna summarizes the arguments for and against the use of 'he' and 'man' as generics in 'Beyond the He/Man Approach: The Case for Nonsexist Language', in *Language, Gender and Society*, pp. 25-37. The 'men' who were created equal according to the U.S. constitution originally excluded women and many men. 'Men' on a restroom sign is understood regularly as a gender-specific term. It is probably intended similarly in an announcement of a 'men's breakfast', but to say that 'man' nurses his young sounds ridiculous. See C. Miller and K. Swift, *Words and Women: New Language in New Times* (Garden City, NY: Anchor Press/ Doubleday, 1976), p. 23. The ambiguity of 'generic' language and pronouns is evident in empirical research, which shows that women and men use and understand such language differently. See Frank and Treichler, 'Introduction', p. 9. Men and boys often assume masculine generic language refers to males, while women and girls tend to read it as inclusive or gender-indefinite. The role played by legislatures and courts shows the problematic nature of the masculine 'generic'. It took a British Act of Parliament in 1850 to decree that 'he' should include 'she'. For a brief history of the development of masculine generic language, see Spender, *Man Made Language*, pp. 147-51. For a lengthier discussion of pronoun use, see A. Bodine, 'Androcentrism in Prescriptive Grammar: Singular *they*, Sex Indefinite *he* and *he* or *she*', *Language in Society* 4.2 (1975), pp. 129-56. When women tried to use 'generic' terms in their favor, American courts in the nineteenth century ruled specifically that 'men' (in some cases) did not include women. For example, in a case that denied a woman entry to the Virginia bar, the Supreme Court in 1894 agreed with a lower court ruling that a 'woman' was not a 'person'. Miller and Swift, *Words and Women*, p. 75.

2.   S. McConnell-Ginet, 'Linguistics and the Feminist Challenge', in *Women and Language in Literature and Society*, p. 6.

3.   Thorne, Kramarae, and Henley cite a study that found 220 terms for a promiscuous woman and only 22 for a promiscuous man; see 'Second Decade', p. 9,

women's marital status (old maid, spinster) that are demeaning (compare bachelor) or have no masculine counterpart (for example, identification of women's marital status by Mrs and Miss).

Beyond the level of individual words and phrases, American feminists note that women and men generally have different conversational styles and roles.[1] Women tend to do more of the conversational support work, introducing and pursuing topics, involving participants, and promoting interaction.[2] Contrary to the popular depictions of women as loquacious, men are more frequent interrupters and dominate more discussion time in mixed sex groups.[3] Men and women may also vary in terms of their use of silence as a strategy, their level of self-disclosure, and their level of politeness (for example, use of 'tag' questions).[4] Feminists differ in how to assess these gender asymmetries in conversational styles and language use. Some feminists, perhaps emphasizing women as victims, interpret the language differences as a sign of women's subordination; others,

citing J.P. Stanley, 'Paradigmatic Woman: The Prostitute', in D.L. Shores (ed.), *Papers in Language Variation* (Birmingham: University of Alabama Press, 1977).

1.   D. Tannen discusses a variety of different conversational styles (though she does not designate the different styles as men's or women's) in her books *You Just Don't Understand: Women and Men in Conversation* (New York: William Morrow and Company, 1990) and *That's Not What I Meant! How Conversational Style Makes or Breaks Relationships* (New York: Ballantine, 1986). See also Thorne, *et al.*, 'Second Decade', pp. 13-17.

2.   Thorne, *et al.*, 'Second Decade', p. 14.

3.   On men's interrupting, see S. McConnell-Ginet, 'Difference and Language: A Linguist's Perspective', in H. Eisenstein and A. Jardine (eds.), *The Future of Difference* (New Brunswick and London: Rutgers University Press, 2nd edn, 1985), p. 163 and McConnell-Ginet, 'Linguistics and the Feminist Challenge', p. 18. Men's dominance of conversation in mixed sex groups may stem from different models of language use. Men seem generally to subscribe to the model of turn-taking and competition for the 'floor'. Women's models tend to be more informal, collaborative, and promoting of interaction. See Thorne, *et al.*, 'Second Decade', p. 18.

4.   A tag question is the 'isn't it' in the sentence: 'The meeting is at ten, isn't it?' R. Lakoff suggests that women's regular use of 'tag' questions is a sign of women's lack of confidence; see *Language and Woman's Place* (New York: Harper & Row, 1975), pp. 14-17. Subsequent research has shown that both men and women use tag questions for multiple purposes. For further discussion of 'tag question' research, see D. Cameron, '"Not Gender Difference But the Difference Gender Makes"—Explanation in Research on Sex and Language', *International Journal of the Sociology of Language* 94 (1992), pp. 17-23.

aiming to revalue the feminine, see women's speech as part of a subculture.[1]

In response to the gender asymmetry of language use, American feminists worked strenuously in the 1970s and 1980s to promote the use of nonsexist language, which they differentiate from gender neutral language. '*Gender-neutral* is a linguistic description...*Nonsexist* is a social, functional description; a nonsexist term works against sexism in society.'[2] Feminists point out that in some instances, such as referring to 'domestic violence' or 'spouse abuse' rather than 'battered women' (when 95% of battering is of women by their husbands or boyfriends), 'it is gender neutral language that obscures the oppression of women and renders sexism invisible'.[3]

Feminists promote nonsexist language because they are convinced that language *does* influence attitudes, perceptions, and behaviors and because sexist language is demeaning to women. Their work takes a variety of forms. Some scholars, like Wendy Martyna, make arguments against the use of 'he' and 'man' as generics.[4] Others encourage publishers and professional organizations to require nonsexist language, and they provide handbooks or guidelines for its use.[5] Some prepare specific resources for particular aspects of nonsexist language use.[6]

1. D. Cameron, 'Not Gender Difference', p. 14.
2. Frank and Treichler, 'Introduction', p. 18.
3. Frank and Treichler, 'Introduction', p. 17.
4. See p. 113 n. 1.
5. A.P. Nilsen *et al.* outline a rationale and provide practical guidelines for nonsexist language use in *Sexism and Language* (Urbana, IL: National Council of Teachers of English, 1977). See also C. Miller and K. Swift, *The Handbook of Nonsexist Writing* (New York: Harper & Row, 1980); R. Maggio, *The Nonsexist Word-finder: A Dictionary of Gender-Free Usage* (Phoenix: Oryx Press, 1987); and B.D. Sorrels, *The Nonsexist Communicator: Solving the Problems of Gender and Awkwardness in Modern English* (Englewood Cliffs, NJ: Prentice-Hall, 1983). In 1974 McGraw Hill was among the first publishers to require use of nonsexist language. See also the recent summary and bibliographies of guidelines for nonsexist language use in the professions by Frank and Treichler, *Language, Gender, and Professional Writing*.
6. The language of worship, including language about and addressed to God has been of particular concern in Christian communities. Numerous worship resources including material for liturgies, hymns, and lectionaries are available. Some denominations have published guidelines, e.g. The 'Guidelines for Inclusive Use of the English Language for Speakers, Writers, and Editors', prepared by the Evangelical Lutheran Church in America Commission for Communication, 1989. See the

Out of Eden

Women, Language and Discourse in French Feminism

French feminists are less concerned with the particular vocabulary and pronouns that dominate American feminists' discussions of nonsexist language use. Rather, they find problematic the whole realm of language and discourse as it relates to women.[1] The work of recent French feminists is more complex (and some feminists might say more compromised) than that of its American feminist counterparts because it builds heavily upon the work of prominent male scholars: the linguistics of Saussure, the psychoanalysis of Freud and Lacan, and the philosophy of Foucault and Derrida, as well as on Simone de Beauvoir's *The Second Sex*.[2] Ann Rosalind Jones describes the target of French feminist criticism this way:

> French theories of femininity, using Derridean deconstruction and Lacanian psychoanalysis, centre on language as a means through which men have shored up their claim to a unified identity and relegated women to the negative pole of binary oppositions that justify masculine supremacy: subject/object, culture/nature, law/chaos, man/woman. Phallocentrism—this structuring of man as the central reference point of thought, and of the

discussions in S. Neufer Emswiler and T. Neufer Emswiler, *Women and Worship: A Guide to Nonsexist Hymns, Prayers, and Liturgies* (San Francisco: Harper & Row, rev. edn, 1984), and B. Wren, *What Language Shall I Borrow? God-Talk in Worship: A Male Response to Feminist Theology* (New York: Crossroad, 1989). Recently, V.R. Mollenkott has argued that 'God' has obviously masculine connotations (as consideration of 'Goddess' makes clear). She concludes that those who think God is beyond gender should balance their use of 'God' with female pronouns. See *Sensuous Spirituality: Out From Fundamentalism* (New York: Crossroad, 1992), pp. 10-11.

1.   T. Moi's *Sexual/Textual Politics: Feminist Literary Theory* (London and New York: Routledge, 1985) provides a detailed, yet brief, introduction to the work of French feminists H. Cixous, L. Irigaray, and J. Kristeva, including relevant background material, bibliography, and critiques. The essays in C.W.M. Kim, S.M. St. Ville, and S.M. Simonaitis (eds.), *Transfigurations: Theology and the French Feminists* (Minneapolis: Fortress Press, 1993) relate French feminist insights to theological concerns. For primary readings in French feminism see the separate works of Cixous, Irigaray, and Kristeva as well as the collections: E. Marks and I. de Courtivron (eds.), *New French Feminisms: An Anthology* (New York: Schocken Books, 1980) and T. Moi, *French Feminist Thought: A Reader* (Oxford: Basil Blackwell, 1987).

2.   S. de Beauvoir, *The Second Sex* (trans. and ed. H.M. Parshley; New York: Vintage Books, 1974).

phallus as the symbol of sociocultural authority—is the target of Franco-feminist criticism.[1]

Many French feminists understand women's relation to language in terms of Jacques Lacan's adaptation and interpretation of Freud's psychoanalytic theories. Lacan associates a child's development and use of language with the child's movement from what he calls the Imaginary to the Symbolic realm. This shift constitutes the development of subjectivity: the child becomes a subject. Coincident with it are submission to what Lacan calls the 'Law of the Father' and a disruption of the union between mother and child, thus splitting the child as subject.

'The Law of the Father is Lacan's formulation for language as the medium through which human beings are placed in culture, a medium represented and enforced by the figure of the father in the family.'[2] The Law of the Father relates to the role of language in teaching us who we are. 'Using language, we internalize the laws of the world, especially those that reflect the patriarchal powers.'[3] While entry into the Symbolic realm is necessary, since language acquisition is vital for survival within society, women's entry into language is difficult. Lacan argues that it is 'organized by lack, or negativity',[4] and Julia Kristeva acknowledges the violence of the Symbolic order.[5]

In spite of the difficulty of the Symbolic realm for women, French feminists would agree with American feminists that women's relationship to language is ambivalent. Language dominates and excludes women, but it also offers them an avenue of escape from patriarchy. The title essay of Luce Irigaray's second major book, *This Sex Which Is Not One*, observes the power of language in subordinating women. Woman in patriarchal discourse is man's Other; she is associated with absence

---

1. A.R. Jones, 'Inscribing Femininity: French Theories of the Feminine', in Green and Kahn (eds.), *Making a Difference*, p. 80.

2. A.R. Jones, 'Writing the Body: Toward an Understanding of *l'écriture féminine*', in J. Newton and D. Rosenfelt (eds.), *Feminist Criticism and Social Change: Sex, Class and Race in Literature and Culture* (New York and London: Methuen, 1985), p. 99.

3. J. Gallop and C. Burke, 'Psychoanalysis and Feminism in France', in Eisenstein and Jardine (eds.), *The Future of Difference*, p. 109.

4. A. Kuhn, 'Introduction to Hélène Cixous's "Castration or Decapitation?"' *Signs: Journal of Women in Culture and Society* 7 (1981), p. 37.

5. A. Hollywood, 'Violence and Subjectivity: *Wuthering Heights*, Julia Kristeva, and Feminist Theology', in Kim *et al.* (eds.), *Transfigurations*, p. 91.

and negativity, and is, hence, outside representation.[1] Women's options
are to be silent, or, if they enter into patriarchal discourse, to mimic male
discourse. To be recognized as something other than babble or chatter,
women's discourse must adopt male norms.[2] Perhaps for this reason,
Julia Kristeva notes that some women find language to be 'secondary,
cold, foreign to their lives'.[3] Thus, one of the major ways French feminists consider language as discourse is by attending to the ways it retains
or reinstates oppression.

While language and discourse may be implicated in women's
oppression, Monique Wittig observes that they also afford a medium for
countering that oppression.[4] As Toril Moi points out, if language can be
interpreted differently (and American feminists have observed that in
many situations men and women do interpret it differently), then the
words, phrases, and syntactical structures are not sexist in themselves.[5]
Kristeva insists that socio-political transformations require transformations in language and in ourselves as subjects.[6]

Following Wittig's lead in her book *Les Guérillères* in 1975, French
feminists developed two conceptions of women's relation to language
and two avenues for taking language back from patriarchy: 'women's
speech (*parole de femmes*) and feminine writing (*écriture-au-féminin*)'.[7]
According to Irigaray, one of its main proponents, women's speech
emerges when women speak with women, but it disappears when men
are present.[8] Irigaray contends that women's speech, like women's
plural or multiple genitalia, is 'plural, autoerotic, diffuse, and undefinable
within the familiar rules of (masculine) logic'.[9]

Similarly, Irigaray maintains that women's writing is based in women's

1.   Moi, *Sexual/Textual Politics*, p. 133.
2.   Moi, *Sexual/Textual Politics*, pp. 135-40.
3.   J. Kristeva, 'A Question of Subjectivity', in P. Rice and P. Waugh (eds.),
Modern Literary Theory: A Reader (London and New York: Edward Arnold, 1989),
p. 129.
4.   Jones, 'Inscribing Femininity', p. 91.
5.   Moi, *Sexual/Textual Politics*, p. 157.
6.   J. Kristeva, 'Woman Can Never Be Defined', in Marks and de Courtivron
(eds.), *New French Feminisms*, p. 141.
7.   C. Makward, 'To Be or Not to Be... A Feminist Speaker,' in Eisenstein and
Jardine (eds.), *The Future of Difference*', p. 95.
8.   Moi, *Sexual/Textual Politics*, p. 144.
9.   C. Burke, 'Irigaray Through the Looking Glass', *Feminist Studies* 7.2 (1981),
p. 289.

bodily differences from men. Irigaray argues that women must invent or find our body's language in order that it may accompany our story.[1] Her own texts seek to 'embody female difference'.[2] For Irigaray, women's writing is a means of escape from the Law-of-the-Father.[3] Kristeva's interest in maternity suggests how this escape might happen. 'Kristeva sees maternity as a conceptual challenge to phallogocentrism... gestation and nurturance break down the oppositions between self and other, subject and object, inside and outside.'[4]

Cixous's theory of *écriture féminine* is perhaps the most elaborated. She contends that there is *marked* writing and that such writing offers the possibility of change, an opportunity for transformation of society and culture.[5] Cixous suggests that it may not be possible to define female writing,[6] but she insists that this writing exists nevertheless.[7] Moi observes that for Cixous, *écriture féminine* is not equated with whatever women write; rather, it consists in texts (by authors of either gender) that 'strive in the direction of difference, struggle to undermine the dominant phallogocentric logic, split open the closure of the binary opposition and revel in the pleasures of open-ended textuality'.[8] Cixous's notion of female writing lives within Lacan's Imaginary world, seeking to get back to or to retain the voice of the Mother.[9] Her writing is full of maternal metaphors.[10] Moi observes that

---

1. L. Irigaray, 'When Our Lips Speak Together', *Signs: Journal of Women in Culture and Society* 6 (1980), p. 76.

2. Irigaray, 'When Our Lips Speak Together', Burke's introductory note, p. 67.

3. Jones, 'Inscribing Femininity', p. 86.

4. Jones, 'Inscribing Femininity', p. 86.

5. H. Cixous, 'The Laugh of the Medusa', in E. Abel and E.K. Abel (eds.), *The SIGNS Reader: Women, Gender & Scholarship* (Chicago: University of Chicago Press, 1983), p. 283.

6. Moi observes the difficulty inherent in rendering *écriture féminine* into English. The distinction, important to American feminists, between 'feminine', indicating the social constructs of gender, and 'female', as the biological aspect of sex, is lost in French because there are not two separate terms: *féminine* represents them both. See Moi (ed.), *Sexual/Textual Politics*, p. 97.

7. Cixous, 'The Laugh of the Medusa', p. 287.

8. Moi, *Sexual/Textual Politics*, 108; this attitude also leads Cixous to abhor the term *écriture féminine* because of its imprisonment within the binary logic she seeks to undo.

9. Moi, *Sexual/Textual Politics*, pp. 117-18.

10. Jones, 'Inscribing Femininity', p. 88.

Cixous's vision of feminine/female writing as a way of reestablishing a spontaneous relationship to the physical *jouissance* of the female body may be read positively, as a utopian vision of female creativity in a truly non-oppressive and non-sexist society.[1]

Yet critics also see problems with Cixous's work. Cixous's essentialism shows little interest in addressing social change.[2] Hélène Vivienne Wenzel warns that '*écriture féminine* perpetuates and recreates long-held stereotypes and myths about woman as natural, sexual, biological, and corporal by celebrating her essences'.[3] Thus, this notion becomes 'little more than a seductive new rhetoric of our times, a rhetoric that tells women what they want to hear about themselves without insisting that they demand political power'.[4] Jones concludes that women's speech and women's writing are both powerful and problematic. They are vital as 'a lens and a partial strategy',[5] but they have also 'been criticized as idealist and essentialist, bound up in the very system they claim to undermine; they have been attacked as theoretically fuzzy and as fatal to constructive political action'.[6]

Kristeva's linguistic theories about discourse and meaning offer a helpful alternative to the problematic theories of women's speech and women's writing. Kristeva refuses to treat meaning as static, but instead focuses 'on the process or production of meaning and subjectivity'.[7] Kristeva understands language as 'a complex signifying *process* rather than a monolithic *system*'.[8] By insisting on both the semiotic and the symbolic (usually associated, respectively, with childish nonsense and magisterial discourse) and by attending to process, Kristeva's 'theory of signification...allows for the breaks in meaning that we sense in puns, the subversion of the authoritative language of the Logos, and the return of the instinctual drives to pleasure'.[9] Kristeva's theories of meaning also

1. Moi, *Sexual/Textual Politics*, p. 121.
2. H.V. Wenzel, 'The Text as Body/Politics: An Appreciation of Monique Wittig's Writings in Context', *Feminist Studies* 7 (1981), p. 272.
3. Wenzel, 'The Text as Body/Politics', p. 272.
4. Wenzel, 'The Text as Body/Politics', p. 272.
5. Jones, 'Inscribing Femininity', p. 96.
6. Jones, 'Inscribing Femininity', p. 91.
7. R.S. Chopp, 'From Patriarchy into Freedom: A Conversation between American Feminist Theology and French Feminism', in Kim *et al.* (eds.), *Transfigurations*, p. 45.
8. Moi, *Sexual/Textual Politics*, p. 152.
9. Gallop and Burke, 'Psychoanalysis and Feminism', p. 111.

insist on the importance of context, thus shifting the focus from language to discourse. Moi explains:

> Kristeva's theory of language as a heterogeneous signifying process located in and between speaking subjects suggests an alternative approach: the study of specific linguistic strategies in specific situations. But this kind of study will not allow us to generalize our findings, In fact, it will take us towards a study of language as specific *discourse* rather than as universal *langue*.[1]

By attending to language as specific discourse, Kristeva's theories overlap with the methodologies of rhetorical critics, to which we now turn.

Rhetorical Criticism
Rhetorical criticism, as practiced in Old Testament studies by the students and followers of James Muilenburg, is something of a misnomer.[2] Muilenburg's version of rhetorical criticism grew out of his dissatisfaction with the form criticism of his day. By attending not only to similarities among texts (as form criticism does) but to unique features of texts, especially in terms of the boundaries of a unit and the literary devices that provide its shape and emphasis, Muilenburg's rhetorical criticism became a kind of Hebrew stylistics. While Muilenburg himself expressed some interest in historical matters and authorial intentions (which might help justify use of the term 'rhetorical'), the 'Muilenburg school' developed in a direction that largely abandoned these interests.[3] Critics in this school attend to the final form of a text and consider only intrinsic matters. Their 'rhetorical criticism' is hard to distinguish from the 'new criticism' of American literary critics in the 1950s and 1960s.

1.   Moi, *Sexual/Textual Politics*, p. 154.
2.   For a helpful discussion of Muilenburg's practice of rhetorical criticism, its relationships with form criticism, and the later differences of the 'Muilenburg school' from Muilenburg's ideas, see T.B. Dozeman, 'Rhetoric and Rhetorical Criticism: OT Rhetorical Criticism', *ABD*, V, pp. 712-15. See also J. Muilenburg's 1968 SBL presidential address: 'Form Criticism and Beyond', *JBL* 88 (1969), pp. 1-18.
3.   Several essays of the Muilenburg school are collected in J.J. Jackson and M. Kessler (eds.), *Rhetorical Criticism: Essays in Honor of James Muilenburg* (Pittsburgh: Pickwick Press, 1974). P. Trible's *God and the Rhetoric of Sexuality* (Philadelphia: Fortress Press, 1978) employs this type of 'rhetorical criticism' to address Genesis 2–3. See also her book *Rhetorical Criticism: Context, Method and the Book of Jonah* (Guides to Biblical Scholarship; Minneapolis, Fortress Press, 1994).

While rhetoric is certainly concerned with literary form and style, it is not limited to these matters.

> Rhetoric has a number of overlapping meanings: the practice of oratory; the study of the strategies of effective oratory; the use of language, written or spoken, to inform or persuade; the study of the persuasive effects of language; the study of the relation between language and knowledge; the classification and use of tropes and figures; and, of course, the use of empty promises and half-truths as a form of propaganda.[1]

These understandings of rhetoric as related to persuasive communication with pragmatic goals develop from the discussion and practice of rhetoric by Aristotle and other classical rhetoricians.

Classical rhetoric involved public oratory designed to achieve consensus by persuading an audience about a particular rhetorical situation. Aristotle discusses three types of rhetoric: judicial (or forensic) rhetoric is employed in legal settings to determine judgments about past actions; epideictic rhetoric is practiced at ceremonial occasions to promote particular public values in the present; and deliberative rhetoric occurs in the political arena, seeking the consensus of an assembly about matters of future action. As the third part of the trivium for classical education,[2] Aristotle presents rhetoric using five elements of oratory: invention, arrangement, style, memory, and delivery. Rhetoric always 'begins with audience-held opinions and uses these as a basis for constructing arguments'.[3] The invention, finding things to say, proceeds with the aid of *topoi* that help a rhetor discern various dimensions of a subject. Aristotle insists that the rhetorical process requires attention to the 'three major sources of influence on audience judgment: the argument of the case itself, *logos*; the perception of the orator's character, *ethos*; and the audience's emotional engagement, *pathos*'.[4]

1. P. Bizzell and B. Herzberg (eds.), *The Rhetorical Tradition: Readings From Classical Times to the Present* (Boston: Bedford Books of St. Martin's Press, 1990), p 1.

2. The first two elements are grammar (syntactics, following Charles Peirce) and logic (semantics). See Bizzell and Herzberg, *The Rhetorical Tradition*, p. 908. Rhetoric becomes pragmatics for Peirce. For the original discussions see Aristotle, *The Rhetoric and the Poetics of Aristotle* (trans. W. Rhys Roberts and I. Bywater; New York: The Modern Library, 1984).

3. G.A. Hauser, *Introduction to Rhetorical Theory* (Speech Communication Series; New York: Harper & Row, 1986), pp. 24-25. Hauser's slim volume provides a helpful introduction to rhetoric from a variety of ancient and modern perspectives.

4. G. Hauser, *Introduction*, p. 109.

Modern discussions of rhetoric have developed from these classical beginnings. Contemporary discussions recognize that rhetoric assumes the maturity of the audience and involves the risk of nonacceptance of an argument.[1] Rhetoric is 'bilateral', not engaging in types of argumentation that one would not willingly entertain oneself. It recognizes that *ethos* does not arise by claim or argument, but through inference. It acknowledges that different types of arguments work best in different situations. For example, inductive arguments may serve as illustrations or for inexperienced audiences who might not understand general rules, while deductive arguments, particularly enthymemes (syllogisms with a missing premise or conclusion), effectively involve reasoning audiences in drawing the desired conclusions.[2]

Rhetorical criticism requires the determination of a 'rhetorical situation'.[3] Rhetorical situations involve persons, events, and objects of conscious attention. They are 'situations that present problems that can be resolved meaningfully through the uses of speech and writing'.[4] The problem, or exigence, is an imperfection that can be eliminated or improved. Rhetorical situations have a life cycle: origin, maturity, deterioration, and disintegration.[5] Their origin occurs as the speaker defines the situation, awakening and heightening awareness. At maturity, an audience is receptive to persuasion and willing to mediate change. Deterioration begins as complicating factors arise, attitudes harden, or interest weakens. When an exigence is no longer perceived as modifiable, disintegration has occurred.

New Testament scholars employ understandings of rhetoric and methods of rhetorical criticism developed from rhetoric's classical use.[6]

---

1.   The revival of rhetoric as Perelman's 'new rhetoric' developed in this century because epistemic uncertainty makes room for rhetorical persuasion and argumentation. See C. Perelman and L. Olbrechts-Tyteca, *The New Rhetoric: A Treatise on Argumentation* (trans. J. Wilkinson and P. Weaver; Notre Dame: Notre Dame University Press, 1969).

2.   S. Toulmin, *The Uses of Argument* (Cambridge: Cambridge University Press, 1958) develops a detailed discussion of argumentation involving data, warrants, claims, backing, rebuttal, and qualifiers.

3.   L. Bitzer's essay 'The Rhetorical Situation', *Philosophy and Rhetoric* 1 (1968), pp. 1-12 is the starting point for recent discussions of 'rhetorical situation'.

4.   G. Hauser, *Introduction*, p. 34.

5.   My discussion is based on G. Hauser, *Introduction*, pp. 39-40.

6.   For analyses of classical rhetoric and its influence on and applicability to the study of New Testament texts, see the works of G.A. Kennedy: in particular, *New*

George Kennedy's method for analyzing New Testament texts involves five steps: (1) definition of the rhetorical unit, (2) specification of the rhetorical situation, (3) identification of the type of rhetoric (judicial, epideictic or deliberative), (4) discussion of invention and style (the arrangement of the argument into a unified discourse), and (5) evaluation of the overall effectiveness of the argument. This type of rhetorical analysis, employing classical categories, is most easily achieved with texts that are clearly persuasive in character, like many of the New Testament epistles.[1] Vernon Robbins employs what he calls socio-rhetorical criticism to narrative texts as well.[2] His method involves four components: internal matters, intertextuality, social and cultural dynamics, and ideology.

Contemporary rhetorical theory shares many assumptions about knowledge, language, and meaning with postmodern critics. In recent decades, social scientists and natural scientists have come to recognize that 'knowledge is a linguistically constructed and consensual arrangement'.[3] Similarly, rather than seeing knowledge as a reflection of reality and language as its neutral medium of transmission, French social theorist Michel Foucault 'argues that knowledge is created by discourse'.[4] These arguments about the nature of knowledge echo those of the classical Sophists, who maintained that rhetoric is epistemic, that it makes knowledge. Agreeing with Foucault, philosopher Jacques Derrida insists that language is not referential or representational, but figurative.

Testament Interpretation through Rhetorical Criticism (Chapel Hill and London: The University of North Carolina Press, 1984). For a helpful introduction to the plethora of terms, see the first chapter of D.F. Watson's dissertation, *Invention, Arrangement, and Style: Rhetorical Criticism of Jude and 2 Peter* (SBLDS, 104; Atlanta: Scholars Press, 1988). Good bibliographies for NT rhetorical criticism are included in Watson, 'The New Testament and Greco-Roman Rhetoric: A Bibliography', *JETS* 31 (1988), pp. 465-72; and C.C. Black, II, 'Rhetorical Criticism and the New Testament', *Proceedings: Eastern Great Lakes and Midwest Biblical Societies* 8 (1988), pp. 77-92.

1.   See, for example, the work of H.D. Betz, *Galatians: A Commentary on Paul's Letter to the Churches in Galatia* (Hermeneia; Philadelphia: Fortress Press, 1979); and N.R. Petersen, *Rediscovering Paul: Philemon and the Sociology of Paul's Narrative World* (Philadelphia: Fortress Press, 1985).

2.   V.K. Robbins, *Jesus the Teacher: A Socio-Rhetorical Interpretation of Mark* (2nd edn with new introduction; Philadelphia: Fortress Press, 1992).

3.   Bizzell and Herzberg, *The Rhetorical Tradition*, p. 921.

4.   Bizzell and Herzberg, *The Rhetorical Tradition*, p. 901.

With the Sophists, Foucault and Derrida recognize all language as rhetorical, as persuasive in intent.[1] Given its epistemic and figurative qualities, rhetoric involves 'the relation of language to the world (to life)'.[2] These changes in the assessments of knowledge and language affect scholars' conceptions of meaning as well. Anthropologists and ethnographers insist that meaning is situated, that 'language means as it is used'.[3] Many literary theorists likewise understand meaning as a function of language use in a social situation.[4]

A rhetorical approach to study of literary texts acknowledges that, as rhetorical works, texts function in a social milieu. Rhetoric recognizes the power of language in shaping knowledge and meaning and in evoking responses from hearers and readers. Rhetorical theory is honest about the ideologies and pragmatic goals of authors, speakers, and interpreters. As Bizzell and Herzberg describe it, rhetoric has become a comprehensive theory.

> [Rhetoric] has grown to encompass a theory of language as a form of social behavior, of intention and interpretation as the determinants of meaning, in the way that knowledge is created by argument, and in the way that ideology and power are extended through discourse. In short, rhetoric has become a comprehensive theory of language as effective discourse.[5]

Rhetorical criticism, especially when it can be practiced with some knowledge of the author or the social setting of a literary work, analyzes texts as communicative acts.

> Rhetorical (or pragmatic) criticism considers a work of art chiefly as a means to an end, as a vehicle of communication and interaction between the author and the audience, and investigates the use of traditional devices to produce an effect in an audience. It is an internal criticism that focuses on the rhetoric of the text itself, but also works outward to considerations of author, audience, and their interrelationships.[6]

Elisabeth Schüssler Fiorenza describes rhetorical criticism as focusing 'on the persuasive power and literary strategies of a text which has a

---

1. Bizzell and Herzberg, *The Rhetorical Tradition*, p. 917.
2. Bizzell and Herzberg, *The Rhetorical Tradition*, p. 907.
3. G. Hauser, *Introduction*, p. 140.
4. Bizzell and Herzberg, *The Rhetorical Tradition*, p. 900.
5. Bizzell and Herzberg, *The Rhetorical Tradition*, p. 899.
6. B. Fiore, 'Rhetoric and Rhetorical Criticism: NT Rhetoric and Rhetorical Criticism', *ABD*, V, p. 716.

communicative function in a concrete historical situation'.[1]

Literary texts undoubtedly functioned differently for their original audiences than they do for subsequent ones. Still, texts continue to function rhetorically for contemporary audiences.[2] Whether or not we are interested or able, as interpreters, to discover an original concrete historical situation for a particular text, we can still consider how a text functions for today's audiences and contexts. Such consideration involves analysis of rhetoric. Schüssler Fiorenza contends that rhetoric 'seeks to instigate a change of attitudes and motivations, it strives to persuade, to teach and to engage the hearer/reader by eliciting reactions, emotions, convictions and identifications. The evaluative criterion for rhetoric is not aesthetics but praxis'.[3] If Schüssler Fiorenza is correct, we should assess the contemporary impact of biblical rhetoric by how it persuades us to live our lives.

Speech Act Theory
Perception of the rhetorical function of language prompted J.L. Austin to develop speech act theory.[4] Austin, a philosopher of language, recognized that not all sentences are statements (i.e., propositions). Rather than dismissing other types of language as 'nonsense', Austin sought, in his 1955 William James lectures at Harvard, to describe them. He calls sentences that *do* something 'performatives'; those that simply *state* something are 'constatives'. While it makes sense to talk about the truth of constatives, Austin discusses the success of performatives by specifying necessary 'felicity conditions' and by categorizing their failures. Austin's later lectures turn to the discussion of illocutionary acts. John R. Searle,[5] H. Paul Grice, Mary Louise Pratt, Emile Benveniste,

---

1. E. Schüssler Fiorenza, 'Rhetorical Situation and Historical Reconstruction in 1 Corinthians', *NTS* 33 (1987), p. 387.

2. At least they function rhetorically for readers who are not constantly preoccupied with other matters of historical, literary, or rhetorical analysis.

3. Schüssler Fiorenza, 'Rhetorical Situation', p. 387.

4. Austin's lecture notes were edited and published by his students under the title *How to do Things with Words* (ed. J.O. Urmson and M. Sbisà; Cambridge, MA: Harvard University Press, 2nd edn, 1975).

5. J.R. Searle, *Speech Acts: An Essay in the Philosophy of Language* (Cambridge: Cambridge University Press, 1970). This book and Searle's other work have prompted lively debate, most notably with S. Fish and J. Derrida. S. Fish, 'How to Do Things with Austin and Searle: Speech-Act Theory and Literary Criticism', chap. in *Is There a Text in this Class?: The Authority of Interpretive Communities*

Susan Lanser, Hugh White, and others have developed aspects of speech act theory and assessed its relation to literature.[1]

An illocutionary act, which for Austin and speech act philosophers of language comes to replace the sentence as the philosophical unit of interest,[2] is perhaps most easily understood in its relation to locutionary acts and perlocutionary acts. A *locutionary* act is the act *of* saying something. It includes the physical utterance itself as well as its sense and reference. A *perlocutionary* act is the act done *by means of* saying something, the act of inducing contingent or consequential effects on the hearer(s). An *illocutionary* act is the act done *in* saying something, such as promising, threatening, announcing.[3] Illocutionary acts, or illocutions, are thus similar to performatives.[4] Like performatives, illocutions are matters of convention. Their force and effectiveness (what Austin called their felicity) depend on social recognition. Austin describes six types of

(Cambridge, MA: Harvard University Press, 1980). J. Derrida, *Limited Inc.* (Evanston, IL: Northwestern University Press, 1988) contains Derrida's essay 'Signature, Event, Context' on Austin and Searle's speech act theory (first published in translation in *Glyph 1*) and his response, 'Limited Inc a b c', to Searle's reply: 'Reiterating the Differences: A Reply to Derrida', *Glyph 1* (Baltimore: Johns Hopkins University Press, 1977), pp. 198-208. See also Fish, 'With the Compliments of the Author: Reflections on Austin and Derrida', chap. in *Doing What Comes Naturally: Change, Rhetoric, and the Practice of Theory in Literary and Legal Studies* (Durham, N.C., and London: Duke University Press, 1989).

1. H.P. Grice presented the William James lectures on speech act theory at Harvard in 1967. An excerpt is included in 'Logic and Conversation', in P. Cole and J.L. Morgan (eds.), *Syntax and Semantics 3: Speech Acts* (New York: Academic Press, 1975), pp. 41-58. See also M.L. Pratt, *Towards a Speech Act Theory of Literary Discourse* (Bloomington: Indiana University Press, 1977) and 'The Ideology of Speech Act Theory', *Centrum* NS 1.1 (Spring 1981), pp. 5-18; E. Benveniste, *Problems in General Linguistics* (trans. M.E. Meek; Coral Gables, FL: University of Miami Press, 1966); and S.S. Lanser, *The Narrative Act: Point of View in Prose Fiction* (Princeton: Princeton University Press, 1981). In relation to biblical studies, see H.C. White (ed.), *Speech Act Theory and Biblical Criticism* (Semeia, 41; Decatur, GA: Scholars Press, 1988). This volume includes helpful bibliographies.

2. M. Hancher, 'Beyond a Speech-Act Theory of Literary Discourse', *Modern Language Notes* 92 (1977), p. 1084.

3. Austin, *How to Do Things with Words*, pp. 99-101.

4. R.E. Sanders contends that 'an *illocutionary act* is the performance of some particular action that can only be performed by means of uttering [something]': 'In Defense of Speech Acts', *Philosophy and Rhetoric* 9 (1976), p. 113.

infelicities to classify ways in which a speech act fails.[1] Both Austin and Searle have also classified illocutions themselves in terms of their function.[2]

Narratology

Speech act theory contributes to an analysis of the rhetoric of direct discourse and focuses its attention on individual sentences. Narrative theory or narratology is the broader category for study of narrative texts as larger units. Much of recent narrative theory has developed out

---

1.   Austin, *How to Do Things with Words*, pp. 14-18. He groups these into two main categories: misfires and abuses. Misfires occur when the procedure is improperly done; abuses have to do with insincerities on the part of participants. Misfires include two types of 'misinvocation', what Austin hesitantly calls 'non-plays', when there is no conventionally accepted procedure, and 'misapplications', when the person(s) or circumstances involved in the speech act are inappropriate. A second pair of misfires are 'misexecutions', called 'flaws' or 'hitches'. A flaw refers to an incorrect or faulty procedure or performance, while a hitch is an incomplete one. Austin divides the third pair of infelicities, the abuses, into 'insincerities' and 'breaches' (or infractions). To avoid insincerities, participants in the speech act must have the appropriate intentions (thoughts and feelings); similarly, to avoid breeches, they must conduct themselves appropriately following the speech act. R.L. Grimes adds two abuses, 'gloss' and 'flop', and several other categories to Austin's list of infelicities. A gloss is a procedure used to cover up problems; a flop is the failure to produce the appropriate mood or atmosphere. Grimes's other categories include 'ineffectuality', an act that fails to precipitate the anticipated empirical change; 'contagion', an act that leaps beyond proper boundaries; 'opacity', an act that is unrecognizable or unintelligible; 'defeat', an act that discredits or invalidates acts of others; 'omission', an act not performed; and 'misframe', an act whose genre is misconstrued. See 'Infelicitous Performances and Ritual Criticism', in White (ed.), *Speech Act Theory and Biblical Criticism*, p. 116.

2.   Austin's categories are verdictives (giving a verdict, finding, assessment, or appraisal), exercitives (exercising power or influence), commissives (committing oneself to a course of action, declaring or announcing intentions), behabitives (expressing attitudes related to social behavior), and expositives (explaining relationships between statements and an argument or conversation). See *How to Do Things with Words*, pp. 151-52. Searle defines five different groups: representatives present a state of affairs; directives are designed to get the addressee to do something; commissives commit the speaker to an action; expressives express the speakers psychological state; and declarations (like Austin's performatives) bring about the state of affairs to which they refer. (This summary follows Pratt, *Towards a Speech Act Theory*, pp. 80-81.)

of the work of Russian formalists and French structuralists.[1] Vladimir Propp's analysis of the folktale and A.J. Greimas's actantial scheme (involving sender, object, receiver, helper, subject, and opponent) have been influential.[2] These theories tend to concentrate on what the narrative is telling, the events that occur among the characters, which Mieke Bal refers to as the 'fabula'. Bal, following Gérard Genette's comprehensive study, distinguishes between the 'fabula' and the 'story' of a narrative.[3] Both terms have to do with events that take place among the characters. The 'fabula' is the reconstruction of events between characters in the order that these events must have occurred. For example, readers deduce that the woman and the serpent in Genesis 3 have heard somehow about the prohibition before their conversation begins. Their hearing is thus part of the fabula, though it is not reported to us in the story as we have it. The 'story' is the way the events of the fabula are told to readers by the narrator, including rearrangements of order, omissions, shifts in perspective, evaluative comments, and so on.[4] For example, the 'story' in Genesis 2–3 delays confirming the serpent's claim about the couple being like God until God's interior monologue in 3.22.

Genette and Bal study several aspects of the relationship of fabula and story time. First, they observe 'order', that is, whether the events in the story are told in the same order in which they occur in the fabula. They note anachronies, analepses, and prolepses when the orders differ.[5]

1.   For a general introduction to the development of these literary theories, see T. Eagleton, *Literary Theory: An Introduction* (Minneapolis: University of Minnesota, 1983).

2.   V. Propp, *Morphology of the Folktale* (ed. L.A. Wagner, trans. L. Scott; Austin: University of Texas Press, 2nd edn, 1968); A.J. Greimas, *Sémantique structurale* (Paris: Librairie Larousse, 1966). For an English introduction to Greimas's work, see D. Patte, *Religious Dimensions in Biblical Texts: Greimas's Structural Semiotics and Biblical Exegesis* (SBLSS; Atlanta: Scholars Press, 1990).

3.   M. Bal, *Narratology: Introduction to the Theory of Narrative* (trans. C. van Boheemen; Toronto: University of Toronto Press, 1985). G. Genette, *Narrative Discourse: An Essay in Method* (trans. J.E. Lewin; Ithaca: Cornell University Press, 1980); and *Narrative Discourse Revisited* (trans. J.E. Lewin; Ithaca: Cornell University Press, 1988).

4.   Bal, *Narratology*, p. 5, includes a third comprehensive level, the text, in which the story is related.

5.   For a discussion of these terms and an adaptation of Genette's work to biblical study, see A.R. Culpepper, *Anatomy of the Fourth Gospel: A Study in Literary Design* (Philadelphia: Fortress Press, 1981).

Second, narratologists compare the relative 'duration' of the telling in story time of fabula events, yielding a continuum from ellipsis and summary to scene, slow-down, and pause. A fabula event may be inferred but left out of the story, indicating an ellipsis, e.g. how the woman heard the prohibition. It may also be summarized, reported in scenic fashion (often using direct discourse), or emphasized in a slow-down, like the woman's contemplation of the tree in 3.6. The story may also include pauses in the telling of the fabula events for description in the story of characters or spaces (like the rivers and lands in Gen. 2.10-14). Third, Bal and Genette note the 'frequency' of the tellings. Some events are told only once, while others are repeated.

Perhaps Genette's most striking contribution, clarified by Bal, is the insistence on the distinction between 'focalization' and 'voice', between the one who sees and the one who tells.[1] Focalization 'is the angle of vision through which the story is filtered in the text'.[2] The advantages of this relatively unknown term, focalization, over other more common terms like perspective or point of view is that, while the common terms tend to conflate seeing and narrating, focalization does not confuse the person who sees with the person who speaks. For example, focalization may be done by a character (such as the woman seeing the fruit), while the telling may still be done by the narrator. Alternatively the same character may both see and tell, but the focalization may occur through the eyes of the character as a young person, while it is told through the mind of the character as a more mature narrator.[3] By analyzing narrative in terms of focalization, Bal is able to show three aspects of narration: telling, seeing, and doing. The narrator A (or character as narrator) *tells* what the focalizer B *sees* (or perceives) the person or object C being or *doing*.[4] In addition to being done by someone and on something, focalization may also be done from within or from without. That is, the focalizer may see only what is observable from the outside to any spectator (focalization from without), or, like an omniscient narrator, the focalizer may perceive inner thoughts or aspects of the person

1.   Bal, *Narratology*, p. 101, and Genette, *Narrative Discourse*, pp. 189-94.
2.   S. Rimmon-Kenan, *Narrative Fiction: Contemporary Poetics* (London and New York: Methuen, 1983), p. 43.
3.   As, for example, Qohelet's narrations of his early investigations in Qohelet 1–2.
4.   Bal, *Narratology*, p. 104.

or object that are not observable from the outside (focalization from within).

Narratology helps critics to analyze the rhetorical interests and strategies of a narrative text by (1) carefully distinguishing fabula and story and their relationships of order, duration, and frequency, (2) separating focalization and voice, and (3) studying plot, characterization, and the relationship of narration and direct discourse.[1]

Conclusions

Given their common interests in language, its nature, uses, and effects, the lack of overlap among the critical discussions of American feminists, French feminists, rhetorical critics, speech act theorists, and narratologists is striking. While American feminists study the differential use and effects of language and promote use of nonsexist language, they tend to ignore the rich philosophical and psychoanalytic background that informs French feminist theories about language. In French criticism, discussions of these theories are abstract, speaking about subjectivity and about language as a system. French feminists are concerned broadly with women's position in or outside language, with the relationship of language to bodies, and with women's status as man's 'Other' in language. Their responses to these abstractions are less concrete than those of pragmatic American feminists. French feminists often essentialize women or ignore the material realities of their lives as they create theories of women's speech and women's writing.

Rhetorical theory, speech act theory, and narratology are similarly disjoint. While classical rhetoric grew out of pragmatic concerns for developing persuasive communication in particular contexts, what has come to be known as 'rhetorical criticism' in Old Testament study generally ignores the rhetorical situations of both original and contemporary audiences. Since it tends to emphasize only a text's surface structure, it does not overlap with speech act theory's interest in the force and effects of spoken discourse as matters of social convention. Speech act theory has remained primarily a descriptive philosophical

---

1.   These last aspects of narratology are more familiar, so I do not include them. For discussion, see Bal, *Narratology*; Rimmon-Kenan, *Narrative Fiction*; R. Alter, *The Art of Biblical Narrative* (New York: Basic Books, 1981); A. Berlin, *Poetics and Interpretation of Biblical Narrative* (Bible and Literature Series, 9; Sheffield: Almond Press, 1983); and M. Sternberg, *The Poetics of Biblical Narrative: Ideological Literature and the Drama of Reading* (Bloomington: Indiana University Press, 1985).

tool, labelling and categorizing various individual speech acts; unlike classical rhetoric, it pays little attention to how various effects can be achieved.

Narratology, by contrast, attends to the rhetorical aspects of literary texts. By observing the choices made among a variety of options for characterization, time (sequence and relative time of story and fabula), space, and focalization, narratology explains what effects a text may produce and analyzes how it achieves them. Thus, of the three literary methodologies, narratology may offer the greatest resources for describing the persuasive techniques of a narrator's discourse. Yet, it too is limited, in many treatments, by emphasizing narration and minimizing analysis of characters' speech (which might be done using classical rhetoric or speech act theory).

Systematic integration of feminist concerns and issues into any of these literary methodologies is partial at best. Feminists adopting a standpoint epistemology would likely concur with rhetorical critics' honesty about ideologies and goals. They would share this theory's understanding of language as persuasive communication with pragmatic aims. Rhetorical critics' insight about the importance of beginning with audience-held opinions suggests that non-Christian feminists and non-feminist Christians should learn each other's perspectives if they wish to have fruitful conversations.

In spite of their limitations, each of these five theoretical areas offers perspectives on the nature and role of language and discourse, and each contributes insights and tools for analyzing the garden narrative in relation to language. The remainder of this chapter explores the role of language in the garden story by analyzing four particular portions of the story, each paired with different aspects of narrative study. First, the 'Language as Power' section addresses Gen. 2.16-17 and 3.14-19, considering God as a rhetor and asking: what kind of a language user is God? Speech act theory and rhetorical criticism provide the analytical tools. The section also examines the role of language as power in the narrative as a whole.[1] Second, 'Language as Possibilities' focuses on Gen. 3.1-7. It considers the balance of narration and discourse and their separate and joint roles in the text, attending particularly to quoted direct speech. The third section, 'Language as Danger', studies Gen. 3.8-13, considering how the use of pronouns contributes to the attainment of

---

1.   Though each of the four sections concentrates on a particular portion of the Genesis 2–3 text, the sections will at times overlap.

subjectivity by the characters. (I include a brief theoretical discussion at this point.) The fourth and final section, 'Language as Delights', begins with an examination of Gen. 2.18-25 and then branches out to a discussion of the effects of repetition and word plays in the rhetoric of entire narrative.

Language as Power: Genesis 2.16-17, 3.14-19 and Divine Rhetoric

What kind of a language user is God? What is God like as a rhetor? Is God's speech immediately understood? Is God's language, or any language for that matter, transparent, or does it require interpretation? Is God simply to be obeyed, or must God function as a rhetor to persuade? How is language connected with reality? Does language shape reality? Does it reflect reality? Does language serve to communicate? Is it a tool giving expression to our thoughts or is it the medium within which we think? Does the Genesis 2–3 text as a whole convey an understanding of language as power?

Commanding V(o)ice?

God's command to the man in 2.16-17 is the first speech act in the garden:

> (16) And YHWH God commanded the man saying,
> 'Of every tree of the garden you may surely eat,
> (17) but of the tree of the knowledge of good and evil
> you shall not eat of it,
> because on the day that you eat of it you will surely die.'

These two verses reveal several things about God. God speaks as one who has control of the garden. God is concerned to provide food for the man (indicated earlier by the narrator in 2.9). God thinks (or at least talks with humans) in terms of concepts: knowledge, good, evil.[1] God also seems to have some knowledge that the man does not have, particularly about the relationship between dying and eating from one specific tree.

---

1.   While I at times insist on God's giving of the command to the man alone, the woman eventually learns of it, so much of my discussion of the command refers to both the man and woman together as humans.

a. *Commands in Genesis 1*

In assessing God's use of language in these verses, readers of the garden narrative recall the power and effectiveness of God's commands in Genesis 1. There, God called forth light, a firmament, and lights in the firmament; and there was light, and a firmament and lights in the firmament. God ordered the waters to be gathered together, the dry land to appear, the earth to put forth vegetation, and the waters and earth to bring forth living creatures; and it was so. The waters were gathered; the dry land appeared; the earth brought forth vegetation; and the waters and earth were populated with creatures. God's commanding voice in Genesis 1 is effective. God's commands there seem almost to be performative in nature, bringing into being that which they command simply by the act of commanding.[1]

Readers may also recall God's charge to the humans in Genesis 1. There, God blessed the humans and gave them several tasks: to be fruitful, to multiply, to fill the earth, to subdue it, and to have dominion over fish, birds, and living creatures. God also gave them (and all the animals and birds) food: every plant and tree with seed in its fruit. While God's permission of every tree of the garden in Gen. 2.16 sounds like the earlier gift of food in Genesis 1, the command in 2.17 shows it has been modified. Now, one tree is specifically excluded: the tree of the knowledge of good and evil. God gives a reason, warning, or threat to the man for its prohibition. Whereas Genesis 1 emphasized the effectiveness of God's command and the goodness of creation, Gen. 2.17 suggests that both good and evil may already be in the world and hints that human obedience is not automatic.

b. *Understanding God's Command*

How do the humans understand God's command? One reading suggests that God's command and the human response are straightforward: God generously permits all trees except one (presumably with the human's

---

1.   Suggesting that the commands are performative need not mean that God's word is magical. The felicity conditions for performatives require appropriate persons and circumstances, properly executed procedures, and proper subsequent conduct. There is room in a performative understanding of God's creative word for God's doing to accompany the saying and for creaturely response. See Austin, *How to Do Things with Words*, pp. 14-15 and T.E. Fretheim, 'Word of God', *ABD*, VI, pp. 964-65.

best interests at heart[1]), and the humans violate that prohibition, bringing the inherent consequences of their act into play in the sentences of 3.14-19. In this scenario, God knows that the created world is interrelated. The command in 2.16-17 and the limits it reveals are structural components of that creation. In these verses, God both warns the humans about their limits and describes for them the inevitable results of their overstepping of boundaries.[2] God, in this interpretation, benevolently places appropriate restrictions on the humans' exercise of their freedom and informs humankind about them.[3] In other readings, however, God's prohibition may seem arbitrary or capricious.[4]

There are several difficulties in assessing God's command in 2.16-17. Foremost, perhaps, is the unavailability of God's intentions. While readers have inside views into God's motives for creating woman (2.18) and for expelling the couple from the garden (3.22), the narrator provides no explanation for God's command in 2.16-17. Second, there is no immediate response to the command, as we had come to expect in Genesis 1. Rather than saying 'and it was so' or commenting on the man's assent or adherence to God's command, the narrative seems to shift to another topic in 2.18-25. We know neither God's intentions nor the man's reception of the command. Third, while God gave purposes to the created things in Genesis 1, God gives no explanation here. Why

1.   The inside views in 2.18 and 3.22 contribute to this understanding. There, God seems concerned about the conditions of human living.

2.   The idea that events entail their own consequences, and that God does not exact retribution but allows or facilitates those consequences emerges from an essay by K. Koch and subsequent discussions. See K. Koch, 'Gibt es ein Vergeltungs-dogma im Alten Testament?', *ZTK* 52 (1955), pp. 1-42; modified ET: 'Is There a Doctrine of Retribution in the Old Testament?', trans. T.H. Trapp, in J.L. Crenshaw (ed.), *Theodicy in the Old Testament* (Philadelphia and London: Fortress Press and SPCK, 1983), pp. 57-87. Further discussion is included in P.D. Miller, Jr, *Sin and Judgment in the Prophets: A Stylistic and Theological Analysis* (SBLMS, 27; Chico, CA: Scholars Press, 1982).

3.   D. Bonhoeffer understands the prohibition as the '*grace* of the Creator towards the creature'. See *Creation and Fall: A Theological Interpretation of Genesis 1-3* (trans. J.C. Fletcher; London: SCM Press, 1959), p. 52. Similarly, von Rad sees it as part of 'God's fatherly care for man'; *Genesis*, p. 82.

4.   J. Barr, *The Garden of Eden and the Hope of Immortality* (Minneapolis: Fortress Press, 1992), p. 12. Against this position, see T.E. Fretheim, who understands the prohibition's placement before the creation of the woman as indicating that 'law is built into the very created order of things'; see 'Is Genesis 3 a Fall Story?', *WW* 14 (1994), p. 148.

God places this tree (and later the serpent) in the garden, given their role in the subsequent events, is mysterious.[1] The effect of these difficulties may be to make the command seem arbitrary or to portray God as authoritarian.

Is the prohibition arbitrary? Is God authoritarian? We may need to distinguish here between how the man hears the prohibition in the fabula and how readers hear it in the story. Whether the prohibition is arbitrary or God authoritarian also depends on our assessment of the man's intellectual abilities and on our own theology about God's relationships with humans.

Speeding Car Analogy? One way to justify God's seemingly authoritarian 'No' to the man as having his best interests at heart is to think of the prohibition as being for the man's own good, similar to a parent shouting 'No' to a toddler about to run into the street. A mother exerts her authority over young children for their own good, preventing them from being hit by speeding cars. A parental 'No' in this instance is definitely authoritarian, but it is clearly in the interests of the child. The point of this unequivocal command with a toddler is to protect the child and to instill safe habits. But any parent or worker with toddlers also knows that such authoritarianism does not go very far. One must most often explain, incessantly answering the 'why?' question, helping the child learn to reason and to value reasons. The streetside prohibition is acceptable, in part, because one can eventually explain, once the toddler becomes a teenager (who has lived that long, in part, thanks to adults' authoritarian care), the reasons for the earlier unequivocal prohibition.

God may indeed have the humans' best interests at heart in forbidding the tree of the knowledge of good and evil, but the speeding car analogy as an explanation for the prohibition is ultimately unsatisfactory. First, the man is not really like the toddler in the analogy. Although the man remains silent in response and has not (up to this point in the narrative) demonstrated any actions that qualify him as being sufficiently intelligent to comprehend it, God's subsequent delegating to the man of the responsibility for naming the animals (2.19-20)

---

1.   D. Jobling, 'Myth and Its Limits in Genesis 2.4b-3.24', chap. in *The Sense of Biblical Narrative: Structural Analyses in the Hebrew Bible II* (JSOTSup, 39; Sheffield: JSOT Press, 1986), p. 36. See also D.N. Fewell and D.M. Gunn, 'Shifting the Blame', chap. in *Gender, Power, and Promise: The Subject of the Bible's First Story* (Nashville: Abingdon Press, 1993), p. 34.

suggests that he is intellectually quite capable. The man's own poetry in praise of the woman (2.23) implies aesthetic and creative abilities as well. Surely this man could competently entertain reasons for the prohibition.[1] Second, the text provides no clue as to what the dangerous 'speeding car' is. Why will the man die? Even if the man is deemed insufficiently aware, unable to comprehend at the time of the prohibition a reason for his death, readers can be presumed to have achieved the 'teenager' status that requires an explanation for God's authoritarian behavior. None is provided.[2]

Presuming God's Intentions. God's intentions in issuing the command are unavailable. Reasons are not given for issuing the restrictive prohibition, either to the man in the fabula or to the readers of the story. Any number of explanations might have served. God may have wanted to test the man (as God tested Abraham in Genesis 22) to see whether he would obey God.[3] Perhaps God wanted to protect the garden (as God takes care of the animals in the flood episode in Genesis 6–9) by insuring that the man does not eat all the fruit. Such a reading might please the ecologically minded among us. If the man insists on eating from *every* tree, he will destroy the ecological balance. God may have wanted to teach the couple learn to make distinctions.[4] Designating a single tree as prohibited would be sufficient to help them learn this skill. Genesis 1 has suggested the importance of distinctions through its enumerations of the days, its emphasis on plants and animals being created 'according to their kinds', and the setting aside of the Sabbath. But if

---

1.   I am aware of the danger of what M. Bal calls the 'retrospective fallacy', attributing features to characters in an earlier portion of a narrative that they only acquire later as the story progresses. Yet, the final clause of 2:17 seems to presume that the man already has the necessary cognitive skills and abilities that one may infer from his later speech and reported actions. See 'Sexuality, Sin, and Sorrow: The Emergence of the Female Character', in *Lethal Love: Feminist Literary Readings of Biblical Love Stories* (Bloomington and Indianapolis: Indiana University Press, 1987), p. 112.

2.   I discuss the final clause of 2.17 as a partial explanation below.

3.   Though not essential for the reading, this motive often seems to lie behind those interpretations that emphasize human disobedience as the key issue in the narrative.

4.   On the importance of learning distinctions to prevent cannibalism, see Bal, *Lethal Love*, p. 123. This taboo requires that humans be able to differentiate themselves from animals.

giving the prohibition is simply a matter of teaching humans to make distinctions, then why this particular tree? Why forbid knowledge? Or, maybe there was something dangerous about the effects of the tree or the knowledge it imparted so that God really was trying to protect the man.

This explanation, perhaps the most likely, requires further discussion. Just what is so dangerous about the tree? Is it death dealing? The serpent in Gen. 3.4 denies the danger of death that the woman quoted God in 3.3 as having maintained. The narrative agrees with both the woman and the serpent. Readers of Gen. 3.3 already know, from having heard the giving of the command in 2.17, that the woman has quoted God correctly (if not entirely accurately in a verbatim sense) with respect to the association of death with eating from the tree, yet the narrative that follows shows the serpent is correct as well. The couple does not die, at least not immediately (and not physically) as God's original command had claimed, nor does God repeat this deathly part of the warning in the investigation or the sentences. In fact, God is worried in 3.22 about potential eternal life for the man. So, if not death, what is it that is dangerous about the tree? If God is protecting the human(s) by issuing the command, from what is God protecting them? The story never really resolves this question.

Rhetorical Difficulty. What this rhetorical difficulty suggests, then, is precisely that—rhetorical difficulty. If the command had been clear and persuasive, the couple might not have relented in the face of an alternative perspective. God's rhetoric in the command is ultimately not successful in preventing the couple from eating from the tree of the knowledge of good and evil.[1] Recognizing this fact, commentators generally take one of several positions. Most often they hide or ignore the ineffectiveness of God's speech by focusing instead on the human sin or rebellion, which seems so clearly evident in the face of what, for them, is a transparently clear, reasonable command of God. Secondly, readers may get God off the hook by insisting that God really wanted the couple to eat the fruit of the prohibited tree anyway. In this interpretation, the story is set up so that the couple will *have* to disobey the prohibition. God and the serpent are in cahoots[2] (or are really the

---

1. S. Dragga claims that God's words are frail and impotent compared to the serpent's: 'Genesis 2-3: A Story of Liberation', *JSOT* 55 (1992), pp. 9-11.
2. Bal claims that Yahweh and the serpent collaborate to trick the humans into

same person[1]), finding a way to get the couple to gain this knowledge. God thus seems like a parent using 'reverse psychology' on an unsophisticated, rebellious preschool child,[2] telling the child not to do precisely what God hopes he *will* do. Both of these positions aim to preserve the goodness of God by highlighting either the rebelliousness or the willful immaturity of the humans. A third option, used more rarely, is to insist that God alone is the source of the problem. God is malevolent, hostile, or jealous like some of the ancient Near Eastern deities,[3] or God tricked the couple.[4]

Learning to Communicate. I suggest a fourth option, related to all three types. I think neither God nor the humans can be absolved of the difficulty. There *is* a rhetorical difficulty in the story. God provides no rationale for the command.[5] This creates an opening for thinking, reasoning human beings to consider other alternatives. Relationships of trust have not yet been established between God and the humans, nor have patterns of regular communication been set up. Perhaps the couple should have trusted God's word over the serpent's alternative portrayal, but the rhetoric is on the serpent's side. The man had relationships with the animals of the field through his naming of them. The woman has

accepting species rather than individual immortality: *Lethal Love*, p. 124.

1. D.E. Burns suggests that the serpent is really God in disguise: 'Dream Form in Genesis 2.4b-3.24: Asleep in the Garden', *JSOT* 37 (1987), p. 9.

2. R.S. Hanson, 'The Snake and I', in *The Serpent Was Wiser: A New Look at Genesis 1-11* (Minneapolis: Augsburg, 1972), p. 46.

3. C.M. Carmichael, 'The Paradise Myth: Interpreting Without Jewish and Christian Spectacles', in P. Morris and D. Sawyer (eds.), *A Walk in the Garden: Biblical, Iconographical and Literary Images of Eden* (JSOTSup, 136; Sheffield: Sheffield Academic Press, 1992), p. 48. This aspect of Carmichael's exegesis follows gnostic interpreters. See E. Pagels, *Adam, Eve, and the Serpent* (New York: Random House, 1987), p. 69.

4. S. Niditch, 'Folklore and Biblical Narrative: A Study of Genesis 3', chap. in *Folklore and the Hebrew Bible* (Minneapolis: Fortress Press, 1993), p. 46. For discussion of Genesis 3 as a Trickster tale, see C.V. Camp, 'Wise and Strange: An Interpretation of the Female Imagery in Proverbs in Light of Trickster Mythology', in J.C. Exum and J.W.H. Bos (eds.), *Reasoning with the Foxes: Female Wit in a World of Male Power* (Semeia, 42; Atlanta: Scholars Press, 1988) pp. 21, 26-28.

5. One might ask whether commands should be persuasive. God's attention to *ethos* at Sinai (Exod. 20.2 reminds the Israelites who God is and what God has done for them) and God's shift to a persuasive strategy with Cain in Gen. 4.6-7 suggest that God is eventually open to this need.

entered into a dialogue with the serpent, a dialogue that neither the man nor the woman seems to have had so far with God in the story. Through the serpent's rhetoric, the threat of immediate death has become at worst a potential possibility, balanced by the positive aspects of the tree: beauty, sustenance, and wisdom. The fourth option for understanding the ineffectiveness of God's speech is to recognize that the human couple and God are just beginning to learn to communicate. They have not yet developed patterns of interaction and trusting relationships that enable communication about the responsible use of human free will and about divine expectations or guidelines for living in the world as human creatures of God. Language is powerful; rhetoric has a force, but the nature of that power and force depends on the relationships of communication among the participants. These relationships are still developing.

P(ron)ouncing Sentences?

Study of the power of language and analysis of God as a rhetor must address God's monologue in 3.14-19. It is difficult even to name God's speech in these verses, for in naming it we evaluate it. Gen. 3.14-19 might represent God's explanation of the unfolding of the inevitable consequences of human violation of the prohibition. These verses may be God's judgments: God's evaluation of human (and serpentine) behavior and God's passing of sentence on it. This passage could *de*scribe a change in the world order, a newly fallen world contrary to God's originally created order of Genesis 2, or it might *pre*scribe the way reality must now be as a result of the human actions.[1] The 'I will' language of 3.15-16 also requires discussion. Do these verses suggest that God is vowing to act in certain ways in relation to the world? Is God cursing, and if so what or whom is God cursing? Perhaps these verses are punishments. God's pronouncements in Gen. 3.14-19 certainly have a rhetorical 'bite',[2] but what kind of bite is it? How do

---

1.   P. Trible, among others, is anxious to distinguish these verses as God's *de*scription rather than God's *pre*scription: *God and the Rhetoric of Sexuality* (Philadelphia: Fortress Press, 1978), p. 128. See also Westermann, *Creation*, p. 100 and Hanson, *The Serpent Was Wiser*, p. 49. For a contrary opinion, see S.S. Lanser, '(Feminist) Criticism in the Garden: Inferring Genesis 2–3', in *Speech Act Theory and Biblical Criticism*, p. 75.

2.   H. Bloom and D. Rosenberg, *The Book of J* (New York: Grove Weidenfeld, 1990), pp. 184-85.

readers hear and evaluate them? Are God's words harsh or incommensurate to the deed? Is God angry? letting off steam? disappointed? relenting? merciful? resigned? Gen. 3.14-19 might also be an alternative portrayal of reality, a way of viewing the world in terms of enmity and opposites.[1] This section considers these possibilities and questions and also addresses how Gen. 3.14-19 functions in the narrative as a whole.

Structural Observations. Commentators make several observations about the structure of Gen. 3.14-19. They note that while God interrogated first the man and then the woman (who refers God to the serpent, though God does not question it) in 3.8-13, God's subsequent speech in 3.14-19 is directed to the characters in the reverse order, addressing first the serpent, then the woman, and finally the man. Scholars observe the similarity between God's remarks to the serpent and to the man: both begin with a 'because... ' clause, refer to eating, and include the phrase 'all the days of your life.' God's remarks to the woman have none of these features.

Some exegetes identify the verbal connections with the earlier narrative as indicating the appropriateness of God's sentences for each of the creatures. The serpent was more crafty than the other animals, now it is cursed among or cursed more than the animals. The disobedience involved eating, so the 'punishments' (at least for the man and the serpent) involve eating. The woman found the tree desirable for insight; now she will desire her husband. Some commentators even suggest that God is reversing relationships, creating (or returning to previously established) hierarchies.[2] The woman and the serpent interacted cooperatively with one another; now they will be enemies. The woman improperly exercised authority over her husband; now he will rule over her. He listened to his woman; now, presumably, she will have to listen to him. The woman and the man are each returned to and made

---

1. M. Buber, *Good and Evil: Two Interpretations* (New York: Charles Scribner's Sons, 1952), p. 79.

2. J.T. Walsh discusses the inversion in terms of orders of creation in 'Genesis 2:4b–3:24: A Synchronic Approach', *JBL* 96 (1977), p. 176. T.E. Boomershine speaks of reversals of actantial roles in 'The Structure of Narrative Rhetoric in Genesis 2–3', in Patte (ed.), *Genesis 2 and 3*, p. 125. B. Och, like Walsh, speaks of divinely ordered hierarchies; see 'The Garden of Eden: From Creation to Covenant', *Judaism* 37 (1988), pp. 152-53.

subject to their material source: the woman to the man, and the man to the ground.[1] Does the rhetoric of the narrative or the structural relationships between these verses and the remainder of the narrative justify interpreting them as punishments?

Punishments? Most readers do interpret God's speech in Gen. 3.14-19 as punishments. Four main reasons support this position. First, if the story as a whole is to serve a rhetorical purpose, such as dissuading Israelites from engaging in foreign religious practices[2] or preventing peasant rebellion,[3] decisive divine action condemning incorrect human choices would be the most effective in achieving these ends. Second, scholars observe a pattern of wrong-wrong–punished[4] or sin-speech-mitigation-punishment[5] in Genesis 1–11. Punishment is essential if the narrative in Genesis 2–3 is to fit this pattern. Third, the story may belong to the genre of an early folktale which explains present difficult human conditions as the result of divine punishment of an improper

1. J. Galambush, '*ʾādām* from *ʾᵃdāmâ*, *ʾiššâ* from *ʾîš*: Derivation and Subordination in Gen 2:4b-3:24', in M.P. Graham, W.P. Brown, and J.K. Kuan (eds.), *History and Interpretation: Essays in Honour of John H. Hayes* (JSOTSup, 173; Sheffield: JSOT Press, 1993), p. 42. The emphasis on this return is especially prominent in 3.19.

2. See A. Gardner, 'Genesis 2.4b-3: A Mythological Paradigm of Sexuality or of the Religious History of Pre-exilic Israel?', *SJT* 43 (1990), pp. 14-16; B. Vawter, *On Genesis: A New Reading* (Garden City, NY: Doubleday, 1977), p. 71; Boomershine, 'Rhetoric', p. 127; and W. Park, 'Why Eve?', *St. Vladimir's Theological Quarterly* 35 (1991), p. 131. Gardner, Vawter, Boomershine, and Park all understand the narrative as functioning rhetorically to argue against foreign religions. Westermann counters that such a polemic is not possible because of the primeval nature of the narrative; see *Creation*, p. 92.

3. J.M. Kennedy, 'Peasants in Revolt: Political Allegory in Genesis 2–3', *JSOT*, 47 (1990), p. 4.

4. For example, R.C. Culley, 'Action Sequences in Genesis 2–3', in Patte (ed.), *Genesis 2 and 3*, p. 28. C. Westermann likewise classifies the narrative as one of 'crime and punishment'; see *Genesis 1–11: A Commentary* (trans. J.J. Scullion S.J.; Minneapolis: Augsburg, 1984), pp. 47-56. For a contrary opinion, see Niditch, 'Folklore', pp. 39-36. Niditch observes that the story exhibits the morphology of a typical folktale in which early humans are somehow responsible for the loss of an irretrievable and better reality; the transgression then becomes simply a necessary part of the story structure.

5. D.J.A. Clines identifies this theme, building on the work of von Rad and Westermann, 'Prefatory Theme', chap. in *The Theme of the Pentateuch* (JSOTSup, 10; Sheffield: JSOT Press, 1978), p. 64.

action taken (knowingly, or unknowingly) by ancient ancestors.[1] Perhaps the most persuasive reason for regarding God's speech as describing punishments is that readers expect punishments.[2] The command was given with a threat or warning of immediate consequences. Readers watched the couple eat the forbidden fruit; we know the command was disobeyed. The investigation in 3.8-13 indicates God's continued interest in the command and in the human actions related to it. As readers, we expect God, at this point, to punish the couple for their violation of the command.

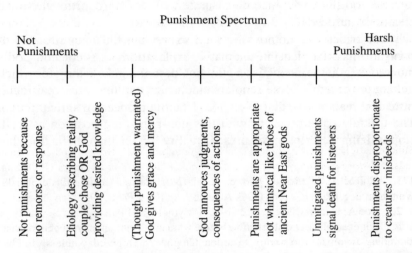

Punishment Spectrum

Yet, if Gen. 3.14-19 conveys God's punishments of the couple, what kind of punishments are they? Commentators differ widely about the nature of the punishments, if they consider God's words in these verses to signal punishments at all. (See chart above.) Some scholars insist that the consequences are intimately linked with the actions of the creatures, that God's role is one of informing the couple of the effects their actions entail and bringing those outcomes into play.[3] Thus, in this view, God's words in 3.14-19 are not punishments at all. Others emphasize God's

---

1.   Niditch, 'Folklore', p. 36.
2.   Lanser, '(Feminist) Criticism in the Garden', p. 75.
3.   Though he seems to struggle with whether 3.14-19 are curses, penalties, or punishments, von Rad describes God's speech as a matter of an offense receiving its consequences: *Genesis*, p. 93. T.E. Fretheim also views these speeches as moral order talk, judgments presenting consequences of creaturely action. See 'The Book of Genesis', *NIB*, I, pp. 363-64, 369.

grace and mercy in withholding immediate death.[1] Closer to the center of the spectrum, scholars observe the justice[2] or appropriateness[3] of these judgments, which are linked with the offenses, in contrast to the whimsical lashing out of other ancient Near Eastern deities.[4] Other exegetes recognize the punishments as associated with pain and death for the listening audience,[5] and contend they are not mitigated.[6] Though these scholars find the punishments difficult, they disagree as to whether the man's[7] or the woman's[8] punishment is worse. At the far end of the spectrum, some readers find the punishments shocking, harsh, terrible, too severe, or incommensurate with or disproportionate to the creatures' misdeeds.[9]

Those critics who do not view God's speech as the announcement of punishments offer plausible alternative explanations of its content. God's monologue, they contend, is an etiology, describing the reality for which the couple opted.[10] Some scholars emphasize that this was a particular historical reality (e.g. that of ancient Israelite pioneering agriculture[11]). The folktale pattern can fit with this non-punishing position as well, emphasizing description of present reality, rather than the action that

1.   S. Dockx, *Le récit du paradis: Gen. II-III* (Paris: Ducelot, 1981), p. 108; Walter Brueggemann, *Genesis* (IBC; Atlanta: John Knox Press, 1982), pp. 49-50.

2.   Boomershine, 'Rhetoric', p. 119.

3.   For example, A.J. Bledstein views the woman's increased pain in childbirth as reminding a woman who wanted to be like the gods (giving birth painlessly) of her humanity: 'Are Women Cursed in Genesis 3.16?' in A. Brenner (ed.), *A Feminist Companion to Genesis* (The Feminist Companion to the Bible, 2; Sheffield: Sheffield Academic Press, 1993), p. 143. Gardner similarly explains the woman's sentence as asserting Yahweh's, not Asherah's, control of fertility: 'Mythological Paradigm', p. 14.

4.   Fishbane, *Text and Texture*, p. 32.

5.   Boomershine, 'Rhetoric', p. 119.

6.   G. Savran, *Telling and Retelling: Quotation in Biblical Narrative* (Indiana Studies in Biblical Literature; Bloomington: Indiana University Press, 1988), p. 71.

7.   F. Watson, 'Strategies of Recovery and Resistance: Hermeneutical Reflections on Genesis 1-3 and its Pauline Reception', *JSNT* 45 (1992), p. 91.

8.   Jobling, *Sense*, p. 34.

9.   Bloom, *The Book of J*, pp. 183-85; Moberly, 'Did the Serpent Get It Right?', *JTS* 39 (April 1988), p. 20.

10.   Bal, *Lethal Love*, p. 125. Though von Rad, *Genesis*, pp. 92, 96 reads 3.14-19 as penalties, he emphasizes their etiological qualities.

11.   C. Meyers, *Discovering Eve: Ancient Israelite Women in Context* (New York: Oxford University Press, 1988), pp. 92-93.

brings it about. Some exegetes maintain that God's address informs the creatures about the lives they will lead, describing real creaturely limitations.[1] Other readers perceive that God's speech gives the human couple precisely the knowledge they desired,[2] noting that it emphasizes tensions[3] or that it portrays the world in terms of opposites, like good and evil.[4]

Perhaps the strongest argument against reading God's words as punishment is the couple's lack of response. At this point (after 3.19), they show no fear or remorse for their deed, no anguish or anxiety about the fates that a punishing God would be here announcing. Unlike Cain, who in 4.13 laments the severity of his punishment or guilt, the couple says nothing in direct response or even acknowledgement. It is almost as if they did not hear God speaking. If the couple did hear, either we may assume them to be stoic, accepting their sentences silently, or we must wonder whether the couple understood God's remarks to them as punishment.

Summary
There is a striking contrast between the power of language in Genesis 1 and in Genesis 2–3. In the first creation account, God's language is creative and effective performative speech, bringing the world into being as God speaks. The second account, however, portrays God's speech with humans as of limited effectiveness. God commands the man, but God's words must be interpreted. The woman's dialogue with the serpent shows that God's words are open to alternative analyses. Critical interpretation of God's speech in Genesis 2–3 is difficult because determining the felicity of a performative utterance or assessing the force of an illocution depends on agreement about language conventions, assigning a genre to the literary form, presuming intentions on the part of the speaker, and knowing responses to a speech. The narrative's

1.   Westermann, *Creation*, p. 98. H. Shank observes in relation to the Cain story that God simply informs the murderer of his fate, but contrasts this with God's punishing in the garden story: 'The Sin Theology of the Cain and Abel Story: An Analysis of Narrative Themes within the Context of Genesis 1–11' (PhD dissertation, Marquette University, 1988), p. 199. Given what sounds like the appeal of Abel's blood to God for justice, Shank's contrast may be more warranted in the opposite direction.
2.   Hanson, *The Serpent Was Wiser*, p. 49.
3.   Galambush, '*ʾādām* from *ʾᵃdāmâ*', p. 44.
4.   Buber, *Good and Evil*, p. 79; Och, 'The Garden of Eden', p. 153.

reticence to supply details about God's reasons and intentions and about human responses to divine speech reinforces the rhetorical difficulties, highlighting the ambiguity, mystery, and nontransparency of God's speech. Yet, while God's motives remain hidden and God's language requires interpretation, God's speech in 3.14-19 suggests that God continues to expect responsible human thought and action. God and humans, it seems, are only beginning to learn to communicate with one another about how to live out of the garden with human freedom and limitations and divine command.

Language as Possibilities: Genesis 3.1-7

In the previous section, I claimed that communication and the effectiveness of God's command was an issue in Gen. 2.16-17, 3.14-19. In Gen. 3.1-7, God's speech and what it means is precisely the topic of discussion. The serpent and the woman discuss God's command, the humans' potential actions, and the implications of both. By employing quotation, the serpent-woman dialogue is necessarily speech about speech, language about language.[1] This dialogue demonstrates that language is not transparent. It is always open to question and capable of a variety of interpretations. Indeed, interpretation is essential and inevitable. Language is never simply a meaning or a message, but always entails rhetoric. The subtle use of rhetoric by the serpent and the narrator, who ultimately frames and shapes the characters' speech and actions, manifests the multiple possibilities of language. In this section I discuss, first, the formal and rhetorical aspects of the speeches themselves as quotations and, second, the narrator's role and the rhetorical effects of framing and shaping the discourse.

Quoting Rhetoric

Before discussing the direct discourse between the serpent and the woman in 3.1-5, a few general comments on their situation in the fabula and story are in order. Readers realize as we hear the interchange between the woman and the serpent that they are discussing something about which, as far as we know, they have no direct knowledge. God's

---

1.   M. Sternberg, 'Proteus in Quotation-Land: Mimesis and the Forms of Reported Discourse', *Poetics Today* 3 (1982), p. 110, citing V.N. Voloshinov, *Marxism and the Philosophy of Language* (trans. L. Matejka and I.R. Titunik; Studies in Language, 1; New York: Seminar Press, 1973), p. 115.

command was spoken to the man in 2.16-17 *before* the woman or the animals, including the serpent, were made, yet they seem to know something about it. Their conversation suggests an ellipsis in the story: something has happened in the fabula which the narrator has chosen not to tell us. We may speculate that the woman and the serpent (while still rib and ground?) heard the command as the man did. We may conjecture that God repeated to the woman and/or to the serpent the same words that God had earlier spoken to the man. In this case, God may have addressed these words to them also, so that the permission and prohibition apply to the woman and serpent as well, or God may simply have informed them about the restriction on the man.

Alternatively, we may posit that the serpent overheard a discussion between man and woman. Similarly, perhaps, the woman overheard a conversation between the man and God. In any case, what the woman and the serpent are discussing in 3.1-5, that is, the original speaking situation and the actual words that were spoken, are not available to us. Their quotations in this sense are 'unverifiable', though we are likely to think otherwise because of the situation we do know.[1] The best we can do, and what we will inevitably do, is to compare the discussion between the woman and the serpent with the command that we know God gave the man in Gen. 2.16-17.

The serpent's first words in 3.1 are usually understood as a question: 'Really, did God say "you (pl) shall not eat of any tree of the garden"?' The quote recalls an earlier situation. Every word corresponds to a word God actually used in 2.16-17. (See the chart on the next page.) Their order has been reversed, however. The phrase 'you shall not eat', comes from 2.17, with the singular 'you' there changed to a plural here; the phrase 'of any tree of the garden' in 3.1 is identical to 'of every tree of the garden' in 2.16.[2] We might also observe that quoters become narrators in a sense, so the introductions to their speeches are significant.

---

1.   Unverifiable is G. Savran's term for a quotation where the original locution is absent. See his *Telling and Retelling*, pp. 7, 105-106. Savran, failing to distinguish fabula and story levels in this instance (though he is aware of them in other examples), incorrectly charges the serpent with offering a 'deceptive quote' (p. 26) or 'deliberate misstatement' (p. 63) in 3.1. Similarly, he assumes the woman has added a phrase (p. 33) in 3.3. While he is not alone among commentators in these evaluative attributions, his topic suggests that the relationships among narrative levels and quoted speech merited more careful attention.

2.   The placement of the negative changes the translation of *kōl* from 'every' in 2.16 to 'any' in 3.1.

Gen. 2.16	*way'ṣaw yhwh ˣlōhîm ʿal-haᵃ̄ādām lᵉᵊmōr*	And YHWH God commanded the man saying,
Gen. 2.17	*mikōl ʿēṣ-haggān ᵊākōl tōᵊkēl*	'*Of every tree of the garden* you may surely <u>eat</u>,
	ûmēˣēṣ haddaᶜat tôb wārāᶜ	but of the tree of the knowledge of good and evil
	lōᵊ tōᵊkal mimmennû	<u>you shall not eat</u> of it,
	kî bᵊyôm ˣᵊkālkā mimmennû môt tāmût	for on the day you eat of it <u>you</u> **will surely <u>die</u>**.'
Gen. 3.1b	*wattōᵊmer ˣel-hāˣiššā ᵊap kî-ˣāmar ˣlōhîm*	So it is said to the woman, 'Really, did God say
	lōᵊ tōᵊklû mikōl ʿēṣ-haggān	"<u>you (pl) shall not eat of any tree of the garden</u>"?'
Gen. 3.2	*wattōᵊmer hāˣiššā ᵊel hannāḥāš*	And the woman said to the serpent,
	mipᵊrî ᶜēṣ-hagān nōᵊkēl	'of the fruit of <u>the trees of the garden we may eat</u>,
Gen. 3.3	*ûmipᵊrî hāᶜēṣ ᵊšer bᵊtôk-hagān*	but, of the fruit of <u>the tree that is in the middle of the garden,</u>
	ˣāmar ˣlōhîm lōᵊ tōᵊklû mimmennû	God said, "<u>You (pl) shall not eat of it</u>
	wᵊlōᵊ tigᵊᶜû bô pen-tᵊmutûn	and you (pl) shall not touch it lest <u>you (pl) die</u>."'
Gen. 3.4	*wayyōᵊmer hannāḥāš ˣel-hāˣiššā lōᵊ-môt tᵊmutûn*	Then the serpent said to the woman, '**You (pl) will not surely die.**
Gen. 3.5	*kî yōdēaᶜ ˣlōhîm kî bᵊyôm ˣᵊkālkem mimmennû*	**For God knows that** *on the day you (pl) eat of it*
	wᵊnipᵊqᵊḥû ᶜênêkem	*your (pl) eyes will be opened*
	wihᵊyîtem kēˣlōhîm yōdᵊᶜê tôb wārāᶜ	*and you (pl) will become like God, knowing good and evil.'*
Gen. 3.7	*wattippāqaḥᵊnā ᶜênê šᵊnêhem*	And the eyes of them both were *opened*,
	wayyēdᵊᶜû kî ᶜêrummim hēm	and they knew that naked [were] they.
Gen. 3.22a	*wayyōᵊmer yhwh ˣlōhîm hēn hāˣādām*	And YHWH God said,
	hāyā kᵊᵊaḥad mimmennû lādaᶜat tôb wārāᶜ	'*Behold, the man has become like one of us, knowing good and evil'.*

key: <u>words quoted by the woman</u>; *words from 2.16, 3.7, or 3.22 'quoted' by the serpent*; **words from 2.17 quoted by the serpent**

The serpent (as narrator) talks about what God 'said', while the narrator of 2.16 described what God 'commanded'.[1]

From the serpent's speech itself it is difficult to determine what caused the divergences between the quotation in 3.1 and what God said in 2.16-17. Again, we do not know what or how either the serpent or the woman knows anything about God's command. The serpent's aims, however, like those of any quoter, depend to some degree on its own knowledge as well as on the knowledge of its conversation partner, the woman. The serpent may be seeking information. It may be expressing real (or feigned) astonishment at God's prohibition. If the serpent knows the prohibition in the same way as we readers have heard it in 2.16-17, the serpent may be deliberately rearranging and misquoting God's words in order to tease, provoke, or manipulate the woman.

We can think of the woman, likewise, as taking on the role of narrator. The woman's response in 3.2-3 begins with free indirect discourse, summarizing in her own words what she understands of God's command. Then she shifts to direct discourse, quoting God.[2] In 3.1, while the serpent's words are individually more nearly identical to those that God spoke in 2.16-17, their rearrangement in the serpent's question alters their meaning considerably. In 3.2-3, the woman's words themselves vary more substantially from God's statement in 2.16-17 than the serpent's words do, but her interpreted version maintains the order and essence of the permission and prohibition more accurately than the serpent's question in 3.1.

The woman's quotation[3] diverges in several ways from God's speech in 2.16-17. The woman specifically mentions the 'fruit' of the trees, and she also includes a phrase about not touching the tree. Her quotation,

1.   Savran observes this distinction: *Telling and Retelling*, p. 70.

2.   Of course, on the first level of narration all of the woman's speech is part of her direct discourse, but when we move to the second level of narration as she begins speaking, we can think of her as a narrator using first free indirect discourse, and then direct discourse when she quotes God. See L.S. Wright, 'Reported Speech in Hebrew Narrative: A Typology and Analysis of Texts in the Book of Genesis', (PhD dissertation, Emory University, 1991) on levels of narration and varieties of discourse types in Genesis.

3.   I use the word 'quotation' to refer to her entire speech since we can consider it to be marked by the serpent's question even before the woman says, 'God said'. I am also careful to avoid attributing modifications in the quoted speech to any quoter since they may not be modifications at all of the speech the quoter is actually quoting. The changes, additions, and omissions all really accrue to the narrator.

like the serpent's, changes the singular 'you' of 2.16-17 to a plural. It also omits the infinitive absolute construction (rendered by 'surely' in my translation), and it omits reference to 'every' tree in the permission. The woman's version changes the immediate and sure death reference of 2.17 'on the day you eat of it you will surely die' to a hypothetical 'lest you die'. Most notably, the woman does not refer to 'the tree of the knowledge of good and evil', but to 'the tree that is in the middle of the garden'.

Again, we *cannot* say what caused the woman to report as God's speech something that we observe differs from a speech situation we readers have heard. The woman may be accurately reporting what she heard at another time from God or from the man. We readers *can* talk about the rhetorical effects, on us, of the divergences between what the woman says and what we heard in 2.16-17. The woman's use of an unmarked quotation in 3.2 may suggest that she has appropriated the command as applying to her. It may also show her respect for God's command and her assent to God's authority. Her less generous version of the permission and her forbidding of even touching the fruit may have no significance, or they may indicate that the serpent's hints about God's stinginess have already begun to affect her. Her mention of 'fruit' may show that the woman is interpreting a command that did not specifically mention fruit; it may suggest an interest in horticulture; or it may accrue to the narrator's interest in puns (see below). Similarly, the woman's restriction of the couple from touching the tree may be a fleshing out of an original command, or it may be an added cautionary measure. Joined with her comment about not touching, the phrase 'lest you die' may be the woman's way of rendering the immediacy of the death threat, or it may change a definite result of the eating into merely a hypothetical consequence.

If the previous divergences between the woman's speech and the earlier command have not made readers wonder about what actually was said, the woman's specification of the tree will make them check their notes or turn back a page to find out just which tree *is* in the middle of the garden. Gen. 2.9 answers the question, noting that both the tree of life and the tree of the knowledge of good and evil are in the middle of the garden. As the serpent's question suggests, we readers may experience some uncertainty at this point about which tree is prohibited. We may also wonder, as a result of the woman's claims, just how dangerous the tree is, what actions precisely are prohibited, and what the consequences of violating the prohibition will be. These effects set us up for the serpent's next claim.

The serpent's initial retort in 3.4, 'You (pl) will not surely die', which may also be translated as 'You (pl) will surely not die', differs from God's pronouncement by only one word: not. Although the serpent is denying the woman's claim, which itself seems to quote God imprecisely, we readers know that the form of the serpent's denial is a direct negation of God's exact words in 2.17. Thus, it seems to us as though the serpent is misquoting or contradicting God with this remark. If our theological sensibilities have been shaped by other texts and other associations with God, they may be scandalized by the thought that God might lie or be wrong. Nevertheless, the serpent's assertion makes it possible to see the world in other ways. Adding the single word 'not' in 3.4 has transformed God's threat or warning of 2.17 into a reassurance.

The continuation of the serpent's response in 3.5 about what God knows combines a retrospective quotation with a prospective one. The serpent's quotation looks back to God's words of 2.17 'for...on the day...', which the woman's speech omitted. It also looks forward to the narrator's words about the couple's open eyes in 3.7 and to God's interior monologue in 3.22 about the man having become like one of the gods, knowing good and evil. Except for the changes in pronouns required for the different forms of discourse in these three verses, the serpent's words again accurately quote those of God and the narrator.

The effects of the serpent's accurate and true statements in 3.4-5 may eventually prove more troubling to readers than the rearrangements of God's speech and altered meanings were in 3.1,4. By the end of the story, readers know that the serpent's words here have proven true. The couple does not die. The narrator confirms, immediately after their eating, that on the day they ate their eyes 'were opened' (3.7), raising reader confidence in the serpent. As we read on, this new trust seems somewhat misplaced when the second element of the serpent's prospective quotation, being like God, does not immediately follow. Instead, the narrator informs us in 3.7 that the couple knew they were naked. When God's interior monologue in 3.22 belatedly informs readers that the couple (or at least the man) has, in fact, become like God, knowing good and evil, readers may grow suspicious of the narrator as well as of God. The serpent ultimately gains in credibility.

At the point where the serpent concludes its speech to the woman, however, its remarks may be more difficult to assess. The serpent

introduces the final indirect quotation as being what 'God knows'. The
conflict among the various quotations and interpretations is escalating.
Readers heard God say one thing to the man. The woman quotes a
second slightly different scenario, suggesting she may have heard a third
version. The serpent raises a question about God's speech, then contradicts what we have heard (thus, presenting a fourth possibility), and
finally claims to have access to what 'God knows'. This divine knowledge may be a fifth option for understanding God's intentions and what
may happen if the couple chooses to eat—an option not revealed by
God or the narrator.

Framing Words
The options raised by the dialogue in 3.1-5 may be confusing precisely
because we readers have been drawn in. We no longer hear the story
from above, as if observing it from a helicopter moving in and out to
observe gardens, rivers of the earth, hoards of animals, and a surgical
operation. Now we watch from the ground, or we hear as if perched in
a nearby tree. Rather than giving the story primarily in summarized
snatches with pauses for descriptions, the narrator offers a scene with
dialogue, full of addresses to a plural 'you' that seem to include us. The
dialogue enhances the verisimilitude of the story, seeming to offer us
access to the thoughts and motives of the characters. So we easily forget
that the quotations the characters make are all ultimately set in a frame
constructed by the narrator. The narrator's framing rhetoric controls
that of the characters' inset dialogue. Thus, the narrator's words 'frame'
theirs, both structurally and ideologically.

The biblical narrator's usual reticence makes it difficult to recognize
the subtle ways the narrator is shaping the story. One aspect of the
shaping is the nature of the quotations themselves, as discussed above.
The narrator has controlled our access to the fabula, preventing us from
hearing what and how the woman and serpent know of God's command, with the result that we inevitably compare their words to those
the narrator has chosen to report between God and the man in 2.16-17.
The narrator's clever distortions, through rearranged repetitions and
negations of God's words, may make the serpent seem to be a liar and
manipulator. The divergences between the woman's rendering of the
command and what we readers have heard may make the woman likewise appear irresponsibly loose with God's words.

Furthermore, by delaying until almost the end of 3.6 the information that the man was 'with' the woman, probably during the entire conversation given the serpent's and woman's use of plural verbs, the narrator requires the woman to speak for the couple. She seems to be the only person there. The serpent is shrewdly introduced in 3.1, perhaps suggesting a warning to readers as well as a reminder that the serpent is, after all, simply a creature. By bringing us into the middle of the conversation, the narrator has also avoided describing who else was there. In addition, the introductions of the speeches may reinforce the idea that only the serpent and woman are present. Each is reported as speaking 'to the woman' or 'to the serpent'. On the other hand, these remarks may hint that others were present. After all, they parallel God's addresses 'to the serpent' and 'to the woman' in 3.14,16, where we can presume the presence of all three creatures. In this case, we may wonder (as many commentators do) why the serpent spoke 'to the woman' if the man was present as well, and we may chide the woman for not speaking to the man or to God instead of speaking only in response to the serpent. The delayed reporting of the man's presence and the narrator's insistence on to whom the speeches were directed may also make reflective readers wonder about God's apparent absence during this crucial conversation.

The critical nature of the dialogue between the serpent and the woman is highlighted by the slow-down and inside view in 3.6. By focalizing through the woman's eyes, the narrator provides access to her thinking and reasoning process. The slower pace provides opportunity for reader involvement. We look, with the woman, at the tree. Our sympathy for her view increases because we can participate in it and because what she sees initially echoes what the narrator has told us already in 2.9: that the tree is 'good for food'. Her second observation, that the tree is 'a delight to the eyes', recalls for readers the narrator's description of all the trees in 2.9 as being 'desirable to see'. Her third thought, that 'the tree was desirable for insight', makes sense to us, not only because of the serpent's recent claims, but also because (unlike? the woman) we know, having been shrewdly guided back to 2.9 already, that the tree in the middle of the garden is the tree of the knowledge of good and evil. The narrator has eliminated all mention of 'command' in 3.1-6 by having the characters quote what God 'said' or what God 'knows'. The dialogue between the serpent and the woman has thrown open several options, seeming to reduce the dangers and increase the potential rewards. The slow-down and inside view enable readers to participate in and concur with the woman's reasoning. Given the absence of 'command' language, the newly opened options, and our access to plausible reasoning, we readers may want to join the woman in eating the fruit from the tree. Our imaginative participation in the couple's act may be precisely what the narrator has cunningly sought to produce.

Readers continue to participate with the couple as the narrator reports in 3.7 not only their new awareness but their actions. The narrator informs us that their eyes are 'opened, and...' we may be surprised to hear that they are not like gods as the serpent contended. They do *know* something, though not, it seems, the good and evil of the serpent's second claim. Rather, the couple knows that they are naked. This change in the type of knowledge they gained from what we may have expected does two things. It recalls the situation in 2.25 before the crafty serpent came on the scene, and it also links 'good and evil' with 'naked': the knowledge that the couple expected with what they got. The nakedness that had once seemed only good, now seems evil as well. The mention of 'naked' and the initial comment that the eyes of 'both' were opened sends readers back to 2.25, reminding us that the man and woman both once were 'naked, and were not ashamed'. The couple's subsequent actions now speak louder than words. By sewing coverings for themselves, the couple's shame at their nakedness is displayed for readers, even though the word 'shame' itself is not mentioned.

The narrator's crafty setting of the serpent-woman dialogue within the frame provided by 2.25 and 3.7 also emphasizes the changes in the couple's lives. The man and woman have clearly moved from being naked to clothed and presumably from unashamed to ashamed, but this movement occurs along with other possible changes. Earlier in the story, the woman and man had potential actions (the vocations of helper and of garden worker and guard) arranged for them, but they have not actually done anything so far in the narrative except to speak,[1] sleep, and eat. The couple's opened eyes and new knowledge prompt a change in them from verbally to physically active: they sew fig leaves together and make coverings for themselves. The last remark, 'for themselves', suggests an additional change. The couple previously seemed dependent on God as the provider of food, beautiful trees, and even the breath of life. Now they act on their own, independently of God, as they make

---

1. The man does name the animals (again out of our hearing), which may require thought and activity on his part. Yet his action, even in naming, is primarily one of speech.

things 'for themselves'. The contrast between 2.25 and 3.7 may suggest other changes in the couple as well: perhaps from naive to conscious, from innocent to knowing, from ignorant of social convention to aware of prudence, from accepting of their differences to fearing or being ashamed of them.

The narrator's framing of the eating discussion and event does not end with the verses immediately surrounding 3.1-6, however. In the subsequent interrogation, God's questions in 3.11, 13 and the man's and woman's responses in 3.12-13 recall the scene. Moreover, the narrator shapes how we are to reflect on the earlier scene through the insistence in divine speech on the command and on the *not* eating. God's question 'who told you...' in 3.11 urges the man to consider the source of his knowledge and God's rationale to the man in 3.17 suggests that the woman's voice is not the one to whom the man should have been listening. The narrator's last reference to elements of the serpent-woman dialogue, however, moves in the opposite direction. By confirming in God's interior monologue of 3.22 that the couple has become 'like one of us', presumably like the gods as the serpent predicted, the narrator in some sense vindicates the serpent and perhaps undermines God.

Conclusions: Rhetoric about Rhetoric
So what can we say about the serpent's dialogue with the woman? Is the serpent's rap conniving and deceitful? Does the serpent have some crude hidden agenda in mind? Or does the serpent's 'bum rap' consist in its characterization by commentators as deceitful or by the narrator as 'shrewd'? The serpent may frame the woman (if it is setting her up for a 'fall'), but the narrator certainly frames them both. Ultimately interpreters frame the entire discussion. Like narrators at a metatextual level, interpreters choose which components of the story to highlight, in what order to discuss various aspects, and most importantly how to characterize, label, and evaluate those elements. The rhetoric of the interpreter herself ultimately frames any discussion of a tale and its rhetoric.

My discussion of Gen. 3.1-7 in this section shows two things: (1) that the serpent opened up a genuine alternative, that is, that language offers possibilities, and (2) that the use of quotation as a strategy ultimately frames not only the characters but the narrator as framer, and the interpreter.

First, language offers possibilities. The serpent-woman dialogue shows that in spite of its seeming transparency and clarity, God's command was not immediately obvious. Like all language, God's speech is always subject to interpretation. God's command is a speech act, making intention, knowledge, convention, and relationship all necessary for proper understanding and evaluation. The serpent's position offers an alternative, but the credibility of any alternative depends on the rhetorical relationships among the speakers.

Second, quotation is speech about speech, language about language. It necessarily involves representation, often repetition. It can never completely reproduce an original speech event because the context of the first speech and of the quotation inevitably vary. Thus, quotation, like language in general, also unavoidably interferes, mediates, and exploits. It involves a second level of narration that puts the characters temporarily in the position of narrator, obviously engaging themselves in rhetoric. Quotation, thus, involves a dual strategy: it represents the original speech situation, but it does so in terms of its own rhetorical purposes. It has a divided allegiance, both to accuracy in reporting and to efficacy in persuading. Yet the rhetoric of the quoting inset is always subject to the rhetorical goals of the narrator's framing.

The couple did fatefully eat from the forbidden tree, but by choosing to portray in detail the serpent-woman dialogue as a prelude to the couple's action, the narrator hints that God-human relations are more complicated than they may seem at first sight. By selecting God's words as the precise topic of discussion and by using quotation as the means of representation, the narrator's telling of the events in the garden highlights the multiple possibilities inherent in language and emphasizes the inevitability of interpretation. Through continued reference to the interpretive event of this scene in the subsequent narrative, the narrator reminds us as readers that there are consequences for our interpretations, that we should pay attention to who is doing the persuading, and that God expects us to act, and to interpret, responsibly.

Language as Danger: Genesis 3.8-13

Interpretation continues in Gen. 3.8-13, where pronouns are prominent. Given their role in facilitating entry into the Symbolic realm, according to French feminist theorists, a brief discussion of the linguistic role of pronouns will facilitate discussion in this section about language as danger.

The Linguistic Role of Pronouns

Just as language use is a defining characteristic of humanity, the existence and use of personal pronouns reveals part of the nature of language. These pronouns are evident in all languages, even in languages that avoid using them.[1] That 'I' and 'you' exist in language as forms in spoken discourse shows that language is self-referential. It can conceive of itself as a form.[2] The pronouns 'I' and 'you' have no content outside the instance of spoken discourse. The 'I' is the one who speaks, the one who says 'you' at the moment of speech, the subjective person.[3] The 'you', reciprocally, is defined only in locution, the one addressed by the 'I', the non-subjective person.[4] As dialogue proceeds, the intersubjective 'I' and 'you' change places.[5] The opposition of 'I' and 'you' is essential for speech and identity. Linguist Emile Benveniste observes,

> Consciousness of self is only possible if it is experienced by contrast. I use *I* only when I am speaking to someone who will be a *you* in my address. It is the condition of dialogue that is constitutive of *person*, for it implies that reciprocally *I* becomes *you* in the address of the one who in his turn designates himself as *I*...Language is possible only because each speaker sets himself up as a *subject* by referring to himself as *I* in his discourse.[6]

Saying 'I' or 'you', thus, indicates something of the identity, consciousness, and subjectivity of the speaker. Yet, the pronouns 'I' and 'you,' by remaining without content except within discourse, serve as reminders that language and discourse exist as *social* phenomena subject to implicitly agreed upon conventions.

In contrast to the 'I' and 'you' that are present in relationship with one another through discourse, the so-called 'third person' pronouns are not persons at all.[7] The 'he', 'she', or 'it' is the one who is absent, the non-person.[8] Defined in terms of reference to objects, the 'she' or 'he'

---

1. Benveniste, *Problems in General Linguistics*, p. 225.
2. H.C. White, *Narration and Discourse in the Book of Genesis* (Cambridge: Cambridge University Press, 1991), p. 33.
3. Benveniste, *Problems in General Linguistics*, pp. 197-218, 201.
4. Benveniste, *Problems in General Linguistics*, p. 224.
5. Benveniste, *Problems in General Linguistics*, p. 199.
6. Benveniste, *Problems in General Linguistics*, pp. 224-25, emphasis in original.
7. Benveniste, *Problems in General Linguistics*, p. 198.
8. Benveniste, *Problems in General Linguistics*, pp. 197-201.

stands outside the I-you discourse.[1] If 'I' and 'you' are the primary pronouns of direct discourse, 'he' and 'she' are referential forms, the pronouns for narration. The appearance of 'she' or 'he' in characters' speech is a sign that they have taken over one of the narrator's roles as focalizer and/or rhetor.

Pronoun Use and Effects in Genesis 2–3

The use of pronouns in Genesis 2 reveals significant aspects of the relationships among God and the humans. If language provides the possibility and discourse the provocation for the emergence of subjectivity,[2] then we should not be surprised that subjectivity is only beginning to develop in Genesis 2. The majority of the narrative there consists of reports of God's actions and prospects for the man and the woman. None of the four verses of direct discourse (2.16-18, 23) is part of a dialogue, enabling the interchange of 'I' and 'you'.

The man's subjectivity begins to emerge as the 'you', the addressee of divine command in Gen. 2.16-17, yet the man does not respond. He does not immediately take on a full subject status by replying with his own 'I' to God's speech. The man begins to define himself in opposition to others through his naming of the animals in 2.19-20. He gains further identity of his own with the advent of his human counterpart, woman, when he speaks in 2.23, claiming 'my bones' and 'my flesh'.

The woman, however, does not have the same level of subjectivity at 2.23. Like the man, she is not in dialogue with God, but unlike him she does not speak herself, nor has anyone yet spoken *to* her. Though both the woman and the man begin in the narrative as a 'lack' (the ground needed a worker; the man needed a helper), the woman does not have the man's stature by the end of Genesis 2. The man has changed from being lack, object, and addressee eventually to becoming speaker and possessor (using 'my'). The woman is still an object. The man's word 'this' in 2.23 does not even recognize the woman as a person, while the narrator's 'his woman' in 2.25 describes her as a possession.

Thus, Genesis 2 reveals differences in the subject status of the characters. God is a subject, speaking internally and to another (the man), able to use 'I'. The man is an incomplete subject, addressed as 'you' by God, partially recognizing himself in speech with his 'my'. The

---

1.   Benveniste, *Problems in General Linguistics*, pp. 197-218.
2.   Benveniste, *Problems in General Linguistics*, p. 227.

woman stands outside discourse, neither speaking her 'I' nor addressed as a 'you'. She is an object and a possession.

The situation at the beginning of Genesis 3 has improved somewhat for the woman. Someone, albeit a snake, finally engages her in dialogue, though not her alone. In spite of the narrator's introductions to the woman's and the serpent's direct discourse as occurring between the two of them alone, the plural pronouns in Gen. 3.1-5 reveal that the woman is neither addressed as an individual, nor does she think of herself independently from the man.

The discussion in 3.1-5 does not center around the humans as subjects.[1] Its focus, rather, is on God as subject—on what God said and what God knows. In spite of being the topic of discussion, God never becomes an object. God is never replaced in the treeside conversation by the non-personal third person pronoun 'he', nor does the narrator even permit the conversationalists to use God's name, YHWH. The dialogue refers simply to what 'God' said or knew.

The narrator reports each human's eating separately in 3.6. Then their actions continue in concert until God's address to the man alone in 3.9. Thus, the woman, now, as well as the man, is the subject of an active verb. Still, neither human has yet claimed their 'I' in speech.

The sound of God in the garden prompts the couple's hiding in Gen. 3.8, and God's questions provoke their continued movement toward full subjectivity. Unlike the serpent, God addresses each of them as individuals. Thus, the man's 'I' in 3.10 contrasts sharply with the woman's 'we' and the plural 'you' in her quotation of God in 3.2-3. The man seems to have forgotten the woman entirely as he tells God only his own activities and feelings. He uses 'I' four times in 3.10, claiming himself as subject of hearing, being afraid, being naked, and hiding, prior to his confession in 3.12 of eating. In contrast, the woman speaks a single 'I', admitting in 3.13 that she ate.

In the interrogation scene, God and humans enter into dialogue for the first time: they exchange the 'I' and 'you' subject positions. The humans again respond as they are addressed. The serpent called to them both as 'you (pl)'. God calls only to the man, 'where are you?' The couple's dialogue shows the rupture of the woman's joint 'we' into the man's and woman's individual 'I', 'me', and 'she'. The woman has not

---

1.   Nor does the serpent ever speak as a subject, using 'I'. Except for the woman's claim 'we may eat' in 3.2 and the serpent's assertion 'you will not die' in 3.4, the dialogue only indirectly refers to the couple's actions as potential subjects.

progressed very far in the man's eyes. From a 'this' in 2.23, she has become a 'she' in 3.12. There is still no dialogue between the man and the woman: neither one, as an 'I', addresses the other as 'you'. The man and woman each talk with God, though the man's address is not very flattering. God, for the first time, becomes an object, an Other, a 'you' who is heard by the man. God is also an accused subject addressed by the man as the 'you' who gave him the woman. The woman seems not to attain full subject status in relation to God, however. While she uses her 'I' in 3.13 in response to God's address to her as 'you', she does not reciprocally address God as 'you'. Perhaps this is due to the more limited relationship between these two characters. God had addressed the man as 'you' in 2.16-17, and in 3.11 God recalls this speech to the man as being what 'I commanded you'. God, so far, has not used God's 'I' in discourse with the woman.

God reasserts God's subject status in the monologue that follows, by retaining control of the speaking voice (stuffing the serpent's mouth with dust, perhaps for fear of what it might say[1]), by asserting God's 'I will' (to the serpent and the woman in 3.15-16), and by reasserting the 'I commanded' (to the man in 3.17). The serpent, woman, and man serve only as addressees in this monologue, and differentially so. The serpent is referred to with the pronouns 'you' or 'your' ten times, the woman only five times, and the man fifteen times. This unevenness is hard to explain. Perhaps the longer address to the man is a function of God's lengthier relationship with him, but then God's greater attention to the serpent than the woman is surprising. After the monologue in 3.14-19, the personal pronouns disappear (except for God's 'us' in 3.22) in favor of non-personal narration.

There are several possible effects of the monologue and resumption of narration. Certainly, the repetition of 'you' and 'your' (30 times) continues drawing the reader in as an addressee. God's 'I will' may add force to the pronouncements to the woman and the serpent (and the overhearing readers). Since the I-you interchange does not occur in monologue, the subtle message to the reader may be that God ultimately controls or judges rhetorical situations, that dialogue with God eventually ends in God's monologue.

---

1.   Fewell and Gunn, 'Shifting the Blame', pp. 33-34.

Conclusions: Language, Subjectivity, and Danger

Study of the use of pronouns in Genesis 2–3 reminds us that language is a social activity. Language requires recognition of ourselves in relationship with or in contrast to others. In these relationships, language and rhetoric are necessary for communication. Lacanians suggest the importance of the mother-father-child triangle in provoking the emergence of language and subjectivity through the recognition of difference. We might make similar observations about the role of difference and triangles in Genesis 2–3. Before the interrogation scene in 3.8-13, characters interact in pairs, in spite of (or perhaps the precise reason for) the delayed mentioning of the man's presence in the serpent-woman scene in 3.1-6. After eating the fruit, the couple seems to recognize their differences in one another's presence (or to evaluate them differently), occasioning their covering.[1] It is their hearing of God in the garden, signaling the advent of a scene involving all three characters, that coincides with the man's and woman's increased subjectivity.

The questioning scene also emphasizes the necessity of language for communication. Though God may already know what has transpired in the garden, the narrator depicts God asking the humans about their actions. Perhaps God is asking for information, or maybe God wants to hear the man's and woman's interpretations of the recent events. Somehow, narrating or speaking the events, confessing their actions, is important for making these actions fully real for the humans. Language is how we make our private realities public. Communication, in this scene, is a rhetorical enterprise. God reminds the man that it was God ('I') who commanded the man and inquires of him 'who' the rhetor was who told him he was naked. The woman recognizes the serpent's persuasion of her when she responds that it 'tricked' her.

The social nature of language and the inevitability of communication and rhetoric also reveal the dangers inherent in language. Language is dangerous because it is powerful, because it involves interpretation and persuasion, because its effects are often unpredictable. The scene in Gen. 3.8-13 reveals the dangers of language. While the couple covered themselves from one another's eyes as soon as they had eaten the forbidden fruit, it is hearing God's voice in the garden that prompts their fearful hiding from God. Their covered nakedness in God's presence is

---

1. Or, if the covering was not prompted by a new or changed recognition of differences, it at least marks difference since now some parts of their bodies are covered while others are revealed.

now a symbol of their status as social beings. It may also be a sign of their own slyness.[1] Their clothing signals that they may repeat the serpent's subtle persuasion and their own crafty interpretations; it reminds them of their perpetual potential betrayal and mistrust of one another. The woman's perception of the serpent's trickery in 3.13 shows the potential danger of persuasion. By remarking that the serpent tricked her, the woman may be 'passing the buck' like the man, and she may also be understanding and acknowledging her misdeed (as I argued in the previous chapter). Whether excuse, confession, or both, the woman's remark about the serpent's trickery shows that she recognizes that there are consequences for her interpretation of the tree, for her acceptance of the serpent's persuasion. Language is potentially dangerous because its use requires responsibility and accountability, and it may have consequences beyond what we can envision. The woman certainly got more than the sustenance, beauty, and wisdom that she bargained for.

Language as Delights: Genesis 2.18-25

While the power and danger of language may subdue or terrify us, and its plural possibilities may confuse us or open our eyes, the multiplicity of language is also a source of delight. Double entendres, similes, metaphors, assonance, jokes, and puns all rely on the sounds and play of words, on the plurivocity of language. Through such word play, abundant in the garden narrative, we acknowledge the pain and power, the division and danger of linguistic rhetoric, but we also celebrate the pleasure of possibilities and the delicious delight of language. We learn to laugh at ourselves and to enjoy our misunderstandings. This discussion of how words play in the garden addresses primarily the creation of woman in 2.18-25, but incorporates references to linguistic play in the remainder of the narrative as well.

Fitting Ventures

God evaluates the situation in the garden in Gen. 2.18 and finds it 'not good' that the man is alone. This assessment may come as a surprise to readers of Genesis 1 who so regularly heard God there deem various aspects of creation 'good' and the whole 'very good'. The 'not good'

1.   Following the Hebrew pun on naked in 2.25 and shrewd/sly in 3.1, the couple's covering suggests they have been transformed from naked to shrewd.

here may be a signal, then, that creation is not finished. It also indicates that God is not an appropriate companion for the man, since God still considers the man to be alone, in spite of God's recent command to the man.[1] God decides to make the man a 'helper as his counterpart'. The Hebrew word *kᵉnegdô*, here translated counterpart, includes both likeness and opposition, the similarity and difference required for metaphor. The 'not good' echo of the goodness of creation in Genesis 1 and the combined likeness and opposition of the man's proposed partner provide verbal clues to the language games ahead.

In Gen. 2.19-20 the fitting ventures begin. Having initially formed the man from the ground by a pun in 2.7, *hā-ʾādām* from *hā-ʾᵃdāmâ*, God returns to the ground to form animals and birds. The man is certainly not alone after this process, especially since God brings all of these creatures to him for naming, but none of them quite fits. The man is beginning to take shape as a character, however, through his use of language. The narrator insists that the man names the newly formed creatures, and through this speech the man enters into the symbolic realm; he begins to fit in the world. Just how the man assigns names to animals we do not know. Is he like a child, delighting in new vocabulary, or is he more like a sophisticated scientist, organizing and classifying, fitting names to species? Is the ordering and assigning of words to living beings pleasurable for the man, or is it a chore? Whatever his attitude toward the project, the man in 2.19-20 shares some of the creative power and function that God exercised as both maker and namer in Genesis 1.[2] Perhaps God hoped that human ability to see goodness would accompany the man's naming role as it did for God in Genesis 1.

This-Woman Fleshed Out
Since the ground proved infertile as a source for a fitting counterpart for the man, God returns to the Genesis 1 tactic of separation, turning the man, like the ground from which he was taken, into a source of building material. After putting the man to sleep, God separates the man, transforming part of his rib or side into a woman. The woman, thus, is

1.   H.C. White observes that God and the man operate on different levels; see 'Direct and Third Person Discourse in the Narrative of the "Fall"', in Patte (ed.), *Genesis 2 and 3*, p. 94.

2.   M. Scriabine, 'La Genèse comme mythe du langage', chap. in *Au Carrefour de Thèbes* (Paris: Gallimard, 1977), p. 47 even suggests that the man may have breathed life into the animals as God did into the man.

both like and unlike the man. She is like him since she is also created by separation from another material; she is unlike him in what that material is. The man was taken from the ground, she from his flesh. Then in 2.22 God brings the woman, as God had brought the animals, to the man. The phrase 'brought...to the man' repeats a phrase from 2.19, just three verses earlier, whose obvious ending in this case, 'to see what he would call [her]', readers can be expected to supply.[1]

Just what the man calls the woman is what we hear next in 2.23. God's fleshing out of the woman certainly meets with the man's approval. He bursts into language, complete with poetry and pun. The man's poem recognizes both the similarity and difference of this fleshed-out woman. She is similar in being bone of his bone and flesh of his flesh. She is different in being distinct, separated from him, taken from him. The pun the man uses in the fabula to describe the woman echoes the narrator's pun in the story. The narrator describes God's creating man: *hā-ʾādām* from *hā-ʾᵃdāmâ*. In the man's pun too, the newly created being is related to its material source. The woman (*ʾiššâ*) is taken from the man (*ʾîš*).[2] The use of suffixes on Hebrew nouns to show feminine gender suggests an additional word play: though the words are from different roots, *ʾiššâ* sounds like a feminine form of the noun *ʾîš* Depending on the text one chooses to translate, a slightly different pun, based on possessive suffixes may be in order: the woman (*ʾiššâ*) might be taken from *her* man (*ʾîšāh*).[3]

Coupling

The creation is complete in Gen. 2.23 with the man's recognition of the importance of the human companionship God sought to provide in 2.18. The next two verses function to link the text to its audience and to move

1. See the discussion on pp. 100-102 about why the man should be considered to have named the woman in Genesis 2.

2. Galambush points out the reversal of grammatical genders as well. The masculine man (*hā-ʾādām*) was taken from the feminine ground (*hā-ʾᵃdāmâ*) in 2.7. Here the feminine (*ʾiššâ*) is taken from the masculine man (*ʾîš*) in 2.23. See her '*ʾādām* from *ʾᵃdāmâ*', p. 43.

3. A. Tosato maintains that 2.23 was changed to read 'from her man' in the late Persian period when 2.24 was added to support marital legislation: 'On Genesis 2:24'. *CBQ* 52 (1990), pp. 397, 398, 407, 409. This word play is clearly evident in 3.6 in any case, as H.C. White observes in '"Who Told You That You Were Naked?" Genesis 2,3', chap. in *Narration and Discourse in the Book of Genesis*, p. 136.

the story to its next phase. The aside to the narrator's audience in 2.24 is tied with the previous verse by the words man, woman, and flesh. It suggests that the companionship and material similarity expressed in the poem about the two humans in the story is the basis for subsequent human communal and sexual relationships. Humans will abandon their parents in order to join as one flesh physically and socially with their spouses.[1] The sexual connotations of this 'one flesh' become clearer in 2.25 as the narrator picks up the story again, commenting on the garden couple's nakedness. The narrator reverts to the earlier term *hā-ʾādām* for the man, suggesting that the same creature formed in 2.7 and his complement in the newly made woman are the characters with whom the story will continue.[2]

The narrator and onlooking readers are the first to discover the couple's nakedness, since their unclothed status is reported in 2.25. The narrator's comment at this point about the couple's unashamed nakedness subtly links them with the man's poem in 2.23 and with the narrator's aside in 2.24 about social and sexual customs. The innuendo tying the man and woman to the clinging, sexy, one-fleshness causes reader suspicions about the couple's activities to mount. Have the garden man and woman joined their bodies like the couple in the narrator's aside in 2.24? In 3.1 the language play continues as a new character is introduced via a pun on the couple's nakedness. They are naked (*ʿarûmmîm*) as the serpent is shrewd, cunning, or crafty (*ʿārûm*). The couple is smooth-skinned; the serpent, the narrator warns readers, is a smooth operator.[3]

Repetition

Repetition of words and phrases abounds in the narrative, reinforcing themes and ringing in the ears of listeners for pure joy in the sound of

1.   The narrator assumes a male–female coupling and reports the leaving and cleaving from the man's perspective.

2.   See my arguments on pp. 102-104 against Trible's claim that the meaning of *hā-ʾādām* changes as a result of the woman's creation. I concur with Galambush that the terms *ʾîš* and *ʾiššâ* are used as relational terms, roughly as 'husband' and 'wife'. (See 2.24; 3.16 and Galambush, '*ʾādām* from *ʾᵃdāmâ*', p. 36.) There is an imbalance, of course, in that *ʾiššâ* does double duty, also designating the woman of the story, while there is a separate word *hā-ʾādām* to designate the man.

3.   On smooth-skinned and smoother-tongued as an appropriate English rendering of the pun, see Bloom and Rosenberg, *The Book of J*, pp. 63 and 181. Strangely, Rosenberg uses smooth-skinned only in 3.10, not in 2.25.

language. One of the most common words in the story is 'eat', *>ākal*. It occurs twenty-three times in the narrative, almost exclusively in direct discourse.[1] The serpent's eating dust (3.14) may play on the man's being dust (3.19).[2] To eat or not to eat certainly seems to be a key question in this text. Adding to the emphasis are two other words with similar sounds: *kōl* occurs nineteen times[3] and *qōl*, 'sound' or 'voice', three times (3.8, 10, 17).

In addition to its interest in eating, the narrative also makes a display of body language. The story uses several bodily terms: (sur)face of ground (2.6), nostrils (2.7), four heads from the river (2.10), rib (2.21, 22), bones (2.23), and flesh (2.23, 24). The bodily references continue as the displayed bodies of Genesis 2 become knowing, covered and hiding bodies of Genesis 3. Their eyes are opened (3.7) as the serpent had predicted (3.5) because they ate fruit that was a delight to the eyes (3.6). The couple first covers their bodies from one another's sight (3.7), then hides them entirely from the newly embodied presence of God walking in the garden (3.8). Later God announces the serpent will go on its belly (3.14); head and heel will be struck (3.15); children will be born (3.16); faces will be sweaty (3.19); and God fears the knowing man's stretched out hand (3.22).

Other Word Plays

In addition to the puns noted above, where *hā->ādām* is made from *hā->ᵃdāmâ*, *>iššâ* is made from *>îš*, and naked and sly people are juxtaposed with a sly and crafty serpent, creative listeners may notice other ironies, assonance, and soundplays. Verbal ironies include God sending man out of the garden in 3.23 to avoid the man sending out his hand to eat from the tree of life (3.22). The man also hears the sound of God in the garden in 3.8 before God sentences him in 3.17 for hearing his wife.

---

1.   In direct discourse, *>ākal* appears nineteen times: 2.16 (×2),17(×2); 3.1, 2, 3, 5, 11 (×2), 12, 13, 14, 17(×3), 18, 19, 22. In the narrator's discourse, *>îš* appears four times: 2.9; 3:6(×3). P.D. Miller, Jr, sees the repetition of terms for eating in the actions and God's speech as signs that there is a correspondence between sin and judgment. See *Genesis 1–11: Studies in Structure and Theme* (JSOTSup, 8; Sheffield: JSOT Press, 1978), pp. 28-30.

2.   D. Louys, *Le jardin d'Eden: mythe fondateur de l'Occident* (Paris: Cerf, 1992), p. 153.

3.   This word is less obvious in English since it is translated according to context as 'all', 'any', 'no', 'whole', or 'every'; see 2:5 (×2), 6, 9, 11, 13, 16, 19 (×3), 20 (×2); 3:1 (×2), 14 (×3), 17, 20.

There is situational irony as well. Eating from a tree causes the couple's awareness of their nakedness, and it is precisely to the cover of the trees that the couple goes to hide this new-found awareness.[1]

The word plays are both aural and visual. The pain/toil/labor (*ʿiṣṣābōn* or *ʿeṣeb*) in 3.16-17 that resulted from the woman's and man's eating recalls the tree (*ʿēṣ*) that occasioned it.[2] The serpent is subtle (*ʿārûm*) in 3.1 and is cursed or banned (*ʾārûr*) in 3.14.[3] Given the similarity of the Hebrew consonants r (ר) and d (ד), one scholar has even suggested there may be a visual play on the naked (*ʿrm*) man (*ʾdm*) in 2.25.[4] The similarity between Eve's name (*ḥawwâ*) and living (*ḥāy*) is reflected in the etymology assigned to her name in 3.20.[5] Further word plays may include the surface similarity of the fig leaves in 3.7 to the pleasant tree in the preceding verse or perhaps to their newly opened eyes.[6] The play is visual between fig (תאנה) and pleasant (תאוה) and aural between fig (*tᵊʾēnâ*) and eyes (*ʿênê*). The sound of the hissing snake echoes in the woman's claim in 3.13 that the serpent tricked (*hiššîanî*) her.[7] There may even be an intertextual pun where the couple responds to the command in Gen. 1.28 to 'be fruitful' (*pᵊrû*) by sewing (*wayyitpᵊrû*) fig leaves together.[8]

In/Conclusion

Given the summaries of sections in the chapter, I keep this section brief. This chapter has had two simultaneous goals: to show that Genesis 2–3

1.   A.J. Hauser, 'Genesis 2–3: The Theme of Intimacy and Alienation' in D.J.A. Clines, P.R. Davies, and D.M. Gunn (eds.), *Art and Meaning: Rhetoric in Biblical Literature* (JSOTSup, 19; Sheffield: JSOT Press, 1982), p. 28.

2.   Hauser, 'Intimacy and Alienation', p. 32.

3.   Trible, *God and the Rhetoric*, p. 124.

4.   D. Damrosch, *The Narrative Covenant: Transformations of Genre in the Growth of Biblical Literature* (San Francisco: Harper & Row, 1987), p. 142.

5.   Bal, *Lethal Love*, p. 129 also suggests a possible visual play between the (unpointed) names of Eve (חוה) and YHWH (יהוה).

6.   R. Hinschberger, 'Une lecture synchronique de Gn 2–3', *RevScRel* 63 (1989), p. 8.

7.   J.W. Rosenberg, *The Harper Collins Study Bible* (New York: Harper Collins, 1993) annotation to Gen. 3.13.

8.   L. Brisman, *The Voice of Jacob: On the Composition of Genesis* (Bloomington: Indiana University Press, 1990), p. 6. Might a play on this verb also account for the introduction in 3.3, 6 of the word fruit (*pᵊrî*) not in the original command?

is interested in language and to uncover and describe the narrative strategies and the possible rhetorical effects of these strategies. The narrator's reticence has rhetorical effects. It makes assessing God's command difficult at the story level, and causes trouble at the text level in determining both whether the sentences are punishments and what is the overall rhetoric of the story. God and language are certainly powerful in this text, but their power is qualified by the rhetorical difficulties experienced by characters and readers. Study of quotation and repetition, of the interplay between direct discourse and narrative framing reveals that language offers genuine alternatives and multiple possibilities. It emphasizes the role of persuasion and interpretation that entail consequences and demand responsibility. Analysis of the use of pronouns in the garden narrative shows the emergence of the characters' different subjectivities and suggests reader participation in the dangerous social realm of language use and accountability. Finally, the delights of language are evident in the puns, word plays, and pleasure in the sounds of language of the Hebrew text. This aspect of the story is often overlooked as commentators seek more serious meanings for the narrative. The text's understanding of language is complex. The narrative recognizes the power and the possibilities of language as well as its dangers and delights.

Chapter 4

OUT OF EDEN—IDEOLOGIES, INTERTEXTS, AND DIFFERENCE

Previous chapters have demonstrated varieties of responses and potential interpretations of the garden narrative. Chapter 1 suggested multiple readerly questions. Chapter 2 showed that even feminist biblical scholars disagree about the significance of Gen. 3.16 and about whether to view the story as affirming the woman's intellectual rigor or to lament its thoroughgoing patriarchy. Chapter 3 focused on how Genesis 2–3 affects readers, exploring the narrative levels and techniques that contribute to its powerful rhetoric. Still, the story remains troubling and unsettled. Scholars disagree about the force of God's words in Gen. 3.14-19, and the narrative presents language ambiguously: as power, possibilities, danger, and delights.

The three chapters thus far have addressed Genesis 2–3 by considering readers, communities (feminist biblical scholars), and the rhetoric of texts, respectively. This chapter combines these ways of thinking about interpretation. It recognizes that as readers we come to the interpretive process with various life experiences. We hold (or perhaps better are held by) several ideologies, just as the ethical assumptions and goals we bring to the task of interpretation are shaped by communities to which we belong. Even the texts themselves are not unmarked by life, because the ways we are affected by them and how we understand them vary according to differing intertexts.

This chapter begins to ask why we are interpreting texts, particularly the Bible. What is at stake for us as individuals and as members of communities in the ways we prepare ourselves to hear and choose to interpret texts? By addressing 'difference' in this chapter, I suggest that issues and concerns of contemporary communities are appropriate conversation partners in reading the Bible. For feminists, the term 'difference' is a shorthand for gender, race, sexual orientation, class, ethnicity, age, ability and other material and socially constructed realities that affect our lives.[1] Before giving much theoretical attention to this topic, it is reasonable to ask whether Genesis is even interested in difference.

Interest in 'Difference'

While not, of course, sharing the nuances of contemporary discussions, the attention to separation, divisions, distinctions, and otherness in Genesis 1–3 suggests that questions about 'difference' arise from the text as well as from interpreters. Readers of the garden narrative are set up for thinking about difference by the attention to careful ordering in Genesis 1. Creation there occurs, at least in part, by means of separation. The poem contrasts day and night, sea and land. In addition to these opposites, God fashions things 'according to their kinds'. God distinguishes humanity from the rest of creation for a particular role and sets aside the sabbath as a special day.

Concern with difference persists in Genesis 2–3. Separations continue in this story: *ʾādām* from *ʾᵃdāmâ* and *ʾiššâ* from *ʾîš*. The river divides into branches, and the man makes distinctions by naming the animals. God puts in the middle of the garden the tree of the knowledge of good and evil, whose name holds the opposites good and evil in a tense unity. God insists on the value of making proper distinctions by singling out this tree as prohibited for human consumption. The man experiences similarity in difference from the woman. Creatures discuss human likeness or otherness from God, and the narrative portrays male-female difference. At the end of the story, God marks the couple by providing clothing and separates them from the garden.[2]

1.   For a survey of similarities and differences among women and the importance of attending to them, see J.B. Cole, 'Commonalities and Differences', in J.B. Cole (ed.), *All American Women: Lines that Divide, Ties That Bind* (New York: The Free Press, 1986), pp. 1-30.

2.   Scholars agree that 'difference' is a concern of Genesis 2–3. M. Bal says that it is 'differentiation that was at issue'. *Lethal Love: Feminist Literary Readings of Biblical Love Stories* (Bloomington and Indianapolis: Indiana University Press, 1987), p. 124. C.M. Carmichael insists that 'an overall concern with certain distinctions motivates the composition of the material': 'The Paradise Myth: Interpreting Without Jewish and Christian Spectacles', in P. Morris and D. Sawyer (eds.), *A Walk in the Garden: Biblical, Iconographical and Literary Images of Eden* (JSOTSup, 136; Sheffield: Sheffield Academic Press, 1992), p. 50. J.D. Crossan claims that the text is 'about the origins of differentiation and especially about the basic one between

My interest in 'difference' as a theme for this chapter arises not only from the text but also from feminist commitments. Because Genesis 2–3 has traditionally contributed to the scaffolding supporting what many feminists now view as the repressive institutions of 'compulsory hetero-sexuality' and socially constructed male dominance, it seems reasonable, perhaps even imperative, to converse with Genesis 2–3 about gender and difference.[1]

As in previous chapters, I begin with theoretical discussions that inform the subsequent readings of Genesis 2–3. I introduce, first, ideology and ideological criticism; second, textuality and intertextuality; and third, various feminist understandings of reality and 'difference'. Because of the complexity of this feminist scholarship and its relative unfamiliarity to most biblical scholars, this third discussion is somewhat longer than the others.

This chapter also revisits some themes of earlier chapters (knowledge, experience, and language) by considering them in relationship to the ways ideologies and intertexts help to create worldviews. After the theoretical discussion, I engage Genesis 2–3 together with several ideologies and intertexts. Feminist scholarship on gender and difference provides one key lens through which I read the Genesis text. Societal ideologies of sexism, racism, and heterosexism constrain our notions of reality and condition our awareness and responses to differences among humans. They also damage people's lives. As an attempt at ethical ideological interpretation for contemporary communities, I first read Genesis 2–3 in relation to ideologies about gender and difference. Next, by

divinity and humanity'. 'Response to White: Felix Culpa and Foenix Culprit', in D. Patte (ed.), *Genesis 2 and 3: Kaleidoscopic Structural Readings* (Semeia, 18; Chico, CA: Scholars Press, 1980), p. 110. D. Jobling views 'the beginning of conceptual differentiation as such' as a 'fall' in this story: *The Sense of Biblical Narrative: Structural Analyses in the Hebrew Bible II* (JSOTSup, 39; Sheffield: JSOT Press, 1986), p. 136. S. Niditch claims: 'The abiding underlying concern in Genesis 3 is the passage from absence of structure—and therefore lack of disharmony—to structure, reality, and differences that lead to enmity'. *Folklore and the Hebrew Bible* (Minneapolis: Fortress Press, 1993), p. 41. H.C. White argues that the 'issue here is the modality of the human's *relation* to differential knowledge'. *Narration and Discourse in the Book of Genesis* (Cambridge: Cambridge University Press, 1991), p. 135. W.H. Willimon suggests: 'The story of Adam and Eve is a story about the difference between being an animal and being human', *Sighing for Eden: Sin, Evil and the Christian Faith* (Nashville: Abingdon Press, 1985), p. 105.

1.   'Compulsory heterosexuality' is defined below.

reading the garden narrative in relation to Cain's story in Gen. 4.1-16 and with biblical wisdom literature, I explore alternatives for understanding our world(s) and our relationships with God.

Ideology: History and Application

Communities of faith may think that the term ideology should be kept as far away from Scripture as possible. Ideology has a bad reputation. While you and I may have beliefs and values, other people have ideologies. In one sense, the term is pejorative; it seems to connote something false. Yet ideologies may also seem neutral, perhaps even helpful. Feminism and environmentalism, for example, might be considered ideologies. While perhaps extreme at times, these movements may also be seen as working for appropriate social changes. Even if we do not participate in activist movements, we may recognize that the mass media plays a role in shaping our reactions and thoughts on a variety of issues. It may be seen as promulgating ideologies. So what is an ideology, and why talk about the Bible in terms of ideologies?

Origins and Marx's Use of the Term Ideology

The wide variety of definitions and connotations for the term ideology grows out of its fairly recent history. A French philosopher, Destutt de Tracy, coined the term in 1796.[1] One of a group, known as materialists, he wanted to found a new science of ideas. Ideology, the understanding of human intellectual faculties, was to be part of the task of zoology. This potentially positive connotation of ideology soon vanished. In the early nineteenth century, Napoleon used a version of the term in a derogatory fashion, referring to those he opposed as 'ideologues'. John Thompson describes this shift in the meaning of ideology.

> It ceased to refer only to the *science of ideas* and began to refer also to the *ideas themselves*, that is, to *a body of ideas which are alleged to be erroneous and divorced from the practical realities of political life*. The sense of the term also changed, for it could no longer lay claim unequivocally to the positive spirit of the Enlightenment. Ideology qua positive and preeminent science, worthy of the highest respect, gradually gave way to

---

1.   J.B. Thompson, *Ideology and Modern Culture: Critical Social Theory in the Era of Mass Communication* (Stanford: Stanford University Press, 1990), p. 29.

ideology *qua* abstract and illusory ideas, worthy only of derision and disdain.[1]

Ideology retained this negative sense as Marx developed the concept.

Marx used the term ideology in at least two different ways, neither positive. In 1845 in *The German Ideology* Marx and Engels used the term ideology polemically to chide their opponents, Hegelians, for disputing about ideas while doing nothing to change conditions in the real world. Thompson characterizes their use of the term this way: 'ideology, on this account, is a theoretical doctrine and activity which erroneously regards ideas as autonomous and efficacious and which fails to grasp the real conditions and characteristics of social-historical life'.[2] By 1859 ideology had become associated specifically with Marxist concerns about class. Thompson describes this Marxian understanding of ideology as 'a system of ideas which expresses the interests of the dominant class but which represents class relations in an illusory form'.[3] Thompson identifies a third conception of ideology, combining aspects of the previous two, as latent in Marxist thought, though never precisely used by Marx in this fashion.

> [I]deology is a system of representations which serves to sustain existing relations of class domination by orientating individuals towards the past rather than the future, or towards images and ideals which conceal class relations and detract from the collective pursuit of social change.[4]

In various ways, ideology has continued to be a key concept within Marxism.

Althusser and Ideological State Apparatuses

Perhaps the most influential use of ideology in recent Marxist thought is that of French theorist Louis Althusser, who combines aspects of Lacan's psychoanalytic theory with Saussure's linguistic structuralism. For Althusser, ideology, like Freud's unconscious, is eternal, though its manifestations in various particular ideologies may vary. Althusser builds on Marxist theory, seeking to explain the reproduction of the conditions of production. Like Marx, he assumes that an economic infrastructure provides a base on which a superstructure of politics, laws, and ideologies

---

1.   Thompson, *Ideology and Modern Culture*, p. 32, emphasis his.
2.   Thompson, *Ideology and Modern Culture*, p. 35.
3.   Thompson, *Ideology and Modern Culture*, p. 37.
4.   Thompson, *Ideology and Modern Culture*, p. 41.

is built. What Althusser refers to as 'state apparatuses' keep the State in power. Repressive state apparatuses (RSAs) are public institutions such as the government, law, army, police, courts, prisons, etc. that operate by violence and repression. While RSAs maintain some order and control, it is ideological state apparatuses (ISAs) that are most effective in ensuring that the State will be able to reproduce the relations of production. ISAs are multiple and distinct private institutions that function (sometimes in contradictory ways) through ideologies. They include 'Churches, Parties, Trade Unions, families, some schools, most newspapers, cultural ventures, etc.'[1]

Althusser considers the educational system, along with the family, to be the dominant ideological state apparatus in modern capitalist societies, filling a role once held by the church. While portraying themselves as neutral environments free of ideologies, schools in fact drum the ruling ideology into students, then eject them into production as 'the agents of exploitation (capitalists, managers), the agents of repression (soldiers, policemen, politicians, administrators, etc.) and the professional ideologists (priests of all sorts, most of whom are convinced 'laymen')'.[2]

Althusser insists that ideologies exist materially in their practices, yet the term ideology retains its negative flavor and its association with illusion. For Althusser, what an ideology does is to represent 'the imaginary relationship of individuals to their real conditions of existence'.[3] It does this through a process Althusser calls 'interpellation' or hailing. When a person responds to the hailing of an ideology, by recognizing herself as being summoned or addressed, she becomes a subject. Terry Eagleton describes this role of ideology in creating a subject.

> I come to feel, not exactly as though the world exists for me alone, but as though it is significantly 'centered' on me, and I in turn am significantly 'centered' on it. Ideology, for Althusser, is the set of beliefs and practices which does this centering. It is far more subtle, pervasive and unconscious than a set of explicit doctrines: it is the very medium in which I 'live out' my relation to society, the realm of signs and social practices which binds

---

1.   L. Althusser, 'Ideology and Ideological State Apparatuses', in D. Latimer (ed.), B. Brewster (trans.), *Contemporary Critical Theory* (San Diego: Harcourt Brace Jovanovich, 1989), p. 73; reprinted from *Lenin and Philosophy and Other Essays* (New York: Monthly Review Press, 1971).

2.   Althusser, 'Ideology and Ideological State Apparatuses', p. 82.

3.   Althusser, 'Ideology and Ideological State Apparatuses', p. 87.

me to the social structure and lends me a sense of coherent purpose and
identity.[1]

The function of an ideology, thus, is to constitute social subjects through
interpellation.[2]

Elizabeth Grosz provides a helpful summary of Althusser's theory of
ideology. Ideology comprises the institutional and cultural framework of
any society. It functions to produce social subjects out of biological 'raw
materials'. Thus, ideology is located in systems of ideas, beliefs, values
and practices, which are internalized and lived as true by the subject.
Because it expresses the unspoken values of the dominant class, ideology
is the distorted representation of real social relations.[3] From Althusser's
notion of ideology, it is not far to Alice Jardine's much quoted definition
of 'ideology as the conceptual glue of culture, that which makes cultural
seem natural, that which holds any cultural system together, that which,
in fact, makes any system of relationships appear natural'.[4] Though
ideology developed in connection with class relations in Marxism,
Althusser's understanding of ideology's naturalizing function makes the
term very useful for feminists. Feminists understand some ideologies as
functioning to maintain sexism.

Describing and Defining Ideology
From the preceding discussion it should be clear that ideology may be
'some kind of especially coherent and rigidly held system of political
ideas',[5] but it is not simply that. Ideology has fundamentally to do with
'what is "obvious"'.[6] It is both 'a guiding vision of future social action'[7]
and 'a generic term for the processes by which meaning is produced,

1.   T. Eagleton, *Literary Theory: An Introduction* (Minneapolis: University of
Minnesota, 1983), p. 172.
2.   Eagleton, *Literary Theory*, p. 96.
3.   E. Grosz, *Sexual Subversions: Three French Feminists* (Sydney and Boston:
Allen & Unwin, 1989), pp. 15-16. I have rearranged and organized as a paragraph,
while still quoting, several items from Grosz's list.
4.   A. Jardine, 'Death Sentences: Writing Couples and Ideology', in S.R.
Suleiman (ed.), *The Female Body in Western Culture: Contemporary Perspectives*
(Cambridge, MA: Harvard University Press, 1986), p. 85.
5.   J.H. Kavanaugh, 'Ideology', in F. Lentricchia and T. McLaughlin (eds.),
Critical Terms for Literary Study, (Chicago: University of Chicago Press, 1990),
p. 305.
6.   Kavanaugh, 'Ideology', p. 318
7.   M. Novak, 'Narrative and Ideology', *This World* 23 (Fall 1988), p. 73.

challenged, reproduced, transformed'.[1] Among various definitions, I find
John Thompson's formulation most helpful: 'to study ideology is to
study the ways in which meaning serves to establish and sustain relations
of domination'.[2] Thompson consciously retains a negative connotation
for ideology. He explains the consequences of his proposal.

> The concept of ideology, according to the formulation proposed here, calls
> our attention to the ways in which meaning is mobilized in the service of
> dominant individuals and groups, that is, the ways in which the meaning
> constructed and conveyed by symbolic forms serves, in particular circum-
> stances, to establish and sustain structured social relations from which
> some individuals and groups benefit more than others, and which some
> individuals and groups have an interest in preserving while others may
> seek to contest. The study of ideology, understood in this sense, thus
> plunges the analyst into a realm of meaning and power, of interpretation
> and counter-interpretation, where the object of analysis is a weapon
> employed in a battle carried out on the terrain of symbols and signs.[3]

Ideology, thus, involves recognizing naturalized social constructions of
'reality' in need of critique; the term serves as a shorthand for a host of
questions and concerns about what it is we should be doing, who gets to
decide, and on what basis (if any).

From this brief survey[4] it should be clear that ideologies are part of
everyday life for everyone, and that they may constrain or empower.[5]
The question is not whether we hold ideologies; we do. Rather, questions
concern how ideologies operate, whether by consent or through social
practices;[6] whether we embrace them critically or uncritically;[7] and,

1.   M. Barrett, 'Ideology and the Cultural Production of Gender', in J. Newton
and D. Rosenfelt (eds.), *Feminist Criticism and Social Change: Sex, Class and Race
in Literature and Culture*, (New York and London: Methuen, 1985), p. 73.

2.   Thompson, *Ideology and Modern Culture*, p. 56.

3.   Thompson, *Ideology and Modern Culture*, pp. 72-73.

4.   For more information on the history of ideology, such as K. Mannheim's
connecting it with utopias and the sociology of knowledge or the concern by the
Frankfurt school (e.g. Benjamin, Marcuse, Horkheimer, Adorno) with the role of
mass culture, see Thompson, *Ideology and Modern Culture* or T. Eagleton, *Ideology:
An Introduction* (London and New York: Verso, 1991).

5.   P. McLaren, 'On Ideology and Education: Critical Pedagogy and the Politics
of Education', *Social Text* 19/20 (1988), p. 179.

6.   Y. Zhao, 'The 'End of Ideology' Again? The Concept of Ideology in the Era
of Post-modern Theory', *Canadian Journal of Sociology/Cahiers canadiens de
sociologie* 18 (1993), p. 72.

7.   Novak, 'Narrative and Ideology', p. 74.

given the critiques of post-structuralism, whether it still makes sense to talk about ideologies as illusions or distortions (that is, presuming notions of truth and representation).[1] Even more critical than the discourse about ideology are the actual contests for determining or defining reality that such recognition of ideologies entails. Rosemary Hennessy observes: 'At issue is the entire ensemble of social relations the construction of reality maintains'.[2] Ideological struggle forges reality through a process Antonio Gramsci calls hegemony, a 'process whereby a ruling group comes to dominate by establishing the cultural common sense, that is, those values and beliefs that go without saying'.[3] If one agrees with Gramsci and ideological critics that reality itself is constructed, one will also observe 'slips or cracks' in the coherence of hegemonic discourse that open it to ideological critique.[4]

Ideological Criticism

Ideological criticism grows out of the relationship between ideology and meaning. It recognizes that all knowledge, and literary theory in particular, is political and interested, and that there are no 'innocent' readings. In fact, it argues that theories claiming purity 'are nowhere more clearly ideological than in their attempts to ignore history and politics altogether'.[5] The language of critique requires consciousness and aims at transformation; it recognizes that ideologies have consequences while acknowledging the impossibility of standing outside ideologies. Political theorist Gayatri Spivak explains: 'One cannot of course "choose" to step out of ideology. The most responsible "choice" seems to be to know it as best one can, recognize it as best one can, and, through one's necessarily inadequate interpretation, to work to change it'.[6] Ideological criticism exposes the ways that texts reflect the conditions of their production, how they function to reproduce particular interests as they are read, and how texts have been, and still serve as, agents of domination.[7]

1. Novak, 'Narrative and Ideology', p. 75.
2. R. Hennessy, 'Women's Lives/Feminist Knowledge: Feminist Standpoint as Ideology Critique', *Hypatia* 8, 1 (1993), p. 22.
3. Hennessy, 'Women's Lives/Feminist Knowledge', p. 22.
4. Hennessy, 'Women's Lives/Feminist Knowledge', p. 23.
5. Eagleton, *Literary Theory*, p. 195.
6. G.C. Spivak, 'The Politics of Interpretations', chap. in *In Other Worlds: Essays in Cultural Politics* (New York and London: Routledge, 1988), p. 120.
7. This threefold formulation loosely follows the task of analyzing literary

John Thompson's discussion of the modes of operation of ideology is helpful in engaging in these tasks of ideological criticism. Thompson offers a typology of five general modes of symbolic construction, each having a few typical strategies: legitimation (rationalization through narrative or universalizing), dissimulation (displacement, euphemism, trope), unification (standardization, symbolization of unity), fragmentation (differentiation, expurgation of the other), and reification (making natural, eternal, or nominal/passive).[1] Thompson's typology may facilitate the descriptive task of ideological critics, helping them 'to become conscious of how unnatural all of this naturalness is'.[2]

Such consciousness may also permit revolutionary and liberative counter-reading of texts,[3] but some biblical scholars have begun to ask whether exposing a text's ideological interests or performing an interpretive counter-reading of those interests should be the ultimate goal of biblical scholarship. They press ideological criticism's question 'Why is there a book of X, and what does it do to you if you read it?'[4] (about historical production and contemporary effects) to its logical end by asking whether it is time in biblical scholarship to move beyond interpretive description to evaluative critique. David Clines suggests 'Perhaps in fact the almost unchallenged assumption that the task of biblical scholars is essentially to *interpret* the text represents a systematic repression of our ethical instincts'.[5] Esther Fuchs agrees, charging that the paraphrasing of biblical exegetes serves only to re-encode the Bible's patriarchal sexual politics, sometimes in worse forms.[6] Elisabeth

ideological effects outlined by E. Balibar and P. Machery, 'On Literature as an Ideological Form', in R. Young (ed.), I. McLeod, J. Whitehead, and A. Wordsworth (trans.), *Untying the Text: A Post-Structuralist Reader* (Boston and London: Routledge & Kegan Paul, 1981), p. 93. For another influential proposal, see F. Jameson, 'On Interpretation: Literature as a Socially Symbolic Act', chap. in *The Political Unconscious: Narrative as Socially Symbolic Act* (Ithaca, NY: Cornell University Press, 1981), especially, pp. 76-77.

1. Thompson, *Ideology and Modern Culture*, p. 60.
2. G. Aichele, 'Text, Intertext, Ideology', paper presented at the SBL Ideological Criticism Group, Washington D.C., 22 November 1993, p. 4.
3. Aichele, 'Text, Intertext, Ideology', p. 7.
4. D.J.A. Clines, 'Possibilities and Priorities of Biblical Interpretation in an International Perspective', *Biblical Interpretation* 1 (1993), p. 85.
5. Clines, 'Possibilities and Priorities', p. 87.
6. E. Fuchs, 'Contemporary Biblical Literary Criticism: The Objective Phallacy', in V.L. Tollers and J. Maier (eds.), *Mappings of the Biblical Terrain: The Bible as*

Schüssler Fiorenza called for this move toward ethical scholarship in her 1987 Society of Biblical Literature presidential address,[1] and there are signs that scholars heard her call.[2] One of the key areas for ideological and ethical scholarship concerns meaning and postmodern notions of textuality.

Textuality and Intertextuality

Fish-ing for Text and Meaning

Stanley Fish's *Is There a Text in this Class?* is a good place to begin a theoretical discussion of text and meaning.[3] Fish's position is that a text is unstable (that is, that there is no text, per se, prior to interpretation) and that determinate meanings are unavailable.[4] Fish demonstrates this position by analyzing an initial misunderstanding by one of his English department colleagues. When one of Fish's former students asked this professor on the first day of a new term 'is there a text in this class?' he responded by telling her the title of the textbook. When she explained that this was not what she was asking about, the professor was able to shift his context of understanding to another category that Fish explains he already had. When the professor understood the student as 'one of Fish's victims' (that is, as having succumbed to Fish's notions about textuality), he was then able to answer the student's query as a question about literary theory.[5]

The point of Fish's example is that two different meanings of the

Text, (Lewisburg, PA: Bucknell University Press, 1990), pp. 134-42.

1.   E. Schüssler Fiorenza, 'The Ethics of Biblical Interpretation: Decentering Biblical Scholarship', *JBL* 107 (1988), pp. 3-17.

2.   See S. Fowl, 'The Ethics of Interpretation or What's Left Over After the Elimination of Meaning', in D.J.A. Clines, S. Fowl, and S. Porter (eds.), *The Bible in Three Dimensions: Essays in Celebration of Forty Years of Biblical Studies in the University of Sheffield* (JSOTSup, 87; Sheffield: Sheffield Academic Press, 1990), pp. 379-98; D. Patte, 'Textual Constraints, Ordinary Readings, and Critical Exegesis: An Androcritical Perspective', in R.C. Culley and R.B. Robinson (eds.), *Textual Determinacy: Part One* (Semeia, 62; Atlanta: Scholars Press, 1993), pp. 59-79; and a potential AAR/SBL consultation on Character Ethics and Biblical Interpretation.

3.   S. Fish, *Is There a Text in this Class?: The Authority of Interpretive Communities* (Cambridge, MA, and London: Harvard University Press, 1980). See discussion on pp. 13-15, 17 of Fish's reading strategies and ideas about interpretive communities.

4.   Fish, *Is There a Text in this Class?*, p. 305.

5.   Fish, *Is There a Text in this Class?*, p. 313.

question were both eventually available. Thus, it is conventions and institutional assumptions that constrain meanings, not simply willful interpreters who 'impose' them, as Fish's opponents complain.[1] In Fish's example, these two contexts might be called 'first day of class questions' and 'literary theory debates'.[2] Because Fish's colleague was familiar with both situations, he was able to shift his context of understanding from the first type to the second. The student's words are equally clear in either context; they are just clear differently.[3] This is why Fish claims that 'there are no determinate meanings and that the stability of the text is an illusion'.[4]

Fish insists that 'it is impossible even to think of a sentence independently of a context', and argues that meaning and context cannot be separated.[5] One does not first understand a sentence and then infer a context. Instead, 'one hears an utterance within, and not as a preliminary to determining, a knowledge of its purposes and concerns'.[6] The point of Fish's essay 'is that communication occurs within situations' and that 'meanings come already calculated...because language is always perceived, from the very first, within a structure of norms'.[7]

The same kind of constraints apply to overall interpretations of texts. While several theorists argue that if Fish is right then there are no norms to judge among interpretations, Fish claims that their position is on one level

> unassailable, but on another level it is finally beside the point. It is unassailable as a general and theoretical conclusion: the positing of context- or institution-specific norms surely rules out the possibility of a norm whose validity would be recognized by everyone, no matter what his situation. But it is beside the point for any particular individual, for since everyone is situated somewhere, there is no one for whom the absence of an asituational norm would be of any practical consequence... So that while it is generally true that to have many standards is to have none at all, it is not true for anyone in particular (for there is no one in a position to speak 'generally'), and therefore it is a truth of which one can say 'it doesn't matter'.[8]

1.   Fish, *Is There a Text in this Class?*, pp. 305-306.
2.   Fish, *Is There a Text in this Class?*, p. 307.
3.   Fish, *Is There a Text in this Class?*, p. 311.
4.   Fish, *Is There a Text in this Class?*, p. 312.
5.   Fish, *Is There a Text in this Class?*, p. 310.
6.   Fish, *Is There a Text in this Class?*, p. 310.
7.   Fish, *Is There a Text in this Class?*, p. 318.
8.   Fish, *Is There a Text in this Class?*, p. 319.

Thus, Fish attempts, ultimately, to console his readers. Solipsism and relativism are not the inevitable result of his position because, while one can speak generally of relativism, one cannot *be* a relativist.[1] Interpretation is thus already constrained by those interpretive communities within which we do our interpreting.

The logical conclusion to Fish's position is that texts come into being only as they are interpreted. Fish claims that a text and the constraints scholars presume to find in it are created by the conventions of the interpreting communities within which a text is read. There is no 'outside' on which critical theory can stand. Fish's quarrel with most scholars who oppose his views is that they want to treat a text separately from its interpretation, as if by existing prior to interpretation a text could provide a corrective or serve as the foundation for judging hermeneutical theories or individual interpretations. Fish argues persuasively that we can only appropriate a text through the lenses of the various interpretive communities to which we belong. A text has no separate existence from its communities of readers.[2]

Responding to a series of *Semeia* articles exploring questions of textual determinacy in biblical studies, Burke Long seems to agree with Fish. Long wonders whether textual constraints can be conceived apart from theory and reading,[3] and he suggests an explanation for our experience and talk about textual constraints.

> It may be that when *we* speak about the possibilities that a text offers, its constraints on allowable readings, that we mask in objectivist language our situational choices about what counts as constraint, or allowable possibility of meaning, in the first place. Perhaps the hermeneutical model, a text

1. Fish, *Is There a Text in this Class?*, p. 319.
2. For clarification of Fish's antifoundationalist position, see: *Doing What Comes Naturally: Change, Rhetoric, and the Practice of Theory in Literary and Legal Studies* (Durham, NC, and London: Duke University Press, 1989). S. Moore discusses the impact of Fish's claims for biblical studies in 'Negative Hermeneutics, Insubstantial Texts: S. Fish and the Biblical Interpreter', *JAAR* 54 (1986), pp. 707-19, and in *Literary Criticism and the Gospels: The Theoretical Challenge* (New Haven: Yale University Press, 1989). See also two essays in G.A. Phillips (ed.), *Poststructural Criticism and the Bible: Text/ History/ Discourse* (Semeia, 51; Atlanta: Scholars Press, 1990): F. Burnett's 'Postmodern Biblical Exegesis: The Eve of Historical Criticism', pp. 51-80 and A.K.M. Adam's 'The Sign of Jonah: A Fish-Eye View', pp. 178-91.
3. B.O. Long, 'Textual Determinacy: A Response', in Culley and Robinson (eds.), *Textual Determinacy*, p. 162, emphasis his.

offering possibilities of meaning to a meaning-creating reader, is best seen as a formulaic reduction of a dynamic interactive process in which our sense of objectivity attached to a text is already embedded in a process of reading.[1]

Meaning As Interpretation

As the above discussion suggests, how to talk about the way readers make meaning with texts is not obvious. It does not become easier when theorists use basic concepts like 'text' in dramatically different ways, but this is precisely the situation for intertextuality, which is based on 'text' being something other than simply words on a page.

Subtlest of All the Terms in the Field: Text. Roland Barthes explains this notion of textuality by contrasting 'work' and 'text'.[2] For Barthes, a 'work' is concrete; it is observable as an object. It was written by an author, can be held in the hand, and is meant for consumption. A 'text', in contrast, is a methodological field; it exists only as discourse, is experienced only as activity, as production. A text, as the etymology of the word suggests, is a tissue—a weave, web, mosaic, or network of irrecoverable quotations, which have long since lost their quotation marks.[3] A text is made of discourse and is polysemic. Thus, Barthes suggests (following the passage in Mark 5 about the demon), its name is Legion.[4] So textuality, as Barthes defines it, is always intertextuality: a text is composed of other texts. An example may help.

Thaïs Morgan's title 'Is there an intertext in this text?' demonstrates deliberately how textuality and intertextuality work in ordinary language.[5] Readers not familiar with Fish's influential essay 'Is there a text

---

1. Long, 'Textual Determinacy', p. 158.

2. R. Barthes, 'From Work to Text', in J.V. Harari (ed. and trans.), *Textual Strategies: Perspectives in Post-Structuralist Criticism* (Ithaca: Cornell University Press, 1979), pp. 73-81.

3. Barthes's point about text consisting of unmarked quotations is that all of the words and phrases we use are bits ¹ pieces of discourse, common language we have heard whose origins we have forgotten. For example, citations of all the essays I have read that describe 'text' using the words tissue, weave, web, mosaic or network would fill at least a page. These words have become part of the common discourse for talking about text à la Barthes.

4. Barthes, 'From Work to Text', p. 77.

5. T.E. Morgan, 'Is There an Intertext in This Text?: Literary and Interdisciplinary Approaches to Intertextuality', *American Journal of Semiotics* 3.4 (1985), pp. 1-40.

in this class?' may presume that Morgan is asking a straightforward question. Those who know Fish's essay, however, read a fuller text: they recognize first the nod to Fish, second the presumed answer 'yes' to the question, and third the playful self-reference thereby included in Morgan's title. The title also demonstrates another aspect of intertextuality: its relationship to discourse. Like the question to Fish's colleague on which it is based, Morgan's title changes in meaning as it is read by readers who are familiar with, or who do not know, the literary theoretical discourse about texts and textuality.

Defining Intertextuality. Because of the particular notion of text it implies, scholars should avoid using the word 'intertextuality' simply to be trendy.[1] The term was coined by Julia Kristeva and developed from her reading of Bakhtin's dialogism.[2] Intertextuality does not depend on authorial intent.[3] It should be distinguished from Lindbeck's proposal of intratextuality[4] and from studies of sources, influences, or redaction.[5] The Bible itself and Jewish midrashim on biblical texts may already be operating with notions of intertextuality.[6]

1. E. van Wolde, 'Trendy Intertextuality?', in S. Draisma (ed.), *Intertextuality in Biblical Writings: Essays in Honour of Bas van Iersel* (Kampen: Kok, 1989), pp. 43-49.

2. O. Miller, 'Intertextual Identity', in M.J. Valdés and O. Miller (eds.), *Identity of the Literary Text*, (Toronto: University of Toronto Press, 1985), p. 36. See also J. Kristeva, 'Word, Dialogue, and Novel', chap. in T. Gora, A. Jardine, and L.S. Roudiez (trans.), *Desire in Language: A Semiotic Approach to Literature and Art* (New York: Columbia University Press, 1980).

3. J. Frow, 'Intertextuality and Ontology', in M. Worton and J. Still (eds.), *Intertextuality: Theories and Practices* (Manchester: Manchester University Press, 1990), p. 46.

4. T.K. Beal describes intratextuality this way: 'Developed most fully by George Lindbeck (1984), intratextuality concerns the life (and life-giving force) of a text through a particular stream of confessional tradition... there is very little room in this theory for the work of the reader... Rather, that textual world/medium acts as a relatively autonomous structure which makes sense of the reader.' See Beal's 'Glossary', in D.N. Fewell (ed.), *Reading Between Texts: Intertextuality and the Hebrew Bible* (Louisville: Westminster/John Knox Press, 1992), p. 23.

5. Miller, 'Intertextual Identity', p. 19; and W.S. Vorster, 'Intertextuality and Redaktionsgeschichte', in Draisma (ed.), *Intertextuality in Biblical Writings*, p. 26.

6. See M. Fishbane's discussion of 'inner-biblical exegesis' in *Biblical Interpretation in Ancient Israel* (Oxford: Clarendon Press, 1985) and D. Boyarin, *Intertextuality and the Reading of Midrash* (Bloomington: Indiana University Press, 1990).

Thaïs Morgan provides a helpful review of the development of the ideas behind intertextuality and of the various theories currently in use. Morgan observes that

> the notion of intertextuality emerges from the cross-fertilization among several major European intellectual movements during the 1960's and 1970's, including Russian formalism, structural linguistics, psychoanalysis, Marxism, and deconstruction, at the least.[1]

Semiotics and structuralism require intertextuality because they presume formal connections among cultural domains. As structuralism's heir and nemesis, deconstruction's emphasis on deferment of signification makes it 'an iconoclastic theory of the *necessary intertextuality of all discourse*'.[2] While some theorists, like Kristeva, see intertextuality as a process governed ultimately by the reader, others posit a more text-driven model. For Michael Riffaterre, intertextuality may be obligatory. It is necessarily presupposed when a word does not make any usual sense in its particular context, but when the word's meaning in an intertext offers a solution.

> There is obligatory intertextuality, where the meaning of certain words of the text is neither that which language permits nor that which context demands but the sense that these words have in the intertext. It is the inacceptability of this sense in the language or in the context which constrains the reader to hypothesize a solution offered in a formal homologue of the text that he will try to decipher. The object is not an object of quotation; it is a presupposed object.[3]

The complexity of the various notions of intertextuality suggests that the term itself, like its meaning, transgresses boundaries as it spills over and avoids definition.[4] While we might define intertextuality broadly with Kristeva as 'the sum of knowledge that makes it possible for texts to have meaning', for the purposes of this chapter, Michael Riffaterre's general definition will suffice: 'Intertextuality is the perception, by the reader, of relationships between one work and others, which have [historically] preceded or followed it'.[5]

---

1. Morgan, 'Is There an Intertext in This Text?', p. 2.
2. Morgan, 'Is There an Intertext in This Text?', p. 17, emphasis his.
3. Miller, 'Intertextual Identity', pp. 30-31, citing Riffaterre, 'La trace de l'intertexte', *La Pensée* 215 (October 1980), p. 9 (my translation).
4. T.K. Beal, 'Ideology and Intertextuality: Surplus of Meaning and Controlling the Means of Production', in Fewell (ed.), *Reading Between Texts*, p. 37.

I use intertextuality in three different ways in this chapter as a means of identifying and addressing questions of the Genesis 2–3 text that are also held by its feminists interpreters. First, feminist scholarship on gender and difference serves as an intertext to help identify questions and sharpen critiques that feminists bring to traditional interpretations of the garden narrative. Second, I read Genesis 2–3 in relation to an obvious intertext, the Cain and Abel story in Gen. 4.1-16. Interpreting this text highlights key issues and develops themes that enhance the understanding of Genesis 2–3. Third, at a more theoretical level, I discuss feminist questions about knowledge, discourse, and reality, as posed by the garden narrative and feminist scholarship on difference, through an analysis of how wisdom literature addresses these same concerns. Before turning to these intertextual readings, I discuss feminist scholarship on difference, which provides a key ideology and intertext.

Defining and Describing 'Difference'

Given the origins of the feminist movement in women's recognitions that they are not treated equally with men, it comes as no surprise that feminist scholarship on the topic of 'difference' is voluminous. I have selected a few positions from the vast array. My choices represent a range of feminist thought about difference and contribute to subsequent readings of Genesis 2–3. I present the feminist scholarship here, offering little critique. The discussion begins with feminist analysis of the dominant worldview as a 'rape culture' or a system of 'compulsory heterosexuality'. Notions of women and gender arising from these constructs of reality are complicated by consideration of interlocking structures and the politics of difference.

Women and Rape Culture
In her two essays on 'Feminism, Marxism, Method, and the State', Catharine A. MacKinnon, a professor, lawyer, and post-marxist radical feminist theorist, analyzes women's sexuality in relation to male power, particularly in the context of rape and rape law.[1] MacKinnon argues that

---

5.   Miller, 'Intertextual Identity', citing Riffaterre, 'La trace', p. 4 (my translation).
1.   C.A. MacKinnon, 'Feminism, Marxism, Method, and the State: An Agenda for Theory', in N.O. Keohane, M.Z. Rosaldo, and B.C. Gelpi (eds.), *Feminist Theory: A Critique of Ideology* (Chicago: The University of Chicago Press, 1981,

sexuality organizes society, 'creating the social beings we know as women and men, as their relations create society'.[1] Sexuality is central to MacKinnon's feminist analysis of society because so many of the realities of women's lives are related to sex. She cites women's concerns about 'abortion, birth control, sterilization abuse, domestic battery, rape, incest, lesbianism, sexual harassment, prostitution, female sexual slavery, and pornography'.[2] Rather than seeing the domination that accompanies these practices as an alien imposition on sexuality, MacKinnon interprets reality from victims' experiences. As a result, she 'sees sexuality as a social sphere of male power of which forced sex is paradigmatic'.[3]

Under this analysis of society, women and women's sexuality are defined in relation to men. In her first essay, MacKinnon observes that women's sexuality is defined as 'the capacity to arouse desire in' men, and a woman 'is a being who identifies and is identified as one whose sexuality exists for someone else, who is socially male'.[4] These definitions lead MacKinnon to wonder whether women's sexuality and women even exist:

> If women are socially defined such that female sexuality cannot be lived or spoken or felt or even somatically sensed apart from its enforced definition, so that it *is* its own lack, then there is no such thing as a woman as such, there are only walking embodiments of men's projected needs.[5]

1982), pp. 1-30 and 'Feminism, Marxism, Method, and the State: Toward Feminist Jurisprudence', in D. Latimer (ed.), *Contemporary Critical Theory* (San Diego: Harcourt Brace Jovanovich, 1989), pp. 605-33. The essays are reprinted from *Signs: Journal of Women in Culture and Society* 7.3 (Spring 1982), pp. 515-44 and 8 (1983), pp. 635-58. I cite the first essay as 'Theory', and the second as 'Jurisprudence'.

1.   MacKinnon, 'Theory', p. 2. While I present MacKinnon's position here, G. Rubin offers a more nuanced understanding of the role of sexuality in societal organization. See 'The Traffic in Women: Notes on the "Political Economy" of Sex', in R.R. Reiter (ed.), *Toward an Anthropology of Women* (New York: Monthly Review Press, 1975), pp. 157-210. Rubin exegetes (her word) Lévi-Strauss's anthropology and Freud's psychoanalysis and concludes that kinship systems in various cultures organize sex/gender systems by means of a sexual division of labor. She defines the neutral concept of a sex/gender system as 'the set of arrangements by which a society transforms biological sexuality into products of human activity, and in which these transformed sexual needs are satisfied' (p. 159).

2.   MacKinnon, 'Theory', p. 15.

3.   MacKinnon, 'Jurisprudence', p. 618.

4.   MacKinnon, 'Theory', p. 19.

5.   MacKinnon, 'Theory', p. 20, emphasis hers.

In the second essay, MacKinnon's analysis of rape and rape law intensifies the definitions of women and gender. MacKinnon observes: 'Male and female are created through the eroticization of dominance and submission.'[1] She concurs with Susan Brownmiller in recognizing 'women's gender status as a function of rape... [because] the threat of rape benefits all men'.[2] Forced sex 'constitutes the social meaning of gender: "Rape is a man's act... and being raped is a woman's experience"', independently of whether the gender designations man and woman correspond to male or female persons.[3] 'To be rap*able*', MacKinnon discerns, 'defines what a woman *is*'.[4] She elaborates: 'Sex makes a woman a woman. Sex is what women are *for*'.[5] MacKinnon's language for defining women becomes more graphic and forceful as the essay progresses and her outrage at the social reality of rape and rape law increases: 'the more the sexual violation of women is routine... the more honestly women can be defined in terms of our fuckability'.[6]

MacKinnon is certainly aware that not all men are rapists and not all women are raped, and she recognizes that 'many (maybe even most) rapes involve honest men and violated women'.[7] But this is precisely the problem. In its designing and adjudicating of rape law, the state, as embodied in the law, is male.[8] In the law, rape is defined in male sexual terms, requiring penetration by the alleged perpetrator and lacking the victim's consent.[9] MacKinnon observes that since 'dominance is eroticized' and 'acceptable sex, in the legal perspective, can entail a lot of force', it becomes difficult, in a society of male dominance, to distinguish sex from rape.[10] As MacKinnon puts it, 'rape consented to is

1. MacKinnon, 'Jurisprudence', p. 605.
2. MacKinnon, 'Theory', p. 623, citing S. Brownmiller, *Against Our Will: Men, Women and Rape* (New York: Simon & Schuster, 1976), pp. 8, 196, 400-407, 427-36.
3. MacKinnon, 'Jurisprudence', pp. 623-4, citing C.M. Shafer and M. Frye, 'Rape and Respect', in M. Vetterling-Braggin, F.A. Elliston, and J. English (eds.), *Feminism and Philosophy* (Totawa, NJ: Littlefield, Adams & Co., 1977), p. 334.
4. MacKinnon, 'Jurisprudence', p. 624, emphasis hers.
5. MacKinnon, 'Jurisprudence', p. 626, emphasis hers.
6. MacKinnon, 'Jurisprudence', p. 628.
7. MacKinnon, 'Jurisprudence', p. 628.
8. MacKinnon, 'Jurisprudence', p. 625.
9. MacKinnon, 'Jurisprudence', p. 622.
10. MacKinnon, 'Jurisprudence', pp. 619, 622, 623.

intercourse'.[1] Consent, again, is determined from the man's perspective:

> When a rape prosecution is lost on a consent defense, the woman has not
> only failed to prove lack of consent, she is not considered to have been
> injured at all. Hermeneutically unpacked, read: because he did not perceive
> she did not want him, she was not violated. She had sex.[2]

The man's perspective, which may differ substantially from the woman's
regarding an alleged rape, is not seen as simply one perspective. Rather,
there is a conflict of meanings, and 'whether a contested interaction is
rape comes down to whose meaning wins'.[3] Rape law does not acknowledge the possibility that there are different realities involved for the
alleged assailant and the victim. MacKinnon reasons:

> The problem is this: the injury of rape lies in the meaning of the act to its
> victims, but the standard for its criminality lies in the meaning of the same
> act to the assailants. Rape is only an injury from women's point of view. It
> is only a crime from the male point of view, explicitly including that of the
> accused.[4]

What is at stake, for MacKinnon's theorizing, for rape victims, and
potentially in the Genesis garden narrative, is the nature of truth and
reality.

MacKinnon recognizes that the male perspective is systemic and
hegemonic, that reality itself is gendered, and that claims of objectivity
are, in fact, insistence on male dominance.

> The male perspective is systemic and hegemonic. The content of the
> signification 'woman' is the content of women's lives. Each sex has its
> role, but their stakes and power are not equal. If the sexes are unequal, and
> perspective participates in situation, there is no ungendered reality or
> ungendered perspective... In this context, objectivity—the nonsituated,
> universal standpoint, whether claimed or aspired to—is a denial of the
> existence or potency of sex inequality that tacitly participates in
> constructing reality from the dominant point of view.[5]

MacKinnon's key insight is that *'Power to create the world from one's
point of view is power in its male form'*.[6] She acknowledges male

1. MacKinnon, 'Jurisprudence', p. 622.
2. MacKinnon, 'Jurisprudence', p. 626.
3. MacKinnon, 'Jurisprudence', p. 625.
4. MacKinnon, 'Jurisprudence', p. 625.
5. MacKinnon, 'Jurisprudence', p. 606.
6. MacKinnon, 'Theory', p. 23, emphasis hers.

power, but displays it as a myth. 'Male power is real; it is just not what it claims to be, namely, the only reality. Male power is a myth that makes itself true'.[1] MacKinnon argues that feminism unmasks the myth of a single reality by exposing the production of truth in the service of power: 'Feminism distinctively as such comprehends that what counts as truth is produced in the interest of those with power to shape reality, and that this process is as pervasive as it is necessary as it is changeable'.[2] Such change in the production of truth and reality, especially in the context of law, is the implicit goal of MacKinnon's feminist theorizing. Feminism's task, then, is the exposure and renegotiation of ideologies.

Compulsory Heterosexuality and Lesbian Existence
The work of two lesbian feminist theorists, American poet Adrienne Rich and French novelist Monique Wittig, shapes the next portion of this discussion of difference. Like MacKinnon, these theorists work from experience, in this case lesbian experience, to question the unitary nature of reality. Wittig sees lesbian existence as a challenge to what she calls the 'straight mind', and Rich posits a 'lesbian continuum' to describe the various ways some women have always resisted what she calls 'compulsory heterosexuality'.[3]

Compulsory Heterosexuality. Though the term 'compulsory hetero-sexuality' is the basis for Rich's essay, she never defines it. Rather than defining it immediately, I first describe the presumed basis, nature, and effects of compulsory heterosexuality as the term is used or implied by Rich and Wittig. Compulsory heterosexuality, which its proponents understand as normal human sexuality, presumes a natural biological division between women and men. Since this view also assumes that sexual desire is heterosexual in nature, the opposition between male and female is thereby naturally produced. Lesbian existence prompts

1. MacKinnon, 'Theory', p. 28.
2. MacKinnon, 'Jurisprudence', p. 611.
3. M. Wittig, 'The Straight Mind', *Feminist Issues* 1.1 (Summer 1980), pp. 103-11; and A. Rich, 'Compulsory Heterosexuality and Lesbian Existence', in E. Abel and E.K. Abel (eds.), *The SIGNS Reader: Women, Gender & Scholarship* (Chicago and London: The University of Chicago Press, 1983), pp. 139-68. The essay is reprinted from *Signs: Journal of Women in Culture and Society* 5.4 (Summer 1980), pp. 631-60. Rich's essay has sparked considerable debate, particularly because sexual relations between women are not necessary for partic-ipation in her lesbian continuum.

theorists like Rich and Wittig to deny the validity of these presumptions. They contend, instead, that the division between men and women is not natural[1] and that it is men's oppression of women, which 'produces the doctrine of the difference between the sexes to justify this oppression'.[2] Heterosexuality is not natural, they insist; it is an ideology. Similarly, the 'heterosexualization of desire' and the consequent male/female opposition are productions of compulsory heterosexuality as a historically contingent social and political institution.[3]

Rich examines compulsory heterosexuality as an institution. She suggests that 'for women heterosexuality may not be a "preference" at all but something that has had to be imposed, managed, organized, propagandized, and maintained by force', an institution akin to capitalism and white supremacy that is 'maintained by a variety of forces, including both physical violence and false consciousness'.[4] Rich cites three pages worth of strictures related to compulsory heterosexuality that she contends men have used to control women.

Because of the cumulative effect of naming these practices, I summarize most of Rich's list here in a reorganized fashion.[5] Men have *controlled women physically and sexually* (even when the strictures are performed by women on other women or girls) through clitoridectomy, infibulation, and genital mutilation; chastity belts; punishment and death; unnecessary hysterectomy; rape; wife beating; incest; prostitution; harem; sexual violence; male control of abortion, contraception, and childbirth; enforced sterilization; female infanticide; and pimping. They have *exploited women* through arranged marriage; marriage and motherhood as unpaid production; token women; women as 'gifts'; bride price; pimping; women as entertainers; women's dressing for male titillation; women as call girls, 'bunnies', geishas, prostitutes, and even as

1. M. Wittig, 'One is not Born a Woman', *Feminist Issues* 1.2 (1981), p. 48.
2. Wittig, 'One is not Born a Woman', p. 53. G. Rubin argues differently in 'The Traffic in Women'. Gender is a 'product of the social relations of sexuality' (p. 179). It is one component of a culture's sex/gender system that can (but need not) result in a variety of oppressions. Most sex/gender systems do have a sexual division of labor, however, whose purpose, Lévi-Strauss concludes, 'is to insure the union of men and women by making the smallest viable economic unit contain at least one man and one woman' (p. 178).
3. J. Butler, *Gender Trouble: Feminism and the Subversion of Identity* (New York and London: Routledge, 1990), pp. 17, 115.
4. Rich, 'Compulsory Heterosexuality', p. 156.
5. Rich, 'Compulsory Heterosexuality', pp. 146-48.

secretaries. They have *controlled women* through the idealization of heterosexual romance; destroying documentation of lesbian existence; socialization that satisfaction of the male sexual 'drive' is a right; pornography; seizure of children from lesbian mothers; sexual harassment; enforced economic dependence of wives; witch persecutions; campaigns against midwives; male pursuits being valued more than female; erasure of female tradition; noneducation of females; sex-role stereotyping; male social/professional bonding; and discrimination in professions. They have *confined women* by means of rape as terrorism; purdah; foot binding; 'feminine' dress codes; the veil; and prescriptions of 'full-time' mothering.[1] Rich's linking of all of these practices to compulsory heterosexuality makes it clear why she deems this institution 'a beachhead of male dominance'.[2]

Perhaps the most striking characteristic of compulsory heterosexuality, is its hegemony. Wittig refers to a conglomerate of prevalent, unexamined philosophical and political categories of the social sciences that function like primitive concepts in what she terms 'the straight mind'. These categories 'concern "woman", "man", "sex", "difference", and all of the series of concepts which bear this mark, including such concepts as "history", "culture", and the "real"'.[3] Wittig characterizes the straight mind as universalizing its concepts into laws that are 'true for all societies, all epochs, all individuals'.[4] This universalizing tendency contributes to the hegemony of compulsory heterosexuality. It defines some people out of existence, as Judith Butler, a critic of Wittig's theory, observes:

> The cultural matrix through which gender identity has become intelligible requires that certain kinds of 'identities' cannot 'exist'—that is, those in which gender does not follow from sex and those in which the practices of desire do not 'follow' from either sex or gender. 'Follow' in this context is a political relation of entailment instituted by the cultural laws that

1.   I am aware that not all cultures view all of these practices negatively. Even women Rich would characterize as being controlled or exploited in these ways might disagree with her. For example, some women may prefer the veil and separation of men and women, as practiced in some Arab countries, to what they view as the dangerous flaunting of sexuality in the West. These women may also feel they exercise considerable power in the private sphere over such matters as arranged marriages.

2.   Rich, 'Compulsory Heterosexuality', p. 141.

3.   Wittig, 'Straight Mind', p. 107.

4.   Wittig, 'Straight Mind', p. 107.

establish and regulate the shape and meaning of sexuality. Indeed, precisely because certain kinds of 'gender identities' fail to conform to those norms of cultural intelligibility, they appear only as developmental failures or logical impossibilities from within that domain.[1]

The main effect of compulsory heterosexuality, according to Wittig and Rich, is oppression. Compulsory heterosexuality requires speech in its own terms;[2] it traps imaginations; it makes marriage seem imperative and inevitable; and it is powerful as a model for other oppressions.[3] It labels single women and widows deviant, and makes women's relation to men a near economic necessity, leading many women to market their attractiveness to men.[4]

Economically disadvantaged, women—whether waitresses or professors—endure sexual harassment to keep their jobs and learn to behave in a complaisantly and ingratiatingly heterosexual manner because they discover this is their true qualification for employment, whatever the job description.[5]

Compulsory heterosexuality simplifies prostitution and pimping and contributes to women's acceptance of incest and battery.[6] It renders the terrorism of rape 'natural' due to the presumably uncontrollable male sex drive.[7] Sanctions for nonparticipation, as in the witch burnings, include death.[8] Due to the bias of compulsory heterosexuality, lesbians, if they are not simply invisible, are deemed abhorrent or labeled deviant.[9]

Some qualifications and clarifications may seem appropriate at this point. First, the general societal expectation of heterosexual marriage is surely not as odious as Wittig and Rich make it seem. Her critic, Ann Ferguson, questions Rich's assumption 'that all heterosexual relations are coercive or compulsory relations'.[10] Some women happily choose and enjoy marriage. Rich would probably counter that their presumed

1. Butler, *Gender Trouble*, p. 17.
2. Wittig, 'Straight Mind', p. 105.
3. Rich, 'Compulsory Heterosexuality', pp. 148, 165, 168.
4. Rich, 'Compulsory Heterosexuality', pp. 142, 149-50.
5. Rich, 'Compulsory Heterosexuality', p. 150.
6. Rich, 'Compulsory Heterosexuality', p. 153.
7. Rich, 'Compulsory Heterosexuality', pp. 152-53.
8. Rich, 'Compulsory Heterosexuality', p. 144.
9. Rich, 'Compulsory Heterosexuality', p. 156.
10. A. Ferguson, J.N. Zita, and K.P. Addelson, 'On "Compulsory Heterosexuality and Lesbian Existence": Defining the Issues', in Keohane, *et al.* (eds.), *Feminist Theory*, p. 159.

choice indicates the hegemonic effectiveness of the institution. Second, neither Wittig nor Rich comments in any detail on the effects of compulsory heterosexuality on men. In fact, careful study of their essays reveals that they are not talking about heterosexuality as compulsory for *both* men and women, but simply its requirement for women.[1] In addition to its effects on women, the societal disdain and abuse of gay men suggest that compulsory heterosexuality might be more accurately defined as the ideology and accompanying societal practices that presume that all people are by nature heterosexual and should therefore behave sexually in accordance with that nature. What makes compulsory heterosexuality visible as an institution, at least to Wittig and Rich, is lesbian existence.

Lesbian Existence and 'Lesbian Continuum'. Lesbians are an anomaly in the hegemonic system of compulsory heterosexuality, and they are the model for resistance.[2] The fact that lesbians exist and may not desire men allows Rich to question the presumption of female heterosexuality. If heterosexuality is natural for women, Rich wonders why so many strictures are needed to keep it in place.[3] She postulates that compulsory heterosexuality might have grown out of men's need for access to women: 'men really fear... that women could be indifferent to them altogether, that men could be allowed sexual and emotional—therefore economic—access to women *only* on women's terms'.[4] Rich contends that the issue feminists need to address is 'the enforcement of hetero-sexuality for women as a means of assuring male right of physical, economical, and emotional access'.[5]

Lesbian existence is important in challenging compulsory hetero-sexuality, but what *is* lesbian existence? Rich and her critics agree on

1.   For discussion of accepted male homosexual practices in ancient Greece and modern Melanesia (contradicting the presumption of universal compulsory hetero-sexuality for men), see G. Moore, O.P., 'Nature and Sexual Differences', *New Blackfriars* 75.878 (January 1994), pp. 52-64.

2.   The remaining discussion refers primarily to lesbians, following Rich and Wittig. In many but not all cases, similar arguments could be made about gay men's relations to societal assumptions.

3.   Rich, 'Compulsory Heterosexuality', p. 145.

4.   Rich, 'Compulsory Heterosexuality', p. 151.

5.   Rich, 'Compulsory Heterosexuality', p. 155. Rubin suggests an alternate focus: feminism should seek 'elimination of the social system which creates sexism and gender'. See 'The Traffic in Women', p. 204.

what it is not. It is falsely conceived when the 'narrow conception of the institution of heterosexuality... defines lesbian existence as bedtime rebellion against compulsory coitus'.[1] It is not simply sexual preference,[2] nor do most lesbian feminists today consider it to be simply a personal, civil rights issue.[3] Lesbian existence is not adequately understood by the term 'gay' or when it is subsumed under male homosexuality.[4]

Rich broadens the scope of lesbian identity by positing a 'lesbian continuum' of women who have in some way resisted the strictures of compulsory heterosexuality.[5] Rich intends 'the term *lesbian continuum* to include a range—through each woman's life and throughout history—of woman-identified experience'.[6] She associates marriage resistance with the continuum and suggests that 'we can see ourselves as moving in and out of this continuum, whether we identify ourselves as lesbian or not'.[7] Ferguson infers from this concept that Rich would define lesbian identity as 'the sense of self of a woman bonded primarily to women who is sexually and emotionally independent of men'.[8]

While Rich's 'lesbian continuum' broadens the meaning of lesbian to include a wide spectrum of women, Monique Wittig claims: 'Lesbians are not women'.[9] It may sound as though Wittig is reinforcing the perception of compulsory heterosexuality that views lesbians in terms of a deviance concept.[10] Instead, Wittig recognizes sexual division itself and the term 'woman' as concepts of compulsory heterosexuality.

1. Zita, 'On "Compulsory Heterosexuality..."', p. 174.
2. Rich, 'Compulsory Heterosexuality', p. 140.
3. R. Hennessy, 'Queer Theory: A Review of the *differences* Special Issue and Wittig's *The Straight Mind*', *Signs: Journal of Women in Culture and Society* 18 (1993), p. 964.
4. Rich, 'Compulsory Heterosexuality', p. 145.
5. While Rich offers the concept of a lesbian continuum as potentially liberating for all women, whom she considers a wasted resource under compulsory heterosexuality (pp. 156,167), the appropriateness and usefulness of the term has been debated. Ferguson rejects it as ahistorical, 'On "Compulsory Heterosexuality..."', (p. 153), while Zita offers several reasons for its use (pp. 169-71,175).
6. Rich, 'Compulsory Heterosexuality', p. 156.
7. Rich, 'Compulsory Heterosexuality', p. 157; quote on p. 159.
8. Ferguson, 'On "Compulsory Heterosexuality..."', p. 148.
9. Wittig, 'Straight Mind', p. 110.
10. For a discussion of the use of deviance concepts in describing lesbians, see Addelson, 'On "Compulsory Heterosexuality"'.

Lesbian is the only concept I know of which is beyond the categories of sex (woman and man), because the designated subject (lesbian) is *not* a woman, either economically, or politically, or ideologically. For what makes a woman is a specific social relation to a man, a relation that we have previously called servitude, a relation which implies personal and physical obligation as well as economic obligation ('forced residence,' domestic corvée, conjugal duties, unlimited production of children, etc.), a relation which lesbians escape by refusing to become or to stay heterosexual.[1]

Rather than considering lesbians to be a third gender, Wittig sees them as problematizing the concepts of sex and gender.[2] The notion that lesbians are not 'real' women (whether from societal bias or Wittig's considered refusal) shows that 'woman' is a constructed category: it 'destroys the idea that women are a "natural group"'.[3]

Summary: Questioning 'Women' and 'Reality'

As we have seen, not all theorists agree on how to talk about women. MacKinnon understands gender as an oppressive male hegemonic construct: women as rapable. While not deriving gender from sex or considering either concept to be a purely physical category, MacKinnon's approach to sex and gender ties the two closely together. Wittig's approach, in contrast, views 'women' as a construction of the institution of compulsory heterosexuality. In fact, for Wittig, women are precisely those females who are closely related to men under this system. Lesbians, according to Wittig, because of their dissociation from men both sexually and economically, are *not* women. Rich does not refuse the label women for lesbians; rather, she broadens the notion of lesbian to include women who resist compulsory heterosexuality in any of several ways. Because of their ties to the construct of compulsory heterosexuality, both Wittig's and Rich's notions of women, like MacKinnon's, depend (even if through denial) on male/female opposition.

The arguments of MacKinnon, Rich, and Wittig agree at several points. First, sexuality, and male domination related to it, affect women's lives in many ways. Secondly, sexuality organizes society and what it means to be man and woman; in particular, sexual dominance determines maleness and femaleness. Thirdly, realities differ, even in what might be considered a single situation or event, for dominant and

1. Wittig, 'One is not Born a Woman', p. 53.
2. Butler, *Gender Trouble*, p. 113.
3. Wittig, 'One is not Born a Woman', pp. 47, 49.

oppressed. Fourthly, the presumed single (hegemonic) reality coincides with a male, heterosexual view. Finally, feminism, as it theorizes from the perspectives of victims and those on the margins, unmasks the socially constructed nature of 'reality' and its core concepts, such as woman, man, sex, gender, and difference. Determining how to understand and interpret 'reality' may be a question in the garden as well, as the serpent's question and conversation in Gen. 3.1-5 suggest.

Complicating 'Women'—Integrating Structures

The above discussion of reality and its key concepts by MacKinnon, Rich, Wittig, and their critics includes almost no mention of race or class.[1] Women of color broaden the category 'woman' by pointing out its racialized nature. They note that it has been and continues to be used by white women in ways that falsely universalize from white women's experience. White women experience their gender with coercive advantages and black women with oppressive torments under white supremacist patriarchy in the U.S.[2] African American writer and cultural critic, bell hooks, points out that

> It was a mark of race and class privilege, as well as the expression of freedom from the many constraints sexism places on working class women, that middle class white women were able to make their interests the primary focus of feminist movement and employ a rhetoric of commonality that made their condition synonymous with 'oppression.'[3]

Such false generalization is inappropriate because white women and women of color face different problems, as Audre Lorde poignantly observes.

1. MacKinnon, Rich, and their critics do acknowledge race as a factor of analysis, but they do so primarily in footnotes. It does not seem to shape their overall discussion of sexuality or the nature of oppression. Wittig does not address race in the essays I reviewed.

2. See the contrast D.S. Williams poses between patriarchy and demonarchy in 'The Color of Feminism: Or Speaking the Black Woman's Tongue', *Journal of Religious Thought* 43.1 (1986), p. 52: 'Patriarchy, *in its white institutional form*, can also be understood as the systemic governance of white women's lives by white women's fathers, brothers, and sons using care, protection, and privilege as instruments of social control. Demonarchy can be understood as the demonic governance of black women's lives by white male and white female ruled systems using racism, violence, violation, retardation, and death as instruments of social control'.

3. b. hooks, *Feminist Theory: From Margin to Center* (Boston: South End Press, 1984), p. 6.

Some problems we share as women, some we do not. You fear your
children will grow up to join the patriarchy and testify against you, we fear
our children will be dragged from a car and shot down in the street, and
you will turn your backs upon the reasons they are dying.[1]

Thus, 'women,' as the term has often been used by white feminists, is
partial.

Critiques by women of color suggest that while still basically dualist,
sex and gender are complicated by attention to race and class.[2] In spite
of the separate literatures that have developed around class, race,
gender, and sexual orientation, recent feminist theory insists on treating
these as interlocking systems rather than as separate features of a
person's identity that could be considered in isolation from one another.
Understanding these interrelated structures is vital, as Lorde contends:

As a Black lesbian feminist comfortable with the many different
ingredients of my identity, and a woman committed to racial and sexual
freedom from oppression, I find I am constantly being encouraged to
pluck out some one aspect of myself and present this as the meaningful
whole, eclipsing or denying the other parts of self. But this is a destructive
and fragmenting way to live.[3]

Tiana Arruda agrees. As a Latina lesbian, she laments the times she has
had to split herself into different people in order to do political work: 'I
would like to be who I am without having to prioritize oppressions, but I

1.   A. Lorde, 'Age, Race, Class, and Sex: Women Redefining Difference', chap.
in *Sister Outsider: Essays and Speeches by Audre Lorde* (Trumansburg, NY: The
Crossing Press, 1984), p. 119.
2.   For a careful discussion of the relationships among sex, race, class, and
gender, see E.V. Spelman, *Inessential Woman: Problems of Exclusion in Feminist
Thought* (Boston: Beacon Press, 1988). Spelman's analysis of gender in ancient
Greece leads her to propose a nondualistic approach to gender. She observes, for
example, that the categories 'women' and 'females' were distinct for Aristotle. Not
all females were women, nor were all males men. Rather a person's social class (as
slave, free, or citizen) determined whether the gender categories man and woman even
applied. For example, 'by "woman" Aristotle means the female companion of a
natural ruler, that is, a free woman, not a slave woman' (p. 41). Aristotle philoso-
phized in terms of more than two genders: men, women, and male and female slaves.
Similarly, to account for the ways in which race and class interact with gender in our
society, Spelman suggests that feminists should adopt a multiple and particular
understanding of gender (not, of course, limiting the category women solely to the
most privileged classes).
3.   Lorde, 'Age, Race, Class, and Sex', p. 120.

don't know if it is always possible'.[1] Class is also factor in this analysis—structuring the neighborhoods in which we live, our level of protection and isolation, the time we spend in leisure or survival tasks, and our access to education and perhaps interest in such abstract discussions.

Race, class, and sexual orientation are not *only* experiences of the nonwhite, the poor, or lesbians and gay men, they are also significant for white, middle-class, heterosexual women and men. Feminist scholarship has begun to recognize that notions of 'white' and 'race' are social constructions.[2] Similarly, both men and women are gendered, and they are gendered differently depending on their position in relation to other social categories. Having power and privilege to determine and *be* the norm is an issue in claims to invisibility that the use of the overgeneralizing term 'women' may imply.

Politics of 'Difference'

Whether and how we talk about difference is related to our response to

1. T. Arruda, 'How Can I Live a Life of Lies?' in J. Ramos (ed.), *Compañeras: Latina Lesbians (An Anthology)* (New York: Latina Lesbian History Project, 1987). See also M. Lugones's recent proposal advocating the intentionally blurred categories that the reality of *mestizaje* suggests: 'Purity, Impurity, and Separation', *Signs: Journal of Women in Culture and Society* 19 (1994), pp. 458-79. G. Anzaldúa addresses similar issues in *Borderlands La Frontera: The New Mestiza* (San Francisco: Spinsters/Aunt Lute, 1987).

2. R. Frankenberg analyzes 'whiteness' as a changing relational category, asymmetrically co-constructed with 'other racial and cultural categories, with class and with gender', *White Women, Race Matters: The Social Construction of Whiteness* (Minneapolis: University of Minnesota Press, 1993), p. 236. Whiteness involves 'dominance rather than subordination, normativity rather than marginality, and privilege rather than disadvantage' (p. 237). Whiteness 'changes over time and space' (p. 236) and thus has a material history that includes colonization in the U.S. and 'the significance of race in the shaping of U.S. society' (p. 9). Frankenberg argues that the daily realities of the social and political constructions of race and racism shape *white* women's daily lives. Peggy McIntosh's list of more than forty unearned advantages that she has daily as a white woman can help white women understand what we otherwise may not 'get' (as a result of our 'white privilege'). See 'White Privilege and Male Privilege: A Personal Account of Coming to See Correspondences through Work in Women's Studies' (Working Paper, no. 189, Wellesley College Center for Research on Women, Wellesley, MA). On the social construction of 'race', see also H.L. Gates, Jr, 'Editor's Introduction: Writing "Race" and the Difference It Makes', in H.L. Gates, Jr (ed.), *'Race', Writing, and Difference* (Chicago: University of Chicago, 1985), pp. 1-20.

differences. One's response is affected by societal values, for instance, whether race (as in the U.S.) or class (as in Britain) may be a more important factor in human interactions. It is theoretically possible, though highly unlikely, *not* to recognize difference. If differences are recognized, responses may range from destruction to celebration. Genocide and holocaust attempt to destroy others deemed to be 'different' (read inferior) in order to achieve purity or sameness (or for economic motives such as access to land or wealth). One may fear or loathe unequal 'others' or terrorize and exploit them through slavery, racism, and sexist oppression. Ignoring or misnaming difference serves primarily to maintain privileges of the dominant group. Denying the importance of differences, with the goal of equality as essential sameness, may be a pathetic pretense for a policy of assimilation. Activists may struggle for the elimination of socially constructed differences that oppress, or they may argue for equality defined as a strategic indifference to difference. Some people may agree to tolerate difference, provided this tolerance entails no changes or challenging of their privilege. Others may affirm or confront difference by welcoming others or celebrating difference. When we celebrate difference, bell hooks challenges us to think about who is throwing the party and whether serving as host functions to maintain privilege.[1] Another response is to attempt to relate across differences, forging solidarity and celebrating the richness of cultural varieties.[2]

Recently, difference and diversity have become popular, the 'politically correct' way to talk. Yet some theorists observe dangers, or at least ambivalence, in such talk about difference. Chief among the complaints is that difference talk is just a fad. Some privileged people argue against fadism, with the hope that talk about difference will soon disappear and we can get on with important matters (without needing to alter social systems of privilege). Others less privileged fear that difference talk is only lip service, a way to avoid implementing actual societal change. Critics of difference talk may argue that it is poorly theorized and that it, in fact, has little impact on those theories, such as

1. b. hooks, *Yearning: race, gender, and cultural politics* (Boston: South End Press, 1990), p. 54.
2. On forming alliances across a variety of differences, see L. Albrecht and R.M. Brewer (eds.), *Bridges of Power: Women's Multicultural Alliances* (Philadelphia: New Society Publishers, 1990).

postmodernism, which regularly employ it.[1] They may also worry that the elitist way much difference talk is carried out, for a very specialized audience and avoiding such politically concrete words as oppression, exploitation, domination, and struggle, further marginalizes people and misnames realities.[2] Difference talk is considered an 'escape to theory', a means to avoid the nuts and bolts work of transforming society,[3] or an unsuccessful attempt at using the 'master's tools' to do something they were never meant to do.[4] Perhaps worst, bell hooks charges that difference talk can simply be a mask:

> I am waiting for them to stop talking about the 'Other,' to stop even describing how important it is to be able to speak about difference. It is not just important what we speak about, but how and why we speak. Often this speech about the 'Other' is also a mask, an oppressive talk.[5]

When difference talk is not simply useless, a failure, or an escape, it may serve as a means of appropriation or exploitation. Difference talk in the U.S. has for centuries facilitated the economic exploitation of groups of slaves, immigrants, illegal aliens, or 'others' who served as forced or cheap surplus labor. When its goal, though acknowledging differences, is actually to reduce difference to an essential underlying sameness, as women or as humans, difference talk appropriates others in a way that preserves privilege. White feminists appropriate different others when we fail to acknowledge that it is women of color who have raised issues related to difference and when we demand that they teach us about their cultures or serve as tokens of otherness on panels and committees we have formed and organized without their leadership.[6] We exploit difference when we commodify blackness or sell Native American spirituality, when we treat others as exotic spice that we would like to taste. Cultural critic, bell hooks, describes how she began thinking and doing research for her essay 'Eating the Other' by talking

1.   hooks, *Yearning*, p. 24.

2.   hooks, *Yearning*, pp. 51, 54, 125.

3.   D.S. Williams, 'Womanist/Feminist Dialogue: Problems and Possibilities', *JFSR* 9.1-2 (1993), p. 69.

4.   A. Lorde, 'The Master's Tools Will never Dismantle the Master's House', chap. in *Sister Outsider: Essays and Speeches by Audre Lorde* (Trumansburg, NY: The Crossing Press, 1984).

5.   hooks, *Yearning*, p. 151.

6.   L. Bethel, 'What Chou Mean WE, White Girl?', *Conditions: Five* [The Black Women's Issue] 2.2 (1979), pp. 86-92.

to folks from various locations about whether they thought the focus on race, Otherness, and difference in mass culture was challenging racism. There was overall agreement that the message that acknowledgment and exploitation of racial difference can be pleasurable represents a breakthrough, a challenge to white supremacy, to various systems of domination. The over-riding fear is that cultural, ethnic, and racial differences will be continually commodified and offered up as new dishes to enhance the white palate—that the Other will be eaten, consumed, and forgotten.[1]

Because difference talk can be so easily used simplistically or in continued service of dominance, Spelman suggests 'dropping the word "difference" except under special conditions'.[2] Difference talk seems ambivalent. There is danger both in focusing on and in ignoring differences. Both assertion and denial of difference can facilitate domination. In this situation, perhaps what matters most is who determines the categories of difference that structure people's lives and what their purposes are.

In spite of the dangers of appropriation, many women of color continue to argue the importance of attending to and speaking about differences. Audre Lorde insists: 'Ignoring the differences of race between women and the implications of those differences presents the most serious threat to the mobilization of women's joint power'.[3] Categorization affects people's lives; difference matters. Differences shape our experiences and our understanding of our experiences.

Difference In and Out of the Garden

How does the previous theoretical discussion contribute to reading Genesis 2–3? The theory is all recent: understandings of ideologies, definitions of textuality and intertextuality, complications of women and gender due to awareness of rape culture, compulsory heterosexuality, unearned privilege, and differences of race and class oppressions. None of these notions would make sense in the same way in original settings of the garden story. But my concern is primarily with how Genesis 2–3 is read today, in contexts within which these matters are relevant, even crucial.

1. b. hooks, *Black Looks: Race and Representation* (Boston: South End Press, 1992), p. 39.
2. Spelman, *Inessential Woman*, p. 174.
3. Lorde, 'Age, Race, Class, and Sex', p. 117.

The garden narrative does not explicitly portray or address rape, lesbian existence, or matters of race and class.[1] It does, however, suggest particular notions of gender and ideologies about relations between men and women. It fashions a world where events have consequences, and it suggests the importance of construals of reality and of paying attention to the place of God in the construals. After a few brief hermeneutical remarks, in this section I first read Genesis 2–3 with feminist theories about difference as an intertext. Then, I relate the garden narrative to an obvious biblical intertext: the story about Cain and Abel.

Conversation, Contexts and Questions

How can we take contemporary theories about ideologies and the intertextual nature of texts into account when engaging a biblical text? David Tracy suggests conversing with the text as an appropriate hermeneutical strategy.[2] How might such a conversation occur? We might try to discern the settings of original hearers of the text, to discover what situations the text was confronting in the life of the community, and to unmask the ideologies of the text in addressing those situations. Several scholars take this historical approach and thereby enhance our understanding of the text's possibilities.[3]

---

1. C.B. Copher cites traditions that view 'the "Negro" as the beast of the field' in Gen. 3.1 and claim that 'Cain was turned black and became the ancestor of black peoples' in his essay 'The Black Presence in the Old Testament', in C.H. Felder (ed.), *Stony the Road we Trod: African American Biblical Interpretation* (Minneapolis: Fortress Press, 1991), pp. 148, 150. Race has been a far more prominent issue in the interpretation of Genesis 9–10. See Copher's essay; Felder, 'Race, Racism, and the Biblical Narratives'; and R.C. Bailey, 'Beyond Identification: The Use of Africans in Old Testament Poetry and Narratives', in *Stony the Road we Trod*. See also K.G. Cannon, 'Slave Ideology and Biblical Interpretation', in K.G. Cannon and E. Schüssler Fiorenza (eds.), *Interpretation for Liberation* (Semeia, 47; Atlanta: Scholars Press, 1989). More work needs to be done on how race and racism affect readings of biblical texts.

2. D. Tracy, *Plurality and Ambiguity: Hermeneutics, Religion, Hope* (San Francisco: Harper & Row, 1987).

3. Here are a few of the most recent proposals for ideological readings of Genesis 2–3 in its historical context. Carol Meyers reads the text as an etiology for the difficult life of pioneering agriculture: *Discovering Eve: Ancient Israelite Women in Context* (New York: Oxford University Press, 1988). S. Niditch reads it as a folktale about a lost community ideal: *Folklore*. J.M. Kennedy sees it as a rhetorical ploy to quench peasant rebellion: 'Peasants in Revolt: Political Allegory in Genesis 2–3', *JSOT* 47 (1990), pp. 3-14. A. Gardner views the text as a subtle warning

We might also converse with the many others who have been in conversation with Genesis 2–3 throughout the centuries between its original hearing and our own. This history of reception and interpretation of the text surely affects our readings as well, so familiarity with interpretations by sages and gnostics, rabbis, apostles, church fathers, and reformers contributes to contemporary understanding of the text.[1] The temptation may be to settle our reading on one of these original or subsequent hearings of the text. Our interpretive task is then delimited to historical study followed by attempts to shape our own imaginations in ways that fit the settings and meanings we discern through this investigation. For example, Christians might take the New Testament times and interpretations of Genesis 2–3 as the canonically normative period and reading. One problem with adopting this approach is that it may lead simply to attempts on our part to 'play first century Bible-land'.[2] This is something that late twentieth century Christians cannot do. Playing tenth or sixth century BCE Israel would be even more difficult.

Yet, the centuries and changes separating our world from the ancient hearers of this text, together with our historical consciousness of this separation, do not make interpretation impossible. They simply suggest that trying to reshape our imaginations into those of premodern Hebrew cultures may not be the most useful approach to reading a text for contemporary communities. Attempts to make past situations and answers fit today's circumstances and questions may be doomed to fail, but questions raised by the text in its original and subsequent contexts

against foreign idol worship: 'Genesis 2.4b-3: A Mythological Paradigm of Sexuality or of the Religious History of Pre-exilic Israel?', *SJT* 43 (1990), pp. 1-18. D. Carr proposes a redactional argument in which the final form of the text aims to undermine wisdom by rewriting an earlier creation story in Genesis 2*: 'The Politics of Textual Subversion: A Diachronic Perspective on the Garden of Eden Story', *JBL* 112 (1993), pp. 577-95.

   1.   See J. Hick, *Evil and the God of Love* (San Francisco: Harper & Row, 1978) and essays by S.N. Lambden, P.S. Alexander, and P. Morris in *A Walk in the Garden* (see bibliography for titles). For a concise summary of the early history of interpretation, see my 'Eve through Several Lenses: Truth in 1 Timothy 2.8-15', in A. Brenner (ed.), *A Feminist Companion to the Hebrew Bible in the New Testament* (Sheffield: Sheffield Academic Press, forthcoming).

   2.   A quip attributed to K. Stendahl by J. Plaskow 'Anti-Judaism in Feminist Christian Interpretation', in E. Schüssler Fiorenza (ed.), *Searching the Scriptures Volume One: A Feminist Introduction* (New York: Crossroad, 1993), p. 123.

may persist. In addition to looking for analogies between former and present contexts and perhaps endeavoring to apply ancient answers to modern and postmodern situations, we might also investigate these questions themselves. An interpretive strategy may emerge from the process. We may learn ways the biblical text speaks to our time and questions by considering how the ancient text raised and responded to similar questions in its own time. We may also need to consider questions and be in conversation with the ancient text about questions and contexts its original audiences could never have imagined. We converse with the text, as Tracy suggests, about its questions and our own.

The standard Christian creation-fall interpretation of Genesis 2–3 emphasizes humanity's relationship with God, as well it should. It leads to questions such as: How are humans like and unlike God? How are we related to God? Can we dare to question God, and with what consequences? How can we combine our experience of the world with what we know of and from God? But the text is surely interested in other matters as well, especially in biblical anthropology. What does it mean to be a man? to be a woman? to be creatures of God? What are human vocations? How are men and women similar, yet different? How are humans related to one another, to creation, and to God? How do human sexual desires work, and why are they so potent? Why is language so delightful? so dangerous? How does language shape our world? Why are words so powerful? How do they hold so many possibilities? How do we make choices? How do we live with the consequences of those choices? Why is bearing and sustaining life so difficult? What is lifegiving? We may also want to ask related questions beyond what the text directly prompts. What is the nature of reality? Do words affect people differently in different communities? How do race and class differences affect our lives and our hearing and interpretation of texts?

Different interpretations suit different ancient and modern communities. For example, African villages struggling to survive on an increasingly deforested land may well hear Genesis 2–3 in ways similar to the early pioneering agricultural communities that Carol Meyers posits were original hearers of the text.[1] For them, the emphasis on eating may speak to a contemporary concern: it may rightly shape their reading of the text. But other contemporary communities need other

---

1.   See C. Meyers, *Discovering Eve*, and M. Oduyoye, *The Sons of the Gods and the Daughters of Men: An Afro-Asiatic Interpretation of Genesis 1–11* (Maryknoll, NY: Orbis Books, 1984).

interpretations. Different readings of the text reflect our varied assessments of what constitutes our most urgent problems. Though our questions may parallel those of a text's first audiences, so that those questions are in some way timeless, the most helpful readings of the text will also address particular situations. They will be timely as well as timeless.

By discussing rape, compulsory heterosexuality, and the dangers of oversimplifying difference, I have suggested that I think some of the most urgent problems currently facing U.S. society are related to gender, race, class, and sexual orientation. These problems concern how we organize society and the ways we categorize people either too quickly, on the basis of socially constructed distinctions, or with insufficient attention to the overlapping and interlocking character of the real historical and lived differences among us. Feminist scholarship on gender and difference serves as an intertext for the following reading of Genesis 2–3.

Gender and Difference in the Garden

Fashioning Compulsory Heterosexuality. Standard theological interpretations of Genesis 2–3 have not emphasized the gender relationships presumed by the story or its interpreters.[1] Yet, when questions about human sexuality become matters for the attention of faith communities, appeals are made to Genesis 1–3. The general presumption is that these texts express a clear understanding of gender differences and that they provide a divine imprimatur solely for sexual relations between one man and one woman under the God-given estate of marriage. Does Genesis 1–3 establish marriage as part of God's created order? While I do not wish to argue against the importance of marriage, I suggest that basing the institution on a divine mandate in Genesis 1–3 is tenuous.

Genesis 1 portrays God as concerned with creation of the entire universe. The earth, sky, and seas are filled with plants, birds, fish, animals, and humans, each according to its kind. God blesses and mandates fertility for all species, urging them to fill earth and seas. Reproduction is certainly created by God and of concern to God, but at a species level. Humankind's creation in terms of male and female in Gen. 1.27 is not necessarily describing an individual human couple. Creation as males and females ensures reproduction; it enables the human race to fulfill God's command in 1.28 to 'be fruitful and

---

1. With the exception of feminist interpretation, of course. See Chapter 2.

multiply'. A single couple could not fill the earth. God is not instituting marriage in Genesis 1, or insisting on individual sexual relationships solely between one man and one woman. God is enabling and commanding the reproduction of the human species.[1]

Genesis 2, however, is clearly a one man and one woman story, but God may not have marriage in mind here either. God is concerned that the man is alone and wants to make a helper and counterpart for him. Companionship seems to be at least part of what is at issue. God's company is insufficient: God is unwilling or unable to be an appropriate helper and counterpart for the man. Another creature is needed. Yet God does not seem to know (or at least is willing to relinquish decision about) what the right creature will be.

Rather than beginning immediately with a woman decked out in bridal regalia,[2] God starts with animals. This is hardly what one would expect if marriage was God's intent, but furry friends seem quite reasonable if companionship is one of the goals. Moreover, it seems that the man makes the choice. The animals will not do, apparently, so God goes back to the drawing board and after considerable effort comes up with a woman. Note that God does not seem sure that the woman is what the man needs either: God brings the woman to the man as God brought the animals, presumably to see how he will respond. This lack of certainty about the woman's appropriateness seems unlikely for a deity in the process of fashioning heterosexual marriage as the sole appropriate institution for sexual human beings.

Furthermore, when the woman is found to be satisfactory, there is no divine command or blessing to be fruitful and multiply.[3] In fact, there is no divine response of any kind to the man's acclamation: no approbation, no congratulations, not even a tacit acceptance. God seems to be off stage. The narrator, in 2.24, certainly does promote a picture of sexual union within a social institution.[4] The narrator has shaped the

1. For further discussion of this position see P. Bird, '"Male and Female He Created Them": Gen. 1.27b in the Context of the Priestly Account of Creation', *HTR* 74 (1981), pp. 129-59.

2. The rabbis note that God dressed up the woman like a bride and brought her to the man (*Gen. R.* 18.1), an image G. von Rad picks up as well: *Genesis: A Commentary* (Philadelphia: The Westminster Press, rev. edn, 1972), p. 84.

3. Granted, that message was part of another story, but its absence here might suggest, at least, that procreation is not a major goal of this story at this point in the narrative.

4. Our English translators betray the Hebrew's assumptions and their own at

Genesis 2 story toward a climax in 2.24 that serves ideologically to naturalize men's attraction toward and sexual union with women. But if marriage as a created order is what God is after in this chapter, why does God follow such a circuitous route in bringing woman and man together, and why is God's response to the man's elation and God's approval of their coupling not noted?

Perhaps Genesis 3 is needed to clarify the requirement of heterosexual marriage. The woman, when the narrator allows her to speak, does not presume that she exists solely in relation to man. She is quite willing to converse with the serpent, unperturbed by what the man with her might think of her actions. This might place the first woman on Rich's 'lesbian continuum' since she is acting somewhat independently of man. She would not, of course, be a 'lesbian' by Wittig's definition, since it is not clear that she is rebelling against compulsory heterosexuality. In fact, it is not clear that this way of organizing society has yet been firmly established. It may seem to some readers, however, that God later prescribes a version of 'couch therapy' for Rich's budding lesbian.[1]

It is Gen. 3.16 that perhaps most strongly contributes to the case for heterosexual marriage, or to the institution of compulsory heterosexuality, depending on how you look at it. God has already announced hierarchy in 3.14 in his curse of the serpent. To this God adds enmity and battering: the mutual striking of 3.15. These situations apply not simply to the woman and the serpent in the story, but continue through their offspring to future generations. Then in 3.16 God increases the woman's pains (that she has not yet felt?) in childbearing. Thus, pain and children are associated a second time. It is hard to imagine that a woman

---

this point. They generally use the term 'wife' in 2.24 and 2.25, while the Hebrew word *'iššâ* for woman/wife remains the same throughout the two verses. There are at least two subtleties we might observe from this translational issue. First, Hebrew sees no need to distinguish between 'woman' and 'wife'. The assumptions of the culture were apparently that being a wife was the appropriate state for a woman, so no confusion ensues by using the same word for both. (A similar dual function applies to the single word *'iš* used here for 'man' and 'husband'.) Secondly, the English translations betray a theology that is promoting heterosexual marriage. By using the term 'wife' both in 2.24 (in the narrator's aside about the norm of marriage in his culture) and in 2.25 (when we have returned to the story of the garden man and woman) the translators suggest that this first human couple was somehow married as well, at least by 2.25.

1. 'Couch therapy' is an unofficial term for the practice of using forced heterosexual intercourse to attempt to alter a gay man's or lesbian's sexual orientation.

would choose such a scenario, yet this is precisely what God claims: woman's desire is for her man, even though it is tied with his rule over her. As MacKinnon would describe it, 'dominance is eroticized'.[1] For what or to whom was the woman's desire previously? It sounds new in 3.16, as if it were not initially for her man. A glance back at 3.6 suggests that woman's desire was originally for sustenance, beauty, and wisdom. Does 3.16 constitute the creation of compulsory heterosexuality as Rich has described it: the arranging, pretending, designing, and punishing that requires or compels woman to be fertile in her desire for man in a situation of male dominance?

If we step back from the text to consider possible ideologies of the human authors, there seems to be a clear attempt, here, to put women in their place, which is essentially barefoot and pregnant. The woman is defined as having babies, desiring her man, and living under his control. She seems no longer to be the thinking woman who acts independently of man as she did in 3.1-6. She has been stripped, ideologically naked, of that independent persona. Portraying woman this way, through divine punishment, suggests several possibilities. First, this is woman's lot in life. Second, she brought this situation on herself by her own actions (in spite of the absence of 'because you have...' in 3.16). Third, this female lot is ongoing. (We infer the 'all the days of your life' from the surrounding passages.) Fourth, perhaps no reason was required since this situation for women was natural or obvious. Fifth, the generic names 'man' and 'woman' used throughout the text suggest that the punishment in 3.16 applies to all women. The narrator tells the story as if this verse describes God's current, if not original, intent for women as a group. The story seems to suggest either that God designed the world with compulsory heterosexuality in mind or that God created a world in which it could result from human actions. God's sanctioning of the situation, whether or not God is pleased with it, remains.

This discussion, informed by feminist ideological analysis, suggests avoiding, or only cautiously using, Genesis 1–3 as support for the limitation of acceptable sexual relations to those of heterosexual marriage. One cannot reasonably claim these chapters as unambiguously support-ing a loving, mutual relationship between husband and wife as the setting in which those sanctioned sexual relations occur. Instead, mutuality is absent throughout the story. Marriage is constructed by the narrator, and from a man's perspective in Gen. 2.24. The description of

---

1.   MacKinnon, 'Jurisprudence', p. 623, and see discussion above.

male/female sexual relations in Gen. 3.16 contributes to the 'eroticization of dominance' that leads feminists like MacKinnon to claim that, in our culture, rape and sexual intercourse are indistinguishable. Such a confusion results, as MacKinnon observes, from adopting a male view of reality as the norm.

Producing Gender and Reality. I am suggesting that one of the ideological functions of the garden narrative may be precisely to construct reality and gender from a male perspective and to treat the resulting concepts as natural and therefore not to be questioned but assumed. This construction of reality has several features that persist in the present day social relations of what feminists call patriarchy.[1] First, the man is the norm for humanity. He is formed first and is the center of God's and the narrative's attention.[2] Secondly, the man's perspective on reality is God-given; it is the way things are. The man becomes a co-creator, of sorts, with God, ordering reality through his naming of the animals. His gaze, determining woman and appraising woman's desirability, is affirmed by the narrator.

Thirdly, woman is 'other' and body. She is defined only in relation to man; she has no independent vocation other than to be his helper and to rectify the situation of his aloneness. The woman is created precisely in the terms MacKinnon described: she is by design a 'walking embodi-ment of the man's projected needs'.[3] The woman's physical existence as body is perceived by the man as deriving *from* him and by the narrator as existing *for* the man. This physical male/female difference is established as natural and significant because it needs covering once the couple's eyes are opened. In this way, the narrator proposes gender not as a construct, but as a natural result of biological sex characteristics.

---

1.   Though the Genesis text leads to discussions of patriarchy primarily in terms of gender, feminist theorists argue for understanding 'the term in the classical sense, specifically, as a complex pyramidal political structure of dominance and subordi-nation, stratified by gender, race, class, religious and cultural taxonomies and other historical formations of domination'. This is E. Schüssler Fiorenza's definition, building on the work of S. Walby, who 'understands patriarchy as a complex system of interrelated social structures'. See Schüssler Fiorenza, *But She Said: Feminist Practices of Biblical Interpretation* (Boston: Beacon, 1992), pp. 115, 241; and S. Walby, *Patriarchy at Work: Patriarchal and Capitalist Relations in Employment* (Minneapolis: University of Minnesota Press, 1986).

2.   For support of this claim, see the discussion in Chapter 2.

3.   Modified to singular from MacKinnon, 'Theory', p. 20.

Fourthly, the story demonstrates that woman's perception of reality is wrong. Her acceptance of the serpent's alternate version of reality is dismissed implicitly through the immediate unwelcome consequences of the couple's eating and explicitly in 3.17-19 when God punishes the man precisely for having listened to her.[1] Fifthly, as described in the discussion above, the reality that some feminists would call 'compulsory heterosexuality' is God-given. Further, there is no narrator's report of God's sorrow about this human condition. In contrast to God's disappointment and grief at human wickedness in Gen. 6.5-6, God expresses no remorse at human behavior or the hierarchies God has newly described for their ongoing life together.[2] Instead, Gen. 3.16 seems to offer striking support for MacKinnon's portrayal of how women as a gender are constructed under compulsory heterosexuality: 'Sex makes a woman a woman. Sex is what women are *for*'.[3]

Producing such an understanding of gender relations as 'reality' seems to be one of the ideological functions of the story. Yet this reality is undermined, by the story itself, as being the *sole* reality. Several features of the narrative recognize this portrayal as a construction: it is not the only way reality could be conceived. Gender is a production, perhaps one whose performance could be changed.

How is the constructed nature of this reality glimpsed in Genesis 2–3? First, the story reveals the narrator's successful defining power to be a construction by contrasting it with the woman's unsuccessful attempt at perceiving reality. The narrator's construction of the world achieves its status as appropriate, in part, because the woman's does not. The existence within the story of *two* realities, rather than one, indirectly suggests the constructed nature of at least one of them.

Secondly, the opposites embedded in the phrase 'knowledge of good and evil' imply that difference exists, if not actual duality. The hegemony of a single construal of reality is not complete if alternatives can be

---

1. See the discussion on pp. 142-145 about whether God's words in 3.14-19 constitute punishments. I suspect that radical feminist theorists would understand God's words in this way.

2. While God's expulsion of the couple from the garden may serve as an alternate expression of a similar mood, perhaps a visual signal of divine disgust at the couple's actions, it does not seem to suggest heavy-heartedness on God's part regarding the pronouncements just made in 3.14-19.

3. MacKinnon, 'Jurisprudence', p. 626. Childbearing as part of women's purpose might be understood as a necessary consequence of the garden woman's imposed desire for her man.

envisioned. Similarly, the woman's talk about having been 'tricked' hints at a misapprehension of reality or of the potential consequences of her action; her choice admits the existence of at least two possibilities.

Thirdly, the talk about eyes being opened and there being some kind of change in the couple's knowledge implies a new way of looking at the world; it acknowledges that the world is a matter of perception. Fourth, aspects of the serpent/woman understanding of reality are confirmed by God's internal monologue in 3.22. Thus, the alternate world is not false; the woman may simply be the wrong person to claim knowledge of it. Finally, and perhaps most obviously, using the generic names 'man' and 'woman' is a clear attempt at universalizing. It shows itself to be a naturalizing maneuver, an indication that the story is an ideological fabrication designed to support or sustain a specific, and a particularly gendered, reality.

A Story Gone Awry. What has gone 'awry' in this portrayal of reality in Genesis 2–3? Phyllis Trible's characterization of the text as a 'love story gone awry' strikes a chord. Something is certainly wrong. I suggest that what has gone 'awry' with this text is not solely the actions and relationships of the characters in the story. It is also social constructions of reality, woman, gender, and difference; it is relationships among human beings in our world today that are 'awry'. What feminists might conclude has gone 'awry' in Genesis 2–3 is not primarily the woman's well-reasoned, if ultimately fateful, decision to eat and share the forbidden fruit and the man's choice to join her in this action.

What feminists might claim is 'awry' in this story is the way the narrator and many of the text's interpreters construct definitions of 'woman' that exist solely in relation to man: woman is designed to help man, to be admired by him, to feed him, and to serve his sexual and reproductive needs. What is 'awry' is compulsory heterosexuality, complete with God-fashioned, 'natural', similarity-in-difference of woman and man that creates sexual desire and binary gender roles from physical differences and works through divine eroticization of male dominance and female submission. What is 'awry' is women's intellectual silence and submission, as readers blame the woman for the fate of humanity, making of her at worst a seductive temptress, bringing death and trouble, or at best a thoughtful theologian—but one whose knowledge cannot be trusted and whose words are best avoided.[1] What is 'awry' is our shame

1. One would have thought that after J.M. Higgins's careful collation and

at being embodied, at being sexual. What is 'awry' is women being controlled by men.

But something is also 'awry' with any reading of the story that stops here, that abandons Eve and women who follow her to their subordination, that accepts this dismal ideology that the narrator and countless interpreters of Genesis 2–3 have promulgated, and which many feminist interpreters have attempted to dismiss or deny. For the story itself provides a clue to its own undoing.

The serpent's question remains available through our reading of the text, even if God and the narrator have stopped its mouth with dust. We are free to ask with the serpent 'Did God *really* say...?' and perhaps to fashion our own questions, such as: 'Shall he rule over you?' We may adopt the serpent's question to interrupt any interpretation that stops at domination. 'What did God really say' may be our perennial human question.

Uncertainty, reflection, decision, action, responsibility, and consequences—this is the way life is. God has provided complexity and freedom. If there were no serpents, we might still be in the garden, and we women might not yet be speaking. Another voice is necessary to separate the oneness, to view the world differently, to challenge our thinking and our easy assumptions. Life is certainly *not* easy when we live knowing difference: hearing that we may not yet be like God, seeing that we are not like one another, hiding our differences if we can, recognizing evil as well as good—even evil embodied in crushing, desiring, dominating hierarchies. But perhaps this recognition of opposites, of difference, of multiple ways of seeing, knowing, and being in the world can contribute to our lives.

We need stories, language, and images. I am not suggesting that the story of Genesis 2–3 will be persuasive to those outside Christian and Jewish communities. As the previous section on reading Genesis 2–3 in conversation with contemporary contexts shows, reading with feminist

refutation of terms inappropriately applied to the woman that interpreters would be more careful in describing her actions: 'The Myth of Eve: The Temptress', *JAAR* 44 (1976), pp. 639-47. Yet two recent essays continue to cast the woman into the role of 'seducer': D. Steinmetz, 'Vineyard, Farm, and Garden: The Drunkenness of Noah in the Context of Primeval History', *JBL* 113 (1994), p. 203; and P.R. Davies, 'Women, Men, Gods, Sex and Power: The Birth of a Biblical Myth', in A. Brenner (ed.), *A Feminist Companion to Genesis* (The Feminist Companion to the Bible, 2; Sheffield: Sheffield Academic Press, 1993), p. 195.

theories as intertexts displays textual ideologies serving precisely those ideological state apparatuses that many feminists find destructive. Feminists may reasonably prefer other stories and visions. But advocates of feminism within Jewish and Christian communities who are willing to read ideologically and intertextually may find resources in this text, in the questions we share with it and in the permission to question—even God—that it suggests. The remainder of this chapter reads Genesis 2–3 with biblical intertexts.

Difference Near the Garden: Reading with Genesis 4.1-16
There are several reasons for reading the Cain and Abel story in Gen. 4.1-16 as an intertext with Genesis 2–3.[1] First, the introductory 'these are the generations...' formula, which separates sections of Genesis, groups these stories together in the Gen. 2.4–4.26 unit. Second, the stories are linked by characters and location. Cain's story begins with the garden narrative's man and his wife, Eve. Both stories end with banishment east of Eden. Moreover, Cain's story completes the cycle begun in 2.4-5. While the garden story begins with the earth (ארץ) and then makes a man from the ground (אדמה), puts him in a garden, and eventually returns him to the ground, it is not until the end of the Cain story (4.12, 14, 16) that the cycle is completed by Cain's return again to the earth.[2] Third, the two stories share common vocabulary. Some repeated words are fairly ordinary, such as ground, earth, face/presence, fruit, till, hand, keep/guard, and field, while others suggest a conscious parallel with Genesis 3: knew, desire, rule over, where, 'what have you done?', voice, cursed, driven out, and east of Eden.[3] Fourth, the plot of the stories is similar. Characters in both narratives take actions involving fruit that affect their relationships with God. Their choices lead to an investigation followed by a curse, a disrupted relationship with the ground, and exile.[4]

1. Comments on the text and translation of Gen. 4.1-16 are included in notes as they are relevant to the discussion.
2. W. Vogels, 'Caïn: l'être humain qui devient une non-personne (Gn 4.1-16)', *NRT* 114 (1992), p. 339. See also Davies, 'Women, Men, Gods, Sex and Power' for a concentric pattern stretching from 2.5 to 9.20.
3. M. Fishbane, 'Genesis 2.4b–11.32/The Primeval Cycle', chap. in *Text and Texture: Close Readings of Selected Biblical Texts* (New York: Schocken Books, 1979), pp. 26-27.
4. For parallels, see T.E. Fretheim, *Creation, Fall, and Flood.* (Minneapolis: Augsburg, 1969), pp. 93-94; A.J. Hauser 'Linguistic and Thematic Links between

The Cain and Abel story is also appropriate because it is concerned explicitly with the chapter's theme: difference. Once the two brothers have been introduced in 4.1-2a, they are immediately distinguished by profession. Contrasts continue as brothers make separate offerings to God.[1] Cain seems to have had the idea first, but Abel appears to best him by offering the firstborn of his flocks. The different offerings and the brothers who give them receive differential regard from God, a response that makes Cain furious.[2] Westermann recognizes the danger of differences as inequalities: 'There come to the surface here those difficulties that endanger community, when one has more than the other, when one is successful and the other not. Inequality enters where there should be equality. This is what the story is all about'.[3] Because of these inequalities and in spite of God's intervention in 4.6-7 (which may suggest that Cain's offering received an appropriate response), Cain reacts in anger and kills his brother. While the narrator and God's speech to Cain emphasize relationship, by repeating seven times in the narrative that Abel was his 'brother', Cain explicitly distances himself, maintaining through his question in 4.9 that he is not his brother's keeper. Attention to difference continues through Cain's banishment from the ground and from God's presence, and in Cain's distinctive mark of divine protection.[4]

Re-Viewing Interrelationships. Cain's story is striking in its portrayal of relationships. It is the differences in the divine-human relationships between God and each of the brothers that sets the story in motion. Cain's disappointment and anger at his brother's preferential treatment and Cain's decision (after God's advice) about how to handle these

Gen 4.1-16 and Gen 2-3', *JETS* 23 (1980), pp. 297-305; and D. Steinmetz, 'Vineyard, Farm, and Garden'.

   1.   G. von Rad finds the division between the brothers to be so deep that it affects their religious practice: they worship at separate altars, *Genesis*, p. 104.

   2.   L. Alonso-Schökel recognizes the story introducing three key differences: culture, cult, and divine acceptance: *¿Dónde está tu hermano? Textos de fraternidad en el libro del Génesis* (Institucíon San Jerónimo, 19; Valencia: Artes Gráficas Soler, 1985), p. 23.

   3.   C. Westermann, *Genesis 1–11: A Commentary* (trans. J.J. Scullion, S.J.; Minneapolis: Augsburg Publishing House, 1984), p. 297.

   4.   H.C. White refers to this sign of perpetual difference as 'the price of eternal liminality, and alienation'. See '"Where Is Your Brother?" Genesis 4', chap. in *Narration and Discourse*, p. 166.

emotions occasions the brother-brother murder. God's description of the brother's blood crying out dramatizes the effects of Cain's choice on his relationship with the ground. After it swallows the brother's blood, the ground will no longer give its strength to the brother's murderer. The man-ground relationship is disrupted as well.

The striking portrayals of the divine-human, brother-brother, and man-ground relationships in Gen. 4.1-16 suggest rethinking and re-viewing relationships and interrelationships in the garden story. The diagram below depicts several of these relationships, while standard interpretations typically focus on only one or two. The creation-fall reading of Genesis 2–3 emphasize the God-human relationship by describing first God's creation of humans and then human alienation from God as a result of sin. The maturation or growth interpretation almost eschews relationship entirely by focusing on changes within human beings as they relate to the humans' developing experience in the story. The text as a whole, however, suggests concern not with only one or two key characters or relationships, but with the complexity of interrelationships among earthly, animal, human, and divine realms.

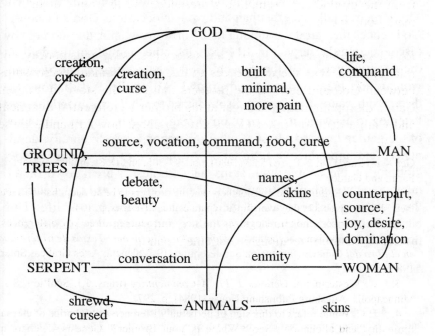

In contrast to the clearly organized and separated parts of creation in Genesis 1, the garden story weaves relationships among various creatures, highlighting their interdependence. For example, the ground is the source for man's creation and for the trees that provide him food. The relationship between man and trees is the subject of God's mandates about eating and not eating. Man's vocation to till the ground becomes more difficult because of the curse on the ground engendered by the man's inappropriate eating from a forbidden tree. The story is interested in other interrelationships as well. The narrator's lengthy description of the garden and rivers may function to give them shape, almost as characters, insuring that the earth and trees, which serve primarily as site and object in the narrative, will not be forgotten because they cannot be actors in the plot. Although she is built or fashioned by God, woman's relationship to God (in contrast to the man's) is minimal. Its nature is uncertain. God announces more toil in childbearing and ongoing wifely desire, but readers of Genesis 2–3 do not know how these words might affect woman's relationship with God.

God's speech in Gen. 3.14-19 and subsequent actions in 3.21-24 embody in a concise framework the interlocking nature of many of these relationships. Disruption of one relationship upsets others as well. The serpent's talk with the man and woman occasions God's response. God echoes the narrator's linking in 3.1 of serpent, animals, and field by disconnecting the serpent in 3.14 from the other animals of the field. In the ensuing verses of the speech, God relates serpent and woman, woman and man, and man and ground. All of these affiliations are disturbed because of the man's disobedience to God's command through listening to his woman. Interruption of man's relationship with the trees of the garden leads to a host of other disruptions as well: enmity, dominance, and unproductive farm labor. At the end of the chapter, God's clothing of the couple with skins may suggest a breakdown of the humans' relationships with animals. The humans are also expelled from the garden in order to avoid their eating from the tree of life. This banishment indicates the ongoing nature and potential permanence of the man's disturbed relationship with the ground.[1]

---

1. I am aware that human relation to the ground is a matter of ongoing concern and that it changes in the primeval narrative. See especially Gen. 5.29 and 8.21 on the curse.

Judging Differences. The stories in Genesis 2–4 emphasize broken relationships. Ruptures in these relationships are often caused by human judging of difference. Here I consider briefly the role of difference and judgment in the Cain story before returning to consider similar matters in Genesis 2–3.

God's preference of one brother's offering over the other's in Gen. 4.4-5 may seem arbitrary or capricious.[1] Certainly, Cain was upset by it. Yet God insists in 4.6-7 on appropriate reactions to difference, on human ability to control one's behavior, and on responsibility for choices and actions. What is the nature of differences and choices in Genesis 4? Commentators sometimes refer to the 'acceptance' of Abel's offering and the 'rejection' of Cain's, but Luis Alonso-Schökel suggests that these terms are too strong. Rather, the language of 'had regard for' simply indicates God's preferences for the younger brother, rather than the older, and for meat over vegetables.[2] God is not the only character making choices. God's choice evokes Cain's response to difference. Hugh White observes that by 'destroying his brother, Cain will eliminate the Other, the one whose difference poses a permanent threat to his success... with the divine'.[3] Walter Brueggemann notes that 'Cain had a choice of embracing a brother preferred over him. But he yielded to the waiting rage'.[4] Cain's choice prompts Brueggemann to characterize the story as 'a statement about the awesome choices daily before us and the high stakes for which we take daily risks'.[5]

Though Cain's story portrays response to difference in individual human terms, we may reasonably extend it in two directions. First, what are the effects and choices related to judging societal differences, and

1. At least the response seems arbitrary if commentators' efforts at explaining and justifying God's differential response are any indication of how readers perceive it. For a review of various proposals, see G. J. Wenham, *Genesis 1–15* (WBC; Waco, TX: Word Books, 1987), p. 104. H. Shank argues for God's permission of ambiguity rather than God's capriciousness; see 'The Sin Theology of the Cain and Abel Story: An Analysis of Narrative Themes within the Context of Genesis 1–11' (PhD dissertation, Marquette University, 1988), p. 199.

2. Alonso-Schökel, *¿Dónde está tu hermano?*, p. 29. S. Levin concurs, arguing that Gen. 8.21 suggests that God prefers the smell of meat over grain offerings; see 'The More Savory Offering: A Key to the Problem of Gen 4.3-5', *JBL* 98 (1979), p. 85.

3. White, 'Where Is Your Brother?', p. 160.

4. W. Brueggemann, *Genesis* (IBC; Atlanta: John Knox Press, 1982), p. 61.

5. Brueggemann, *Genesis*, p. 61.

second, is a God whose creation of difference and whose judgments about difference seem to enable or perhaps even to provoke human crisis acting justly? The targums on the Cain story reflect this second question. They variously portray Cain and Abel as arguing (during the ellipsis of 4.8 before Cain kills Abel) that God rewards the just and punishes the wicked, thus attempting to understand or to explain God's preference of one offering and one brother over the other.[1] E.A. Speiser also recognizes this wisdom theme: God's response to Cain is that 'good conduct should result in exaltation, not dejection! The whole would then be a "wisdom" motif, suitably applied to the case in question'.[2] Before turning to wisdom literature as an intertext for Genesis 2–3 that takes up several of the questions raised here, we consider the choices and judgments of the garden narrative.

The story of the first man and woman displays a profound interest in human judging of differences and freedom to act. God's command in Gen. 2.16-17 of permission and prohibition, of eating and not eating, affords great freedom within some boundaries. The man is expected to

1.   J.M. Bassler, 'Cain and Abel in the Palestinian Targums', *Journal for the Study of Judaism* 17 (1986), pp. 56-64. See also J. Kugel, 'Cain and Abel in Fact and Fable: Genesis 4.1-16', in R. Brooks and J.J. Collins (eds.), *Hebrew Bible or Old Testament? Studying the Bible in Judaism and Christianity*, (Notre Dame: University of Notre Dame Press, 1990), p. 178. Kugel explains that, according to *Targum Neofiti*, Cain 'feels that the rejection of his sacrifice was entirely arbitrary, and this leads him to conclude that the world in general is run in a cold and ultimately random fashion: sinners are not punished, the righteous are not rewarded, "there is no judgment and no divine judge"'.

2.   E.A. Speiser, *Genesis* (AB; Garden City, NY: Doubleday, 1964), p. 33. Alonso-Schökel, in contrast, opposes reading this text in terms of a doctrine of retribution. Regarding what he claims as Westermann's conclusion that 4.6-7 is an insertion and that Cain's behavior is justified before, during, and after the offering, Alonso-Schökel says (my translation), 'if God does not reward justly, humans do well in rebelling. To attribute such an attitude to a supposedly primitive story is to advance by centuries the passion of Job before an inexplicable God', *¿Dónde está tu hermano?*, p. 29. But could not these early Genesis narratives be precisely foregrounding the inexplicable nature of God, not necessarily for the purposes of promoting rebellion; Cain, after all, does not fare well. Rather the narrative may be part of an overall arrangement in Genesis that says that the inexplicable God, the God who poses unmotivated commands from the outset, the God who accepts and rejects at God's whim, this God of all the earth, who destroyed the world and vowed never to destroy it again, who scattered the peoples and created their languages, this God chose us, Israel.

distinguish between the one forbidden tree and the others from which he may eat. Evidence of human freedom and judging of difference continues in the man's naming of the animals and in his unsolicited poetic response to the woman. The story of woman's creation in 2.18-23 shows man's recognition of woman's difference and his exercizing freedom responsibly to make choices. The man had preferences: he fancied woman over the animals. The narrator in 2.24 describes ongoing male choice as being exercised responsibly when men leave their parents to cling to their women. The narrator hints that such responsible behavior (the heterosexual monogamy portrayed in 2.24) allows humans to judge difference (the garden couple's response to their nakedness in 2.25) in ways that permit appropriate intimacy.

The serpent-woman conversation in 3.1-5 and the couple's subsequent action and its effects described in 3.6-8 serve as an example of difference misjudged, of human freedom abused. The serpent's initial question explicitly asks the woman to judge God's command and implicitly challenges the reader to discern the differences between this command and the serpent's phrasing. The woman's response recognizes the need to distinguish among the trees; it acknowledges the importance of choosing actions carefully. The serpent tempts the woman with promises of divine-likeness, of differences minimized between humans and gods. The woman judges the tree and acts freely in eating from it, as does her man in his eating. The aftermath of the eating reveals the misjudgment. The couple's new knowledge of their nakedness prompts a covering of their physical differences, suggesting, perhaps, a new-found shame, in contrast with their shameless nakedness of 2.25. Yet, even these coverings might be seen as an appropriate response to new knowledge, were it not for the hiding and fear that the couple displays in 3.8 at God's arrival in the garden. The interrogation in 3.8-13 reveals the couple's free choices as misjudgments. The sentences in 3.14-19 reimpose distinctions, now as harsh differences between serpent and woman, woman and man, and man and ground. God's clothing of the couple in 3.21 distinguishes them as humans from both animals and gods. God's concern in 3.22 with human godlikeness recognizes the importance of difference, and God's decision in 3.23-24 to banish the couple insures that future human choice will not permit their eventual crossing the border to potential immortality.

Developing Relationships. The parallelism evident in the two stories of
Gen. 2.5–4.16 suggests that attention to the development of relationships
between them may be appropriate. The first relationships that seem to
have developed are Eve's. Her claim in 4.1 to have created 'a man with
YHWH' suggests that she may be responding both to God and to her
man.[1] At her creation, woman hears the man in 2.23 claiming to be the
source of woman. Now aware that birth proceeds through woman, Eve
claims woman's role in creating man: whereas man claimed that *ʾiššâ*
came from *ʾîš*, Eve counters that she (who has heard herself in 2.23 to
be an *ʾiššâ*) gives birth to *ʾîš*.[2] In contrast to man's failure to mention
God's role in creating woman in 2.23, Eve acknowledges God's part in
parturition in 4.1. By naming her first child, the woman also asserts her
power to name as the man did in 3.20. The absence in 4.1 of any
mention of toil, coupled with what seems to be a fairly triumphant cry,
suggests that Eve does not acquiesce to the position God assigned her in
3.16. While she accepts her role as mother, she seems to rebel against
subordination by putting herself, as a co-creator, at the level of God. She
has gotten a man just as God did in Genesis 2. She bears an *ʾîš* from
ʾiššâ just as God had made an *ʾādām* from *ʾᵃdāmâ*. If Gen. 4.1 signals
Eve's delayed response to her sentence in 3.16, she may be making the

1. There are many issues with the translation of *qānîtî ʾiš ʾet-yhwh* in 4.1.
Translating *qānîtî* as 'gained' might preserve the Hebrew pun between *qānîtî* and
Cain's name, *qaîn*, but it loses the strength that this word may have as a word of
creation when used with God as subject. For discussions of the translation, see
U. Cassuto, *A Commentary on the Book of Genesis: Part I From Adam to Noah
Genesis I – VI 8* (trans. I. Abrahams; Jerusalem: The Magnes Press, 1961) and
B. Vawter, 'Prov. 8.22: Wisdom and Creation', *JBL* 99 (1980) pp. 205-206. Puzzling
also is Eve's use of *ʾîš* for what must have been a male infant. The phrase 'with
YHWH' startles readers who expect human male rather than divine agency in begetting
offspring. There is no textual basis, however, for adding 'help of' to a translation that
aims at verbal correspondence.

2. To be careful about narrative levels here, we note that it is the narrator who
reminds us in 4.1 that the man knew his *ʾiššâ*. One might think that the narrator, then,
should get the credit for reversing the birth-giving roles in this verse. But while the
narrator's words may refer readers back to 2.23, there we may presume that the
woman hears the man's speech about the *ʾiššâ*'s relationship to *ʾîš*. It is part of the
fabula where the characters interact, as well as being part of the narrator's story level.
Ultimately, of course, the narrator casts the roles of the characters, so perhaps the
narrator is not as tied to male dominance as ideological analysis of the earlier story
suggested.

best of the situation described above as 'compulsory heterosexuality', or she may be rebelling against it.

God's relationship to humans in terms of God's desires and God's expectations for them develops as the two stories proceed. In Genesis 2–3, man is related to the trees through God's command, and violation of that command disrupts man's relation with the ground. God spells out the command clearly, and a separate character provokes the disobedience. Human decision is entirely free, since God is off stage when the couple chooses to eat from the forbidden tree. The judgments God dispenses in 3.14-19 seem to be purely God's decision. Though God refers to the creatures' actions ('because you have... ') as a reason for their punishment, God points to no direct consequences of their deeds as occasioning the particular sentences that God pronounces. In this sense, though related thematically to the actions that provoked them, God's discipline seems somewhat arbitrary. Furthermore, God is personally involved in meting out some of the penalties: God says 'I will... ' to the serpent and woman.

God interacts differently with humans in the Cain and Abel story. There, divine expectations for the nature of familial relationships are unspecified, allowing Cain to ask whether he is to be his brother's keeper. Moreover, it is precisely God's responses to the brothers and their sacrifices (not the machinations of another character) that provoke the crisis in the story. But while God is off stage at the crucial moment of the garden narrative in Gen. 3.6, God stays 'on the scene' in 4.6-7 as Cain struggles with his emotions. God intervenes, in this story, at the decisive moment, not to prevent the eventual murder, but to attempt to instruct or to persuade human choice. Alonso-Schökel notes that, whereas Eve was not taught about the evil arts of the serpent nor told that she should discern false oracles, God does teach Cain, in what Alonso-Schökel calls the first instruction that God offers in the Bible.[1] Cain, however, does not accept this counsel. Human freedom to act remains, but because of God's teaching it is informed freedom and freedom exercised in relation to God. The consequences of human action also differ: they are not solely by divine fiat, for God's response is

---

1. Alonso-Schökel, *¿Dónde está tu hermano?*, p. 34. H.C. White also recognizes the new nature of this divine–human interaction, but he suggests that God is not really interested in 'genuine intersubjective dialogue' with Cain and observes that God fails 'to elicit a real dialogue about the causes of his anger'. See 'Where Is Your Brother?', pp. 158, 160.

motivated in part by the cries of Abel's blood from the ground. The ground's infertility results *explicitly* as a consequence of Cain's action, rather than seeming to occur solely through divine decision as it did in 3.17-19. Cain hints that some responsibility for the events accrues to God as well. Perhaps God, rather than Cain, should have been the brother's keeper. The symbol marking the sinner now has explicit rather than implicit meaning. God promises sevenfold vengeance and offers a mark as protection for Cain in 4.15, whereas the motivation and function of the clothing in 3.21 is uncertain. Finally, the banishments in the two stories differ. While God drives the man out of the garden in 3.24, it is Cain who either recognizes the necessity of exile or chooses it for himself in the brothers' story. Cain claims to have been driven away (4.14) and eventually goes away on his own (4.16) from God's presence, even though God does not affirm Cain's interpretation of his burden.

What do these comparisons suggest about the development of relationships in Genesis 2–4? What have humans and God learned in these two stories? The spare nature of both stories makes such inferences tenuous, but I suggest a few possibilities. The humans seem to have learned or developed further resistance. Eve's naming claims authority, rather than submitting to subordination and silence. Cain has recognized in 4.4-5, perhaps more than his parents did, the arbitrariness of God's interactions with humans. He may also have learned anger (by hearing about God's reactions to the garden debacle?). Cain's prayer, lamenting his punishment or confessing the weight of his guilt before God, suggests that humans can dialogue with God for justice and mercy, rather than simply silently accepting God's judgment. Cain's self-imposed banishment suggests his further recognition that human relationship with God can be refused: Cain can choose to leave God's presence.

Having provided the occasion for human disobedience in Genesis 3, through the commandment that distinguished a particular tree, God more boldly stirs up human relations in Genesis 4 through God's differential response to the brothers and their offerings. God seems almost to be experimenting with the trouble God can cause humans, or at least to be exercising divine freedom without regard for its potential human effects. God does seem to have learned from the garden events that a 'hands off' policy is ineffective in guaranteeing appropriate human action. So, God tries intervention and direct instruction in 4.6-7. Though potentially beneficial, these strategies emerge as ineffective, at least in this instance. God may learn from Cain's implicit challenge about who should be his brother's keeper that, as creator, God should shoulder some responsibility for human interactions. God takes up this responsibility by providing protection for the remaining brother, Cain. God will also exercise this responsibility later in the primeval narrative in God's decision to destroy much of creation because of human wickedness and out of God's sorrow at having made them (Gen. 6.5-7). After the flood, God affirms this responsibility by requiring a reckoning for human life (Gen. 9.5). God has learned to attempt to maintain relationships in Cain's story by being 'on the scene' during most of the narrative, by explaining rather than simply announcing the consequences of human actions, and by being protective, even of a murderer.

Intertextual reading of the garden narrative with Cain's story helps us to re-view interrelationships, to judge differences, and to recognize developing relationships. Yet questions for feminists still remain in relation to Genesis 2–3.

Out of Eden: From Genesis to Wisdom

Feminists are troubled with the way traditional interpretations of Genesis 2–3 portray gender relations. Feminist theories about difference presented earlier in this chapter imply that discussion of what it means to be a woman or a man needs to be more complicated than what these standard readings of Genesis 2–3 suggest. If 'reality' is to some degree socially constructed, as study of ideologies proposes, then as societies we must be responsible for the gendered worlds we help to construct. I have perhaps played the role of the serpent in reading Genesis 2–3 in terms of compulsory heterosexuality. By proposing an alternate perspective, as the serpent does, this interpretation raises some of the garden story's questions all over again. How should we understand our world and our relationship with God? If we do not have a clear word from God about sex/gender systems, then, like the garden woman, we must consider whether to regard feminist theories and my alternate reading as potentially dangerous distractions or to risk tasting new knowledge.

Speculation about knowledge and experience, discourse and reality, does not occur simply in the abstract. The lived experience of various individuals and communities, within systems of oppression based on real and constructed differences, compels feminist interpreters to seek practical approaches to these questions. It demands respectful ways of recognizing difference and of living our lives. Interpreters of the garden narrative, especially in relation to Cain's story, may ask about God's role in these matters. Does God orchestrate the construction of difference? Is God a model for the arbitrary wielding of power? Feminists may also be troubled about the way God is portrayed in the garden narrative, especially in relation to the woman. The narrator reveals so little about this relationship. What we hear may suggest either that God is indifferent to the woman or that God punishes her too harshly. We yearn for more details. We are frustrated by limits to knowledge.

Reading Genesis 2–3 with other intertexts may be helpful in addressing feminist questions about knowledge, discourse, reality, and God as posed by the garden narrative and feminist scholarship on difference. Biblical wisdom literature, particularly in Proverbs 1–9, acknowledges that discourses compete to determine reality.[1] It addresses limits to knowledge and apparent indifference in Qohelet, and in Job it considers divine-human relationships of worship and judgment. Biblical wisdom literature is at home with opposites. It recognizes the complexity of life. It urges the pursuit of wisdom and knowledge, the competent use of understanding. It reminds us that, while we should think and plan, God is also involved in our lives and will work with how life turns out. Wisdom literature has room, that is, for both human intellect and God's activity. This combination is not only helpful for reading Genesis 2–3, but for thinking about ways to read the Bible in contemporary post-Enlightenment contexts. Wisdom literature allows difference. It acknowledges our desire for clear-cut categories like the 'righteous' and the 'wicked', but it knows that life is often considerably muddier than these sharp separations suggest. It urges our wise judgment, acknowledges our limited perspectives, expresses our rage or despair, and compels our trust in God.

Biblical wisdom literature is also an appropriate intertext because of its links to the garden narrative. First, it uses vocabulary reminiscent of the early chapters of Genesis. Perhaps most obviously, the 'insight' that makes the tree desirable for woman is a common word in Proverbs (10.5, 19; 14.35; 16.20; 17.2; 21.11-12). The tree of life is a symbol for wisdom in Prov. 3.18 (cf. 11.30; 13.12; 15.4). Proverbs also speaks regularly of good and evil (for example 14.19, 22; 31.12), eating, and fruit (for example 1.31). Qohelet's theme word *hebel*, often translated

1. My discussion of wisdom literature will address only Proverbs, Qohelet (Ecclesiastes), and Job, though I may make occasional reference to wisdom traditions in Sirach (Ecclesiasticus) and Wisdom of Solomon.

'vanity', is the name of the garden couple's second son, Abel. Qohelet also talks of evil, knowledge, and the return of man to dust (3.20; 12.7). The book of Job gets off the ground because its protagonist, like the wise men of Proverbs, turns away from evil (1.1, 8; 2.3). It continues when, counter to his wife's advice, Job accepts evil from the hand of God as well as good (2.10). Job 15.7 refers to the first man, and dust is a prominent word in the book. Good, evil, eating, fruit, knowledge, man (ʾādām), dust, and *hebel* all recall the Eden narrative.

Secondly, wisdom literature and Genesis 2–3 share a common interest in the theme of this chapter: difference.

> The book of Proverbs, for example, lays out a wealth of distinctions that are, in many instances, polar in character—wise and foolish, rich and poor, diligent and slothful, virtuous woman and loose woman. This polar feature even extends, as can be readily observed in the book of Ecclesiastes, but also in the book of Proverbs ('Answer not a fool according to his folly', 26.4; 'Answer a fool according to his folly', 26.5), to a fondness for bringing together contradictory views in a deliberately unresolved way.[1]

The book of Job's portrayal of various views on divine retribution may share this approach.

Thirdly, questions raised by wisdom literature are similar to those raised by feminists in relation to the garden story. Both ask about the relationship between language and reality, the role of experience in developing knowledge, and the involvement of God in human troubles. The garden story and wisdom literature wrestle with the same question: how appropriately to pursue wisdom.

Scholars have recognized relationships between wisdom literature and Genesis 2–3. While not specifically claiming a connection with Israel's wisdom tradition, Crossan recognizes in the story of the first man and woman a dilemma that Qohelet faced: the choice between life with no pain or knowledge of differences that includes pain.[2] Scholars note parallels between the garden narrative and wisdom literature. Carmichael observes that, like Genesis 2–3, wisdom associates women, sex, and serpents (Prov. 30.19).[3] Luis Alonso-Schökel identifies several wisdom

---

1.   C.M. Carmichael, 'The Paradise Myth: Interpreting without Jewish and Christian Spectacles', in P. Morris and D. Sawyer (eds.), *A Walk in The Garden: Biblical, Iconographical and Literary Images of Eden* (JSOTSup, 136; Sheffield: JSOT Press 1992), p. 50.

2.   Crossan, 'Felix Culpa and Foenix Culprit', p. 111.

3.   Carmichael, 'The Paradise Myth', p. 53.

motifs in the Eden narrative: knowledge of good and evil, the snake's slyness, Adam as a sage classifying reality, attention to the ordinary world (for example the rivers in Gen. 2.10-14), and a 'stylistic dexterity' and 'literary knack' comparable to that of wisdom literature.[1] He also speculates about how the story developed as a narrative growing out of a sage's reflections about the origins of sin and evil.[2] Franco Festorazzi argues similarly that wisdom takes a story form in Genesis 2–3.[3] Other scholars read the garden narrative specifically as an anti-wisdom text, one that condemns autonomous thinking.[4]

Choosing wisdom literature as an intertext is certainly an interpretive move, but another ideological choice is deciding how to do the intertextual reading. In the previous section, Cain's story served as an intertext to facilitate the understanding of Genesis 2–3. The ultimate goal was an enhanced interpretation of the garden narrative. The intertextual reading in this section moves in the opposite direction: from feminist theological questions raised in relation to Genesis 2–3, through engagement with wisdom literature, to implications for living with difference in today's world. That is, the goal of this section is not primarily a better understanding of the garden narrative but additional conversation about issues and questions provoked by feminist engagement with Genesis 2–3.

Three clusters of texts and questions are considered in turn. First, analysis of the role of discourse in Proverbs, in relation to worldview, builds from the discussion of language in Chapter 3 and earlier portions

---

1.   L. Alonso-Schökel, S.J., 'Sapiential and Covenant Themes in Genesis 2–3', in J. L. Crenshaw (ed.), *Studies in Ancient Israelite Wisdom* (New York: KTAV, 1976), pp. 472-73; translation of 'Motivos sapienciales y de alianza en Gn 2–3', *Bib* 43 (1962), pp. 295-315.

2.   Alonso-Schökel, 'Sapiential and Covenant Themes', p. 479.

3.   F. Festorazzi, 'Gen. 1–3 e la sapienza di Israele', *Rivista Biblica* 27 (1979), p. 50.

4.   G.E. Mendenhall argues that Genesis 3 is a *mashal* written in the sixth century (using deliberately archaizing language) out of the Job-like wisdom traditions to suggest that obedience to Yahweh is better than the knowledge of wisdom that had led to the recent collapse: 'The Shady Side of Wisdom: The Date and Purpose of Genesis 3', in H.N. Bream, R.D. Heim, and C.A. Moore (eds.), *A Light unto My Path: Old Testament Studies in Honor of Jacob M. Myers* (Philadelphia: Temple University Press, 1974), pp. 319-334. Sharing Mendenhall's position on the narrative as being anti-wisdom (but disagreeing with him on the dating) are J. Blenkinsopp, *The Pentateuch: An Introduction to the First Five Books of the Bible* (Anchor Bible Reference Library; New York: Doubleday, 1992), p. 67 and Brueggemann, *Genesis*, pp. 51-52. See also Carr's proposal mentioned on p. 203.

of this chapter about notions of reality. Secondly, Qohelet raises questions about human knowledge that extend the discussion of Chapter 2 and express concerns about societal relations similar to this chapter's interest in matters of difference. Thirdly, Job's battle with God about justice and integrity, in view of a potential doctrine of retribution, proves helpful in feminist grappling with God and in thinking about the role and sentence of the woman in the garden narrative.

Wise or Foolish: Discourse and Reality in Proverbs

Chapter 3 examined language and discourse in the garden narrative. Discussion of ideologies and intertextuality in this chapter raises feminist questions about the relationships among discourse, reality, and worldview. With these questions in mind, we consider the resources Proverbs provides for thinking about these relationships. The discussion is in three main parts: first, description and analysis of Proverbial rhetoric, including the two women in Proverbs 1–9; second, exploration of the relationship between discourse and reality; and third, consideration of intertextual relationships between Proverbs and Genesis 2–3.

Proverbial Rhetoric. Proverbs 1–9 consists almost entirely of poetic speeches, which function to shape reading of the sentence proverb collection in chs. 10–31. In many of the poems, a speaker (a teacher or parent, probably a father[1]) admonishes a listener (a son or male student) to heed the speaker's advice. Personifications of both wisdom and folly as women calling out in the streets suggest that the silent interlocutor is male (and presumably heterosexual). These chapters urge the reader to seek wisdom and to avoid folly by accepting the father's counsel and woman wisdom's invitation.

Rhetorically, Proverbs recognizes the critical role of language as discourse in shaping reality. Proverbs 1-9 promote and attempt to inculcate in readers a particular worldview. They portray wisdom's discourse *as* reality and any other discourse as folly, illusion: 'Wisdom is not one discourse among others but the stuff of reality itself. The values

---

1.   Prov. 4.3-4 reveals the speaker in Proverbs 1–9 as a father, though A. Brenner suggests that these discourses may contain 'suppressed, misquoted or misread F[emale] discourses': 'Some Observations on the Figurations of Woman in Wisdom Literature', in H.A. McKay and D.J.A. Clines (eds.), *Of Prophets' Visions and the Wisdom of Sages: Essays in Honour of R. Norman Whybray on his Seventieth Birthday* (JSOTSup, 162; Sheffield: Sheffield Academic Press, 1993), p. 193.

of the father are built into the structures of the world'.[1] If the world is a realm of competing discourses, then the rhetorical task is to inculcate the correct discourse. Vivid depictions of wisdom and folly, personified as women inviting and alluring the listening young man, contribute to this task.

Analyzing Proverbial Discourse: A Tale of Two Women. In order to address the feminist questions about language and reality mentioned earlier, discussion here focuses on the portrayals of 'woman wisdom' and the 'strange woman'[2] and on the battle waged between them in Proverbs 1–9 for the hearer's and reader's attention.

Proverbs 1–9 personifies wisdom as a woman. As a character, wisdom is the most prominent woman of the Bible.[3] She speaks three times in Proverbs, calling out from the public places.[4] In the first speech (1.22-33) wisdom laments the inattention of fools and scoffers (1.22), urging them to listen (1.23), and warning of the consequences of their continued refusal. Wisdom's second address (8.4-36) mirrors the father's counsel in the previous seven chapters. Both woman wisdom and the father commend the 'words of my mouth' (4.5; 5.7; 7.24; 8.8). Wisdom urges listeners to take her instruction, as the father recommends his (1.8; 8.10). She promises sound wisdom that the father has urged his son to keep (8.14; 3.21). In both of their speeches, wisdom is to be valued and

1.   C.A. Newsom, 'Woman and the Discourse of Patriarchal Wisdom: A Study of Proverbs 1–9', in P.L. Day (ed.), *Gender and Difference in Ancient Israel* (Minneapolis: Fortress Press, 1989), p. 151.

2.   Discussion below will clarify use of the terms 'woman wisdom' and 'strange woman' as representing competing discourses. Feminist scholars view various terms in Proverbs as constituting a single metaphorical cluster, usually referred to as the 'strange woman'. See C.V. Camp, 'What's so Strange about the Strange Woman?' in D. Jobling, P.L. Day, and G.T. Sheppard (eds.), *The Bible and the Politics of Exegesis: Essays in Honor of Norman K. Gottwald on His Sixty-Fifth Birthday*, (Cleveland: The Pilgrim Press, 1991), pp. 97-108; G.A. Yee, '"I Have Perfumed my Bed with Myrrh": The Foreign Woman (*ʾiššâ zārâ*) in Proverbs 1–9', *JSOT* 43 (1989), pp. 53-68; and footnotes by Camp and C. Fontaine at Prov. 1.20-33 and *ad. loc.* in the *HarperCollins Study Bible*.

3.   In length of treatment in the Hebrew Bible, C.R. Fontaine ranks wisdom fifth among all characters, after God, Job, Moses, and David: 'Wisdom in Proverbs', in L.G. Perdue, B.B. Scott, and W.J. Wiseman (eds.), *In Search of Wisdom: Essays in Memory of John G. Gammie*, (Louisville, KY: Westminster/John Knox, 1993), p. 113.

4.   See also descriptions of her in 1.20-21; 3.13-18; 4.5-9; 7.4-5; 8.1-3; 9.1-3.

treasured (2.4; 3.14-15; 4.8; 8.10-11) as leading to wealth, position, and honor (3.16; 4.8-9; 8.15-18, 21).[1] In an unprecedented move, wisdom grounds her authority in her ancient participation with God in creation (8.22-31). She concludes her appeal by promising happiness and life, and by warning of death for those who hate her (8.32-36). Wisdom's third address in Proverbs 9 pits her against the strange woman in calling listeners to a banquet.[2]

A cluster of terms portrays woman wisdom's rival in Proverbs 1–9, whom I call 'strange woman'. (See chart below.) She first appears as a strange woman (*ʾiššâ zārâ*) or foreigner (*nokrîyâ*) in 2.16. This pair of terms is repeated in 7.5, and a similar pair occurs in 5.20. The translation of *ʾiššâ zārâ* by 'strange woman,' rather than 'loose woman' or 'adulteress', is justified by observing how the same pair is translated in 5.10 when it applies to men: they are simply strangers and aliens. Parallel to the foreign woman in 6.24 is an evil woman (*ʾiššâ rāʿ*). The trio of terms (strange woman, foreigner, evil woman) is linked with notions of woman's marital infidelity. Prov. 2.17 describes the woman as having left her partner, and 6.26 and 7.10-23 describe her attempts at seductive behavior. By Prov. 7.10, her behavior warrants no special adjectives: she is simply 'woman'. It is not use of vocabulary in parallelism that ties the 'foolish woman' of 9.13 to the earlier terms. Rather, the foolish woman's seductive behavior is rhetorically framed as deceptive because her words in 9.16 are nearly identical with wisdom's in 9.4. By using such smooth talk and functioning as wisdom's rival, the foolish woman is framed as guilty by association. She deserves to join the cluster 'strange woman'.

Terms for the 'strange woman'

'Literal' translation	Hebrew	Reference	Translations	
strange woman	*ʾiššâ zārâ*	2.16a; 7.5a	NRSV	loose woman
			NIV	adulteress

1. It is not clear how to assess the similarities in their discourses. Does the father's counsel gain its stature and influence through association with woman wisdom, or might personified wisdom function as a puppet proclaiming the father's worldview?

2. The situations and speeches in 9.1-6 and 9.13-18 are similar.

strange	*zārā* (f. sg.)	5.3	NRSV	loose woman
			NIV	adulteress
		5.20a	NRSV	another woman
			NIV	adulteress
strangers	*zārîm* (m. pl.)	5.10a	NRSV	strangers
			NIV	strangers
foreigner (f.)	*nokrîyâ* (f. sg.)	2.16b; 6.24b;	NRSV	adulteress
		7.5b	NIV	wayward wife
		5.20b	NRSV	adulteress
			NIV	another man's wife
foreigner (m.)	*nokrî* (m. sg.)	5.10b	NRSV	alien
			NIV	another man
evil woman	*ʾēšet rāʿ*	6.24a	NRSV	wife of another
			NIV	immoral woman
prostitute	*zônâ*	6.26a; 7.10b	NRSV/NIV	prostitute
woman of man wife of husband	*ʾēšet ʾiš*	6.26b	NRSV	wife of another
			NIV	adulteress
woman (wife)	*ʾiššâ*	7.10a	NRSV/NIV	woman
foolish woman	*ʾēšet kᵉsîlût*	9.13	NRSV	foolish woman
			NIV	woman Folly

In contrast to woman wisdom, who speaks directly (1.23-33; 8.4-36; 9.4-6), strange woman's speech is almost exclusively reported by the narrator. She is always introduced by the nature of her speech, which is thickly coated with derisive, warning adjectives: it is smooth (2.16; 5.3; 6.24; 7.5, 21) or loud (9.13). While woman wisdom is associated with value and confers honor wealth and prestige (3.14-16; 4.8-9; 8.10-21), strange woman is described bodily, with honey-dripping lips (5.3), or in terms of her beauty (6.25) or dress (7.10). Getting entangled with her leads to loss of honor and wealth (5.9; 6.31, 33). Yet both women speak in public places (1.20-21 and 8.1-3; 7.12 and 9.14); both call the simple and senseless to turn in to their houses (9.4, 16); and both invite their guests to eat bread and to drink (9.5, 17).

Discourse and Reality[1]. It is the similarities of the discourses of these two women, more than their differences, that reveal how language and discourse can be dangerous. As their final speeches demonstrate, the editor of Proverbs has created a deliberate confusion of the two women.[2]

> Those who are lovers of language, and the sages are most certainly among them, can expect to taste the fruits of both the Strange Woman's deceit, namely death, and Woman Wisdom's truth, the life that comes from Yhwh (8.35). The fundamental duality that exists in human intercourse is inescapable. Language may, in the abstract, separate truth and deceit, but in experience the two often become one.[3]

Language is dangerous when it unites truth and deceit, and because it displays deception at all. Strange woman's very existence in the discourse of Proverbs, as someone operating outside the bounds of society, shows that disorder is possible. Her speech, moreover, by suggesting only sweet consequences (9.17) for moral impropriety, disrupts society. Proverbs 1–9 reveals the manipulative power and subtlety of human speech when it is used as

> a smoke screen, blinding its listeners to the effect of their actions upon themselves and society. In this manner, not only is morality threatened, but the use of language is perverted, its relationship to what the sages considered reality sundered, and the discourse of the sage, on which the intellectual endeavor depends, thus rendered suspect.[4]

The strange woman threatens the sage because the deception inherent in her speech renders suspicious the claimed straightforwardness of his words.

The battle between woman wisdom and the strange woman also

---

1. In this chapter, I am interested in the relationship between discourse and reality in Proverbs primarily in terms of how the text continues to function in contemporary communities.

2. J.N. Aletti, 'Séduction et parole en proverbes I-IX', *VT* 27 (1977), p. 133.

3. C.V. Camp, 'Wise and Strange: An Interpretation of the Female Imagery in Proverbs in Light of Trickster Mythology', in J.C. Exum and J.W.H. Bos (eds.), *Reasoning with the Foxes: Female Wit in a World of Male Power* (Semeia, 42; Atlanta: Scholars Press, 1988), pp. 24-25.

4. C.V. Camp, 'Woman Wisdom as Root Metaphor: A Theological Consideration', in K.G. Hoglund, E.F. Huwiler, J.T. Glass and R.W. Lee (eds.), *The Listening Heart: Essays in Wisdom and the Psalms in Honor of Roland E. Murphy, O. Carm.* (JSOTSup, 58; Sheffield: JSOT Press, 1987), p. 52.

reveals that discourses shape reality not through conspiracies, but by consensus. In Althusser's terms, discourses are ideological state appara-tuses, hailing individuals who then recognize themselves as being addressed. At stake is the formation of the subject—the listener, learner, or reader.

> The striking prominence of the pronouns 'I' and 'you' and the repeated use of vocative and imperative address in Proverbs 1–9 are clear indicators of what is at stake in these chapters: the formation of the subjectivity of the reader.[1]

Proverbs 1–9 recognizes this social character of discourse in several ways. The two competing discourses hail their would-be adherents in public places (1.20-21; 8.2-3; 7.11-12; 9.14). The dominant rhetoric urges listeners to follow straight paths and to avoid ways that 'lead' to death. Carol Newsom observes that the image of a path represents 'customary social behavior'.[2]

> A path is a social product, made by many feet over a period of time. But its purely physical record of customary social behavior is often transposed in terms of a teleology and a will ('Where does that path lead?'). A path does not, in fact, exclude movement in any direction. It only makes its own direction the easiest, most natural, most logical way of proceeding.[3]

In a world of multiple hailings, of conflicting discourses, paths signal past traditions, potentially helpful habits, but they do so with the recognition that other walks are possible. Proverbs does not welcome alternatives, however. Newsom observes: 'Far from valuing the plurality of discourses that intersect a culture, Proverbs 1–9 seeks the hegemony of its own discourse'.[4] Still, in 'giving discourse a privileged position and in representing the world as a place of conflicting discourses, Proverbs 1–9 appears to acknowledge the socially constructed nature of reality and the problematic status of truth'.[5]

It is because worlds are constructed, as Proverbs 1–9 reluctantly admits, that the need for interpellation and instruction is so great. Proverbs demonstrate their value as teaching and world-shaping counsel for listeners who are willing to learn from authorities, who appreciate

1. Newsom, 'Woman and the Discourse of Patriarchal Wisdom', p. 143.
2. Newsom, 'Woman and the Discourse of Patriarchal Wisdom', p. 147.
3. Newsom, 'Woman and the Discourse of Patriarchal Wisdom', p. 147.
4. Newsom, 'Woman and the Discourse of Patriarchal Wisdom', p. 147.
5. Newsom, 'Woman and the Discourse of Patriarchal Wisdom', p. 149.

tradition. The sages' world exists, however, only by shaping students who accept its teaching. 'A world made of discourse, a symbolic order, an ideology exists only by consensus. If it cannot recruit new adherents and if those whom it reinterpellates do not recognize themselves in its hailing, it ceases to have reality'.[1] The world of Proverbs is a fragile one.

Some feminists question whether the reality Proverbs constructs should continue to be promoted. They recognize that one's symbolic worldview affects behavior and worry that Proverbs operates out of a male construction of reality. Prov. 4.3-4 suggests a father passing along to his son wisdom that he learned from his own father. This fatherly wisdom, however, operates via potentially dangerous male stereotypes about women.

Camp observes that the view of women in Proverbs is male; it exhibits the understanding of women referred to earlier in the chapter as 'compulsory heterosexuality'. In Proverbs, '"woman" is defined in quintessentially male terms, namely, as "one with whom one has some form or another, socially sanctioned or not, of sexual relationship"'.[2] Constructions of sexual difference form the basis for this conception of women. Camp suggests the further possibility that the view of women in Proverbs 1–9 grows out of a social setting and 'gender ideology in which woman *qua* woman has become the symbol of the strange'.[3]

1.   Newsom, 'Woman and the Discourse of Patriarchal Wisdom', p. 146.
2.   Camp, 'Strange Woman', p. 23.
3.   Camp, 'Strange Woman', p. 24. Scholars recognize the portrayals of woman wisdom and strange woman as metaphorical texts, but they differ on the relationship they envision between these symbolic texts and the social realities within which they may have developed. J. Blenkinsopp dates Proverbs 1–9 to the postexilic period when exogamous marriages were a matter of debate and public policy: 'The Social Context of the "Outsider Woman" in Proverbs 1–9', *Bib* 72 (1991), pp. 457-73. He sees woman wisdom as a literary creation designed to mirror favorably the undesirable reality of foreign women in Israel's midst portrayed in Proverbs by the strange woman. In his view, intermarriage and syncretism are 'Proverbs' sole concern (so says Camp, 'Strange Woman?', p. 19).

Camp has proposed two different theories for the social context of the symbolic women in Proverbs. In the first theory, Camp suggests that woman wisdom functions to embody a type of wisdom that could more easily survive the challenge of the exile. She sets Proverbs 1–9 in the context of early postexilic Israel when practical wisdom and women's roles in the family were more predominant and valuable than royal theology. See *Wisdom and the Feminine in the Book of Proverbs* (Bible and Literature, 11; Sheffield: Almond Press, 1985). It was wisdom's 'orientation of the tradition toward daily life, articulated in female imagery, that allowed it to withstand

In any case, Camp questions whether these symbolic women in Proverbs can continue to function profitably for contemporary feminist theologies.[1] She asks whether women in Proverbs have been co-opted, 'put on a pedestal or, [in] the case of the strange woman, vilified, to serve men's purposes of creating an orderly society that would put men back in full control?'[2] Camp warns that perhaps 'once again, images of women are being used by men to support their own place of power in the social structure and the view of reality that supports it'.[3] Newsom identifies one way that this co-optation occurs. The 'speeches of personified wisdom... serve to buttress what the father has said...and belong to the same cultural voice that speaks through the father'.[4] Woman wisdom is a literary creation serving strong ideological and rhetorical functions.

Proverbial rhetoric, feminists justifiably warn, is dangerous. Analysis of Proverbs 1–9 reveals that its rhetoric interpellates the reader in particular ways: as a silent son, already at fault, and expected to be obedient to authority. Wisdom's opening cry in Prov. 1.22 'How long... will you love being simple?' may provide a clue to the son's silence. Newsom observes that wisdom's first words mark the son/reader with a guilty past: 'The reader discovers himself in the text as always, already at fault. And the fault is recalcitrance before legitimate authority'.[5] The son is silent, perhaps because he is *not* attending to his father's (or wisdom's) teaching. The son's silence, like strange woman's alluring

---

the shock of exile in such a creative manner, when the official religion associated with the state cult had been demolished': 'Woman Wisdom as Root Metaphor', p. 59.

In a later article, 'What's so Strange about the Strange Woman?', Camp begins, like Blenkinsopp, with social realities behind the strange woman. Camp proposes that this metaphor may suggest an even later period when attitudes may be closer to those of Sirach. Women have begun to be understood as the primary 'other'. As in Sirach, woman is portrayed in Proverbs as a force of evil associated with sex and death because some women break social boundaries. Their social and sexual deviance is embodied as the adulteress in Proverbs. Woman's foreignness, thus, is not a matter of her nationality but of her willingness to cross borders of what is acceptable behavior. Woman is foreign simply by virtue of her role as man's 'other'. Imagined (or real) male lack of control of women's sexuality, Camp contends, threatens men.

1.   Camp, 'Woman Wisdom as Root Metaphor', p. 47.
2.   Camp, 'Woman Wisdom as Root Metaphor', p. 48.
3.   Camp, 'Trickster', p. 33.
4.   Newsom, 'Woman and the Discourse of Patriarchal Wisdom', p. 145.
5.   Newsom, 'Woman and the Discourse of Patriarchal Wisdom', p. 146.

discourse, suggests that resistance to paternal authority is possible. Newsom's insights merit quoting at length.

> Certainly Proverbs 1–9 makes its own claims to universality and transcendent authority, but its explicit self-consciousness about the central role of discourses in competition provides an internal basis for questioning its own claims. Having learned from the father how to resist interpellation by hearing the internal contradictions in discourse, one is prepared to resist the patriarchal interpellation of the father as well. For the reader who does not take up the subject position offered by the text, Proverbs 1-9 ceases to be a simple text of initiation and becomes a text about the problematic nature of discourse itself. Not only the dazzling (and defensive) rhetoric of the father but also the pregnant silence of the son and the dissidence that speaks from the margin in the person of the strange woman become matters of significance.[1]

Proverbial rhetoric allows feminists to suggest, based on its example, that some discourses should be resisted.

From Tending a Garden to Fashioning a World. What intertextual relationship does Proverbs have with Genesis 2–3? Proverbs 1–9 displays much more directly than Genesis 2–3 male discomfort with female sexual behavior beyond male control. It not only warns men to avoid liaisons with such strange women deemed out of bounds, but it specifically describes these women as evil. It explicitly constructs gender by labeling the acceptable (good) and unacceptable (evil) range of women's behavior. More obviously than Genesis, Proverbs 1–9 displays the world from a male perspective. Thus, feminist reading of Proverbs 1–9 reinforces my earlier reading of Genesis 2–3: that women's sexuality is designed for men and that this construction is held in place through repressive and ideological state apparatuses.

By dramatizing the importance of discourses, Proverbs also depicts the contrast between proper and improper women's behavior as being a human construct. Acknowledgment of the role of discourse in shaping reality also suggests a way out of the garden debacle. By recognizing paths and worldviews as naturalized social constructions, Proverbs commends resistance to illusory or dangerous world-shaping rhetoric. Perhaps in contrast to the behavior of the woman in the garden, who may have acceded too quickly to the serpent's view of the world,

---

1. Newsom, 'Woman and the Discourse of Patriarchal Wisdom', p. 159.

Proverbs advises human discernment and thinking to sort out competing constructions of reality. It recognizes the ambiguous and ideological nature of reality, but allows a role for human planning, in conjunction with God, in transforming the world (cf. Prov. 16.1).[1]

Knowing Difference and Indifference in Qohelet

Qohelet is both similar to and different from Proverbs. Like Proverbs, this book both discusses the value of wisdom and gives examples of it. While Proverbs dramatizes the competition of discourses in shaping reality, through the vivid portrayals of woman wisdom and the strange woman, Qohelet is concerned with knowledge. Qohelet demonstrates *how* we know. His story of seeking wisdom highlights the role of experience and the value of human reflection and reason. He addresses *what* we know: the differences in human societies and the indifference of death. Qohelet is concerned with limits to our knowing and with God as the limiter. He also provides example and counsel about how we *respond* to our knowledge and to the limits of knowing and being. By addressing how and what we know and how we respond to our knowledge, Qohelet takes up questions raised in the garden.

Experiencing Knowledge. Qohelet's method 'is grounded in individual experience'.[2] Qohelet is explicitly empirical in his approach: applying his mind, searching, testing, and considering. He reflects consciously and reports his observations. The book is filled with comments about Qohelet's search for knowledge and its results: 'I considered...', 'I saw...', 'I said (to myself)...', 'I perceived...', 'I have seen...', and 'I thought...' First person narration emphasizes the sage's involvement in creating and refining knowledge.

Qohelet's challenging and testing of tradition suggest that he is willing to learn new knowledge and to use human reason to do so. Qohelet incorporates

> the fundamental tenet of Greek philosophy—the autonomy of individual reason, which is to say, the belief that individuals can and should proceed with their own observations and reasoning powers on a quest for

---

1.   Camp's 'Trickster' essay, which reads Proverbs 1–9 through the lens of the Native American 'trickster', offers another way of thinking about reality.

2.   M.V. Fox, 'Wisdom in Qoheleth', in Perdue *et al.* (eds.), *In Search of Wisdom*, p. 121.

knowledge and that this may lead to discovery of truths previously unknown.[1]

By combining experience and intellect in this way, Qohelet extends the scope of human wisdom. Michael V. Fox views Qohelet's work as an innovation: 'the idea of using one's independent intellect to discover new knowledge and interpret data drawn from individual experience is radical and, I think, unparalleled in extant wisdom literature'.[2] Qohelet's method certainly seems appropriate for feminist theologians struggling to come to grips with received traditions, and the content of his observations and counsel may be fruitful for contemporary questions as well.

Knowing Difference and Indifference. Much of Qohelet discusses difference and indifference to difference. Qohelet knows that differences help make the world work. He sees that toil and skill come from envy (4.4): competition perhaps contributes to competence. He is aware that the poor are kept poor by a system which looks out for itself, preserving its own privileges (5.8-9). Yet he also perceives that status is changeable and ephemeral. While a poor prisoner may replace a king, neither occasions rejoicing (4.13-16).

Qohelet is aware of oppression. He observes in 4.1 that neither the oppressed nor the oppressors have comfort, but he does not suggest that they are thereby the same. Rather, they are distinguished by what they do have: one group has tears, while the other has power. When authority is exercised by one person over another to that one's hurt, Qohelet is a realist (8.2-9). He recognizes that kings can do what they please and that no one can question them. So, he advises prompt, unterrified obedience (as leading to no harm, 8.5) and calm steadfastness in the face of a ruler's anger (10.4). Yet his talk in 8.5-6 about every matter having its time and its way hints at the possibility of well-timed seditious resistance.

Qohelet recognizes class differences (5.8-20). He seems to know the woes of both wealthy and poor. The lonely rich are discontent because no one will inherit their wealth (4.8). Lovers of money are not satisfied (5.10). Their surplus does not let the rich sleep, while, Qohelet claims, the sleep of laborers is sweet (5.12). Wealth, like status, may disappear,

1. Fox, 'Wisdom in Qoheleth', p. 123.
2. Fox, 'Wisdom in Qoheleth', p. 121.

even when the newly-bankrupt rich have children to feed (5.14). On the
one hand, Qohelet suggests that wealth offers no gain, but leads only to
vexation, darkness, sickness, and resentment (5.16-17). On the other
hand, he counsels the rich to enjoy their wealth and status *if* they are
able to do so, because this enjoyment is a gift of God (5.19). Qohelet is
well aware that God does not always permit such enjoyment (6.2-6). It is
not clear whether Qohelet's observations stem from a wealthy man
deposed from his privilege (10.6) or trying to make peace with it, or
from a shrewd but satisfied poor man, whose close contact with the rich
and whose necessary 'double vision' affords keen insights into his
master's distress.[1]

While conscious of differences, Qohelet advocates collaboration and
alliances (4.8-12). Three are better than two, and a couple is superior to
being alone. Such solidarity is not easily broken; it provides warmth,
uplift, and satisfaction.

Limits of Knowing and Being. What disturbs Qohelet is not so much
difference, but indifference to difference. He regularly bemoans the fact
that all have the same fate (2.14; 3.20; 6.6; 12.5). In life, that fate is time
and chance (9.11), but the ultimate equalizer is death. Death is indifferent
to human difference (2.16). It does not come swiftly to the wicked, nor
is it delayed for the righteous (7.15; 8.11). All humans share this fate
(9.2-3)—even with the animals (3.19). Wisdom's value seems ques-
tionable (2.15) in view of such 'crude egalitarianism'.[2]

Qohelet takes death seriously. Death disturbs him because there is no
gain from one's labor: we come and go naked (5.15-16). Nor is there
any remembrance of either the wise or fools (2.16). The dead, Qohelet
suggests, are more fortunate than those living with oppression, and the
unborn better still than one, like him, who sees evil deeds (4.2-3).
Initially, Qohelet's awareness of death leads him to despair and to hate
life (2.17, 20). But though death is a limit, even a bitter reality (7.26),
death ultimately makes Qohelet consider life.[3]

---

1.   The term 'double vision' refers to the experience of members of oppressed
groups who have their own culture but who also, for survival, must learn the dominant
culture. I believe this notion was expressed by W.E.B. DuBois, and the term may
have been coined by him.
2.   Fox, 'Wisdom in Qoheleth', p. 125.
3.   A comment is perhaps in order about Qohelet's finding woman even more
bitter than death in 7.26. It is seen by many, perhaps rightly, as an example of cruel

Death's frustration arises in part from Qohelet's struggles with the principle of retribution. Qohelet observes that judgment does not always correspond to deed: 'there are righteous people who are treated according to the conduct of the wicked, and there are wicked people who are treated according to the conduct of the righteous' (8.14). Qohelet seems to expect, though he does not always experience, that a principle of retribution is in place. In spite of its inconsistent application, and his recognition that God is 'free to ignore human merit',[1] Qohelet expects ultimate justice before God, both for the wicked and for those who fear God (8.12-13; 12.14). Wisdom does not permit escape from God.

Qohelet recognizes God as the limiter of human being and knowing. God has given humans life as it is: a sometimes 'unhappy business...to be busy with' (1.13). Moreover, 'God obstructs human wisdom'.[2] God has designed appropriate things and times, but humans cannot know them (3.11). In spite of human toil and seeking, we cannot know all the work of God (8.17). Part of the world, for example, that babies are made and bodies breathe, remains a mystery (11.5). It is not knowing, particularly not knowing the future (2.19; 8.7; 9.12; 10.14; 11.2), that makes troubles lie heavy and that hinders acceptance of a principle of retribution. 'God has created the world in such a way as to make it impossible to "discover what may happen afterwards" (7.14b), and thus to ascertain the consequences of an action'.[3]

How does Qohelet respond to God's limiting human knowing and being? Fox claims that Qohelet argues for wisdom, even against God. 'An absurd world thwarts understanding. Qoheleth's complaints are not a polemic against wisdom, but a protest against life—and God—on

misogyny, on the way to that of Sirach in 25.16-26. R. van Leeuwen's commentary in the *HarperCollins Study Bible* suggests instead that 'it echoes Proverbs' warning against adultery'. I wonder whether this comment cannot be made even more precise. In Qoh. 7.25 the sage sets out to know wisdom and folly. Though the argument would need to be developed, it may be that the woman 'more bitter than death' in 7.26 is woman folly of Proverbs (whom I called 'strange woman' above) and the woman Qohelet seeks but is unable to find in 7.28 is woman wisdom. Language describing the woman in Qoh. 7.26 echoes that of Prov. 5.4, 22.

    1.   J.L. Crenshaw, 'The Concept of God in Old Testament Wisdom', in Perdue *et al.* (eds.), *In Search of Wisdom*, p. 7.

    2.   Fox, 'Wisdom in Qoheleth', p. 123.

    3.   Fox, 'Wisdom in Qoheleth', p. 123.

wisdom's behalf'.[1] Crenshaw suggests, instead, that 'divine arbitrariness generated skepticism'.[2] I disagree with both these scholars. Qohelet's realism about the ultimate unknowability of everything that God does is not grumbling or protest. Qohelet complains neither to God nor about God as Job does. Nor is Qohelet a thoroughgoing skeptic. Qohelet doubts neither the possibility of knowledge nor the reliability of God.

Rather, Qohelet acknowledges God's power. God's work is unchangeable, even if crooked (7.13). Unlike ephemeral human achievements, God's works endure and inspire awe (3.14). Since God makes both prosperity and adversity, humans should enjoy the one and consider the other (7.14a). God's doing of both is a deliberate frustration: 'so that mortals may not find out anything that will come after them' (7.14b). But if God is powerful and God's ways mysterious, God is also gracious, providing life and enjoyment of it.

Enjoy the living of life is Qohelet's ultimate advice, and it is not a recommendation of either skepticism or despair. Rather, Qohelet counsels enjoying life because he knows both the limitations of human knowledge and God's power and mystery. Delighting in life, in the normal activities of eating and drinking, is 'from the hand of God' (2.24). Eating, drinking, and pleasure are God's gifts (3.13), human actions that God has long ago approved (9.7). Enjoyment must be from God—how else could one savor life, given knowledge of its futility and of the permanence of death? Qohelet recognizes that this gift is not always given. Finding pleasure in one's possessions or in one's toil and lot in life, rather than brooding over them, is God's gift (5.19-20), one that God does not always permit the wealthy to enjoy (6.2).

Qohelet makes a sort of peace with the principle of retribution by recognizing that life is not a matter of seeking treasures, of toiling with the expectation of ultimate rewards. Thus, in its futility, life 'is not to be reckoned as cruel fate or a savage joke, but as God's gift. Though life is *absurd*, it is *given* to humans'.[3] Pleasure in the activities themselves, in

1. Fox, 'Wisdom in Qoheleth', p. 126.
2. Crenshaw does not explicitly claim this position for Qohelet in this essay, though his other work suggests that he probably has Qohelet in mind here, as a skeptic in contrast to others (presumably Job?), whose response to divine arbitrariness consists in 'surrender before a merciful deity': 'Concept of God', p. 14.
3. D.J.A. Clines, 'The Wisdom Books', in Stephen Bigger (ed.), *Creating the Old Testament: The Emergence of the Hebrew Bible* (Oxford: Basil Blackwell, 1989), p. 279, emphasis his.

the doing and being, *is* the reward. That is why Qohelet suggests that being stillborn would be preferable to life without enjoyment (6.3). Recognizing death's inevitability and egalitarianism and knowing the pain that wisdom reveals, Qohelet counsels enjoyment of life (2.24-26; 3.22). In full view of the limitations of human knowledge and of divine freedom, Qohelet advises, to rephrase 11.9-10 in the words of Bobby McFerrin's song: 'Don't worry. Be happy'.

Similarly, although knowledge is partial, and in spite of the vexation and sorrow it brings (1.18), Qohelet advocates wisdom and knowledge.

> To the degree that wisdom—that is, intellect—succeeds in gaining knowledge, it causes pain... For wisdom reveals life's absurdity...The wise man—Qoheleth is projecting his own experience—uses wisdom (reason) in examining life, and this leads him to the conclusion that all is absurd and irreparable.[1]

Qohelet reports the truth, even when painful, because we must know it. Qohelet ferrets out and reports maddening absurdities and injustices because he feels that it is imperative that he—and we—know these truths, a knowledge that belongs to wisdom'.[2] In spite of its fragility (10.1), Qohelet recommends wisdom as superior to folly (2.13). Qohelet has considered (2.12), sought (7.25), used (2.19), acquired (1.16), experienced (1.16), tested (7.23), and known (1.17) wisdom. Although he knows wisdom can be despised (9.16), Qohelet recommends it as better than might and weapons (9.16, 18): a good inheritance (7.11) that gives strength (7.19), helps one succeed (10.10), and makes one's face shine (8.1). Before discussing implications of Qohelet in relation to the garden story and feminist theology, we turn to another response to the injustices and absurdities of life: the book of Job.

Job: Protesting Injustice or Justifying God
The book of Job may be the most well known literary work in the Bible. Whether we deem it a festal tragedy with Samuel Terrien or a comedy with William Whedbee, Job moves readers both by its beauty and by the powerful questions it raises about the nature of human relations with God.[3]

---

1. Fox, 'Wisdom in Qoheleth', p. 126.
2. Fox, 'Wisdom in Qoheleth', p. 128.
3. W. Whedbee, 'The Comedy of Job', in Y.T. Radday and A. Brenner (eds.), *On Humour and the Comic in the Hebrew Bible* (JSOTSup, 92; Sheffield: Almond Press, 1990), pp. 218-19, referring to S. Terrien, 'The Yahweh Speeches and Job's

In the opening scenes, Satan, the accuser, challenges God to find out whether God's servant Job fears God for nothing (1.9). God, like the narrator, maintains that Job is righteous. But God's willingness to permit Satan to take Job's wealth, kill his servants and children, and afflict him with sores puts the principle of retribution and the question of God's goodness squarely on the table. The concluding verses (42.7-17), which together with the first two chapters form the narrative frame for the book, maintain interest in these issues. God restores Job's wealth and gives him new children.

The poetic section, comprising the bulk of the book, emphasizes the principle of retribution through the voices of Job's lecturers (a more appropriate term, it seems, than friends or comforters since they are neither). Job's complaints, protests, and challenges raise questions about the nature and character of God—questions which the divine speeches in chs. 38–41 may seem only indirectly to address.

Knowledge and Experience. The structure of the book of Job suggests that the different levels of the characters' knowledge and experience affect their judgments. We readers hear God's affirmation of the narrator's assessment of Job's righteousness in 1.1, 8. From the narrative introduction we also have some clue about why Job suffers—knowledge that neither Job nor his dialogue partners have.

Job and his 'friends' operate on the basis of their own experience and knowledge of God, Job, and the way the world works. As Matitiahu Tsevat describes it, Job's advisors know that God is good and that the world operates by a system of retribution.[1] Therefore, since Job is suffering, he must have sinned. Job has a different perspective, however. He insists on his own integrity, but shares his cohorts' assumptions about retribution. Thus, Job questions the goodness of God. The deity, we readers have heard in the prologue, claims that Job is righteous, a view God also supports publicly in the concluding scene by affirming Job's speech over that of his lecturers (42.7-8). Presumably God maintains God's own goodness. So, Tsevat argues, if both Job and God are good and still Job suffered, then the world must not work by the principle of retribution.

But what does belief in such a principle suggest about God? Is God a

Responses', *Review and Expositor* 68 (1971), pp. 497-509.
    1.   M. Tsevat, 'The Meaning of the Book of Job', *HUCA* 37 (1966), pp. 73-106, especially pp. 104-106.

God who intervenes in human affairs? Does God simply react mechanically to human actions? When made into a guarantor of retribution by Job's dialogue partners, Crenshaw observes, God is imprisoned: 'Ironically, by depicting God as a "merciless engineer of the mechanization of divine retribution" they imprison the deity in a rigid system that human beings actually control by their conduct'.[1] The issue is not simply retribution. The integrity of God is also at stake.[2]

Discourse, Reality, and God. The whirlwind speeches in chs. 38–41 suggest that God and the world are more complicated than a doctrine of retribution allows, or at least they insist that retribution cannot be the only concept taken up for discussion. Unlike Job or his advisors, God does not speak of justice or retribution. The viewpoint expressed by the character God neither affirms nor denies the doctrine. Instead, God discusses other matters, such as the inaccessibility to humans of the divine design. God portrays God's concern with a wide range of human and non-human creation.[3] Justice, in this view, is not primarily concerned with one human being, but with sustaining life in all of its complexity.[4] God balances the needs of the world as a parent.[5] What seems to be at stake in the divine speeches is not Job-style justice, but trust. 'All that Job learns from God is that the issue is not retribution, but whether God can be trusted to run his world'.[6]

The whirlwind speeches alter Job's understanding and response to God and reality. In the dialogues Job is convinced that reality is related to his experience. If his world has fallen apart, Job calls forth chaos in the whole creation (Job 3).

> An epistemological and religious crisis leads the poet of Job to a serious questioning of the worldview that traditional wisdom had constructed, a reality that was both just and benign and overseen by a God at work in

1.   Crenshaw, 'Concept of God', p. 13.
2.   L.G. Perdue, 'Wisdom in the Book of Job', in *In Search of Wisdom*, p. 84.
3.   J.G. Janzen observes that because they are addressed to Job, the questions of the divine speeches suggest that humans are the creatures with whom God consults about creation. God is concerned with humans and non-humans. See *Job* (IBC; Atlanta: John Knox, 1985), p. 229.
4.   Perdue, 'Wisdom in the Book of Job', p. 95.
5.   D. Jacobson, 'Creation, Birth, and the Radical Ecology of the Book of Job' (Convocation Lecture presented at Luther Northwestern Theological Seminary, 9 February 1992).
6.   Clines, 'Wisdom Books', p. 288.

creation and history to sustain the righteous and to bring the wicked to destruction.[1]

In contrast to Job's lament in ch. 3 and to the view of traditional wisdom, the divine speeches portray a world not centered on Job. They omit, except perhaps by inferences which they expect Job to draw, 'any providential nurturing of human life, perhaps suggesting in a rather shocking way that reality is not anthropocentric, as Job's railings against God would imply'.[2] Job's views of reality and God change as Job gains a double perspective, both divine and human.[3] According to Norman Habel, the divine speeches challenge

> Job, and any who would listen, to discern God as the sage who designed a world of rhythms and paradoxes, of balanced opposites and controlled extremes, of mysterious order and ever-changing patterns, of freedom and limits, of life and death. Within this complex universe God functions freely to monitor the intricacies of the system, to modulate its ebb and flow and to balance its conflicting needs.[4]

Job's response in 42.6 suggests that he is satisfied with a new knowledge and wisdom: 'his new wisdom is that he does not know all, his new perception is that he does not see all; but he now knows enough and sees enough'.[5]

The portrayal of God also changes as the book of Job progresses. God in Job is a God at risk, willing to take Satan's challenge about Job, knowing that God could lose.[6] The God of the prologue

> is fiercely jealous about one successful mortal and allows himself, by his own admission, to be enticed into a wager with the accuser (Job 2.3). Here

---

1. Perdue, 'Wisdom in the Book of Job', p. 89.
2. Perdue, 'Wisdom in the Book of Job', p. 93.
3. Whedbee, 'The Comedy of Job', p. 240.
4. N.C. Habel, 'In Defense of God the Sage', in L.G. Perdue and W.C. Gilpin (eds.), *The Voice from the Whirlwind: Interpreting the Book of Job* (Nashville: Abingdon Press, 1992), p. 38.
5. Whedbee, 'The Comedy of Job', p. 243. While Whedbee's proposal is plausible and shared by a number of scholars, I am intrigued with another possibility that I learned in August 1994 in conversation with Walter Michel. Leery of the translations, Michel observes the poetic form of 42.5-6: 'With my ear I heard *you*, but now my eye has seen *you*, therefore I despise... and I repent in dust and ashes'. And the reader is left to fill in the blank. Michel suggests that by refusing to cave in to God's egotistical power moves in the bombastic divine speeches, Job has in fact passed the last test, and therefore God rewards him.
6. Perdue, 'Wisdom in the Book of Job', p. 96.

is a God like the God of the prophets, who makes decisions in the council on high and intervenes in the lives and history of his people. Unlike the God of the prophets, however, there is here no 'Thus says the Lord' to explain the reason for Yahweh's act of intervention.[1]

This God, thus, seems to be a ruthless bully, 'one who stops at almost nothing, even murder, to prove a point'.[2]

The poetic dialogues portray varied understandings of God. Job's counselors do not expect God to take initiative. 'The character of their God must remain unimpeachable. There is no just world if God is not the moral God of their tradition, the God who reacts'.[3] Job has experienced a God gone berserk.

> This is the mighty *gibbôr*, the hero, the warrior who attacks Job with poisoned arrows and seeks to overwhelm him with terror and dread (6.4). This is God the merciless hunter... the violent and cruel warrior who smashes and rends Job personally... the warrior king... the 'God Who Acts' gone berserk in the life of one mortal... This God... promotes cosmic destruction and social disorder...anarchy... fosters violence... [This] God exercises wisdom by demolishing what humans have constructed... [This God] fosters darkness; instead of stirring the human intellect, God creates morons... activates a chaos... releases darkness... God is an anarchist—a violent anarchist.[4]

God's whirlwind speeches imply another understanding of God, a view that throws some of the others into question. Here God does not primarily intervene, react, or attack. Rather, these speeches portray 'a wise God who has made the world the way it is for his own inscrutable purposes... [They insist] that God must be allowed to know what he is doing, and lies under no obligation to give any account of himself'.[5] In spite of Job's courage in the dialogues to confront God, these speeches suggest that God, finally, is not the problem.

Wisdom Re-Visioned. The book of Job does not resolve the questions it raises, nor does it posit a single acceptable way of understanding the world. The book's

> chief literary feature is that it does not expound or defend a dogma from one point of view, but portrays a debate in which conflicting points of view

1. Habel, 'In Defense of God the Sage', p. 26.
2. Crenshaw, 'Concept of God', p. 12.
3. Habel, 'In Defense of God the Sage', p. 28.
4. Habel, 'In Defense of God the Sage', pp. 28-30.
5. Clines, 'Wisdom Books', p. 287.

are put forward, none of them being unambiguously presented as
preferable to the others. This makes it perhaps the most intellectually
demanding book of the Hebrew Bible, requiring of its readers a mental
flexibility and even a willingness, in the end, to be left with no unequivocal
message.[1]

Because of the multiple points of view in Job, readers are left wondering
whether the world operates through a system of retribution, and what
kind of God God is. God's whirlwind speeches may attempt to chasten
Job, but their 'question form, like God the sage, keeps the wise seeking
and learning in the search for theological wisdom'.[2]

Wisdom is a treasure buried in the earth, whose dwelling God alone
knows (Job 28). Yet, Job may paradoxically have access to her. The
wisdom poem in chapter 28 concludes that to fear God is wisdom, to
shun evil is discernment. Habel observes that this is precisely what Job is
said to have done. He is a blameless and upright man who fears God
and shuns evil (1.8).[3] Through this indirect allusion, the book of Job may
agree with Qohelet that humans have some limited access to wisdom
and that reflection on human experience plays a legitimate role in
understanding the world. Yet, like Qohelet, it does not resolve all of the
issues. 'In the world of the wise there are no absolute solutions to the
open-ended questions of life'.[4] Perhaps wisdom's method of addressing,
but not answering, key questions of life, in the midst of uncertainty,
affords a worthy model for our time:

> by using their powers of observation and the ability to think rationally, the
> sages sought to understand God, social institutions, and the moral life
> through their reflections on creation and human experiences, including
> their own. Yet they never deified their own powers of understanding, for
> they recognized the limits of their capacity to comprehend reality.[5]

From Texts to World: Living the Wisdom
The garden narrative in Genesis 2–3 raises feminist questions about
knowledge and experience, discourse and reality, to which wisdom
literature attends. While Proverbs promotes a single reality, that of
woman wisdom and the teacher/father, Job and Qohelet more directly

1.   Clines, 'Wisdom Books', p. 281.
2.   Habel, 'In Defense of God the Sage', pp. 33-34.
3.   Habel, 'In Defense of God the Sage', p. 25.
4.   Habel, 'In Defense of God the Sage', p. 37.
5.   Perdue, 'Wisdom in the Book of Job', p. 76.

struggle with concerns about human limitations, the role of wisdom in view of multiple perspectives, and God's potentially troubling involvement in the world. Their content, methods, and theologies build from questions the garden narrative raises and contribute to feminist approaches to living wisely.

Qohelet invites us to consider the value of wisdom and the choices we make in living life within limits. Why be wise, Qohelet queries in 2.15? Feminists would also ask: given our knowledge of the injustices and absurdities of life, can we, like Qohelet, both enjoy living life and recommend such enjoyment to others? In so doing are we being co-opted by an indifferent wealthy wisdom (like Qohelet's?) that lives by its privilege? Moving beyond the concerns of Qohelet and Job, can we enjoy living life in ways that work toward others being able to enjoy living as well?

Qohelet makes astute observations about a world of difference. It recognizes the systemic nature of injustices and the potential of individuals, even those outside the hierarchies of power, to effect change. Both Qohelet and Job may be misogynist, classist, and conservative, in the sense of maintaining or seeking to reinstate privilege, rather than calling for reform as do many of the biblical prophets. Yet they also recognize the fleeting nature of privilege and the ultimate equality of humans—even our position as only one part of God's cosmic design. These sages may not have grand ideas for transforming the world, but they do commend honesty in our dealings in it.

One aspect of such honesty is valuing experience and embracing wisdom. Thinking intertextually with the Genesis garden narrative, Qohelet seems to affirm the woman's choice: to value thinking and experimenting, even when new knowledge brings with it awareness of pain and death. Qohelet affirms the importance for feminism of pursuing and reporting knowledge, especially of injustices. Job likewise commends taking positions, even challenging God, based on one's experience with and understanding of the world, and doing so with the awareness (thanks to the book's conclusion) that such understanding is partial.

Both Qohelet and Job, like feminism and the garden narrative, operate within a context of multiple perspectives. Qohelet incorporates these into his own story of testing wisdom. By acknowledging despair as an initial response, and by his constant refrain about the vanity, fleetingness, or absurdity of life, Qohelet demonstrates that his ultimate counsel of enjoying life as a gift of God is *not* the only reasonable approach to

living. Still, he is willing to take a stand: he recommends enjoying life.
Job, likewise, through the various positions of the dialogues, by God's
silence on the question, and via the frame narrative's reinstatement of
Job's wealth, refuses to resolve the question of divine retribution. Thus,
wisdom literature seems to suggest that we are not always called to
resolve issues or to box the world into a single correct 'reality'. Rather,
sometimes it is more important to seek temporary pragmatic solutions
and to discuss questions and take positions, even amid uncertainty.

Qohelet's and Job's methods of valuing experience and testing
tradition provide models for contemporary feminist theologizing. For
feminists, questioning and refashioning theology as one's own need not
mean rejecting either God or tradition, but rather a willingness to live
within the world on God's terms (while perhaps challenging them) and
with an openness to new knowledge about God, the world, and our
living.[1] Wisdom literature affirms for feminist theology the importance
of testing tradition and making it our own, of evaluating it in relation to
our experience and by means of our reason. Feminists would modify
this method in at least one significant way. While Qohelet and Job seem
to have operated primarily as individuals, feminists urge doing theology
in broader communities.

Wisdom literature may contribute most to feminist theology through
its insistence on addressing God questions. Feminists struggle with many
aspects of the garden narrative, with woman's secondary status, with the
fashioning of compulsory heterosexuality, with attempts to silence
women or to dismiss their reliance on experience and reason, with
portrayal of their thinking and speaking as dangerous. But ultimately,
feminists struggle in the garden with God.

Job reassures feminists that we are not alone in finding God troubling.
God, for the Job of the dialogues, has moved beyond being a mysterious
limiter of human life and knowledge to an active, possibly capricious,
harasser. Together, Job and Qohelet provide language for talking about
our experiences of God, difference, and oppression, and they offer
models for responding to these perceptions: despair, skepticism,

---

1.   On feminists refashioning theology, see M.F. Bednarowski, 'The Spirit of
Re-Imagining: Setting the Stage', *Church & Society* 84 (May/June 1994), pp. 12-19.
On wisdom literature as an appropriate, untapped resource for contemporary
theologizing, see W. Brueggemann, 'Scripture and an Ecumenical Life-Style: A
Study in Wisdom Theology', *Int* 24 (1970), pp. 3-19.

suspicion, surrender, untroubled faith, rage, protest, challenge, and enjoyment of life.

Conclusion

The goal of this chapter, as the goal of thesis as a whole, has not been to promote a single interpretation of Genesis 2–3 designed to unseat previous interpretations. Rather, it has been to complicate the interpretive process, to suggest that we as readers come with multiple perspectives on what constitutes reality and that these different understandings affect our readings. We use and hear language differently. We have different knowledge and experiences that we bring to interpretation. We read in relation to different intertexts. We read with values and interests shaped by different questions and communities. Reading through multiple lenses need not be an obstruction to identifying meaning, but can be a resource in appreciating the rich possibilities of a text.

The theoretical discussions at the beginning of this chapter provided a necessary framework for the intertextual readings that followed. They introduced ideologies as systems in which 'meaning serves to establish and sustain relations of domination'[1] and suggested that the ways that we understand ourselves as subjects are shaped by the ideologies through which we are interpellated. Ideologies are thus related to interpretive communities, which form the basis within which texts are understood. Meaning, with this notion of textuality, does not reside in a text, waiting to be ferreted out by cunning interpreters. Rather, intertextuality posits that because texts are weavings of other texts, a text means (and perhaps means differently) through the various discourses within which it is read.

As an example of feminist ideological criticism which would subsequently serve as an intertext for a reading of Genesis 2–3, I described how various ideologies of gender shape feminist theories of reality and difference in selected works of MacKinnon, Rich, and Wittig. MacKinnon analyzes rape law and concludes that we live in a culture in which reality is construed from a male perspective. Rich argues that societal pressures and constraints compel women's heterosexuality and suggests that any women who rebel against this system fit into a 'lesbian continuum'. Wittig takes Rich's thesis a step further by claiming that lesbians are not 'women' at all, because women exist only within heterosexuality, where they are constructed on the basis of men's needs. Theorizing about

---

1. Thompson, *Ideology and Modern Culture*, p. 56.

'difference' requires attention to race, sexual orientation, gender, and class as interlocking structures that are both social constructions and lived realities.

Rape culture and compulsory heterosexuality are not the constructs of reality usually presumed by standard biblical interpretations, yet, they inform many feminist understandings of society and shed a revealing light on ideologies informing readings of Genesis 2–3. I argued that, read through the feminist lenses of this chapter, Genesis 2–3 functions not to institute marriage as a relationship of mutuality between husband and wife but to produce 'compulsory heterosexuality', complete with its 'eroticization of dominance', as the nature of gender and reality. But I also insisted that interpreters need not be satisfied with such an interpretation. The serpent's question opens the way to alternate understandings of reality.

Reading the Cain and Abel story as an intertext showed that the garden narrative is not interested solely in divine-human interaction, but in a variety of interrelationships. This reading emphasized ways in which both stories are concerned with judging difference. It also observed a development in relationships from the first to the second human generation. For example, God teaches and learns differently.

The concluding set of intertextual readings shifted direction from the earlier analyses. Rather than using intertexts to achieve better understandings of the Genesis 2–3 text, these readings began with feminist questions raised in relation to the garden narrative. Then they branched out to consult wisdom literature, whose discussions of discourse, knowledge, and reality were helpful. This literature affirms the feminist insistence on attending to multiple perspectives on reality. It acknowledges the role of ideologies and intertexts in shaping one's understanding and ways of living in the world. Qohelet and Job, in particular, deal directly with ambiguity and the problems God poses for humans, with which feminist readers of the paradise story have also struggled. Wisdom literature thus provides a way to talk and think about a question the garden story raises: what does it mean to be human creatures of God? And it does so with understandings of the roles of knowledge, discourse, ideologies, and reality that are congenial to contemporary feminist theory and critique. Wisdom literature does not provide a solution to the challenges that Genesis 2–3 poses for feminists, but a way, using canonical intertexts, to continue the conversation and to consider what is at stake in our answers for how we live.

CONCLUSION

Interpretation matters. I have shown that Genesis 2–3 claims that interpretation matters, that there are consequences for the actions we take on the basis of our interpretations, and that we should engage this process carefully. This conclusion summarizes and integrates ideas from several chapters, and it poses a few questions and directions for future work.

This book is a work of integrative scholarship. Each chapter brought feminist and critical theories into conversation with the Genesis 2–3 text, focusing on a particular theme. Chapter 1 surveyed varieties of reader-response criticism and then provided a 'slow' reading of the garden narrative with special attention to God. Chapter 2 applied feminist literary criticism and epistemologies to investigate the role of knowledge and experience in the garden. Chapter 3 observed a striking divergence among five theories about language and discourse: American feminist theory, French feminist theory, rhetorical criticism, speech act theory, and narratology. Analysis of Genesis 2–3 using these theories showed that language functions ambivalently in the narrative as power and possibilities, danger and delights.

While the first two chapters focused on individual readers and the third chapter examined the rhetorical effects of the text on readers, chapter four brought the study to the social realm by attending to ideology, intertextuality, and feminist scholarship on 'difference.' When read through the lens of this scholarship, the garden narrative seemed to exhibit what feminists call 'compulsory heterosexuality' and to produce a reality where the male is the norm. I also read Genesis 2–3 in relation to Gen. 4.1-16 and observed interrelationships, developing relationships, and judging of differences. The chapter concluded by moving from feminists' questions raised in relation to Genesis 2–3 to conversations with Proverbs, Qohelet, and Job about discourse, reality, knowledge, difference, and God. These conversations with wisdom literature provided some hints for moving from interpreting texts to living in the world.

Combining feminist scholarship with literary theories to address

Genesis 2–4 and wisdom literature enables drawing a few conclusions about knowledge, discourse, reality, and difference. Feminist phase theory exhibits a variety of approaches to knowing. Feminist epistemologies suggest that 'what we know depends on where we stand', in terms of both our life experiences and our political agendas. Our experiences and knowledge are constrained by the ideologies within which we live. Similarly, intertextuality suggests that interpretation depends on what we know. The garden woman interpreted on the basis of her knowledge and experience and got into trouble. Wisdom literature suggests, however, that personal experience, thought, and reflection are appropriate. It urges us to recognize the limits of our knowledge and to take stands and make commitments in spite of uncertainty.

This study brings several ideas to a conversation about language, discourse, and rhetoric. Language operates through social conventions. It is a matter of agreement and consensus. Language is the means of making our private realities public. Because it is a social phenomenon, rhetorical difficulties may occur: language sometimes fails. The garden story suggests that we beware of how we respond to persuasive rhetoric. Both Genesis 2–3 and Proverbs remind us that discourse is powerful: it may have dangerous or unpredictable effects. Multiple discourses vie for our allegiance, and some lead to death. Rhetoric may also attempt hegemony, making it difficult to sort out competing construals.

Feminist scholarship on 'difference' observes that there are genuine alternatives. There are multiple ways of understanding what it means to be the different materially and socially constructed humans we are. A third party (like the serpent in Gen. 3.1-5 or God in 3.8-13) or outside voices (for example, lesbian perspectives in a straight community) can make some of these possibilities clear. The ways we experience reality are mediated through language, rhetoric, and ideology. Discourse is important because through it we fashion worlds, but those parts of our world that are socially constructed can also be changed or resisted. Biblical wisdom literature encourages us to speak honestly about the systematic injustices in a world of difference, and feminist goals prompt our work to transform these realities.

Interpretation matters both in the garden and out of Eden. Genesis 2–3 hinges on a discussion in 3.1-5 about interpretation. That God's words are the topic of this first conversation in the Bible suggests both the inevitability and the importance of interpretation. Interpretation matters in the garden. Genesis 2–3 speaks profoundly to contemporary communities about life within limits. God's word was and continues to be an issue among us. Interpretations still affect (and effect) the effectiveness of God's speech. Interpretation matters both in and out of the garden: there are consequences for interpretations both in the story and in our lives. God is interested in our interpretations and expects responsible thought and action. Finally, interpretations matter out of the garden. Women have had difficulty with God's words in Gen. 3.16. Many find the garden story troubling; it remains unsettled. Interpretations matter out of Eden, particularly for women, because we continue to experience the effects of this Genesis text and its often oppressive readings.

The bulk of this study consists of bringing feminist scholarship and literary critical theories into conversation with Genesis 2–3. While these conversations are interesting, a question may remain. How should we understand and interpret the garden story? Is Genesis 3 a fall story, as one writer has recently asked?[1]

Moving temporarily beyond the question of which interpretation to adopt for the story, we might also ask whether interpretation, finally, is what biblical scholars should be about. Observing that what a text *means* is a recent question in the millenia of literary study,[2] some scholars contend that what a text *does* should be the object of our scrutiny. While this return to rhetoric, this renewed regard for the power of a text to shape its hearers and readers, is an important corrective to interpretive approaches that attempt to box a text into a single meaning, both the interpretive and rhetorical approaches usually pay insufficient attention to the complexity of interpretive communities that ideological analyses and feminist theories require.

Lutherans may have a particular stake in how these questions are resolved. For Luther, the contrast between letter and spirit (cf. 2 Cor. 3.6) suggests that interpretation 'does not give life'.[3] Genesis 2–3 might be thought of as playing out this Lutheran position that interpretation

1. T.E. Fretheim, 'Is Genesis 3 a Fall Story?', *WW* 14 (1994), pp. 144-53.

2. J.P. Tompkins makes this observation and argues for interacting with texts in ways that are conscious of the political character of the study of language; see her essay 'The Reader in History: The Changing Shape of Literary Response', in J.P. Tompkins (ed.), *Reader-Response Criticism: From Formalism to Post-Structuralism*, (Baltimore: The Johns Hopkins University Press, 1980), pp. 201-32.

3. G.O. Forde, 'Law and Gospel in Luther's Hermeneutic', *Int* 37 (1983), p. 245.

'kills'. Certainly, there were devastating consequences for the garden couple. We wrestle with similar situations. We do not escape our embeddedness in ambivalent language. We may observe, however, that the couple does not die right away: humans have to live with our knowledge of good and evil. Right after the judgments in Gen. 3.14-19, the man bursts into life-affirming pun. Interpretation has its positive side. Because we are stuck in it, we can use interpretation responsibly to live our lives. So, though it will not solve the problem of God,[1] interpretation still matters.

It may still be possible to talk about what a text 'does' or to offer an interpretation that is compelling for an interpretive community. One way to achieve this end, of course, is to define the interpretive community (or the goals of interpretation) so narrowly that it includes very few people. Lutheran feminist scholars, for example, might be able to agree on the effects of Genesis 2–3 or to decide how to interpret this story. Another approach, far more common I fear, is to define the interpretive community broadly (for example, as all biblical scholars, all theologically committed readers, or all Christians) and to presume that everyone in the community shares the same reading of the text or understanding of its rhetorical effects. The ways we define our interpretive communities and the ways we hear texts and understand them are shaped by our positions as members of interpretive communities and by our ideological assumptions and goals in relation to particular texts and communities.

My discussion has shown that even within interpretive communities texts can be heard and interpreted in opposing ways. Chapter 1 offered a broad range of questions that readers with different backgrounds might pose. Chapter 2 suggested that both positive and negative appraisals of the woman's role in the narrative are reasonable. The woman is, in some ways, both a model moral thinker and the victim of a patriarchy that suffuses the entire story (not simply appearing after the 'fall'). Chapter 3 showed that even a particular theme, language, could

---

1.   Donald Juel makes this point. See 'The Authority of the Scriptures: An Assessment of a Conversation' (paper presented at the Convocation of Teaching Theologians on 'Renewing Biblical Authority: A Challenge for the ELCA', Chicago, Illinois, 14 August 1994). My work here is aiming toward some of the 'other matters' that Juel observes remain for our discussion: 'how adequately to render ancient books in our own language and idiom... to consider what difference it will make if "strangers" of all sorts are included in that conversation... [and] what to make of the Bible as a moral guide' (p. 7).

be heard in several ways. Language might be understood as powerful or dangerous, or a reader might appreciate the possibilities or delights of how language plays in the story. Chapter 4 demonstrated that the intertexts (including life experiences) that a reader brings may greatly influence how she hears and interprets a text. Readers familiar with realities described by feminist theories about 'compulsory hetero-sexuality' or 'difference' may experience what the Genesis 2–3 text 'does' differently from those unfamiliar with this scholarship.

To talk about what scripture 'does', then, or about how to interpret it requires paying attention to the lives of real readers in interpretive communities. It insists that we recognize our different experiences and consider how they may shape our reading and hearing. This rhetorical or hermeneutical task acknowledges the multitude of possibilities avail-able in a text as rich as Genesis 2–3 and understands that a text's overall effect or an interpreter's reading is shaped to a large degree by ideologi-cal commitments of the individual interpreter and communities of which she or he is a part.

The claim is not that scripture interprets itself, but that interpreters, shaped by ideological commitments (some of which may include listening for and seeking the guidance of the Holy Spirit), inevitably interpret within communities. Similarly, rather than asking 'Is Genesis 3 a fall story?' (which may sound as if a text's proper interpretation is inherent within the text itself rather than occurring between text and community), it may be more important to consider the ways in which reading Genesis 2–3 *as* a creation-fall story is appropriate for a particular interpretive community. Moving in this direction, I think, is not asking about rhetoric or hermeneutics (how do texts function or how does understanding happen). Nor is it asking what is the best analysis of a particular text's effects or about the superlative overall rendering of the narrative. Instead, it presumes ideological commitments and asks about the ethics of interpretation. Why do we hear or understand Genesis 2–3 in particular ways, and what is at stake for our communities in the ways we choose to describe a text's meaning or effects?

By avoiding selecting a single reading of Genesis 2–3 in terms of either the traditional creation-fall or growth interpretations, I have suggested that neither of these approaches, alone, is adequate for the contemporary communities of which I am a part, as a Lutheran feminist scholar. This does not mean that I do not find helpful aspects in each rendering, but I think that choosing only one of these interpretations is inadequate.

Let me briefly address the creation-fall stream.[1] Ignore for a moment the devastating consequences that this branch of tradition has had for women, and ignore, as well, the gender differences my work has suggested it is important to consider. Instead, think of this interpretation of the story as telling some truths. God does create, enliven, permit, prohibit, and call to account. Humans do disobey. We do sin. But it matters for our communities how we describe that 'sin' and why we choose this particular text (rather than Genesis 4 or Psalm 51, for example) as our primary occasion for discussing human sinfulness.[2]

Early feminist scholarship observed that theological concepts like sin may need to be reassessed in terms of how they apply to women. Valerie Saiving suggested that 'negation of self' may be a more appropriate characterization of sin for women than 'pride'.[3] While more recent scholarship does not want to divide contrasting human experiences of sin so neatly along gender lines, the point remains that we need a variety of characterizations of 'sin' to describe adequately the range of disrupted human relationships with creation, with one another, and with God.

To talk about 'sin' in Genesis 2–3 only as 'failure to trust God' or to insist that this form of sin is primary or fundamental may precisely condemn some members of faith communities at the place they are most vulnerable. Mary Potter Engel reviews several different ways of describing sin and evil by beginning not with the powerful but with victims.[4] She observes that for survivors of sexual or domestic violence,

1.   Similar points could be made against limiting one's reading of the narrative to the growth tradition. While helpfully acknowledging the gifts of reason and human freedom to make decisions, this interpretive strand minimizes other realities of divine–human and interhuman relationships, such as disobedience, shame, and failure to trust or betrayal of trust.

2.   Paul's discussion in Romans 5 is certainly one reason Christians turn to Genesis 2–3 for understanding human sinfulness.

3.   V. Saiving, 'The Human Situation: A Feminine View', in C.P. Christ and J. Plaskow (eds.), *Womanspirit Rising: A Feminist Reader in Religion* (San Francisco: Harper & Row, 1979), p. 37; the essay is reprinted from *The Journal of Religion* 40 (1960), pp. 100-12.

4.   M. Potter Engel, 'Evil, Sin, and Violation of the Vulnerable', in S. Brooks Thistlethwaite and M. Potter Engel (eds.), *Lift Every Voice: Constructing Christian Theologies from the Underside* (San Francisco: Harper & Row, 1990), pp. 152-68.

it may be more appropriate to talk about sin as 'betrayal of trust'.[1] Rape victims, for example, may find it particularly difficult to trust a God so often portrayed in the Bible and in faith communities as male. 'Failure to trust God' is an important and helpful way to talk about human sin, and it may be the best way to talk about sin in the garden narrative. Feminist scholarship suggests, however, that we may need to nuance discussion of sin in these terms (and with this Genesis 2–3 text) by supplementing it (through interpretations of other texts or perhaps new interpretations of this one) with other characterizations of sin, perhaps as 'betrayal of trust'. As this example shows, work remains to be done in thinking about the ethics of interpretation among and for interpretive communities and in considering the implications for how we do theology.

The garden story shows us that interpretation matters. Critical literary theories and feminist scholarship suggest some of the issues involved with interpreting texts for and among contemporary communities: these include awareness of intertextuality, ideologies, and 'difference'. Faith communities today must assume that they include, for example, both perpetrators and victims of abuse, both gays and lesbians who feel constrained by 'compulsory heterosexuality' and straight people who are often oblivious to this view of the world. Lives are at stake in the ways such communities interpret scripture. One challenge for communities of faith that recognize biblical authority is to hear and include all of these voices in serious, thoughtful conversations about hermeneutical processes and interpretation matters that affect the ways we live our lives 'out of Eden'.

---

1. Potter Engel's essay exemplifies the kind of plural approach I am advocating. She reviews several traditional characterizations of sin, discussing situations in which they may still apply but also how they may be 'problematic from the perspective of the victim's survival and recovery' (p. 157). She also offers several new options: distortion of feeling, lack of care, distortion of boundaries, and distortion of the dependence/freedom dynamic (lack of consent to vulnerability). The essay explicitly avoids substituting a single 'new absolute definition of sin' for the old one (p. 154).

APPENDIX: TRANSLATION WITH NOTES

(2.4)[1] These are[2] the generations of the heavens and the earth[3] when they were created, on the day YHWH God[4] made earth and heavens.[5] (5) When no bush of the field was yet on the earth and no grass of the field had yet sprouted, for YHWH[6] God had not caused it to rain upon the earth, and there was not a man[7] to work[8] the ground,[9] (6) but *a stream*[10] would go up from the earth, and it watered the whole face of the ground, (7) then YHWH God formed the man out of dust from the ground, and breathed into his nostrils living breath, so that the man became a living being.

(8) Then YHWH* God planted a garden[11] in Eden,[12] to the East,[13] and he put there the man whom he had formed. (9) And YHWH* God made to sprout from the ground every[14] tree [that is] desirable to see and good to eat, and the tree of life in the middle of the garden, and the tree of the knowledge of good and evil. (10) And *a river* would

---

1. Gen. 2.4 as a whole introduces the following narrative. See T. Stordalen, 'Genesis 2,4: Restudying a *locus classicus*', *ZAW* 104 (1992), pp. 163-77.
2. The LXX has 'This is the book of' in place of 'These are'.
3. The LXX uses the article in 'the heavens and the earth' in 2.4b, not 2.4a.
4. I transliterate the divine name (the tetragrammaton) as YHWH. In the Pentateuch, the name YHWH God appears only in Genesis 2–3 and in Exod. 9.30. For discussion of its meaning see J. L'Hour, 'Yahweh Elohim', *RB* 81 (1974), pp. 524-56.
5. The Samaritan Pentateuch and the LXX reverse the order of these two nouns, possibly due to eye skip or to coincide with the usual order in 2.4a.
6. The LXX omits YHWH here and in several other places that I indicate with an asterisk.
7. I translate *'ādām* consistently as 'man', because, contra Trible, I think that the first human creature throughout this story is portrayed as a man. See discussion on pp. 102-104.
8. *'bd* is a common verb for work or serving, that of a slave or servant to a master or of a priest to God.
9. Hebrew listeners would hear a word play on the words man, *'ādām*, and ground *'ᵃdāmâ*. Close English options are human... humus, and earthling... earth.
10. I italicize words in the translation when unusual Hebrew word order indicates emphasis. There has been considerable scholarly discussion of this particular word, used only here and in Job 36.27, where the translation 'mist' seems appropriate. See E.A. Speiser, ' *'ED* in the Story of Creation', *BASOR* 140 (1955), pp. 9-11.
11. The LXX translates the Hebrew word for garden, *gan*, as 'paradise'.
12. Eden is related to Akkadian and Sumerian words for 'plain' or 'steppe', but sounds like the etymologically unrelated Hebrew noun for 'enjoyment'.
13. The adverb 'to the East' could also be translated temporally: 'from ancient times'.
14. *kōl* is the same word used in 2.5 for 'every'; it means 'all' or 'every'. Here it might be better translated as 'all kinds of'.

go up from Eden to water the garden, and from there it divided and became[1] four branches. (11) The name of the first is Pishon; it is the one that goes around the whole land of Havilah, where there is gold; (12) and the gold of that land is good.[2] There is bdellium[3] there and shosham[4] stone. (13) And the name of the second river is Gihon. It is the one that goes around the whole land of Cush. (14) And the name of the third river is Hidqel (Tigris). It is the one that goes east of Asshur. And the fourth river is the Euphrates.

(15) Then YHWH God took the man[5] and settled him in the garden of Eden[6] to work it and to guard it. (16) And YHWH God commanded the man[7] saying, 'Of every tree of the garden you may surely[8] eat, (17) but of the tree of the knowledge of good and evil you shall not eat of it, because on the day that you eat of it you will surely die.'[9]

(18) Then YHWH God said '[It is] not good [that] the man be alone; I[10] will make for him a helper as his counterpart'.[11] (19) So YHWH* God[12] formed out of the ground every[13] animal of the field and every bird of the heavens, and he brought [them] to the man* to see what he would call them,[14] so that whatever the man* called the living being, that is its name. (20) So the man* gave names to all cattle and birds[15] of the heavens and to every animal of the field, but [as] for the man* he[16] did not find

1.   These two verbs could be translated with a historical present.

2.   One Samaritan manuscript says 'very' good.

3.   Bdellium is the standard transliteration. Some translations say 'aromatic resin' (NIV), 'gum resin' (REB), 'fine resin' (Westermann), and 'rare perfume' (TEV), all following KB.

4.   Another transliteration variously translated as 'onyx' or 'onyx stone' (NRSV, RSV, KJV, NIV), 'lapis lazuli' (JPS, Speiser, *Book of J*), 'cornelians' or 'cornelian stone' (NEB, REB, NJB), or 'precious stones' (TEV).

5.   The LXX adds 'whom he had formed', resuming the construction at the end of 2.8.

6.   The LXX reads garden 'of delights'.

7.   The LXX reads 'the Adam' or 'Adam' in place of 'the man' or 'man' here and in other places that I indicate with an asterisk.

8.   The infinitive absolute construction intensifies the permission; it is often rendered 'freely'.

9.   The infinitive absolute construction in the warning parallels that of the permission in 2.16, and is so translated. There is no cause (except perhaps embarrassed theology) for translating the phrase as 'doomed to die' (REB, NJB) or 'death touches you' (*Book of J*).

10.   The LXX has 'let us make' as in Gen. 1.26.

11.   The translation 'counterpart' captures both the oppositeness and likeness inherent in the Hebrew word *kᵉnegdô*.

12.   The Samaritan Pentateuch and the LXX add 'again'.

13.   The Samaritan Pentateuch includes the definite object marker before 'every'; it is absent in the Masoretic text.

14.   Literally 'it'; presumably the animals were brought individually.

15.   English requires 'birds'; the Hebrew singular noun is collective.

16.   The verb is a *qal* active, third masculine singular and may be translated that way. There is no textual evidence for emending it to a *niphal*. Westermann *ad loc.* agrees. There may be some ambiguity about the subject 'he' of the verb. The man is naming the animals, but it is not clear he knows God is hoping he will find a counterpart.

a helper as his counterpart. (21) So YHWH* God caused a deep sleep[1] to fall upon the man*, and he slept. Then he took one of his ribs, and he closed [with] flesh its place. (22) Then YHWH* God built[2] the rib that he had taken from the man* into a woman, and he brought her to the man*. (23) And the man* said,

> 'This one, this time,[3]
>> bone of my bones and flesh of my flesh;
> this one shall be called woman,
>> for from man[4] was taken this one.'[5]

(24) Therefore a man[6] leaves his father and his mother and clings to his woman,[7] and they[8] become one flesh. (25) And the two of them were naked, the man* and his woman, and they were not ashamed.

(3.1) Now the serpent was more shrewd[9] than all the animals of the field that YHWH God had made. So it said to the woman, 'Really, did God say "you[10] (pl) may not eat from any tree of the garden"?' (2) And the woman said to the serpent, 'of the fruit of[11] the trees of the garden we may eat, (3) but, of the fruit of the[12] tree that is in the middle of the garden, God said, "You (pl) shall not eat from it and you (pl) shall not touch it lest you (pl) die"'. (4) Then the serpent said to the woman, 'You (pl) will not surely die.[13] (5) For God knows that on the day you (pl) eat of it your (pl) eyes

---

1. The 'deep sleep' often occasions a special divine action. See Gen. 15.12-13.
2. The verb is literally 'built' (Westermann, Trible, Vawter, Cassuto, NEB, REB), not 'made' (NRSV, RSV, KJV, NIV), which is used elsewhere in the passage.
3. The first 'this' is indicated by the word *zōʾt*, which is repeated three times in this verse in reference to the woman. The second 'this' is indicated by the definite article on the word for 'occurrence' or 'time'.
4. The Hebrew word for man as male, *ʾîš*, is used here. The LXX, the Samaritan Pentateuch, and targums read 'her man', *ʾîšāh*, which in Hebrew sounds the same as 'woman', *ʾiššâ*, thus reinforcing the pun.
5. The LXX omits the final 'this one'.
6. While Hebrew has the (male) 'man', the LXX has the '(hu)man'.
7. I translate *ʾiššâ* here as 'woman' to parallel the 'man' in the first half of the verse. Since it has no other words for wife and husband, Hebrew uses the words 'woman' and (male) 'man'. For balance, both terms or neither should be translated as referring to marriage.
8. The LXX, Syriac, Vulgate, and *Targum Jonathan* read 'the two of them', agreeing with 2.25.
9. Depending on one's theology and assessment of the serpent, the word *ʿārûm* is translated as 'crafty' (NRSV, NIV, NEB), 'cunning' (Cassuto, REB, TEV), 'subtle' (RSV, KJV, NJB), 'shrewd' (JPS), 'astute' (Westermann), 'sly' (Trible), or 'smooth-tongued' (*Book of J*, to capture the pun with the smooth-skinned couple in 2.25).
10. The serpent's 'you' is plural, referring to both the woman and the man. To remind English readers, I include (pl) in the translation.
11. Some versions add 'all', probably to parallel 2.16 more closely.
12. The Samaritan Pentateuch reads 'this tree'.
13. The serpent's denial uses an infinitive absolute construction like 2.17.

will be opened[1] and you (pl) will be like God,[2] knowing good and evil'. (6) Then the woman saw that good [was] the tree for eating and that a delight it [was] to the eyes and [that] the tree was desirable for insight; so she took of its fruit, and she ate. Then she gave [some] also to her man[3] [who was] with her,[4] and he[5] ate. (7) And the eyes of them both were opened, and they knew that naked [were] they. So they sewed fig leaves, and they made for themselves coverings.[6]

(8) Then they heard the voice[7] of YHWH God walking around[8] in the garden at the breezy time of the day, and they hid themselves, the man* and his woman, from (the face of) YHWH God among the trees of the garden. (9) And YHWH God called to the man* and said to him, 'Where[9] are you?' (10) And he said, '*Your voice* I heard[10] in the garden, and I was afraid because naked [am] I, so I hid'. (11) And he[11] said, 'Who told you that naked [are] *you*?[12] Of the tree which I commanded you not to eat of it did you eat?' (12) And the man* said, 'The woman whom you gave [to be] with me, she gave to me[13] of the tree, and I ate'. (13) Then YHWH God said to the woman, 'What [is] this [that] you have done?' And the woman said, '*The serpent* tricked me, so I ate'.

(14) So YHWH God said to the serpent,
'Because you have done this,
cursed are *you* among[14] all the cattle
and among all animals of the field.

1. The *niphal* also has a middle sense 'be open'.
2. Translating *ᵓelōhîm* as 'gods' would also be appropriate.
3. Hebrew and Greek both use (male) 'man'.
4. There is no reason to omit the phrase 'with her' as several translations do (RSV, JPS, NEB, REB, TEV).
5. The Samaritan Pentateuch and the LXX read 'they ate'.
6. It is not clear what the couple covered, but the sense of the word is something that goes around the body. Aprons (RSV, KJV, Westermann, Cassuto), belts and girdles (other dictionary options) all have connotations that are too specific in English. Loincloths (NRSV, Vawter, NEB, REB, NJB) may be accurate.
7. God's voice while he was walking or the 'sound' of this walking.
8. The *hithpael* participle has an iterative or durative sense.
9. The LXX adds vocative 'Adam' before 'where are you?' Note the singular 'you'.
10. The LXX adds 'walking', presumably understanding Hebrew as 'sound'. Perhaps a dittography from 3.8.
11. The LXX specifies 'God'.
12. The 'you' remains masculine singular in God's questions here.
13. The word 'fruit' (as in most translations) is presumably understood, but it is not in the Hebrew text.
14. Scholars differ on the sense of the preposition *min* here and in the next line. It may mean that the serpent is cursed 'above' or 'more than' all cattle and animals of the field (RSV, KJV, NIV, JPS, Trible, Cassuto, NEB). Or the serpent could be 'banned from' them (Vawter). The serpent alone may be designated 'of' or 'from' the animals as cursed (REB, NJB, TEV). My translation follows NRSV and Westermann in suggesting that serpent is cursed 'among' them, that is, in relation to the animals.

Upon your belly you will go,
and dust you will eat all the days of your life.
(15) *Enmity* I will make between you and the woman
and between your seed and her seed.
They[1] will strike[2] your head,
 and *you* will strike their heel'.

(16) To the woman he said,
'I will greatly multiply[3] your toil and your pregnancies;[4]
with toil[5] you will[6] bear children.[7]
To your man[8] will be your longing,[9]
and he will[10] rule over you'.

(17) And to [the] man* he said,
'Because you[11] listened to the voice of your woman
and you have eaten of the tree
[about] which I commanded you saying,
"you shall not eat of it",
cursed [is] the ground on your account,[12]

---

1.   The pronoun agrees with the masculine singular collective noun 'seed'. I use 'they' and 'their' since the offspring are plural. This pronoun has an interesting history in the versions. See B. Vawter, *On Genesis: A New Reading* (Garden City, NY: Doubleday, 1977), p. 83 for a quick summary. The LXX translates the Hebrew pronoun as 'he', though 'seed' in Greek would use a neuter pronoun. Philo apparently reads the Hebrew 'he' as a 'she' (as it is regularly used), referring to the woman. Old Latin uses the masculine pronoun, but the Vulgate uses 'she' at this point, reading 3.15 as a *protoevangelium*, with the 'she' referring to Mary and the masculine singular 'seed' being Christ. For more details, see J.P. Lewis, 'The Woman's Seed (Gen 3.15)', *JETS* 34 (1991), pp. 299-319.

2.   This verb, the same for both subjects, occurs only here and in Ps. 139.11 and Job 9.17. It is variously rendered as 'bruise' (RSV, KJV, NJB), 'crush' (NIV, Westermann, Cassuto, TEV), 'snap at' (Westermann), 'crave' (Cassuto), 'bite' (TEV), and 'strike' or 'strike at' (NIV, JPS, Trible, Vawter, NEB, REB, NJB).

3.   This is the same root as 'be fruitful' and 'multiply' from Gen. 1.22, 28.

4.   Or 'conception'. With C. Meyers, *Discovering Eve: Ancient Israelite Women in Context* (New York: Oxford University Press, 1988), I prefer *not* to treat 'your toil and your pregnancies' as a hendiadys: 'pain in childbearing'. See discussion of her translation in Chapter 2.

5.   I use 'toil' because it also works in 3.17 and fits the idea of labor in childbirth. The Hebrew word also means 'pain' or 'hurt'. The Samaritan Pentateuch has the plural, so 'pains' or 'labors'.

6.   The LXX uses a subjunctive here: 'may you'.

7.   Following the Masoretes' accents I divide the sentences here.

8.   Hebrew and the LXX use specifically male 'man' or 'husband' here.

9.   This word 'longing' or 'desire' occurs only here, in a parallel passage in Gen. 4.7, and in Song 7.11 [ET 7.10]. See the discussion of Bledstein's translation of this line and the next in Chapter 2.

10.   The imperfect need not be simple future: it includes the options of 'can', 'ought to', 'must', 'shall', and Steinbeck's famous 'may'.

11.   The pronouns are all second person masculine singular, referring only to the man.

12.   The LXX translates 'in your working' reading בעבורך as בעבדך (without the ו ?).

with labor you will[1] eat of it
all the days of your life;
(18) thorns and thistles it will sprout for you,
and you will[2] eat the grass of the field.
(19) By the sweat of your face[3] you will[4] eat bread
until you return[5] to the ground,
for[6] from it you were taken.
For *dust* [are] *you*,
and to dust[7] you will return'.

(20) And the man* called the name of his woman Eve[8] (*Ḥawwah*), for she was[9] the mother of all living. (21) Then YHWH God made for [the] man* and for his woman tunics of skins, and he clothed them. (22) And YHWH* God said, 'Behold,[10] the man* has become like one of us, knowing good and evil; and now lest he send[11] out his hand and take also from the tree of life and eat and live forever...' (23) So YHWH God sent him out of the garden of Eden[12] to work the ground from which he was taken. (24) And he drove out the man*, and he stationed[13] to the east of the garden of Eden[14] the cherubim, and the flame of the turning sword to guard the way to the tree of life.

1.   The LXX has subjunctive 'may you' here as in 3.16.
2.   The LXX has the subjunctive 'may you' again.
3.   The whole introductory phrase in Hebrew is in emphatic position.
4.   The LXX has the subjunctive again.
5.   The LXX uses a future tense here.
6.   The LXX does not read this 'for', instead translating the next words as 'from which'.
7.   The LXX uses 'earth' here in place of the 'dust' it had in 2.7.
8.   The LXX has 'Zoe' (life) here, though it knows the name Eve in 4.1. Commentators regularly note both the relation of Eve's name to the Hebrew word for life and its Arabic and Aramaic cognates meaning serpent.
9.   The LXX omits 'she was'.
10.   The inaccurate 'Behold' is tied to the 'now' in the second half of the verse, but the 'now that... what if' construction suggested by Speiser and adopted in several recent translations makes it difficult to render the nuance of the 'lest'.
11.   I use 'send' here to match 'sent' in 3.23.
12.   The LXX has garden 'of delights'.
13.   The LXX reads 'banished him', referring to the man, and inserts 'put' before the cherubim. Hebrew syntax and Masoretic vowel pointing suggest the cherubim as what was 'stationed'.
14.   The LXX has garden 'of delights' again.

BIBLIOGRAPHY

A. General, Feminist, and Literary Criticism and Theory

Abel, E., and E.K. Abel, *The SIGNS Reader: Women, Gender & Scholarship* (Chicago: University of Chicago Press, 1983).

Albrecht, L., and R.M. Brewer (eds.), *Bridges of Power: Women's Multicultural Alliances* (Philadelphia: New Society Publishers, 1990).

Alcoff, L., 'Cultural Feminism Versus Post-structuralism: The Identity Crisis in Feminist Theory', *Signs: Journal of Women in Culture and Society* 13 (1988), pp. 405-36.

Alcoff, L., and E. Potter, *Feminist Epistemologies* (New York and London: Routledge, 1993).

Althusser, L., 'Ideology and State Apparatuses', in Latimer (ed.), *Contemporary Critical Theory* , pp. 60-102.

Anzaldúa, G., *Borderlands La Frontera: The New Mestiza* (San Francisco: Spinsters/Aunt Lute, 1987).

Aristotle, *The Rhetoric and the Poetics of Aristotle* (trans. W. Rhys Roberts and I. Bywater; New York: The Modern Library, 1984).

Arruda, T., 'How Can I Live a Life of Lies?', in Ramos (ed.), *Compañeras: Latina Lesbians (An Anthology)*, pp. 214-17.

Austin, J.L., *How to do Things with Words* (eds. J.O. Urmson and M. Sbisà; Cambridge, MA: Harvard University Press, 2nd edn, 1975).

Bal, M., *Narratology: Introduction to the Theory of Narrative*, (trans. C. van Boheemen; Toronto: University of Toronto Press, 1985).

Balibar, E., and P. Machery, 'On Literature as an Ideological Form', in Young (ed.), *Untying the Text*, pp. 79-99.

Barrett, M., 'Ideology and the Cultural Production of Gender', in Newton and Rosenfelt (eds.), *Feminist Criticism and Social Change*, pp. 65-85.

Barthes, R., 'From Work to Text', in Harari (ed.), *Textual Strategies*, pp. 73-81.

Beach, R., *A Teacher's Introduction to Reader-Response Theories* (Urbana, IL: National Council of Teachers of English, 1993).

Beal, T.K., 'Glossary', in Fewell (ed.), *Reading Between Texts*, pp. 21-24.

Belenky, M.F., B.M. Clinchy, N.R. Goldberger, and J.M. Tarule, *Women's Ways of Knowing: The Development of Self, Voice, and Mind* (New York: Basic Books, 1986).

Benstock, S. (ed.), *Feminist Issues in Literary Scholarship* (Bloomington: Indiana University Press, 1987).

Benveniste, E., *Problems in General Linguistics* (trans. M.E. Meek; Coral Gables, FL: University of Miami Press, 1966).

Bethel, L., 'What Chou Mean WE, White Girl?', *Conditions: Five* [The Black Women's Issue] 2.2 (1979), pp. 86-92.

Bitzer, L.F, 'The Rhetorical Situation', in W.R. Fisher (ed.), *Rhetoric: A Tradition in Transition in Honor of Donald C. Bryant* (n.p.: Michigan State University Press, 1974), pp. 247-60; reprinted from *Philosophy and Rhetoric* 1 (1968), pp. 1-12.

Bizzell, P., and B. Herzberg (eds.), *The Rhetorical Tradition: Readings From Classical Times to the Present* (Boston: Bedford Books of St. Martin's Press, 1990).

Bleich, D., *Readings and Feelings: An Introduction to Subjective Criticism* (Urbana, IL: National Council of Teachers of English, 1975).

—*Subjective Criticism* (Baltimore: The Johns Hopkins University Press, 1978).

Bodine, A., 'Androcentrism in Prescriptive Grammar: Singular *they*, Sex Indefinite *he* and *he* or *she*', *Language in Society* 4.2 (1975), pp. 129-56.

Boyer, E.L., *Scholarship Reconsidered: Priorities of the Professoriate* (Princeton: The Carnegie Foundation for the Advancement of Teaching, 1990).

Brantenberg, G., *Egalia's Daughters: A Satire of the Sexes* (Seattle: The Seal Press, 1977, 1985).

Bunch, C., and S. Pollack, *Learning Our Way: Essays in Feminist Education* (Trumansburg, NY: The Crossing Press, 1983).

Burke, C., 'Irigaray Through the Looking Glass', *Feminist Studies* 7.2 (1981), pp. 288-306.

Butler, J., *Gender Trouble: Feminism and the Subversion of Identity* (New York: Routledge, 1990).

Cameron, D., '"Not Gender Difference But the Difference Gender Makes"— Explanation in Research on Sex and Language', *International Journal of the Sociology of Language* 94 (1992), pp. 13-26.

—*Feminism and Linguistic Theory* (New York: St. Martin's, 2nd edn, 1992).

Chatman, S., *Story and Discourse: Narrative Structure in Fiction and Film* (Ithaca, NY: Cornell University Press, 1978).

Cixous, H., 'The Laugh of the Medusa', translated by K. Cohen and P. Cohen, in Abel and Abel (eds.), *The SIGNS Reader*, pp. 279-97. Reprinted from *Signs: Journal of Women in Culture and Society* 1 (1976), pp. 875-94.

Cohen, R., (ed.) *The Future of Literary Theory* (New York and London: Routledge, 1989).

Cole, J., 'Commonalities and Differences', in J.B. Cole (ed.), *All American Women: Lines that Divide, Ties that Bind* (New York: The Free Press, 1986), pp. 1-30.

Cole, P., and J.L. Morgan (eds.), *Syntax and Semantics 3: Speech Acts* (New York: Academic Press, 1975).

Collins, P. Hill, *Black Feminist Thought: Knowledge, Consciousness, and the Politics of Empowerment* (London: HarperCollins Academic, 1990).

—'On Our Own Terms: Self-Defined Standpoints and Curriculum Transformation.' *NWSA Journal* 3 (1991), pp. 367-81.

Culler, J., *On Deconstruction: Theory and Criticism after Structuralism* (Ithaca: Cornell University Press, 1982).

Culley, M., and C. Portuges (eds.) *Gendered Subjects: The Dynamics of Feminist Teaching* (Boston: Routledge & Kegan Paul, 1985).

Daly, M., *Gyn/Ecology: The Metaethics of Radical Feminism* (Boston: Beacon Press, 1978).

de Beauvoir, S., *The Second Sex* (ed. and trans., H.M. Parshley; New York: Vintage Books, 1974).

Derrida, J., *Limited Inc* (Evanston, IL: Northwestern University Press, 1988).

Eagleton, T., *Literary Theory: An Introduction* (Minneapolis: University of Minnesota, 1983).

—*Ideology: An Introduction* (London: Verso, 1991).

Ebert, T.L, 'The "Difference" of Postmodern Feminism', *College English* 53 (1991) pp. 886-904.

Eisenstein, H., and A. Jardine (eds.), *The Future of Difference* (New Brunswick and London: Rutgers University Press, 2nd edn, 1985).

Ferguson, A., J.N. Zita, and K.P. Addelson, 'On "Compulsory Heterosexuality and Lesbian Existence": Defining the Issues', *Signs: Journal of Women in Culture and Society* 7 (1981), pp. 158-99.

Fetterley, J., *The Resisting Reader: A Feminist Approach to American Fiction* (Bloomington: Indiana University Press, 1978).

—'Reading about Reading: "A Jury of Her Peers", "The Murders in the Rue Morgue", and "The Yellow Wallpaper"', in Flynn and Schweickart (eds.), *Gender and Reading*, pp. 147-64.

Fiol-Matta, L., and M.K. Chamberlain (eds.), *Women of Color and the Multicultural Curriculum: Transforming the College Classroom* (New York: Feminist Press, 1994).

Fish, S., 'Interpreting the *Variorum*', *Critical Inquiry* 2 (Spring 1976), pp. 465-85.

—*Is There a Text in this Class?: The Authority of Interpretive Communities* (Cambridge, MA: Harvard University Press, 1980).

—*Doing What Comes Naturally: Change, Rhetoric, and the Practice of Theory in Literary and Legal Studies* (Durham and London: Duke University Press, 1989).

Flax, J., 'Postmodernism and Gender Relations in Feminist Theory', *Signs: Journal of Women in Culture and Society* 12 (1987), pp. 621-43.

Flynn, E.A, 'Gender and Reading', in Flynn and Schweickart (eds.), *Gender and Reading*, pp. 267-88.

Flynn, E.A., and P.P. Schweickart, (eds.) *Gender and Reading: Essays on Readers, Texts, and Contexts* (Baltimore: The Johns Hopkins University Press, 1986).

Frank, F.W., and P.A. Treichler (eds.), *Language, Gender, and Professional Writing: Theoretical Approaches and Guidelines for Nonsexist Usage* (New York: The Modern Language Association of America, 1989).

Frankenberg, R., *White Women, Race Matters: The Social Construction of Whiteness* (Minneapolis: University of Minnesota Press, 1993).

French, M., *Beyond Power: On Women, Men, and Morals* (New York: Ballantine Books, 1985).

Frow, J., 'Intertextuality and Ontology', in Worton and Still (eds.), *Intertextuality*, pp. 45-55.

Fuss, D., 'Reading Like a Feminist', *Differences* 1 (Summer 1989), pp. 77-92.

Gallop, J., and C. Burke, 'Psychoanalysis and Feminism in France', in Eisenstein and Jardine (eds.), *The Future of Difference*, pp. 106-21.

Gardiner, J.K., 'Psychoanalytic Criticism and the Female Reader', *Literature and Psychology* 26 (1976), pp. 100-107.

Gates, H.L., Jr, *'Race,' Writing, and Difference* (Chicago: University of Chicago, 1985).

Genette, G., *Narrative Discourse: An Essay in Method* (trans. J.E. Lewin; Ithaca: Cornell University Press, 1980).

—*Narrative Discourse Revisited* (trans. J.E. Lewin; Ithaca: Cornell University Press, 1988).

Gilligan, C., *In a Different Voice: Psychological Theory and Women's Development* (Cambridge, MA and London: Harvard University Press, 1982).

Glaspell, S., 'A Jury of Her Peers', in M.A. Ferguson (ed.), *Images of Women in Literature* (Boston: Houghton Mifflin, 1973), pp. 370-85.

Goetsch, L.A., 'Feminist Pedagogy: A Selective Annotated Bibliography.' *NWSA Journal* 3.3 (1991), pp. 422-29.

Gore, J., *The Struggle for Pedagogies: Critical and Feminist Discourses as Regimes of Truth* (New York: Routledge, 1993).

Greene, G., and C. Kahn (eds.), *Making a Difference: Feminist Literary Criticism* (London and New York: Methuen, 1985).

Greimas, A.J., *Sémantique structurale* (Paris: Librairie Larousse, 1966).

Grice, H.P., 'Logic and Conversation', in Cole and Morgan (eds.), *Syntax and Semantics 3*, pp. 41-58.

Grimes, R.L., 'Infelicitous Performances and Ritual Criticism', in White (ed.), *Speech Act Theory*, pp. 103-22.

Grosz, E., *Sexual Subversions: Three French Feminists* (Sydney and Boston: Allen & Unwin, 1989).

Hall, R.M., with B.R. Sandler, 'The Classroom Climate: A Chilly One fc Women?' (Association of American Colleges' Project on the Status and Education of Women, Washington, DC, 1982).

Hancher, M., 'Beyond a Speech-Act Theory of Literary Discourse', *Modern Language Notes* 92 (1977), pp. 1081-98.

Harari, J.V. (ed.), *Textual Strategies: Perspectives in Post-Structuralist Criticism* (Ithaca: Cornell University Press, 1979).

Haraway, D., 'Situated Knowledges: The Science Question in Feminism and the Privilege of Partial Perspective', *Feminist Studies* 14 (1988), pp. 575-99.

Harding, S., 'Is Gender a Variable in Conceptions of Rationality? A Survey of Issues', *Dialectica* 36.2-3 (1982), pp. 225-42.

—*Whose Science? Whose Knowledge? Thinking from Women's Lives* (Ithaca, NY: Cornell University Press, 1991).

—'Rethinking Standpoint Epistemology: What Is "Strong Objectivity"?', in Alcoff and Potter (eds.), *Feminist Epistemologies*, pp. 49-82.

Hauser, G.A., *Introduction to Rhetorical Theory* (Speech Communication Series; New York: Harper & Row, 1986).

Hawkesworth, M.E., 'Knowers, Knowing, Known: Feminist Theory and Claims of Truth', *Signs: Journal of Women in Culture and Society* 14 (1989), pp. 533-57.

Heilbrun, C., 'Millett's *Sexual Politics*: A Year Later', *Aphra* 2 (1971), pp. 38-47.

Hennessy, R., 'Queer Theory: A Review of the *differences* Special Issue and Wittig's *The Straight Mind*', *Signs: Journal of Women in Culture and Society* 18 (1993), pp. 964-73.

—'Women's Lives/Feminist Knowledge: Feminist Standpoint as Ideology Critique', *Hypatia* 8.1 (1993) pp. 14-34.

Hirsch, E.D., Jr, *Validity in Interpretation* (New Haven: Yale University, 1967).

Holland, N.N., *5 Readers Reading* (New Haven: Yale University Press, 1975).

—'Unity Identity Text Self', in Tompkins (ed.), *Reader-Response Criticism*, pp. 118-33.

Holland, N.N., and L.F. Sherman, 'Gothic Possibilities', in Flynn and Schweickart (eds.), *Gender and Reading*, pp. 215-33.

Holub, R.C., *Reception Theory: A Critical Introduction* (New York: London and Methuen, 1984).

hooks, b., *Feminist Theory: From Margin to Center* (Boston: South End Press, 1984).

—*Yearning: Race, Gender, and Cultural Politics* (Boston: South End Press, 1990).

—*Black Looks: Race and Representation* (Boston: South End Press, 1992).

Irigaray, L., 'When Our Lips Speak Together', *Signs: Journal of Women in Culture and Society* 6 (1980), pp. 66-79.

Iser, W., *The Act of Reading: A Theory of Aesthetic Response* (Baltimore: The Johns Hopkins University Press, 1978).

Jameson, F., *The Political Unconscious: Narrative as Socially Symbolic Act* (Ithaca, NY: Cornell University Press, 1981).

Jardine, A., *Gynesis: Configurations of Woman and Modernity* (Ithaca, NY and London: Cornell University Press, 1985).

—'Death Sentences: Writing Couples and Ideology', in Suleiman (ed.), *The Female Body in Western Culture*, pp. 84-96.

Jardine, A., and P. Smith (eds.), *Men in Feminism* (New York: Methuen, 1987).

Jones, A.R., 'Inscribing Femininity: French Theories of the Feminine', in Greene and Kahn (eds.), *Making a Difference*, pp. 80-112.

—'Writing the Body: Toward an Understanding of *l'écriture féminine*', in Newton and Rosenfelt (eds.), *Feminist Criticism and Social Change*, pp. 86-101.

Kavanaugh, J.H, 'Ideology', in Lentricchia and McLaughlin (eds.), *Critical Terms for Literary Study*, pp. 306-20.

Kelly, J., *Women, History and Theory: The Essays of Joan Kelly* (Chicago and London: University of Chicago Press, 1984).

Kennard, J.E., 'Ourself behind Ourself: A Theory for Lesbian Readers', in Flynn and Schweickart (eds.), *Gender and Reading*, pp. 63-80.

Keohane, N.O., M.Z. Rosaldo, and B.C. Gelpi (eds.), *Feminist Theory: A Critique of Ideology* (Chicago: The University of Chicago Press, 1981, 1982).

Kolodny, A., 'Dancing through the Minefield: Some Observations on the Theory, Practice, and Politics of a Feminist Literary Criticism', *Feminist Studies* 6 (Spring 1980), pp. 1-25.

—'A Map for Rereading: Gender and the Interpretation of Literary Texts', in E. Showalter (ed.), *The New Feminist Criticism: Essays on Women, Literature, and Theory* (New York: Pantheon, 1985), pp. 46-62.

Kristeva, J., 'Woman Can never be Defined', trans. M.A. August, in Marks and de Courtivron (eds.), *New French Feminisms: An Anthology* (New York: Schocken Books, 1980). pp. 137-41.

—*Desire in Language: A Semiotic Approach to Literature and Art* (trans. T. Gora, A. Jardine, and L.S. Roudiez; New York: Columbia University Press, 1980).

—'A Question of Subjectivity', in Rice and Waugh (eds.), *Modern Literary Theory*, pp. 128-34.

Kuhn, A., 'Introduction to Hélène Cixous's "Castration or Decapitation?"', *Signs: Journal of Women in Culture and Society* 7 (1981), pp. 36-40.

Lakoff, R., *Language and Woman's Place* (New York: Harper & Row, 1975).

Lanser, S.S., *The Narrative Act: Point of View in Prose Fiction* (Princeton, NJ: Princeton University Press, 1981).

Latimer, D. (ed.), *Contemporary Critical Theory* (San Diego: Harcourt Brace Jovanovich, 1989).

Lentricchia, F., and T. McLaughlin (eds.), *Critical Terms for Literary Study* (Chicago: University of Chicago Press, 1990).

Lorde, A., 'Age, Race, Class, and Sex: Women Redefining Difference,' 'An Open Letter to Mary Daly,' and 'The Master's Tools will never Dismantle the Master's House', chapters in *Sister Outsider: Essays and Speeches* (Trumansburg, NY: The Crossing Press, 1984).

Lugones, M., 'Purity, Impurity, and Separation', *Signs: Journal of Women in Culture and Society* 19 (1994), pp. 458-79.

MacKinnon, C.A., 'Feminism, Marxism, Method, and the State: An Agenda for Theory', in Keohane, Rosaldo and Gelpi (eds.), *Feminist Theory*, pp. 1-30. Reprinted from *Signs: Journal of Women in Culture and Society* 7.3 (Spring 1982), pp. 515-44.

—'Feminism, Marxism, Method, and the State: Toward Feminist Jurisprudence', in Latimer (ed.), *Contemporary Critical Theory*, pp. 605-33. Reprinted from *Signs: Journal of Women in Culture and Society* 8 (1983), pp. 635-58.

Maggio, R., *The Nonsexist Word-finder: A Dictionary of Gender-Free Usage* (Phoenix: Oryx Press, 1987).

Makward, C., 'To Be or not to Be... A Feminist Speaker' (trans. M. Barsoum, A. Jardine, and H. Eisenstein), in Eisenstein and Jardine (eds.), *The Future of Difference*, pp. 95-105.

Marks, E., and I. de Courtivron, *New French Feminisms: An Anthology* (New York: Schocken Books, 1980).

Martyna, W., 'Beyond the He/Man Approach: The Case for Nonsexist Language', in Thorne, Kramarae and Henley (eds.), *Language, Gender and Society*, pp. 25-37. Reprinted from *Signs: Journal of Women in Culture and Society* 5 (1980), pp. 482-93.

McConnell-Ginet, S., 'Linguistics and the Feminist Challenge', in McConnell-Ginet, Borker and Furman (eds.), *Women and Language in Literature and Society* (New York: Praeger, 1980), pp. 3-25.

—'Difference and Language: A Linguist's Perspective', in Eisenstein and Jardine (eds.), *The Future of Difference*, pp. 157-66.

McConnell-Ginet, S., R. Borker and N. Furman (eds.), *Women and Language in Literature and Society* (New York: Praeger, 1980).

McDavid, A., 'Feminism for Men: 101 Educating Men in "Women's Studies"'. *Feminist Teacher* 3.3 (1988), pp. 25-33.

McIntosh, P., 'Interactive Phases of Curriculum Re-Vision: A Feminist Perspective' (Working Paper, no. 124; Wellesley College Center for Research on Women, Wellesley, MA).

— 'White Privilege and Male Privilege: A Personal Account of Coming to See Correspondences through Work in Women's Studies' (Working Paper, no. 189; Wellesley College Center for Research on Women, Wellesley, MA).

McLaren, P., 'On Ideology and Education: Critical Pedagogy and the Politics of Education', *Social Text* 19/20 (1988), pp. 153-85.

Miller, C., and K. Swift, *Words and Women: New Language in New Times* (Garden City, NY: Anchor Press/Doubleday, 1976).

—*The Handbook of Nonsexist Writing* (New York: Harper & Row, 1980).

Miller, O., 'Intertextual Identity', in Valdés and Miller (eds.), *Identity of the Literary Text*, pp. 19-40.

Millett, K., *Sexual Politics* (New York: Doubleday and Company, 1969).

Minnich, E.K., *Transforming Knowledge* (Philadelphia: Temple University Press, 1990).

Moi, T., *Sexual/Textual Politics: Feminist Literary Theory* (London and New York: Routledge, 1985).

—*French Feminist Thought: A Reader* (Oxford: Basil Blackwell, 1987).

Moore, G.O.P., 'Nature and Sexual Differences', *New Blackfriars* 75.878 (January 1994), pp. 52-64.

Morgan, T.E., 'Is there an Intertext in this Text?: Literary and Interdisciplinary Approaches to Intertextuality', *American Journal of Semiotics* 3.4 (1985), pp. 1-40.

Newton, J., and D. Rosenfelt (eds.), *Feminist Criticism and Social Change: Sex, Class and Race in Literature and Culture* (New York and London: Methuen, 1985).

Nilsen, A.P., *et al.* (eds.), *Sexism and Language* (Urbana, IL: National Council of Teachers of English, 1977).

Novak, M., 'Narrative and Ideology', *This World* 23 (Fall 1988), pp. 66-80.

O'Barr, J.F. (ed.), *Reconstructing the Academy*; special issue of *Signs: Journal of Women in Culture and Society* 12.2 (1987).

Pearson, C.S., D.L. Shavlik, and J.G. Touchton, (eds.), *Educating the Majority: Women Challenge Tradition in Higher Education* (New York: American Council on Education/Macmillan, 1989).

Perelman, C., and L. Olbrechts-Tyteca, *The New Rhetoric: A Treatise on Argumentation* (trans. J. Wilkinson and P. Weaver; Notre Dame: Notre Dame University Press, 1969).

Pratt, M.L., *Towards a Speech Act Theory of Literary Discourse* (Bloomington: Indiana University Press, 1977).

—'The Ideology of Speech Act Theory', *Centrum* NS 1.1 (Spring 1981), pp. 5-18.

—'Interpretive Strategies/Strategic Interpretations: On Anglo-American Reader Response Criticism.' *Boundary 2* 2 (1982) pp. 201-31.

Propp, V., *Morphology of the Folktale* (ed. L.A. Wagner; trans. L. Scott; Austin: University of Texas Press, 2nd edn, 1968).

Ramos, J. (ed.), *Compañeras: Latina Lesbians (An Anthology)* (New York City: Latina Lesbian History Project, 1987).

Reiter, R.R. (ed.), *Toward an Anthropology of Women* (New York: Monthly Review Press, 1975).

Rice, P., and P. Waugh (eds.), *Modern Literary Theory: A Reader* (London and New York: Edward Arnold, 1989).

Rich, A., 'Compulsory Heterosexuality and Lesbian Existence', in Abel and Abel (eds.), *The SIGNS Reader*, pp. 139-68. Reprinted from *Signs: Journal of Women in Culture and Society* 5 (Summer 1980), pp. 631-60.

Richards, I.A., *Practical Criticism* (New York: Harcourt, 1929).

Rimmon-Kenan, S., *Narrative Fiction: Contemporary Poetics* (London and New York: Methuen, 1983).

Rosenblatt, L.M., *Literature as Exploration* (New York and London: D. Appleton-Century Company, 1938).

—'The Poem as Event', *College English* 26.2 (November 1964), pp. 123-28.

—'Towards a Transactional Theory of Reading', *Journal of Reading Behavior* 1 (Winter 1969), pp. 31-47.

—*The Reader, the Text, the Poem: The Transactional Theory of the Literary Work* (Carbondale and Edwardsville: Southern Illinois University Press, 1978).

Rubin, G., 'The Traffic in Women: Notes on the "Political Economy" of Sex', in R.R. Reiter (ed.), *Toward an Anthropology of Women*, pp. 157-210.

Sanders, R.E., 'In Defense of Speech Acts', *Philosophy and Rhetoric* 9 (1976), pp. 112-15.

Schibanoff, S., 'Taking the Gold out of Egypt: The Art of Reading as a Woman', in Flynn and Schweickart (eds.), *Gender and Reading*, pp. 83-106.

Scholes, R., 'Reading like a Man', in Jardine and Smith (eds.), *Men in Feminism*, pp. 204-18.

—*Protocols of Reading* (New Haven and London: Yale University Press, 1989).

Searle, J.R., *Speech Acts: An Essay in the Philosophy of Language* (Cambridge: Cambridge University Press, 1970).

Showalter, E., 'Critical Cross-Dressing: Male Feminists and the Woman of the Year', *Raritan* 3 (1983), pp. 130-49.

—'Women's Time, Women's Space: Writing the History of Feminist Criticism', in Benstock (ed.), *Feminist Issues in Literary Scholarship*, pp. 30-44.

—'A Criticism of Our Own: Autonomy and Assimilation in Afro-American and Feminist Literary Theory', in Cohen (ed.), *The Future of Literary Theory*, pp. 347-69.

Shrewsbury, C.M., 'Feminist Pedagogy: An Updated Bibliography', *Women's Studies Quarterly* 21.3-4 (Fall/Winter 1993), pp. 148-60.

Slatoff, W.J., *With Respect to Readers: Dimensions of Literary Response* (Ithaca: Cornell University Press, 1970).

Smith, B., 'Racism and Women's Studies', *Frontiers* 5 (Spring 1980), p. 48.

Sorrels, B.D., *The Nonsexist Communicator: Solving the Problems of Gender and Awkwardness in Modern English* (Englewood Cliffs, NJ: Prentice-Hall, 1983).

Sosnoski, J.J., 'A Mindless Man-driven Theory Machine: Intellectuality, Sexuality and the Institution of Criticism', in L. Kauffman (ed.), *Feminism and Institutions: Dialogues in Feminist Theory* (Oxford and Cambridge, MA: Basil Blackwell, 1989), pp. 55-78.

Spelman, E., *Inessential Woman: Problems of Exclusion in Feminist Thought* (Boston: Beacon Press, 1988).

Spender, D., *Man Made Language* (London and Boston: Routledge & Kegan Paul, 2nd edn, 1980).

Spivak, G.C., 'The Politics of Interpretations', chap. in *In Other Worlds: Essays in Cultural Politics* (New York and London: Routledge, 1988).

Steinem, G., 'If Men Could Menstruate', chap. in *Outrageous Acts and Everyday Rebellions* (New York: Signet, 1986).

Sternberg, M., 'Proteus in Quotation-Land: Mimesis and the Forms of Reported Discourse', *Poetics Today* 3 (1982), pp. 107-56.

Suleiman, S.R. (ed.), *The Female Body in Western Culture: Contemporary Perspectives* (Cambridge, MA: Harvard University Press, 1986).

Suleiman, S.R., and I. Crosman (eds.), *The Reader in the Text: Essays on Audience and Interpretation* (Princeton, NJ: Princeton University Press, 1980).

Swanson, K.H., 'The Relationship of Interpersonal Cognitive Complexity and Message Design Logics Employed in Response to a Regulative Writing Task' (PhD dissertation, University of Minnesota, 1990).

Tannen, D., *That's Not What I Meant! How Conversational Style Makes or Breaks Relationships* (New York: Ballantine, 1986).

—*You Just Don't Understand: Women and Men in Conversation* (New York: William Morrow and Company, 1990).

Thompson, J.B., *Ideology and Modern Culture: Critical Social Theory in the Era of Mass Communication* (Stanford: Stanford University Press, 1990).

Thorne, B., and N. Henley (eds.), *Language and Sex: Difference and Dominance* (Cambridge, MA: Newbury House, 1975).

Thorne, B., C. Kramarae and N. Henley (eds.), *Language, Gender and Society* (Cambridge, MA: Newbury House, 1983).

Thorne, B., C. Kramarae and N. Henley, 'Language, Gender and Society: Opening a Second Decade of Research', in Thorne, Kramarae and Henley (eds.), *Language, Gender and Society*, pp. 7-24.

Tompkins, J.P., 'Criticism and Feeling', *College English* 39 (1977), pp. 169-78.

—'The Reader in History: The Changing Shape of Literary Response', in Tompkins (ed.), *Reader-Response Criticism*, pp. 301-20.

Tompkins, J.P. (ed.), *Reader-Response Criticism: From Formalism to Post-Structuralism* (Baltimore: The Johns Hopkins University Press, 1980).

Tong, R., *Feminist Thought: A Comprehensive Introduction* (Boulder and San Francisco: Westview Press, 1989).

Toulmin, S., *The Uses of Argument* (Cambridge: Cambridge University Press, 1958).

Valdés, M.J., and O. Miller, (eds.) *Identity of the Literary Text* (Toronto: University of Toronto Press, 1985).

Vetterling-Braggin, M., F.A. Elliston and J. English (eds.), *Feminism and Philosophy* (Totawa, NJ: Littlefield, Adams & Co., 1977).

Voloshinov, V.N., *Marxism and the Philosophy of Language* (Studies in Language, 1; trans. L. Matejka and I.R. Titunik; New York: Seminar Press, 1973).

Walby, S., *Patriarchy at Work: Patriarchal and Capitalist Relations in Employment* (Minneapolis: University of Minnesota Press, 1986).

Walker, A., *The Color Purple* (New York: Washington Square Press, 1982).

—*In Search of Our Mother's Gardens: Womanist Prose* (New York: Harcourt Brace Jovanovich, 1983).

Warhol, R.R., and D. Price Herndl, *Feminisms: An Anthology of Literary Theory and Criticism* (New Brunswick, NJ; Rutgers University Press, 1993).

Wenzel, H.V., 'The Text as Body/Politics: An Appreciation of Monique Wittig's Writings in Context', *Feminist Studies* 7 (1981), pp. 264-87.

Whorf, B.L., *Language, Thought, and Reality: Selected Writings of Benjamin Lee Whorf* (ed. J.B. Carroll; Cambridge: M.I.T. Press, 1956).

Williams, D.S., 'The Color of Feminism: Or Speaking the Black Woman's Tongue.' *Journal of Religious Thought* 43.1 (1986), pp. 42-58.

Wimsatt, W.K., Jr, and M.C. Beardsley, 'The Affective Fallacy', in W.K. Wimsatt, Jr (ed.), *The Verbal Icon: Studies in the Meaning of Poetry,* (n.p.: University of Kentucky Press, 1954), pp. 21-39.

Wittig, M., 'The Straight Mind', *Feminist Issues* 1.1 (Summer 1980), pp. 103-111.

—'One is not Born a Woman', *Feminist Issues* 1.2 (1981), pp. 47-54.

Worton, M., and J. Still (eds.), *Intertextuality: Theories and Practices* (Manchester: Manchester University Press, 1990).

Young, R. (ed.), *Untying the Text: A Post-Structuralist Reader* (Boston and London: Routledge & Kegan Paul, 1981).

Zhao, Y., 'The "End of Ideology" again? The Concept of Ideology in the Era of Post-modern Theory', *Canadian Journal of Sociology/Cahiers canadiens de sociologie* 18 (1993), pp. 70-85.

B. Biblical Criticism and Theology

Adam, A.K.M., 'The Sign of Jonah: A Fish-Eye View', in Phillips (ed.), *Poststructural Criticism and the Bible*, pp. 178-91.

Aichele, G., 'Text, Intertext, Ideology' (Paper presented at the SBL Ideological Criticism Group, Washington DC, 22 November 1993).

Aletti, J.N., 'Séduction et parole en proverbes I-IX', *VT* 27 (1977), pp. 129-44.

Alexander, P.S., 'The Fall into Knowledge: The Garden of Eden/Paradise in Gnostic Literature', in Morris and Sawyer (eds.), *A Walk in the Garden*, pp. 91-104.

Alonso-Schökel, L.S.J., 'Sapiential and Covenant Themes in Genesis 2–3', In Crenshaw (ed.), *Studies in Ancient Israelite Wisdom*, pp. 468-80.

—¿*Dónde Está Tu Hermano? Textos de fraternidad en el libro del Génesis* (Institucíon San Jerónimo, 19; Valencia: Artes Gráficas Soler, 1985).

Alter, R., *The Art of Biblical Narrative* (New York: Basic Books, 1981).

Anderson, J.C., 'Mapping Feminist Biblical Criticism: The American Scene, 1983-1990', *Critical Review of Books in Religion* 4 (1991), pp. 21-44.

Bailey, R.C., 'Beyond Identification: The Use of Africans in Old Testament Poetry and Narratives', in Felder (ed.), *Stony the Road we Trod*, pp. 165-84.

Bal, M., 'Sexuality, Sin, and Sorrow: The Emergence of Female Character (A Reading of Genesis 1–3)', in Suleiman (ed.), *The Female Body in Western Culture*, pp. 317-38.

—*Lethal Love: Feminist Literary Readings of Biblical Love Stories* (Bloomington and Indianapolis: Indiana University Press, 1987).

Barr, J., 'The Authority of Scripture: The Book of Genesis and the Origin of Evil in Jewish and Christian Tradition', in Evans (ed.), *Christian Authority*, pp. 59-75.

—*The Garden of Eden and the Hope of Immortality* (Minneapolis: Fortress Press, 1992).

Bassler, J.M. 'Cain and Abel in the Palestinian Targums', *Journal for the Study of Judaism* 17 (1986), pp. 56-64.

Beal, T.K, 'Glossary', in Fewell (ed.), *Reading Between Texts*, pp. 21-24.

—'Ideology and Intertextuality: Surplus of Meaning and Controlling the Means of Production', in Fewell (ed.), *Reading Between Texts*, p. 27-39.

Beattie, D.R.G., '*Peshat* and *Derash* in the Garden of Eden', *Irish Biblical Studies* 7 (1985), pp. 62-75.

Bednarowski, M.F., 'The Spirit of Re-Imagining: Setting the Stage', *Church & Society* 84 (May/June 1994), pp. 12-19.

Berlin, A., *Poetics and Interpretation of Biblical Narrative* (Bible and Literature Series, 9; Sheffield: Almond Press, 1983).

Betz, H.D., *Galatians: A Commentary on Paul's Letter to the Churches in Galatia* (Hermeneia; Philadelphia: Fortress Press, 1979).

Bigger, S., (ed.) *Creating the Old Testament: The Emergence of the Hebrew Bible* (Oxford: Basil Blackwell, 1989).

Bird, P., '"Male and Female He Created Them": Gen 1.27b in the Context of the Priestly Account of Creation', *HTR* 74 (1981), pp. 129-159.

—'Genesis I–III as a Source for a Contemporary Theology of Sexuality', *Ex Auditu* 3 (1987), pp. 31-44.

Black, C.C., II, 'Rhetorical Criticism and the New Testament', *Proceedings: Eastern Great Lakes and Midwest Biblical Societies* 8 (1988), pp. 77-92.

Bledstein, A.J., 'The Genesis of Humans: The Garden of Eden Revisited', *Judaism* 26 (1977), pp. 187-200.

—'Are Women Cursed in Genesis 3.16?', in Brenner (ed.), *A Feminist Companion to Genesis*, pp. 142-45.

Blenkinsopp, J., 'The Social Context of the 'Outsider Woman' in Proverbs 1–9', *Bib* 72 (1991), pp. 457-73.

—*The Pentateuch: An Introduction to the First Five Books of the Bible* (Anchor Bible Reference Library ; New York: Doubleday, 1992).

Bloom, H., and D. Rosenberg, *The Book of J* (New York: Grove Weidenfeld, 1990).

Bonhoeffer, D., *Creation and Fall: A Theological Interpretation of Genesis 1–3* (trans. J.C. Fletcher; London: SCM Press, 1959).

Boomershine, T.E., 'The Structure of Narrative Rhetoric in Genesis 2–3,' in Patte (ed.), *Genesis 2 and 3*, pp. 113-29.

Boyarin, D., 'The Politics of Biblical Narratology—Reading the Bible Like/As a Woman', *Diacritics* 20.4 (1990), pp. 31-42.

—*Intertextuality and the Reading of Midrash* (Bloomington: Indiana University Press, 1990).

Brenner, A., 'Some Observations on the Figurations of Woman in Wisdom Literature', in McKay and Clines (eds.), *Of Prophets' Visions and the Wisdom of Sages*, pp. 192-208.

Brenner, A. (ed.), *A Feminist Companion to Genesis* (Sheffield: Sheffield Academic Press, 1993).

Brenner, A., and F. van Dijk-Hemmes, *On Gendering Texts: Female and Male Voices in the Hebrew Bible* (Leiden: Brill, 1993).

Brisman, L., *The Voice of Jacob: On the Composition of Genesis, 1–8* (Bloomington: Indiana University Press, 1990).

Brooks, R., and J.J. Collins (eds.), *Hebrew Bible or Old Testament? Studying the Bible in Judaism and Christianity* (Notre Dame: University of Notre Dame Press, 1990).

Brueggemann, W., *Genesis* (IBC; Atlanta: John Knox Press, 1982).

Buber, M., *Good and Evil: Two Interpretations* (New York: Charles Scribner's Sons, 1952).

Burnett, F.W., 'Postmodern Biblical Exegesis: The Eve of Historical Criticism', in Phillips (ed.), *Poststructural Criticism and the Bible*, pp. 51-80.

Burns, D.E., 'Dream Form in Genesis 2.4b-3.24: Asleep in the Garden', *JSOT* 37 (1987), pp. 3-14.

Bussert, J.M.K., *Battered Women: From a Theology of Suffering to an Ethic of Empowerment* (New York: Lutheran Church in America, Division for Mission in North America, 1986).

Cady Stanton, E., *et al.*, *The Woman's Bible* (Seattle: Coalition on Women and Religion, 1974[1898]).

Camp, C.V., *Wisdom and the Feminine in the Book of Proverbs* (Bible and Literature, 11; Sheffield: Almond Press, 1985).

—'Woman Wisdom as Root Metaphor: A Theological Consideration', in Hoglund *et al.* (eds.), *The Listening Heart*, pp. 45-76.

—'Wise and Strange: An Interpretation of the Female Imagery in Proverbs in Light of Trickster Mythology', in Exum and Bos (eds.), *Reasoning with the Foxes*, pp. 14-36.

—'What's so Strange about the Strange Woman?', in Jobling *et al.* (eds.), *The Bible and the Politics of Exegesis*, pp. 97-108.

Cannon, K.G., and E.S. Fiorenza (eds.), *Interpretation for Liberation* (Semeia, 47; Atlanta: Scholars Press, 1989).

Carmichael, C.M., 'The Paradise Myth: Interpreting Without Jewish and Christian Spectacles', in Morris and Sawyer (eds.), *A Walk in the Garden*, pp. 47-63.

Carr, D., 'The Politics of Textual Subversion: A Diachronic Perspective on the Garden of Eden Story', *JBL* 112 (1993), pp. 577-95.

Cassuto, U., *A Commentary on the Book of Genesis: Part I From Adam to Noah Genesis I – VI 8* (trans. I. Abrahams; Jerusalem: The Magnes Press, 1961).

Childs, B.S., *Old Testament Theology in a Canonical Context* (Philadelphia: Fortress Press, 1985).

Chopp, R.S., 'From Patriarchy into Freedom: A Conversation between American Feminist Theology and French Feminism', in Kim *et al.* (eds.), *Transfigurations*, pp. 31-48.

Clines, D.J.A., 'Prefatory Theme', in *The Theme of the Pentateuch* (JSOTSup, 10; Sheffield: JSOT Press, 1978), pp. 61-79.

—'The Wisdom Books', in Bigger (ed.), *Creating the Old Testament*, pp. 269-91.

—'Reading Esther From Left to Right: Contemporary Strategies for Reading a Biblical Text', in Clines *et al.* (eds.), *The Bible in Three Dimensions*, pp. 31-52.

—*What Does Eve Do to Help? and Other Readerly Questions to the Old Testament* (JSOTSup, 94; Sheffield: JSOT Press, 1990).

—'The Story of Michal, Wife of David, in Its Sequential Unfolding', in Clines and Eskenazi (eds.), *Telling Queen Michal's Story*, pp. 129-40.

—'Metacommentating Amos', in McKay and Clines (eds.), *Of Prophets' Visions and the Wisdom of Sages*, pp. 142-60.

—'Possibilities and Priorities of Biblical Interpretation in an International Perspective', *Biblical Interpretation* 1 (1993), pp. 67-87.

Clines, D.J.A., D.M. Gunn and A.J. Hauser (eds.), *Art and Meaning: Rhetoric in Biblical Literature* (JSOTSup, 19; Sheffield: JSOT Press, 1982).

Clines, D.J.A., and T.C. Eskenazi (eds.), *Telling Queen Michal's Story: An Experiment in Comparative Interpretation* (JSOTSup, 119; Sheffield: JSOT Press, 1991).

Clines, D.J.A., S. Fowl and S. Porter (eds.), *The Bible in Three Dimensions: Essays in Celebration of Forty Years of Biblical Studies in the University of Sheffield* (JSOTSup, 87; Sheffield: JSOT Press, 1990).

Coats, G.W., 'The God of Death: Power and Obedience in the Primeval History', *Int* 29 (1975), pp. 227-39.

Copher, C.B., 'The Black Presence in the Old Testament', in Felder (ed.), *Stony the Road we Trod*, pp. 146-64.

Crenshaw, J.L., 'The Concept of God in Old Testament Wisdom', in Perdue *et al.*
(eds.), *In Search of Wisdom: Essays in Memory of John G. Gammie*, pp. 1-18.

Crenshaw, J.L. (ed.), *Studies in Ancient Israelite Wisdom* (New York: KTAV, 1976).

—*Theodicy in the Old Testament* (Philadelphia: Fortress Press; London: SPCK, 1983).

Crossan, J.D., 'Response to White: Felix Culpa and Foenix Culprit', in Patte (ed.),
Genesis 2 and 3, pp. 107-11.

Culley, R.C., 'Action Sequences in Genesis 2–3', in Patte (ed.), *Genesis 2 and 3*, pp.
25-33.

Culley, R.C., and R.B. Robinson (eds.), *Textual Determinacy: Part One* (Semeia, 62;
Atlanta: Scholars Press, 1993).

Culpepper, A.R., *Anatomy of the Fourth Gospel: A Study in Literary Design*
(Philadelphia: Fortress Press, 1983).

Damrosch, D., *The Narrative Covenant: Transformations of Genre in the Growth of
Biblical Literature* (San Francisco: Harper & Row, 1987).

Davies, P.R., 'Women, Men, Gods, Sex and Power: The Birth of a Biblical Myth', in
Brenner (ed.), *A Feminist Companion to Genesis*, pp. 194-201.

Day, P.L., *Gender and Difference in Ancient Israel* (Minneapolis: Fortress Press, 1989).

Detweiler, R., *Reader Response Approaches to Biblical and Secular Texts* (Semeia, 31;
Decatur, GA: Scholars Press, 1985).

Dewey, J., 'Teaching the New Testament from a Feminist Perspective', *Theological
Education* 26.1 (1989), pp. 86-105.

Dockx, S.O.P., *Le Récit du Paradis: Gen. II–III* (Paris: Ducelot, 1981).

Dozeman, T.B., 'Rhetoric and Rhetorical Criticism: OT Rhetorical Criticism', in *ABD*,
V, pp. 712-15.

Dragga, S., 'Genesis 2–3: A Story of Liberation', *JSOT* 55 (1992), pp. 13-31.

Draisma, S. (ed.), *Intertextuality in Biblical Writings: Essays in Honour of Bas van
Iersel* (Kampen: Kok, 1989).

Durber, S., 'The Female Reader of the Parables of the Lost', *JSNT* 45 (1992), pp. 59-
78.

Emswiler, S.N., and T.N. Emswiler, *Women and Worship: A Guide to Nonsexist Hymns,
Prayers, and Liturgies* (San Francisco: Harper & Row, rev. edn, 1984).

Evans, G.R. (ed.), *Christian Authority: Essays in Honour of Henry Chadwick* (Oxford:
Clarendon Press, 1988).

Exum, J.C., 'Raped by the Pen', chap. in *Fragmented Women: Feminist (Sub)versions
of Biblical Narratives* (Valley Forge, PA: Trinity Press International, 1993).

Exum, J.C., and J.W.H. Bos (eds.), *Reasoning with the Foxes: Female Wit in a World of
Male Power* (Semeia, 42; Atlanta: Scholars Press, 1988).

Felder, C.H., 'Race, Racism, and the Biblical Narratives', in Felder (ed.), *Stony the Road
we Trod*, pp. 127-45.

Felder, C.H. (ed.), *Stony the Road we Trod: African American Biblical Interpretation*
(Minneapolis: Fortress Press, 1991).

Festorazzi, F., 'Gen. 1–3 e la sapienza di Israele', *Rivista Biblica* 27 (1979), pp. 41-51.

Fewell, D.N. (ed.), *Reading Between Texts: Intertextuality and the Hebrew Bible*
(Louisville: Westminster/John Knox Press, 1992).

Fewell, D.N., and D.M. Gunn, *Gender, Power, and Promise: The Subject of the Bible's
First Story* (Nashville: Abingdon Press, 1993).

Fiore, B., 'Rhetoric and Rhetorical Criticism: NT Rhetoric and Rhetorical Criticism', in
ABD, V, pp. 715-19.

Fishbane, M., 'Genesis 2.4b-11.32 / The Primeval Cycle', chap. in *Text and Texture: Close Readings of Selected Biblical Texts* (New York: Schocken Books, 1979).

—*Biblical Interpretation in Ancient Israel* (Oxford: Clarendon Press, 1985).

Fontaine, C.R., 'Wisdom in Proverbs', in Perdue *et al.* (eds.), *In Search of Wisdom*, pp. 99-114.

Forde, G.O., 'Law and Gospel in Luther's Hermeneutic', *Int* 37 (1983), pp. 240-52.

Fowl, S., 'The Ethics of Interpretation or What's Left Over after the Elimination of Meaning', in Clines *et al.* (eds.), *The Bible in Three Dimensions*, pp. 379-98.

—'Texts Don't Have Ideologies', *Biblical Interpretation* 3 (1995), pp. 15-34.

Fowler, R.M., *Let the Reader Understand: Reader-Response Criticism and the Gospel of Mark* (Minneapolis: Fortress Press, 1991).

Fox, M.V., 'Wisdom in Qoheleth', in Perdue *et al.* (eds.), *In Search of Wisdom*, pp. 115-31.

Fretheim, T.E., *Creation, Fall, and Flood* (Minneapolis: Augsburg, 1969).

—'Word of God', in *ABD*, VI, pp. 961-68.

—'Is Genesis 3 a Fall Story?', *WW* 14 (1994), pp. 144-53.

—'The Book of Genesis', *NIB*, I, pp. 321-674.

Froula, C., 'Rewriting Genesis: Gender and Culture in 20th Century Texts', *Tulsa Studies in Women's Literature* 7.2 (1988), pp. 197-220.

Fuchs, E., 'Contemporary Biblical Literary Criticism: The Objective Phallacy', in Tollers and Maier (eds.), *Mappings of the Biblical Terrain*, pp. 134-42.

Galambush, J., ' *ʾādām* from *ʾᵃdāmâ, ʾiššâ* from *ʾîš*: Derivation and Subordination in Gen. 2.4b-3.24', in Graham *et al.* (eds.), *History and Interpretation*, pp. 33-46.

Gardner, A., 'Genesis 2.4b-3: A Mythological Paradigm of Sexuality or of the Religious History of Pre-exilic Israel?', *SJT* 43 (1990), pp. 1-18.

Gordis, R., 'The Knowledge of Good and Evil in the Old Testament and the Qumran Scrolls', *JBL* 76 (1957), pp. 123-38.

Graham, M.P., W.P. Brown and J.K. Kuan (eds.), *History and Interpretation: Essays in Honour of John H. Hayes* (JSOTSup, 173; Sheffield: JSOT Press, 1993).

Habel, N.C., 'In Defense of God the Sage', in Perdue and Gilpin (eds.), *The Voice from the Whirlwind*, pp. 21-38.

Hanson, R.S., 'The Snake and I', chap. in *The Serpent Was Wiser: A New Look at Genesis 1–11* (Minneapolis: Augsburg, 1972).

Hauser, A.J., 'Linguistic and Thematic Links between Gen 4.1-16 and Gen 2–3', *JETS* 23 (1980), pp. 297-305.

—'Genesis 2–3: The Theme of Intimacy and Alienation', in Clines *et al.* (eds.), *Art and Meaning*, pp. 20-36.

Hess, R.S., 'Splitting the Adam: The Usage of *ʾadam* in Genesis I–V', in J.A. Emerton (ed.), *Studies in the Pentateuch* (VTSup, 41; Leiden and New York: Brill, 1990) pp. 1-15.

Hick, J., *Evil and the God of Love* (San Francisco: Harper & Row, 1978).

Higgins, Jean M., 'The Myth of Eve: The Temptress', *JAAR* 44 (1976), pp. 639-47.

Hinschberger, R., 'Une lecture synchronique de Gn 2–3', *RevScRel* 63 (1989), pp. 1-16.

Hoglund, K.G., E.F. Huwiler, J.T. Glass and R.W. Lee (eds.), *The Listening Heart: Essays in Wisdom and the Psalms in Honor of Roland E. Murphy, O. Carm* (JSOTSup, 58; Sheffield: JSOT Press, 1987).

Jackson, J.J., and M. Kessler (eds.), *Rhetorical Criticism: Essays in Honor of James Muilenburg* (Pittsburgh: Pickwick Press, 1974).

Jacobson, D.,'Creation, Birth, and the Radical Ecology of the Book of Job' (Convocation Lecture presented at Luther Northwestern Theological Seminary, 9 February 1992).

Janzen, G.J., *Job* (IBC; Atlanta: John Knox, 1985).

Jobling, D., P.L. Day and G.T. Sheppard (eds.), *The Bible and the Politics of Exegesis: Essays in Honor of Norman K. Gottwald on his Sixty-Fifth Birthday* (Cleveland: The Pilgrim Press, 1991).

Jobling, D., 'Myth and Its Limits in Genesis 2.4b-3.24', chap. in *The Sense of Biblical Narrative: Structural Analyses in the Hebrew Bible II* (JSOTSup, 39; Sheffield: JSOT Press, 1986).

Joines, K.R., 'The Serpent in Gen 3', *ZAW* 87 (1975), pp. 1-11.

Juel, D.H., 'The Authority of the Scriptures: An Assessment of a Conversation' (Paper presented at the Convocation of Teaching Theologians on 'Renewing Biblical Authority: A Challenge for the ELCA', Chicago, Illinois, 14 August 1994).

Kennedy, G.A., *New Testament Interpretation through Rhetorical Criticism* (Chapel Hill and London: The University of North Carolina Press, 1984).

Kennedy, J.M. 'Peasants in Revolt: Political Allegory in Genesis 2-3', *JSOT* 47 (1990), pp. 3-14.

Kim, C.W.M., S.M. St. Ville and S.M. Simonaitis (eds.), *Transfigurations: Theology and the French Feminists* (Minneapolis: Fortress Press, 1993).

Koch, K., 'Is there a Doctrine of Retribution in the Old Testament?', in Crenshaw (ed.), *Theodicy in the Old Testament*, pp. 57-87.

Kugel, J., 'Cain and Abel in Fact and Fable: Genesis 4.1-16', in Brooks and Collins (eds.), *Hebrew Bible or Old Testament?*, pp. 167-90.

L'Hour, J., 'Yahweh Elohim', *RB* 81 (1974), pp. 524-56.

Lambden, S.N., 'From Fig Leaves to Fingernails: Some Notes on the Garments of Adam and Eve in the Hebrew Bible and Select Early Postbiblical Jewish Writings', in Morris and Sawyer (eds.), *A Walk in the Garden*, pp. 74-90.

Lanser, S.S., '(Feminist) Criticism in the Garden: Inferring Genesis 2-3', in White (ed.), *Speech Act Theory*, pp. 67-84.

Levin, S., 'The More Savory Offering: A Key to the Problem of Gen 4.3-5', *JBL* 98 (1979), p. 85.

Lieberman, S.R., 'The Eve Motif in Ancient Near Eastern and Classical Greek Sources' (PhD thesis, Boston University, 1975).

Loades, A., and M. McLain (eds.), *Hermeneutics, the Bible, and Literary Criticism* (New York: St. Martin's Press, 1992).

Lonergan, B., *Method in Theology* (New York: Herder & Herder, 1972).

Long, B.O., 'Textual Determinacy: A Response', in Culley and Robinson (eds.), *Textual Determinacy: Part One*, pp. 157-63.

Louys, D., *Le jardin d'Eden: mythe fondateur de l'Occident* (Paris: Les éditions du Cerf, 1992).

Malina, B.J., 'Reader-Response Theory: Discovery or Redundancy?', *Creighton University Faculty Journal* (Omaha) 5 (1986), pp. 55-66.

McKay, H.A., and D.J.A. Clines, (eds.), *Of Prophets' Visions and the Wisdom of Sages: Essays in Honor of Norman Whybray on his Seventieth Birthday* (JSOTSup, 162; Sheffield: JSOT Press, 1993).

McKenzie, J.L., 'The Literary Characteristics of Genesis 2–3', *TS* 15 (1954), pp. 542-72.

McKnight, E.V., (ed.), *Reader Perspectives on the New Testament* (Semeia, 48; Atlanta: Scholars Press, 1989).

Mendenhall, G.E., 'The Shady Side of Wisdom: The Date and Purpose of Genesis 3', in H.N. Bream, R.D. Heim and C.A. Moore (eds.), *A Light unto My Path: Old Testament Studies in Honor of Jacob M. Myers* (Philadelphia: Temple University Press, 1974), pp. 319-34.

Meyers, C.L., 'Gender Roles and Genesis 3.16 Revisit(ed.)', in Meyers and O'Connor (eds.), *The Word of the Lord Shall Go Forth*, pp. 337-54.

Meyers, C.L., and M. O'Connor (eds.), *The Word of the Lord Shall Go Forth: Essays in Honor of David Noel Freedman in Celebration of His Sixtieth Birthday* (Philadelphia: American Schools of Oriental Research, 1983).

Meyers, C., *Discovering Eve: Ancient Israelite Women in Context* (New York: Oxford University Press, 1988).

—'Everyday Life: Women in the Period of the Hebrew Bible', in Newsom and Ringe (eds.), *The Women's Bible Commentary*, pp. 244-51.

Miller, P.D., Jr, *Genesis 1–11: Studies in Structure and Theme* (JSOTSup, 8; Sheffield: JSOT Press, 1978).

—*Sin and Judgment in the Prophets: A Stylistic and Theological Analysis* (SBLMS, 27; Chico, CA: Scholars Press, 1982).

Milne, P.J., 'Eve and Adam: Is a Feminist Reading Possible?', *BibRev* 4 (June 1988), pp. 12-21, 39.

Moberly R.W.L., 'Did the Serpent Get it Right?', *JTS* 39 (April 1988), pp. 1-27.

Mollenkott, V.R., *Sensuous Spirituality: Out From Fundamentalism* (New York: Crossroad, 1992).

Moore, S., 'Negative Hermeneutics, Insubstantial Texts: Stanley Fish and the Biblical Interpreter', *JAAR* 54 (1986), pp. 707-19.

Morris, P., 'Exiled from Eden: Jewish Interpretations of Genesis', in Morris and Sawyer (eds.), *A Walk in the Garden*, pp. 117-66.

Morris, P., and D. Sawyer (eds.), *A Walk in the Garden: Biblical, Iconographical and Literary Images of Eden* (JSOTSup, 136; Sheffield: JSOT Press, 1992).

Muilenburg, J., 'Form Criticism and Beyond', *JBL* 88 (1969), pp. 1-18

Munich, A., 'Notorious Signs, Feminist Criticism and Literary Tradition', in Greene and Kahn (eds.), *Making a Difference*, pp. 238-59.

Newsom, C.A., 'Woman and the Discourse of Patriarchal Wisdom: A Study of Proverbs 1–9', in Day (ed.), *Gender and Difference in Ancient Israel*, pp. 142-60.

—'Cultural Politics and the Reading of Job', *Biblical Interpretation* 1 (1993), pp. 119-38.

Newsom, C.A., and S.H. Ringe (eds.), *The Women's Bible Commentary* (Louisville and London: Westminster/John Knox and SPCK, 1992).

Niditch, S., 'Folklore and Biblical Narrative: A Study of Genesis 3', chap. in *Folklore and the Hebrew Bible* (Minneapolis: Fortress Press, 1993).

Och, B., 'The Garden of Eden: From Creation to Covenant', *Judaism* 37 (1988), pp. 143-56.

Oden, R.A., Jr, 'Grace or Status? Yahweh's Clothing of the First Humans', chap. in *The Bible without Theology: The Theological Tradition and Alternatives to It* (San Francisco: Harper & Row, 1987).

Oduyoye, M., *The Sons of the Gods and the Daughters of Men: An Afro-Asiatic Interpretation of Genesis 1–11* (Maryknoll, NY: Orbis Books, 1984).

Pagels, E., *Adam, Eve, and the Serpent* (New York: Random House, 1987).

Park, W., 'Why Eve?', *St Vladimir's Theological Quarterly* 35 (1991), pp. 127-35.

Patte, D., *Genesis 2 and 3: Kaleidoscopic Structural Readings* (Semeia, 18; Chico, CA: Scholars Press, 1980).

—*Religious Dimensions in Biblical Texts: Greimas's Structural Semiotics and Biblical Exegesis* (SBLSS; Atlanta: Scholars Press, 1990).

—'Textual Constraints, Ordinary Readings, and Critical Exegesis: An Androcritical Perspective', in Culley and Robinson (eds.), *Textual Determinacy*, pp. 59-79.

Perdue, L.G., 'Wisdom in the Book of Job', in Perdue *et al.* (eds.), *In Search of Wisdom*, pp. 73-98.

Perdue, L.G., and W.C. Gilpin (eds.), *The Voice from the Whirlwind: Interpreting the Book of Job* (Nashville: Abingdon Press, 1992).

Perdue, L.G., B.B. Scott and W.J. Wiseman (eds.), *In Search of Wisdom: Essays in Memory of John G. Gammie* (Louisville, KY: Westminster/John Knox, 1993).

Petersen, N.R., *Rediscovering Paul: Philemon and the Sociology of Paul's Narrative World* (Philadelphia: Fortress Press, 1985).

Phillips, G.A. (ed.), *Poststructural Criticism and the Bible: Text/ History/ Discourse* (Semeia, 51; Atlanta: Scholars Press, 1990).

Plaskow, J., 'Anti-Judaism in Feminist Christian Interpretation', in Schüssler Fiorenza (ed.), *Searching the Scriptures Volume One*, pp. 117-29.

Potter Engel, M., 'Evil, Sin, and Violation of the Vulnerable', in S.B. Thistlethwaite and M.P. Engel (eds.), *Lift Every Voice: Constructing Christian Theologies from the Underside* (San Francisco: Harper & Row, 1990), pp. 152-68.

Pritchard, J.B. (ed.), *Ancient Near Eastern Texts relating to the Old Testament* (Princeton: Princeton University Press, 3rd edn, 1969).

Rad, G. von, *Genesis: A Commentary* (Philadelphia: The Westminster Press, rev. edn, 1972).

Radday, Y.T., and A. Brenner (eds.), *On Humour and the Comic in the Hebrew Bible* (JSOTSup, 92; Sheffield: Almond Press, 1990).

Ramsey, G.W., 'Is Name-Giving an Act of Domination in Genesis 2.23 and Elsewhere?', *CBQ* 50 (1988), pp. 24-35.

Ratner, R.J., '"Garments of Skin" (Genesis 3.21)', *Jewish Bible Quarterly* 18 (1989), pp. 74-80.

Richardson, R.M., 'The Theology of Sexuality in the Beginning: Genesis 3', *AUSS* 26 (1988), pp. 121-31.

Robbins, V.K, *Jesus the Teacher: A Socio-Rhetorical Interpretation of Mark* (Philadelphia: Fortress Press, 1992 [1984]).

Saiving, V., 'The Human Situation: A Feminine View', in C.P. Christ and J. Plaskow (eds.), *Womanspirit Rising: A Feminist Reader in Religion* (San Francisco: Harper & Row, 1979), pp. 25-42; reprinted from *JR* 40 (1960), pp. 100-12.

Santmire, H.P., 'The Genesis Creation Narratives Revisited: Themes for a Global Age', *Int* 45 (1991), pp. 366-79.

Sarna, N.M., *The JPS Torah Commentary: Genesis* (Philadelphia: The Jewish Publication Society, 5749/1989).

Savran, G., *Telling and Retelling: Quotation in Biblical Narrative* (Indiana Studies in Biblical Literature; Bloomington: Indiana University Press, 1988).

Sawyer, J.F.A., 'The Image of God, the Wisdom of Serpents and the Knowledge of Good and Evil', in Morris and Sawyer (eds.), *A Walk in the Garden*, pp. 64-73.

Schüssler Fiorenza, E., 'Missionaries, Apostles, Coworkers: Romans 16 and the Reconstruction of Women's Early Christian History', *WW* 6 (1986), pp. 420-33.

— 'Rhetorical Situation and Historical Reconstruction in 1 Corinthians', *NTS* 33 (1987), pp. 386-403.

— 'The Ethics of Biblical Interpretation: Decentering Biblical Scholarship', *JBL* 107 (1988), pp. 3-17.

— *But She Said: Feminist Practices of Biblical Interpretation* (Boston: Beacon, 1992).

Schüssler Fiorenza, E. (ed.), *Searching the Scriptures* (2 vols.; New York: Crossroad, 1993–1994).

Scriabine, M., 'La Genèse comme mythe du langage', chap. in *Au carrefour de Thèbes* (Paris: Gallimard, 1977).

Shank, H., 'The Sin Theology of the Cain and Abel Story: An Analysis of Narrative Themes within the Context of Genesis 1–11' (PhD dissertation, Marquette University, 1988).

Speiser, E.A., *Genesis* (AB; Garden City, NY: Doubleday, 1964).

Steinmetz, D., 'Vineyard, Farm, and Garden: The Drunkenness of Noah in the Context of Primeval History', *JBL* 113 (1994), pp. 193-207.

Sternberg, M., *The Poetics of Biblical Narrative: Ideological Literature and the Drama of Reading* (Bloomington: Indiana University Press, 1985).

Stitzinger, M.F., 'Gen 1–3 and the Male/Female Role Relationship', *GTJ* 2 (1981), pp. 23-44.

Stordalen, T., 'Genesis 2.4: Restudying a *locus classicus*', *ZAW* 104 (1992), pp. 163-77.

Stratton, B.J., 'Dirtying our Hands: Ideologies, Pedagogies, and Scriptures' (Paper presented to the Society of Biblical Literature's Ideological Criticism Group, Chicago, 21 November 1994).

— 'Eve through Several Lenses: Truth in 1 Timothy 2.8-15', in A. Brenner (ed.), *A Feminist Companion to the Hebrew Bible in the New Testament* (Sheffield: Sheffield Academic Press, forthcoming).

Swidler, A., and W.E. Conn, *Mainstreaming: Feminist Research for Teaching Religious Studies* (Lanham, MD: University Press of America, 1985).

Tavard, G., *Woman in Christian Tradition* (Notre Dame: University of Notre Dame Press, 1973).

Terrien, S., 'The Yahweh Speeches and Job's Responses', *Review and Expositor* 68 (1971), pp. 497-509.

Tollers, V.L., and J. Maier (eds.), *Mappings of the Biblical Terrain: The Bible as Text* (Lewisburg, PA: Bucknell University Press, 1990).

Tosato, A., 'On Genesis 2.24', *CBQ* 52 (1990), pp. 389-409.

Tracy, D., *Plurality and Ambiguity: Hermeneutics, Religion, Hope* (San Francisco: Harper & Row, 1987).

Trible, P., 'Depatriarchalizing in Biblical Interpretation', *JAAR* 41 (1973), pp. 30-48.

— *God and the Rhetoric of Sexuality* (Philadelphia: Fortress Press, 1978).

Tsevat, M., 'The Meaning of the Book of Job', *HUCA* 37 (1966), pp. 73-106.

Turner, L.A., 'The Primeval History', in *Announcements of Plot in Genesis* (JSOTSup, 96; Sheffield: JSOT Press, 1990), pp. 21-49.

van Wolde, E., 'Trendy Intertextuality?', in Draisma (ed.), *Intertextuality in Biblical Writings*, pp. 43-49.

Vawter, B., *On Genesis: A New Reading* (Garden City, NY: Doubleday, 1977).

—'Prov. 8.22: Wisdom and Creation', *JBL* 99 (1980), pp. 205-16.

Vogels, W., 'L'être humain appartien au sol: Gen 2.4b-3.24', *NRT* 105 (1983), pp. 515-34.

Vorster, W.S., 'Intertextuality and Redaktionsgeschichte', in Draisma (ed.), *Intertextuality in Biblical Writings*, pp. 15-26.

Walsh, J.T., 'Genesis 2.4b-3.24: A Synchronic Approach', *JBL* 96 (1977), pp. 161-77.

Watson, D.F., 'The New Testament and Greco-Roman Rhetoric: A Bibliography', *JETS* 31 (1988), pp. 465-72.

—*Invention, Arrangement, and Style: Rhetorical Criticism of Jude and 2 Peter* (SBLDS, 104; Atlanta: Scholars Press, 1988).

Watson, F., 'Strategies of Recovery and Resistance: Hermeneutical Reflections on Genesis 1–3 and its Pauline Reception', *JSNT* 45 (1992), pp. 79-103.

Wenham, G.J., *Genesis 1–15* (WBC; Waco, TX: Word Books, 1987).

Westermann, C., *Creation* (trans. J.J. Scullion, S.J.; Philadelphia: Fortress Press; London: SPCK, 1974).

—*Genesis 1–11: A Commentary* (trans. J.J. Scullion, S.J.; Minneapolis: Augsburg, 1984).

Whedbee, W., 'The Comedy of Job', in Radday and Brenner (eds.), *On Humour and the Comic in the Hebrew Bible*, pp. 217-49.

White, H.C., 'Direct and Third Person Discourse in the Narrative of the "Fall"', in Patte (ed.), *Genesis 2 and 3*, pp. 91-106.

—*Narration and Discourse in the Book of Genesis* (Cambridge: Cambridge University Press, 1991).

White, H.C. (ed.), *Speech Act Theory and Biblical Criticism* (Semeia, 41; Decatur, GA: Scholars Press, 1988).

Whitehead, J.D., and E.E. Whitehead, *Method in Ministry: Theological Reflection and Christian Ministry* (Minneapolis: Seabury, 1980).

Widengren, G., *The King and the Tree of Life in Ancient Near Eastern Religion*. (Uppsala: Lundequistka, 1951).

Williams, J.G., 'Genesis 3', *Int* 35 (1981), pp. 274-79.

Willimon, W.H., *Sighing for Eden: Sin, Evil and the Christian Faith* (Nashville: Abingdon Press, 1985).

Wismer, P.L., 'The Myth of Original Sin: A Hermeneutic Theology Based on Genesis 2–3' (PhD dissertation, University of Chicago, 1983).

Wordelman, A.L., 'Everyday Life: Women in the Period of the New Testament', in Newsom and Ringe (eds.), *The Women's Bible Commentary*, pp. 390-96.

Wren, B., *What Language Shall I Borrow? God-Talk in Worship: A Male Response to Feminist Theology* (New York: Crossroad, 1989).

Wright, L.S., 'Reported Speech in Hebrew Narrative: A Typology and Analysis of Texts in the Book of Genesis' (PhD dissertation, Emory University, 1991).

Yee, G.A., '"I Have Perfumed my Bed with Myrrh": The Foreign Woman (ʾiššâ zārâ) in Proverbs 1–9', *JSOT* 43 (1989), pp. 53-68.

Zelechow, B., 'God's Presence and the Paradox of Freedom', in Loades and McLain (eds.), *Hermeneutics, the Bible, and Literary Criticism*, pp. 162-76.

INDEXES

INDEX OF REFERENCES

INDEX OF AUTHORS

JOURNAL FOR THE STUDY OF THE OLD TESTAMENT

Supplement Series